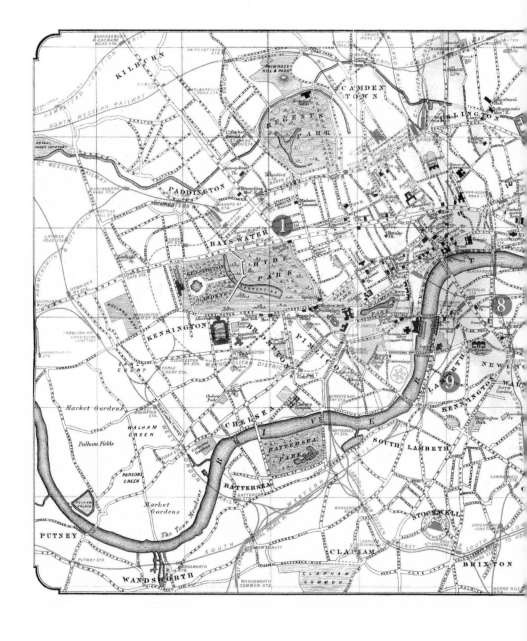

LONDON

Adapted from
Waltham Bros. map of London 1875
From the *Golden Guide to London*

1. Elizabeth Banks' 1st *Cap and Apron* investigation, Portman Square

2. Father Jay's Holy Trinity Mission, Shoreditch and setting of Mrs. Meade's *Princess of the Gutter*

3. Oxford House, Bethnal Green

4. William Booth's first mission, Mile End

5. Frederick Charrington's Tower Hamlets Mission

6. Dr. Barnardo's Boys' Home, Stepney Causeway

7. Toynbee Hall, Whitechapel

8. Women's University Settlement, Blackfriars, Southwark

9. Lambeth Workhouse

Slumming

SLUMMING

SEXUAL AND SOCIAL POLITICS
IN VICTORIAN LONDON

SETH KOVEN

PRINCETON UNIVERSITY PRESS

PRINCETON AND OXFORD

Copyright © 2004 by Princeton University Press
Published by Princeton University Press, 41 William Street, Princeton, New Jersey 08540
In the United Kingdom: Princeton University Press, 3 Market Place, Woodstock,
Oxfordshire OX20 1SY

Third printing, and first paperback printing, 2006
Paperback ISBN-13: 978-0-691-12800-9
Paperback ISBN-10: 0-691-12800-6

The Library of Congress has cataloged the cloth edition
of this book as follows

Koven, Seth, 1958–
Slumming : sexual and social politics in Victorian London / Seth Koven.
p.   cm.
Includes bibliographical references and index.
ISBN 0-691-11592-3 (cl. : alk. paper)
1. Poor—England—London—History—19th century. 2. Slums—England—London—
History—19th century. 3. Sex customs—England—London—History—19th
century. 4. Voluntarism—England—London—History—19th century. 5. Charities—
England—London—History—19th century. 6. London (England)—Social condition.
I. Title.

HV4085.L6K68   2004
306.7'086'94209421—dc22   2003060514

British Library Cataloging-in-Publication Data is available

This book has been composed in Sabon

Printed on acid-free paper. ∞

pup.princeton.edu

Printed in the United States of America

10   9   8   7   6   5   4   3

To William Koven

CONTENTS

LIST OF ILLUSTRATIONS

ACKNOWLEDGMENTS

BOOKS, LIKE their authors, live at the intersection of many different communities, intellectual and personal. I am grateful for this opportunity to acknowledge them—and many individuals within them—whose inspiration and support enabled me to complete this project according to my own lights.

My first debt of gratitude is to Villanova University and the departments of History and Women's Studies for giving me such a lively home. The sort of intellectual and social comradeship I have enjoyed day by day, year after year, has happily made it hard for me to disentangle work from play. For their willingness to comment on whatever bits of this book—from sentences to entire chapters—I have thrust on their desks over the years, I thank my colleagues Scott Black, Mine Ener, Marc Gallicchio, Maghan Keita, Donald B. Kelley, Ann Lesch, Larry Little, Lucy McDiarmid, Evan Radcliffe, Vincent Sherry, Lauren Shohet, and Paul Steege. Adele Lindenmeyr, finding just the right balance between empathic enthusiasm, supportive friendship, and incisive intellectual candor, generously discussed, read, and reread chapters as I wrote them and pushed me to clarify my prose and think harder about my arguments.

My year as a Visiting Associate Professor of History at the University of California, Berkeley, was full of salutary intellectual provocations that transformed this manuscript and emboldened me to take my arguments in new directions. For their insights and challenges, comments and conversations about various chapters, I thank Margaret Anderson, who inspired me to become a historian, as well as Kamilla Elliott, Paula Fass, Carla Hesse, Martin Jay, Alan Karras, Tom Laqueur, David Lieberman, and Mary Ryan. Past and present members of the Delaware Valley British Studies Seminar—in particular Andrew August, Caroline Levine, Mary Procida, Stuart Semmel, Tom Smith, and Julie Taddeo—offered me a forum to discuss my work and, perhaps more importantly, an ongoing community of scholars in Philadelphia whose researches and approaches have enriched my own. I have benefited from Lynn Lees's friendship and mentorship as well as her own vast knowledge of the history of the poor and London. In addition to offering shrewd criticisms of my work, Lynn arranged for me to be a visiting scholar at the University of Pennsylvania and lent me her own office during a year of research leave. Many friends and colleagues in London have opened their homes to me and my family over the years. I extend my warmest thanks to Fiona Gibbs and Vimal Thavathurai, Merle and Joel Osrin, Olivia Dix and Michael Mockridge,

Ruth Ehrlich and Peter Mandler, Pat Thane, and Anna Davin for making my life in London so rewarding and stimulating.

I benefited greatly from astute reader's reports of the entire manuscript by James Epstein, Susan Pedersen, and Martha Vicinus, as well as one anonymous reader. I hope they can find traces of their ideas which guided my revisions. Sonya Michel remains an inspiring friend whose own work and readiness to engage with my own made this a better book. My bulging file labeled "Comments on *Slumming* from friends and colleagues" includes thoughtful responses to specific chapters (or conference papers which turned into chapters) from James Eli Adams, George Behlmer, Catherine Cocks, Anna Davin, William Fishman, Regenia Gagnier, Frances Gouda, Kali Israel, Lori Lefkovitz, Jean Lutes, Joseph McLaughlin, Douglas Mitchell, Deborah Nord, Yopie Prins, Mary Louise Roberts, Ellen Ross, James Sheehan, Kathryn Kish Sklar, Peter Stansky, Pat Thane, Pamela Walker, Judith Walkowitz, Chris Waters, Patricia Yaeger, and Julian Yates. Diana Maltz not only introduced me to Vernon Lee's *Miss Brown* and commented on several chapters but has also shared her own ongoing work on aesthetic philanthropy in Victorian London. My thanks to Lorraine Blair for sharing her discovery of the Wadham House journal at Toynbee Hall. I am also grateful for the skills and dedication of able graduate research assistants, in particular Dana Bielicki, Carmen Breslin, Stephanie Fineman, Thomas Hajkowki, Kathryn Miele, Keith Rolfe, and Kevin Switaj. As this project moved into its final stages, Laura Salvucci provided extraordinary assistance with notes and copyediting. Mara Delcamp efficiently transcribed Elizabeth Banks's letters at the University of Tulsa Special Collections Library. Brigitta van Rheinberg at Princeton University Press far surpassed my highest hopes for what an editor could be. Her excitement about this book was matched by frank editorial advice and substantive critical engagement with the arguments of each chapter. My thanks to the entire team of editors at Princeton University Press including Alison Kalett, Dimitri Karetnikov, Sara Lerner, and Gail Schmitt. The collective efforts of all these people have greatly enriched this book, but its limitations and errors remain entirely my own.

Many librarians and archivists on both sides of the Atlantic provided expert guidance and assistance in finding my way through their collections, including the staff at the British Library and Newspaper Library, Colindale; British Library of Political and Economic Science, London School of Economics; Bodleian Library, Oxford; Cambridge University Library; Colby College, Maine; Kings College, Cambridge; Lambeth Palace Library; Library of Congress; London Metropolitan Archives (formerly the Greater London Record Office); Moffitt Library, University of California, Berkeley; New York Public Library; Public Record Office;

Senate House Library, London University; Swarthmore College, Peace Collection; Tower Hamlets Local History Library; Van Pelt Library, University of Pennsylvania; Victoria and Albert Museum Library; Widener Library, Harvard University; the Women's Library (formerly the Fawcett Library), London Metropolitan University. I am also grateful to the staff at various philanthropic and social welfare institutions who helped me track down materials in their archives, including Frank Emott at Barnardo's Library; Kate Bradley at Toynbee Hall; Tower Hamlets Mission; Oxford House; Lady Margaret Hall Settlement; and the Women's University Settlement. Closer to home, the interlibrary loan wizards at Villanova University's Falvey Library—Therese Dougherty, Ann Ford, and Phylis Wright—have been indefatigable sleuths in tracking down my requests. Bernadette Dierkes and Donna Blaszkowski of Falvey Library' Graphic Services Department offered exceptional expertise and good cheer in organizing images. In countless ways, the staff of Villanova's history department—Christine Filiberti, Edith Iannucci, and Georgiana Kilroy—has contributed to this book. For their assistance in procuring images this book, my thanks to Stephen Povers and Carolyn Rich at Barnardos; Mary Shields at the Carnegie Library, Pittsburgh; Alan Thomas at Save the Children; Kate Bradley at the Barnett Research Centre, Toynbee Hall; Patricia Burdick at Colby College; Rey Antonio at the library of the University of Virginia. My thanks to the *Radical History Review* for permission to reproduce materials from my article "Dr. Barnardo's 'Artistic Fictions': Photography, Sexuality, and the Ragged Child in Victorian London," in chapter 2 of this book. Research for this project was funded by grants and fellowships from the National Endowment for the Humanities, the American Philosophical Society, and Villanova University.

While Joan and our children, Daniel, Zoe, and Eli, may not have read this book, they certainly have lived with it. Their love has sustained me during its composition. Our family adventures on athletic fields across America have taken me far from the slums of Victorian London and remind me that the joys of the present are every bit as important as the lessons of the past.

This book is dedicated to my father William Koven, whose compassion, wisdom, and love of learning continue to guide me.

Slumming

Introduction

SLUMMING: EROS AND ALTRUISM
IN VICTORIAN LONDON

FOR THE BETTER part of the century preceding World War II, Britons went slumming to see for themselves how the poor lived. They insisted that firsthand experience among the metropolitan poor was essential for all who claimed to speak authoritatively about social problems. To a remarkable degree, the men and women who governed church and state in late-nineteenth- and twentieth-century Britain and dominated social welfare bureaucracies and the emerging profession of social work felt compelled to visit, live, or work in the London slums at some point in their careers of public service. Even the fiery Welsh radical Lloyd George, champion of popular rights against aristocratic privileges, sought out a friend to take him on a tour of the East London slums soon after he arrived in London in 1890 to assume his seat in parliament.[1] Lloyd George may have been intent to witness the scenes of human misery and sexual degradation made famous the world over by the serial murderer Jack the Ripper, but he also embarked on a journey routed for him by thousands of well-to-do men and women. By the 1890s, London guidebooks such as Baedeker's not only directed visitors to shops, theatres, monuments, and churches, but also mapped excursions to world renowned philanthropic institutions located in notorious slum districts such as Whitechapel and Shoreditch.[2]

We will never know precisely how many men and women went slumming, but the fact that slums became tourist sites suggests it was a very widespread phenomenon. At any given time there were hundreds of private charitable institutions and agencies in the metropolitan slums, each visited regularly by scores of donors, trustees, and volunteer and paid workers. No doubt slumming was merely an evening's entertainment for many well-to-do Londoners,[3] but for many others, the slums of London exercised powerful and tenacious claims over their minds and hearts, drastically altering the course of their lives.

One such man was James Granville Adderley. Adderley was far too iconoclastic to be representative of anything, but his life provides one point of entry into the world of the women and men whose philanthropic labors are the subject of this book. Even those who disliked Adderley's radical ideas liked the man himself. He bristled with righteous indignation about the world's injustices, but he also radiated an inner calm and a joyful enthusiasm that drew people of all sorts and conditions to him. Well-born, charming in conversation, blessed with even-featured good looks, and bright without being ostentatiously intellectual, Adderley seemed destined for a lucrative career in law and politics. However, within a short time of leaving Oxford in the mid-1880s, he found himself the toast of philanthropic London as head of one of the metropolis's newest institutions for translating vague ideals about cross-class brotherly love into concrete form: the Oxford House in Bethnal Green. A residential colony of idealistic university men planted in a slum district, it was devoted to constructing bridges of personal friendship between rich and poor through Christian work and wholesome "rational" recreation. There was something absurd about Adderley's instant celebrity as an expert on social questions, and he knew it better than anyone else. He cannily recognized that his contemporaries saw him not as he actually was but rather as an embodiment of a new type of man: the " 'ecclesiastical young man,' " called upon to "address all kinds of meetings, and looked upon as a sort of freak—the fellow who might live in luxury in Belgravia but preferred [the poverty of] Bethnal Green."[4]

Impatient with the unending stream of visitors, reporters, and transient do-gooders to Oxford House, Adderley took his clerical vows and moved farther east into ever less glamorous slum districts. He joined the Catholic prelate Cardinal Manning and the trade unionist Ben Tillett in championing the cause of London's grossly exploited dock laborers in their world-famous strike in 1889; he defended the rights of laboring men against puritanical attempts to deny them the pleasures of the stage and music hall; he threw his heart and soul into club work with the "rough lads" in his adopted neighborhood of Poplar and invited large numbers of them for holidays on the grounds of his ancestral home, Hams Hall. He helped form a new religious community within the Church of England that was founded on the rules of St. Francis: The Society of Divine Compassion. Adderley and his brothers in poverty exalted the beautiful while despising the exuberant materialism of late Victorian London. Jolly fellowship among men went hand in hand with severe austerity. "There was no carpet on the floors, a fire only in the common room, and the brothers did their own crude cooking," one visitor recalled. A bare plank served as his only bed. Adderley felt that even this self-denying regimen kept him too far removed from the gritty struggles of the homeless poor. He spent weeks at a time disguised as a tramp, often sleeping rough on the streets. The depth of his compassion was matched by the breadth of his tolerance. He extended his hand not only to social outcasts but also to sexual outlaws like the celebrated playwright Oscar Wilde, convicted in 1895 for committing same-sex acts of gross indecency. Living in East London placed Adderley far from the starched-collar respectability and top-hatty conventions of bourgeois domesticity and freed him to develop distinctly heterodox ideas about class relations, male sexual celibacy, and social purity. When Adderley died in 1942, it was another man, Arthur Shearly Cripps, his "comrade in tramping, dossing, and in preaching the gospel," who memorialized their loving friendship in a tender poem of chaste but sensual couplets: "He to whose lips the taste of old wine clings/ Asks no new wine. Ah me! My friend's loss brings/ No wish for some new friend to fill his place."[5]

Why did Adderley renounce the privileges of aristocratic birth and the comforts of family to live for six decades in voluntary poverty and sexual celibacy among the London poor as a bachelor slum priest? His only biographer discouraged readers from seeking the psychological roots of Adderley's singular devotion because he was "a man of simple ways and thoughts and friendships" who never worried about himself and instead did God's work as a parish priest.[6] We need not posthumously coerce Adderley onto the psychoanalyst's couch to suggest that the private and public, sexual and social forces shaping his life choices may not have been as "simple" as his "ways."

This book tries to make sense of the ideas and movements, institutions and practices that made the slums of London and "slumming" seem so necessary to Adderley and thousands of members of the "comfortable classes." It examines the complex historical and cultural circumstances in which such women and men found themselves and to which they importantly contributed. I attempt to save them from the misguided goodwill of those who would make them into saints and the smugness of those who would dismiss them as marginal cranks, or worse yet, as hypocrites. They were none of these. Instead, I try to recapture the altogether messier mingling of good intentions and blinkered prejudices that informed their vision of the poor and of themselves. While exploring deep structures of thought and feeling in nineteenth- and early-twentieth-century British culture, I attend to individuals' particularities. I portray slum reformers and workers not as mere tools of social or discursive forces outside their control—though such forces did influence their agendas—but as human beings who confronted ethical dilemmas and made difficult choices.[7] I examine the interplay of sexual and social politics both at the micro-level of how women and men came to express and understand who they were and at the macro-level of public debates about poverty and welfare, gender, and sexuality. By so doing, I work within, but also reorient, a tradition of scholarship linking private conscience and public duty in Victorian culture and society.[8]

The intimate, turbulent, and often surprising relationship between benevolence and sex, rich and poor, in Victorian London is my subject. I came to this topic circuitously through the history of elite men's and women's philanthropic endeavors to bring "sweetness and light" to the dark spaces and dirty inhabitants of the metropolis. As I immersed myself deeply in the sources, I found it impossible to keep sex, sexual desire, and sexuality out of their story. So what began as an inquiry into class-bridging institutions and social welfare programs took on a life of its own, propelled by several insights. First, it became clear that debates about "social" questions such as homelessness, social hygiene, childhood poverty, and women's work were often sparked by and tapped into anxieties about sex, sexuality, and gender roles. To understand how elite men and women thought about the poor required me to reckon with how they thought about sex, gender, and themselves. Second, I discovered that the widely shared imperative among well-to-do men and women to traverse class boundaries and befriend their outcast brothers and sisters in the slums was somehow bound up in their insistent eroticization of poverty and their quest to understand their own sexual subjectivities. But how and why were these movements, both literal and imaginative, connected? And what were the consequences of such linkages for the histories of class, gender, sexuality, and welfare? An inquiry into the set of social practices and relations that Britons called slumming promised a means to untangle and knit together in a new way the history of sexual and social politics.[9] Once I started looking for slumming, it was hard not to find it everywhere.

The Oxford-educated journalist Henry Wood Nevinson, who lived with his talented wife Margaret and their growing family in an insect-infested slum flat in the 1880s, astutely observed that slumming expressed both "shamed sympathy" with the poor and an irresistible "attraction of repulsion" for them.[10] Nevinson's paradoxical formulation points to the double optic through which elites viewed the slums of London. Men and women like the Nevinsons knew only too well that slums were real places of monotonous material deprivation and quiet human suffering which both rightly elicited their sympathy and called them to action. At the same time, when elites wrote about slums, they tended to romanticize and exoticize them as sites of spectacular brutality and sexual degradation to which they were compulsively drawn.[11] Slums were anarchic, distant outposts of empire peopled by violent and primitive races; but they were also conveniently close, only a short stroll from the Bank of England and St. Paul's, inhabited by Christian brothers and sisters. They were prosaically dull and dangerously carnivalesque.

The metropolitan slums provided well-to-do philanthropic men and women with an actual and imagined location where, with the approval of society, they could challenge prevailing norms about class and gender relations and sexuality.[12] These men and women may well have needed the freedom the slums offered them more than the poor in their adopted neighborhoods benefited from their benevolent labors. Such claims capture the complex social dynamics of philanthropic encounters between rich and poor, as well as my own ambivalence about them. Reformers' creativity and passion, their sincerely felt and lived ethos of service, inspire admiration. At the same time, many were deeply invested in the titillating squalor of the slums, which they used as stages upon which they enacted emancipatory experiments in reimagining themselves. Synonymous with squalid tenements and soiled lives, the slums of London ironically functioned as sites of personal liberation and self-realization—social, spiritual, and sexual—for several generations of educated men and women.[13]

Upper-class men and women had long ventured into the low haunts of London in pursuit of illicit pleasure. In 1670, the Queen and the Duchesses of Richmond and Buckingham caused a public uproar when they disguised themselves as "country lasses" at Bartholomew Fair to mingle undetected with the common people. "They had all so over done it in their disguise," Sir Henry Ingilby reported in his diary, that they quickly drew the attention of the mob, which angrily pursued them all the way to the Court gate. Ingilby concluded his entry "thus by ill conduct was a merry frolic turned into a penance."[14] It would be easy to trace an unbroken history of such self-serving escapades from the seventeenth to the twentieth centuries. But by the mid-nineteenth century, altruists began to rival pleasure seekers in shaping public perceptions of the purpose and meaning of descents into the spaces of the poor. Well-to-do philanthropists justified their slum journeys as a way to do penance for the sins of their class, to investigate and study the poor, and to succor them. Far from concealing their slum explorations, they did their best to publicize them in the name of social science, civic duty, and Christian love. They used the materials they gathered—statistical, anecdotal, visual—to write sociological reports, political-economic treatises, novels, passionate sermons, and revelatory newspaper articles; to secure jobs in private voluntary associations and in expanding social welfare bureaucracies within local and national government; to bolster their credentials as expert witnesses before parliamentary commissions of inquiry and as members of parliament.

If slumming was an indispensable method of gathering knowledge about urban poverty, it also revealed the extent to which charity was, according to the expatriate American novelist Henry James, "a kind of passion." But what was the nature of this "passion"? How did this "passion" affect the ways in which well-to-do Victorians came to define social problems and their solutions? James's understanding of the London poor was at best superficial. He was, however, an astute observer of the inner longings of his English peers, those extraordinarily articulate "public moralists" who molded opinion and devised policies on social questions.[15] His writings suggest that the Victorians' "passion" for charity was fueled by unconsummated and unacknowledged desires for all sorts of taboo intimacies between rich and poor, the clean and the dirty, the virtuous and the verminous, men and women, women and women, and men and men.[16] James could not help thinking that there was "something indecent" about so much goodness.[17]

Many kinds of love, sexual and nonsexual alike, animated Britons' engagement with philanthropy. I investigate how the histories of sexuality and sexual desires usually associated with the private lives of individuals intersected with the public histories of benevolence to shape metropolitan philanthropy and social welfare. While I do not anachronistically impose the vocabulary of twentieth-century psychoanalysis on my nineteenth-century subjects, I do attempt to illuminate their psychological and sexual complexities. I examine the motives, representations, meanings, and consequences of their forays into the slums of Victorian and Edwardian London. At the same time, I reconstruct as best I can the responses of the poor to their uninvited visitors. The circumstances and survival strategies of the poor necessarily shaped their vision of the world and of their social betters.[18] This book reveals the extent to which politics and erotics, social and sexual categories, overflowed their boundaries, affecting one another in profoundly consequential ways for our understanding of poverty and its representations, social policies, and emerging sexual and gender identities in modern Britain.

SLUMMING DEFINED

How did Victorian men and women define the activity "slumming" and its closely associated verb forms "to slum" or "to go slumming?" What meanings did they associate with these terms? How do I define and use them in this study? Let me answer each of these questions in turn.

In August 1893, Adderley tried to answer the question "Is Slumming Played Out?" for the middle-brow *English Illustrated Magazine*. "The fashionable slumming of eight years ago," he assured readers, "is given up as a wholesale practice." He quickly defined "fashionable slumming" by offering several egregious examples of its excesses. He conjured "the languid lady" driven down to the docks to see a flesh-and-blood "stevedore" for the sole purpose of impressing her dinner guests that evening (841). He blasted the "provoking rich people" who arrived in East London so filled with literary preconceptions that actual slums were not nearly "slummy enough" for them.[19] Fashionable slumming encouraged some observers to trivialize poverty, transform it into self-serving entertainment, and perpetuate absurd misconceptions about the savagery of the poor.[20] It disguised prurient curiosity in the garb of social altruism. There was no reason to lament its passing as a fad.

The clarity of Adderley's moral judgments matched the slipperiness of his rhetoric and arguments. Despite his condemnation of fashionable slumming, he claimed that the attitudes promoting it spurred new approaches to charity, foremost among them the growing belief that "cheque-book philanthropy" (merely giving cash donations) was no substitute for giving one's own best self to the poor in friendship. Adderley contrasted one set of practices he abhorred—fashionable slumming—with another he admired but to which he attached no name. However, the weight of the evidence he put forward undermined his own attempt to construct straightforward distinctions. The very institutions he singled out for doing genuine Christian work among the poor, such as Dr. Barnardo's schemes to rescue street children and the university settlement in Whitechapel, Toynbee Hall, were also the epicenters of fashionable slumming in the 1880s and '90s.[21] Unable to wrest the word "slumming" from its association with prurient curiosity, Adderley nonetheless wanted to harness its social and cultural resources for benevolent ends. He concluded his article with a rousing call for thoughtful university men to join him in serving the London poor.

> Let no young man think his education complete until he has come to know the poor, their lives and their needs. Let the sons of the upper classes strike out courageously beyond the conventional philanthropy of their parents and get over their suspicions of "Socialism." Let them investigate that creature whom they call a "cad" and discover his lurking heart and soul.

Why did Adderley provide examples of fashionable slumming but yet never explain what "slumming" itself meant or how it related to the charitable schemes detailed in his article? His inclusions and exclusions provide several important clues. His article conspicuously ignored the vast army of philanthropic women—from the elite Ladies Bountiful to the working class Ranyard Bible nurses and Salvation Army "slum lassies" (estimated at 500,000 in 1893)—who were rapidly making benevolence into a feminized enclave of social life.[22] While Adderley's article ostensibly denounced the idle rich regardless of their sex, he subtly associated the vices of fashionable slumming with women by his choice of examples (recall the "languid lady") and by the close identification of femininity and fashion. Excluding female benevolence in all its many forms made his appeal to the "sons of the upper class"—and not their daughters—seem inevitable and logical.[23] My point here is not to show that Adderley was mean-spirited toward women. He was not. Rather, I am arguing that Adderley's attempt to preserve Christian work among the poor from contamination by fashionable slumming depended on an unstated set of assumptions about gender and his own unacknowledged investment in making philanthropy appealing to men at a time when women were coming to dominate it.

Slumming, the word and the activities associated with it, was distinguished historically by a persistent pattern of disavowal. It was a pejorative term used to sneer at the supposedly misguided efforts of other people. As a form of urban social exploration, it bore the obloquy of sensationalism, sexual transgression, and self-seeking gratification, not sober inquiry and self-denying service to others. Clergymen, journalists, novelists, philanthropists, social investigators, and reformers, therefore, went to great lengths to contrast their supposedly high-minded engagement with social problems with the activities of casual "slummers."[24] Attaching the rhetorical label "slumming" to a social practice was a very effective way to discredit it and to distance oneself from it. An editorial published in the radical journal the *Link* in October 1888 blasted the "gorgeously plumed birds of passage" who "slummed because . . . the horrors they brushed by threw into more brilliant relief the daintinesses of their own fair surroundings . . . because a morbid curiosity, sated with novelistic pruriences, craved the stronger sensations of real abominations."[25] The *Link's* outspoken editors, Annie Besant and William T. Stead, had themselves undertaken hundreds of slum journeys, seeking to bring justice to the disinherited through their inflammatory articles. Just as slumming itself brought together the high and the low, it confounded clear-cut distinctions between true and false charity.[26]

Casual slumming often merged imperceptibly into sustained attempts not just to grapple with the costs of poverty in individual lives, but also to formulate systemic critiques of social and economic injustices. In the letters, memoirs, and autobiographies of leading reformers and politicians, we encounter a recurring pattern: an early episode of slumming, motivated largely by curiosity, sets the stage for deeper awareness of and commitment to redressing the evils of urban poverty. When William Beveridge first visited Toynbee Hall, he felt like "an American tourist doing Whitechapel in two days," but by the time he left, he had begun to analyze the structures of wages and work that caused unemployment and to propose solutions to them.[27] Jane Addams, the American feminist-internationalist, condemned the way in which slumming produced an "unfair," "fragmentary," and "lurid view of poverty." But she also acknowledged that her midnight tour of East London in the autumn of 1883, perched safely atop an omnibus hired by a West London Missioner, left an indelible and salutary imprint on her imagination. The socialist H. M. Hyndman heaped scorn upon slumming as a general social phenomenon:

it was one of the odious privileges of the bourgeoisie, a symptom of the ills of capitalist Britain rather than a means to solve them. But he, like Addams, confessed in his memoir that a "tremor of fitful sympathy among the well-to-do" in 1866 had pricked his social conscience and led him to join "guardsmen and girls of the period, rich philanthropists and prophets of Piccadilly, students of human nature and cynics on the make" to betake themselves "with hearts and pockets bursting with charity to the choicest rookeries to be found along the riverside."[28] Just as spiritual autobiographers following Augustine emphasized their youthful carnality to demonstrate God's grace in leading them to sanctity, so, too, social reformers and political activists confessed their own guilty pleasures of "slumming" in order to criticize them.

The urban historian H. J. Dyos has argued, and I think cogently so, that the word "slum" has "no fixity" and "was being used in effect for a whole range of social and political purposes."[29] The fundamental instability of meanings attached to the "slum" and its associated word forms is reflected in the *Oxford English Dictionary*'s definitions. According to the *OED*, "slumming" is "the visitation of slums, esp. for charitable purposes." But it referred readers to the verb "to slum," which it defined in several ways: "to go into, or frequent, slums for discreditable purposes; to saunter about, with a suspicion, perhaps, of immoral pursuits" and "to visit slums for charitable or philanthropic purposes, or out of curiosity, esp. as a fashionable pursuit." "Slummers" usually referred to those who "slummed" or engaged in "slumming"; but, maddeningly, "slummers" also described the poor residents of slums. Charity and philanthropy mingle with immoral pursuits and voyeuristic curiosity in these definitions, which refuse to be definitive.[30]

Following Dyos's lead, I have made mobility, not fixity, central to my definition of slumming. I use slumming to refer to activities undertaken by people of wealth, social standing, or education in urban spaces inhabited by the poor. Because the desire to go slumming was bound up in the need to disavow it, my history of slumming includes the activities of men and women who used any word except slumming—charity, sociological research, Christian rescue, social work, investigative journalism—to explain why *they* had entered the slums. My definition of slumming depends upon a movement, figured as some sort of "descent," across urban spatial and class, gender and sexual boundaries. The sermon preached by Rev. Prebendary W. Rogers in Balliol College Chapel on Sunday, February 4, 1883, captures well the spatial dynamics of slumming with its sanctioned immersion in an otherwise forbidden world. Rev. Rogers invited his audience "to descend with him" into the streets of East London to confront the rampant "coarseness and vulgarity," "poverty and meanness written upon the countenances of the wayfarers . . . vice flaunting itself in gaudy apparel." Not satisfied with the grotesque spectacle of the street, Rogers beckoned churchgoers to penetrate even more intimate interior spaces of the poor: "Follow these people home to their wretched houses in which they are huddled together like the beasts that perish, and you will find them grossly ignorant, semi-paupers."[31] If, as cultural anthropologists tell us, dirt is matter out of order, then slumming required elite men and women to go where they did not belong, out of their expected places. While most justified their slum expeditions as part of an effort to expose and clean up the filth of city life, their roles as urban housekeepers existed in uneasy tension with their own disordering of class, gender, and sexual norms.

Contemporaries imposed a wide range of meanings and distinctions on their forays into the precincts of the poor as they vied with one another for preeminence in the crowded world of metropolitan philanthropy. While underscoring these differences, each of the following chapters identifies shared cultural assumptions about the social and sexual relations between rich and poor, men and women, that bound together the varied forms of slumming examined in this book.

WHO WENT SLUMMING? SOURCES AND SOCIAL CATEGORIES

The socioeconomic backgrounds of those who went slumming and those they went to see ranged very broadly. Throughout this study, I will often use terms such as "rich," "elite," and "well-to-do" to characterize slummers. These terms lack precision for they include men and women whose social worlds had little in common beyond their sense that they commanded resources entitling them to gawk at or help the poor. The capaciousness of these terms reflects the heterogeneity of slummers, who included members of the royal family, such as Princess Alice of Hesse; scions of Britain's most eminent aristocratic dynasties, such as the prime minister Lord Salisbury, whose sons William and Hugh lived in Oxford House in Bethnal Green; upper-middle-class political elites, for example, William Gladstone, whose daughter Helen lived in the south London slums as head of the Women's University Settlement; the offspring of clergymen and professionals aspiring to gentility; and merchants and their children for whom slumming marked their own recent social ascent. Some, such as the journalist James Greenwood, came from very modest backgrounds and used their slumming to earn their living rather than as a way to share their wealth.[32]

The so-called poor, the objects of all this unsolicited benevolence, likewise spanned a considerable spectrum from the homeless to sweated workers packed into one-room tenements to seasonally employed unskilled laborers to regularly employed skilled artisans, whose wages surpassed those of junior clerks. Once again, this grouping defies the commonsense categories of social history.[33] Why lump together such diverse people under the umbrella of "the poor" or "laboring men and women" or "the working class"? After all, the late-Victorian pioneers of empirical sociology such as Charles Booth and Ernest Aves, Jesse Argyle, Beatrice Potter, and Clara Collet, themselves deeply involved in the mania for slumming in the 1880s, went to great pains to offer fine-grained distinctions between different groups based on earnings and social and cultural habits. A highly skilled "labour aristocrat" had no more in common with an out-of-work member of the so-called "residuum" or "submerged tenth" than a titled noblewoman did with the daughter of a tradesman who, by dint of intelligence and determination won a scholarship to Girton or Newnham College before embarking on a paid career as a social worker in the slums. "Elite," "poor," "well-to-do," and "laboring people" remain useful though descriptively imprecise terms because they signal the social distance—and contemporaries' own perception of that distance—which lay at the heart of slumming and slum benevolence. Terms such as "the poor" also convey the social reality that even skilled and relatively well-paid laboring men and women, over the course of their lives, did often experience periods of want and poverty occasioned by sickness and unemployment.[34] Many who went slumming came to appreciate the crudeness of their own initial ideas about poverty and understood the vast differences in outlook separating denizens of penny-a-night lodging houses from those pillars of working-class respectability who took pride in their immaculate broom-swept front stoops and lace curtains. Other less careful observers did not bother to make such distinctions, generalized about the poor based on their observations of a few sensational cases of misery, or felt cheated when the men and women they encountered seemed altogether too respectable.

I pay scrupulous attention to the widely varying reasons for and contexts surrounding the many forms of slumming analyzed in this book. For example, we need to understand the particular bureaucratic and moral imperatives which led David Edwards, a licensing inspector for the London County Council, to go undercover and inspect a music and dance hall, the Rose and Crown, on December 29, 1890. The Rose and Crown so happened to be located in one of the most impoverished quarters of East London near the Docks. Neither a craving to see how the poor lived nor charity motivated Edwards. No love of disguise led him to go undercover; inspectors were expected to blend into their surroundings to better observe them. He had a job to do that night, and he did it. But the way he wrote about and interpreted his experiences tapped into much broader ways of thinking and writing about slum life. Edwards could have chosen simply to note that some female prostitutes and their customers frequented the Rose and Crown. Instead, he transformed a routine report of inspection into a tale of disgust and titillation. He reproduced his conversations with a prostitute who importuned him to go home with her. And then, as if anxious to avoid incriminating himself, he opined that "my reason for making such a long report is because I can find no other name for such a place than a hell."[35]

Edwards's sweeping moral condemnation of the dance hall and all its female habituées as prostitutes did not go unchallenged. The official case file of the administrative hearing noted that during the ensuing interrogation, "A Voice from the Hall" cried out, "many a respectable woman goes there." We will never know to whom that disembodied voice belonged, though we can surmise it may have been a woman (or her husband) who went to the Rose and Crown and believed that Edwards's words had besmirched her reputation.[36] Readers will encounter many other such voices throughout this book, ranging from the indignant accusations of several children Dr. Barnardo "rescued" to the self-assertive political rhetoric of laboring men in a Bethnal Green club who refused to play the deferential part their Oxford sponsors had assigned to them. These voices are potent reminders that those positioned as objects of slumming readily challenged their social betters' characterization of them and had their own ideas about the affluent men and women in their midst. The poor asserted themselves in their daily encounters with philanthropists, but they did so within circumstances of grotesquely unequal power.

Men and women who went slumming left behind an extraordinary abundance of sources—letters, diaries, memoirs, books, articles, speeches, newspaper stories, annual reports, visual images—which the historian can use to recreate their social and mental landscapes. Sometimes we are fortunate enough to have autobiographies (published and unpublished) and letters written by laboring men and women, which give a fuller sense of their perspective and their use of language to express themselves. However, most residents of working-class and poor neighborhoods in London, while increasingly active participants as readers in Victorian and Edwardian print culture, did not usually have the time, desire, or need to write down their thoughts and feelings.[37] We more often than not hear their voices through texts produced by the well-to-do. For example, the spinster housing reformer Ella Pycroft wrote to her colleague Beatrice Potter, daughter of a wealthy merchant and railway executive, recounting the reactions of several East Londoners to an article on unemployment and slum housing that Potter published in the *Pall Mall Gazette*.[38] Pycroft had circulated Potter's article among residents in the Katherine

Buildings, at least one of whom was not edified by what he read. Pycroft explained to Potter that three of the poor residents "having read the article dispassionately, understand it and agree with it all." But one, a man named Joseph Aarons, "was specially angry at your saying the Buildings were 'designed and adapted' for the lowest class of workmen partly because he will take 'low' to mean 'disreputable'; partly because he shares our feelings about the construction of the Bgs. [buildings]. But I told him you did not mean to express approval of their construction, but on the contrary had written strongly against it."[39]

Pycroft's letter offers a fragmentary glimpse, albeit filtered through her own grid of personal and political preoccupations, of an independent-minded working man's response to the elite slummers in his midst. Far from deferring to Potter as either a "lady" or an amateur sociologist, Aarons objected to her choice of words, which he recognized would adversely mold public perceptions of the social and moral status of the building's residents. Pycroft, as the author of the letter, gets the final word here as she often, though not always, did in her dealings with her clients. At the same time, her letter captures an otherwise irretrievable moment of intellectual and personal negotiation between an elite woman reformer and a poor man—a sort of tug of war Pycroft and Potter daily enacted with the residents of Katherine Buildings in their philanthropic rounds as lady rent collectors.[40] While extant sources make it possible to trace the evolution of Potter's and Pycroft's ideas about class relations, poverty, and gender, we can recover little more about Aarons' thoughts.

The great social statistician Herbert Spencer was, like Joseph Aarons, quite critical of the way his gifted protégée Beatrice Potter depicted social problems. Spencer distrusted the reliability of information gathered through slumming and urged Potter to put a halt to her risky "doings in London" investigating sweated labor disguised as a poor Jewish seamstress. "Bear in mind," Spencer admonished, "that the experiences which you thus gain are misleading experiences; for what you think and feel under such conditions are unlike what is felt and thought by those whose experiences you would describe."[41] For Spencer, Potter's incognito slumming could not possibly serve either her best interests as a young single woman or those of the emerging scientific and objective discipline of sociology.[42] Such methods of collecting data were inherently flawed because they blurred the line between participant and observer, social facts and individual fancies. Spencer's objections to Potter's escapades (which she herself later dismissed as a "lark") can be restated in more general terms: slumming was antithetical to seeing society as it truly was. We need not share Spencer's confidence in the superiority of his own sociological methods to concur with him that slumming *did* shape how elite men and women represented their experiences among the poor, defined social problems, and developed solutions to them. This is precisely what makes its history so important.

EROS AND ALTRUISM: JAMES HINTON AND THE HINTONIANS

Punch, Victorian Britain's ever vigilant monitor of shifting cultural norms, seemed quite certain that slum benevolence was neither wholly pure nor wholly disinterested. In 1884, it published "In Slummibus," an ironic visual satire depicting a preening clergyman surrounded by two demurely attractive young ladies carrying presumably wholesome literature for the heathen poor (figure below). The title of the image undoubtedly makes fun of the fad for hiring omnibuses to take visitors through East London's poorest neighborhoods without soiling their shoes and clothes.[43] As the three philanthropists gaze upon the squalid slumscape through which they stroll, they are far from masters of all they survey. They are subjected to the stares and impudent commentary of the poor, including one "small Eastendian" who remarks (in *Punch*'s best version of proper Cockney): "'Ello! 'Ere's a Masher! Look at 'is Collar an' 'At!" In *Punch*'s commentary, the man of God is mistaken for a "masher," a slang phrase for a male sexual predator. Apparently, the poor can see through the clergyman's upright appearance to discern his base motives. He is no different from thousands of West End gentlemen "mashers" who regularly ventured to East London to sample its illicit pleasures: sex, drugs, penny gaffes, and music halls.

As *Punch*'s imagery suggests, slumming raised troubling ethical questions about the very nature of the philanthropy itself. Was philanthropy a laudable form of self-denial, an expression of a deep human impulse to witness and enter sympathetically into the suffering of others in order to diminish it? Or was benevolence merely a cover for egoistic self-gratification, a means imaginatively and literally to enter otherwise forbidden spaces, places, and conversations, to satisfy otherwise forbidden desires? What was the right relation between serving others and pleasure? Was eros compatible with altruism?[44]

These questions loomed large in the life and writings of the mid-nineteenth-century aural surgeon and social philosopher James Hinton and lay at the very heart of this book. Hinton's private history and the public history of his ideas and their reception closely parallel that of slumming itself: it is a story of unruly desires and their disavowal, of high ideals and vexed realities. Victorian reformers drew inspiration from many sources, but it was Hinton who most deeply and explicitly articulated how the problems of slum life and the attractions of slumming were enmeshed in a

IN SLUMMIBUS.
Small Eastendian. "Ello! 'ere's a Masher! Look at 'is Collar an' 'At!"

The stiffly erect, gaitered clergyman appears utterly disdainful of and disconnected from the squalid scene that offers a virtual ethnography of slum types in
the imagination of elite observers: barefoot ragged children, a powerful and
defiantly-posed working woman with her laundry behind her, and a group of
seemingly drunk men clustered in front of the pub, one of whom is so degenerate that he has a simian rather than a human face. (*Punch*, May 3, 1884, 210.)

complex matrix of sexual and social politics. My own discovery of Hinton and my surprise that his ideas touched so many men and women involved in slum benevolence helped to shape the questions I pose in this
book. Using Hinton as the philosophical point of departure for my history of slumming—instead of other more familiar thinkers such as
Thomas Carlyle or John Ruskin or T. H. Green—signals my intention to
construct a genealogy of benevolence and social welfare in which gender
experimentation and heterodox sexuality figure prominently.

As slumming gathered momentum in the early 1880s, some claimed
that society was beginning to reap the harvest of enlightened altruism
Hinton had sown in the years before his death in 1875.[45] Hinton devoted
his life to unraveling the mysterious sources of the desire to serve others
as part of his larger project to liberate women and men from the body-
denying and soul-withering values which he believed inhibited human
self-development.[46] He could find unity in his philosophy only by mixing
"intimately with and becom[ing] the friend of the lowest and poorest
class." He traced the origins of this impulse to his experiences as an apprentice to a woolen draper in Whitechapel, where he daily witnessed the

sexual degradation of laboring women. He ached to live among the poor "as a man longs for his wedding-day"[47] and insisted that the rich could only realize their fullest selves by sympathizing with and serving those in need. He decried the spiritual deadness of conventional morality, which cut men and women off from nature and the life-affirming wellsprings of genuine altruism.[48] Rejecting the belief that women's moral authority was based on their "passionlessness," Hinton insisted that it was not only moral but essential for women, as much as men, to enjoy sexual pleasure. He anticipated the day when all women would be emancipated from ruinous "social disabilities," which kept them from realizing their god-appointed tasks to rule by serving others.[49] Men would only reach their human potential once they had been "womaned"—subjected to women's beneficent influence.[50]

Hinton was a philanthropic hedonist. Refusing to play the part of self-sacrificing do-gooder, Hinton urged contemporaries to seek pleasure through altruism which would in turn result in social and sexual freedom. At the very heart of his project was the imperative to train human desires to serve others and by so doing unlock those natural "pleasures, instincts, impulses" that society was so determined to repress.[51] The conduct of his life, his outward appearance, and his manners were as striking and unconventional as his ethics and explain in part his impact on contemporaries. He wore ill-fitting and conspicuously plain clothes and had no tolerance for social formalities. In the eyes of Edith Lees Ellis, an ardent proponent of women's rights and lesbian wife of the founder of British sexology, Havelock Ellis, Hinton was "the ascetic and the sensualist alike," "a muscularly strong man with the tenderness of a woman."[52] Hinton's body became the mirror of his social and sexual ethics: he was both masculine and feminine, self-denying and pleasure-seeking.

Now forgotten by all but a small handful of scholars, Hinton exercised a magnetic personal and intellectual hold over his disciples, whose substantial contributions to Victorian debates about sexual and social problems bore no relation to their small numbers.[53] In the 1870s and '80s, Hinton's followers included not only Edith Lees but also her future husband, Havelock Ellis.[54] Ellis, along with Hinton's wife, Margaret, and her sister Caroline, were original members of the Fellowship of the New Life, the precursor of the much better known socialist Fabian Society. The Fellowship consisted of approximately thirty men and women committed to discussing decidedly unorthodox ideas about society—including Hinton's—and enacting them in their daily lives.[55] Hinton's teachings left an enduring mark on one of Britain's best-known female social purity campaigners, Ellice Hopkins, who worked among prostitutes and demanded that men be held to the same standards of chastity as women.[56] Hinton was a spiritual guide and mentor to the Oxford historian of the industrial revolution, Arnold Toynbee, and influenced Toynbee's friends Henrietta and Samuel Barnett, who founded Toynbee Hall in 1884, the university settlement in Whitechapel named in Toynbee's memory.

Hinton's writings may have focused exclusively on sex between men and women, but his ideas about sexual freedom struck a particularly resonant chord among well-educated philanthropic men and women like Edith Lees Ellis who were attracted to members of their own sex. The married aristocratic poet Roden Berkeley Wriothesley Noel (third son of the Earl of Gainsborough), possessed with "a soul Bisexual," found in Hinton's theories a way to combine his zeal to better the plight of poor children with his equally absorbing passion for describing and enjoying beautiful male bodies.[57] Other university-educated men shared Noel's interest in Hinton's ideas as well as his search for an ethical creed compatible with their love of male comrades. When the Arts and Crafts socialist Charles Ashbee returned to Kings College, Cambridge, after a sojourn in the Whitechapel slums at Toynbee Hall, he talked over Hinton's theories with his circle of friends and with Edward Carpenter, the age's most outspoken defender of homosexual rights and one of Roden Noel's confidants.[58]

If Hinton mattered so much to thoughtful men and women destined to leave their mark on modern British history, why has he languished in such obscurity? Hinton's virtual erasure from history must in part be attributed to the opacity of his prose and his lack of a coherent philosophical system.[59] But his disappearance from history was also the result of a deliberate campaign of rumor and innuendo in the 1880s intended to discredit him and his ideas at precisely the time his disciples tried to secure his reputation as a first-rate thinker and social visionary. Hinton was pilloried for violating a litany of sexual norms: espousing free love and the virtues of nakedness; engaging in an affair with his sister-in-law; and offering attractive women an opportunity to experience the joys of sexual liberation with him.[60] When his son Howard actually did abandon his wife and position as science master at Uppingham and entered into a free union with Mrs. Maud Weldon in 1884, many felt that the son's transgressions vindicated their worst suspicions about his long-dead father.[61] Hinton became persona non grata with many late-Victorian proponents of frank discussion of sex and social reform who felt too vulnerable to criticisms about the conduct of their private lives to risk association with the disgraced Hinton.[62] The quicksand of sexual scandal, based wholly on unsubstantiated rumor, swallowed up Hinton's good deeds and philosophy, leaving behind few visible traces of his once formidable influence on contemporaries' understanding of the dynamics of eros and altruism.

Even this cursory overview of the dense networks of discipleship and affiliation surrounding Hinton demonstrates that his ideas contributed substantially to innovative philanthropic movements and social purity crusades and formed part of the intellectual lineage of ethical socialism, radical sex reform, and the "science" of sexuality. In the chapters that follow, I reintroduce many of his followers as they wrestled with the legacy of his life and ideas in their day to day work in the slums. Just as men and women whose sexual subjectivities spanned a wide spectrum of same- and opposite-sex desires found spiritual and intellectual sustenance in Hinton, so, too, this book brings together their histories as they sought to integrate their approaches to urban poverty with their ideas about gender and sexuality.

Each of the next five chapters delves into the tension between eros and altruism at a particular moment in the history of slumming in London. I offer neither a continuous nor comprehensive narrative, but rather a series of case studies presented in loosely chronological order. The weight of my evidence and arguments are drawn from the period from the 1860s to World War I, but I will also reach backward to the 1840s and forward to the interwar period and beyond. I will move freely across traditional disciplines including history, literature, art history, and sociology in bringing together men's and women's, cultural and political, feminist and queer histories.

I am unashamedly opportunistic in my deployment of a wide range of methodologies and theoretical approaches but my championship of no one of them. My approach has been guided by pragmatic considerations: if a methodology makes it possible to tease out meaning from my evidence, I have used it to the best of my abilities. At the same time, I also have tried to interpret the words of my informants according to their own time-bound social and cultural logic. Understanding men and women from the past on their own terms is quite different from uncritical acceptance of them. I have sought to balance respect for the depth and extent of reformers' commitment to serving the poor with awareness that they imposed their own assumptions about sexuality, gender, and class on the poor. A great deal of useful scholarly energies have been devoted to sorting out whether the flowering of Victorian philanthropy grew out of genuine Christian empathy for the downtrodden or fear of the disruptive powers of the underclass; out of a desire to love the poor or to dominate them. The evidence gathered in this book suggests that we stand to gain deeper insights by exploring how these seemingly contradictory approaches and impulses co-existed and fed off one another without reducing one to the other. Consequently, I often provide more than one way to think about specific evidence and broader arguments rather than artificially disciplining my findings to support a narrower and more apparently coherent interpretation. While some readers may find this approach frustrating or equivocal, it constitutes less a refusal to make up my mind than an interpretation sustained throughout the book.

The book has a two-part structure. Part one, "Incognitos, Fictions, and Cross-Class Masquerades" consists of three chapters, each of which explores elites use of deceptive practices (incognitos, undercover investigative journalism, falsified photographs) to reveal "truths" about the poor that they claimed would otherwise have remained hidden. I explore contemporaries' responses to the ethical conundrums raised by these techniques for producing knowledge about and images of the poor. All three of these chapters interpret texts and images of the poor, the context of their production and circulation, and their impact on the subsequent histories of social policy, sexology, literature, journalism, and photography. These chapters address broad themes in Victorian society, but I approach them through the narrower lens of the work of an individual or a key episode in that person's life. While my aims are not those of the biographer, I hope that readers will feel as though they have had a chance to get to know my subjects in their complexly flawed humanity.

These chapters build on the insight that clothing was both a metaphor and a marker of class and sexual identities.[63] Given the vast scale of life in London and its limitless possibilities for encounters with strangers, most had no choice but to assume that the clothes a person wore defined who a person was. At the same time, Londoners knew all too well that clothes were unreliable signifiers of identity because they could be removed as easily as they were put on. The slum explorers, reformers, and journalists discussed in part one cast off their clothing—and with it the constraints though not privileges of their social status—to gain insights into the poor and themselves.[64]

Disguise and the homoerotic possibilities of nakedness were key issues in the workhouse scandal and press sensation examined in chapter one, "Workhouse Nights: Homelessness, Homosexuality and Cross-Class Masquerades." This chapter recreates the chain of social, cultural, and political responses to a series of newspaper articles published in January 1866 by the journalist James Greenwood, who audaciously disguised himself as a tramp and spent the night in the state-regulated ward for homeless men in the Lambeth Workhouse. Greenwood's claim that the casual ward had been transformed into a male brothel for the "hideous" enjoyment of homeless men and youths unleashed a moral panic and led Londoners to wonder whether Greenwood was a selfless crusader exposing the cruel treatment of the homeless poor or an unscrupulous adventurer gratifying his own morbid curiosity. I trace the enduring impact of this workhouse scandal on the British state's construction and regulation of male homosexuality and homelessness.

A decade later, Londoners once again found themselves discussing the truthfulness and sexual morality of a man who claimed to be a champion of the outcast poor. Chapter two, "Dr. Barnardo's Artistic Fictions: Photography, Sexuality, and the Ragged Child" recovers the meanings of photographs of street children, whose tattered garments not only revealed their vulnerable bodies but also beseeched viewers to act on their behalf. Such images have a long history—beginning in the 1870s, when the renowned evangelical philanthropist Dr. Thomas John Barnardo first photographed "street arabs" in his care, ostensibly to document the conditions under which he originally found them and to advertise his own benevolence. This chapter examines the 1877 arbitration hearing in which Barnardo defended himself against charges that he kept company with a prostitute, abused the children in his Home and circulated falsified and sexually provocative images of them (his so-called artistic fictions). The Barnardo controversy, like the workhouse scandal examined in chapter one, led contemporaries to contemplate the relation between eros and altruism. Was Barnardo an upstanding Christian or a sexual miscreant? Did his staged photographs of children, taken in his studio, capture the essential truths about their harrowing lives on the streets or did these images memorialize Barnardo's self-serving exploitation of his helpless charges?

Chapter three, "The American Girl in London: Gender, Journalism, and Social Investigation in the Late Victorian Metropolis" recreates the transatlantic world of female investigative journalists in the slums of New York and London from the 1880s to 1920s. I highlight the transatlantic migrations and elaborate self-inventions of one woman, Elizabeth Banks, who claimed for women the right to imitate James Greenwood by disguising herself as a laboring girl to garner copy for her articles. Unlike either Greenwood or Barnardo, Banks never pretended to be motivated by a desire to help others. This chapter explains why Londoners were so disconcerted and intrigued by Banks's refusal to play the part of either the crusading journalist or Lady Bountiful. It sets Banks's exploits against the backdrop of shifting constructions of femininity and the social and cultural history of women's incognito slumming and their journalistic accounts of female labor and urban poverty.

Part two, "Cross-Class Sisterhood and Brotherhood in the Slums" consists of two chapters analyzing the tensions between the rhetoric and practice and erotics and politics of brotherly and sisterly love for the poor. I move away from the biographical approach deployed in part one and offer a more panoramic view of philanthropic and religious institutions and movements in late-nineteenth- and early-twentieth-century London. While scandals about sex (or, more accurately, about putative sex acts) figure centrally in part one, part two delves deeply into the subtle but also elusive articulation of sexual desire, sexual subjectivity, and gender ideologies. These closely linked chapters underscore how conceptions of fraternity and sorority shaped reformers' programs and policies for the poor and their efforts to understand themselves as individuals. At the same time, I analyze how poor men, women, and children negotiated with their would-be benefactors and manipulated elite preconceptions about them to extract what resources they could.

Part two extends my engagement with the impact of imperialism on slumming, a theme that enters briefly into part one. These two chapters demonstrate the ways in which the metropolitan slums and distant outposts of empire were linked in the British imperial imagination as places of freedom and danger, missionary altruism and sexual opportunity. Many male and female reformers discussed in part two not only constructed rhetorical analogies between the two but literally moved between them during the course of their own careers. The American philosopher William James was appalled by precisely the tendency to conflate slums with colonial possessions, which he detected in Rudyard Kipling's writings. "Kipling knows perfectly well," James complained, "that our camps in the tropics are not college settlements or our armies bands of philanthropists, slumming it; and I think it a shame that he should represent us to ourselves in that light."[65]

Dirt as a material phenomenon and as a sexually charged metaphor in the daily lives and writings of educated independent women forms the subject of chapter four, "The Politics and Erotics of Dirt: Cross-Class Sisterhood in the Slums." The first part asks why elite women were so fascinated by dirt and shows how this influenced their analysis of the economics and sexual politics of female poverty in London. The second part turns more fully to the "erotics" of dirt by focusing on the relationship between dirt, dirty bodies, and dirty desires in women's writings about slum life. Chapter five, "The New Man in the Slums: Religion, Masculinity, and the Men's Settlement House Movement" opens with an overview of the history of fraternity and fraternal ideologies in Victorian Britain and then analyzes the interplay of religion and sexuality in benevolent institutions devoted to cross-class brotherhood. I focus on the first two settlement houses, pan-denominational Toynbee Hall and High Anglican Oxford House, as sites where elite men destined to play leading roles in church and state in the twentieth century experimented with unconventional ideas about politics and class relations, brotherhood and democracy, gender and sexuality.

Asserting the historian's peculiar prerogative to dwell in the past, I have largely left it to readers to discern for themselves the implications of this study for the world in which we live. In several chapters, I provide epilogues which briefly trace some of the more striking post–World War I legacies of the particular stories I have told. This book emphasizes the challenges several generations of energetic and compassionate men and women confronted in their efforts to better the lives of the London poor. In simplest terms, it shows just how difficult it was—and is—to translate the desire to be good into actually doing good for others. I hope that this study may perhaps inspire and chasten those intent to better the world to reflect deeply on the implications of the choices made by like-minded men and women a century ago.

PART ONE

INCOGNITOS, FICTIONS, AND

CROSS-CLASS MASQUERADES

Chapter One

WORKHOUSE NIGHTS:

HOMELESSNESS, HOMOSEXUALITY,

AND CROSS-CLASS MASQUERADES

I N THE SUMMER of 1865, the reform-minded medical journal the *Lancet* commissioned three doctors, led by Ernest Hart, to investigate the deplorable conditions of infirmaries attached to London's forty-three Poor Law Union Workhouses, those despised institutions of last resort for the indigent, the disabled, the aged, and the sick of the metropolis.[1] In 1864, "wretched [Timothy] Daly," had died in the Holborn Workhouse through the malign neglect of untrained nurses, themselves paupers, and of the Guardians of the Poor who had been too cheap to provide nighttime care for sick inmates. This case was followed by the equally harrowing death of Richard Gibson in the St. Giles and St. George Workhouse in Bloomsbury in 1865.[2] Many of Britain's most influential poor-law and sanitary reformers threw their weight behind the *Lancet*'s campaign, including the redoubtable champion of modern nursing Florence Nightingale, who entered the fray over the medical care of the London poor with the same gusto that had made legendary her work in Scutari during the Crimean War.[3] Nonetheless, the *Lancet*'s articles failed to capture the imagination of the broader public who, understandably, lacked an appetite for administrative details about pauper diets, the cubic space requirements of the sick, and the professional qualifications and emoluments of workhouse nurses and doctors.[4]

However, the *Lancet*'s articles did catch the eye of Frederick Greenwood, the enterprising editor of the fledgling newspaper written by and for "gentlemen" readers, the *Pall Mall Gazette*.[5] He believed that the *Lancet* had hit upon a story he could transform from a worthy public-health controversy into a media sensation. Frederick decided to launch his own investigation into workhouses. He recruited his brother James to undertake an audacious and unprecedented task, one he hoped would more effectively capitalize on public anxieties about the metropolitan underclass than had the *Lancet*'s initial campaign to make infirmaries into free hospitals for the poor. He asked James to disguise himself as a homeless tramp to see and hear for himself what it meant to spend a night locked up in the casual ward for destitute wayfarers and vagrants that was attached to the Lambeth Workhouse.[6]

By mid-January 1866, a series of articles entitled "A Night in a Work-house," written by James Greenwood but reprinted under the pseudonym "The Amateur Casual," appeared in the *Pall Mall Gazette* and overnight created a new mode of journalistic reporting—incognito social investigation using cross-class dress—and a new style of sensational and self-consciously theatrical writing about the poor.[7] In the previous two decades, Charles Dickens and Henry Mayhew had trawled the back streets and alleyways of London seeking scenes of destitution to reproduce for their eagerly indignant readers, but they had remained sympathetic outsiders and observers of life among the poor. The Amateur Casual had undertaken a more daring assignment: he had masqueraded as one of the poor to experience firsthand what it meant to be an inmate in a ward for indigent wayfarers, tramps, and other homeless people.

"A Night" helped establish the *Pall Mall Gazette* as Victorian Britain's leading paper devoted to exposing social evils and launched James Greenwood's long career as one of the preeminent chroniclers of London's netherworlds. Greenwood's articles made the degrading conditions in the casual wards of workhouses an instant cause célèbre. The *London Review* feigned bored indifference to the stir but aptly captured the public's perverse mingling of injured virtue with licentious hunger for scandal: "We are remarkably subject to periodical fits of reformation," its writer explained. "The parochial gruel is not now more diluted than it was six months ago, and just as many paupers may have died on it then as at present; but our virtue is at this season roused to the point, and we must have our craving satisfied."[8]

Greenwood's series circulated widely on all levels of British society. In the midst of his first week as leader of the House of Commons, William Gladstone took time out from his worries about the fate of parliamentary reform to read "A Night."[9] The week before, "Conductor 1548" of a southbound Hampstead omnibus stole "a minute or two" from his work to peruse "A Night" "while his vehicle was slowly progressing over London-bridge."[10] The series sold by the thousands in penny broadsides for the poor and in shilling pamphlets for the well-to-do, in turn spawning popular broadsides responding to it[11] (figures 1.1a and b). For a brief moment, Britons across the social and political spectrum put aside their anxieties about the attacks of Fenian nationalists in Ireland to contemplate horrors all too close to home. Reprinted in papers throughout the metropolis and Great Britain, "A Night" also attracted international notice. The socialist and historian of revolution, Louis Blanc, digested them for *Le Temps*, leading some French newspapers erroneously to attribute Greenwood's discoveries to Blanc himself and to chide the

English for needing a Frenchman to show them "the real state of their workhouses."[12]

What had Greenwood discovered—or at least purported to have uncovered—during his single night in the workhouse? Why did it, and not the graphic descriptions of bodily misery and official ineptitude published in the *Lancet*, become a Victorian sensation? What have scholars had to say about "A Night" and its enduring significance? While less well known today than the exposés of poverty and vice of Henry Mayhew's *London Life and Labour* series in the 1850s, Andrew Mearns's *Bitter Cry of Outcast London*, and W. T. Stead's "Maiden Tribute" series in the 1880s,[13] "A Night" has not languished in obscurity. I first encountered it almost twenty years ago in the pioneering work of literary historian P. J. Keating, who had reprinted it entirely as the first selection of his anthology of Victorian writing about the slums and offered a perceptive critical assessment. Anthologized again more recently, "A Night" has been studied closely by historians of journalism and the press, theater historians, literary critics, and social historians of the urban poor.[14] Quite remarkably, none of these scholars has noticed the "startling revelation" that made "A Night" a sensation rather than yet another assault on poorhouses: the supposed transformation of the male casual ward of the Lambeth Workhouse into a male brothel. According to Greenwood, public authorities were using public money to create the conditions that encouraged the most vicious male members of the metropolitan underclass to engage in sodomy.

Greenwood's "A Night" established an ongoing tradition of imagining the precincts of poverty in London as "queer" and "eccentric"[15] spaces in which social investigators, clergymen, reformers, philanthropists, social workers, and writers could explore and represent heterodox sexual desires and practices.[16] The historical significance of "A Night" depends in part on the ways in which Greenwood and his diverse audiences linked together concerns about male sexuality with attitudes about the metropolitan underclass and social policies and practices. The publication of the articles precipitated a moment of remarkable convergence between high and low reading publics, between sensational journalism, social reform, and sexual politics. Unlike so many other Victorian exposés, "A Night" *did* have a lasting impact on how contemporaries perceived and represented the poorest of the poor in the metropolis and contributed significant momentum to those forces calling for reform of the Poor Laws and the government of London.[17] The format, language, themes, and images Greenwood deployed in this series recur over and over in the writings of philanthropists, journalists, and reformers for the next seven decades.[18] It served as a kind of template upon which renowned slum explorers, such as W. T. Stead, Jack London, and George Orwell, necessar-

STARTLING PARTICULARS!

A NIGHT

IN A

WORKHOUSE.

From the PALL MALL GAZETTE.

By James Greenwood.

January 1866.

HOW THE POOR ARE TREATED IN LAMBETH!

THE CASUAL PAUPER!

"OLD DADDY," THE NURSE!

THE BATH!

The Conversation of the Casuals!

THE STRIPED SHIRT!

THE SWEARING CLUB!!

'Skilley" and "Toke" by Act of Parliament!

The Adventures of a Young Thief!

&c. &c. &c.

BOWERING, 211, BLACKFRIARS ROAD,
SELL & SON, King Street, Borough, and all Newsagents.

PRICE ONE PENNY.

FIGURE 1.1a. "A Night in a Workhouse" was a publishing sensation that captured readers across the entire social and economic spectrum. While it was initially published in the *Pall Mall Gazette*, the newspaper for gentlemen, it soon sold in the thousands in the streets of London. The cover of the penny edition, intended for the working poor, emphasized the sensational disclosures awaiting readers.

A NIGHT

IN A

WORKHOUSE.

Reprinted from the

"PALL MALL GAZETTE."

LONDON:

OFFICE OF THE PALL MALL GAZETTE,

14, SALISBURY STREET, STRAND, W.C.

Figure 1.1b. The cover of the shilling pamphlet, intended for well-to-do readers, conveys the seriousness of the topic and physically resembles countless other tracts on sanitary and social questions. Both editions were published in 1866. (Figure 1.1a reproduced with permission from the Albert and Shirley Small Special Collections Library, University of Virginia.)

ily inscribed their own stories about the slums and against which we in turn can reread their narratives.

Claiming that "A Night" was a scandal about the putative sexual practices of homeless poor men raises the question: Why have other scholars *not* noticed the single most salient and salacious "fact" Greenwood disclosed about men's casual wards?[19] In what sense were sexual secrets at the heart of the text of "A Night" and public responses to it? How and why did its homoerotic dimensions come to be so securely and safely closeted? Recovering the diverse ways in which Greenwood's mid-Victorian contemporaries understood the social and sexual dimensions of his investigation makes it possible to analyze the consequences of "A Night" for perceptions of the homeless and their treatment. What impact did "A Night" have on ongoing debates about metropolitan poverty and elite slumming, private benevolence and public policy, male sexuality and its regulation? The four parts of this chapter provide some answers to these questions. The first introduces Greenwood and the political and social setting of London in January 1866. Because "A Night" was first and foremost a news story written to satisfy the particular needs of a specific moment in time, understanding the context of its immediate production and reception is important. It helps to delineate some of the public preoccupations of Greenwood's first readers that he skillfully mobilized in writing the series. The second offers a close—and sequential—reading of the individual articles comprising "A Night" as each originally appeared in installments in the *Pall Mall Gazette* during the week of January 12, 1866. By so doing, this section preserves the problematic striptease-like structure Greenwood chose to impose on his tale—with its partial disclosure of the naked truths he claimed to have discovered—in order to call attention to it as a rhetorical strategy. It also underscores the ways in which he used the literal limits of the newspaper page to create in his readers a desire to read the next installment. The third analyzes how Greenwood's readers across the social and political spectrum responded to and appropriated "A Night" to serve their own varied agendas. This section charts the ways in which social responses to "A Night" simultaneously fed off but also occluded the story's sexual dimensions. The sheer overwhelming number and variety of social responses threatened, but never quite succeeded, to dissipate entirely the initial sexual charge that animated the public's interest in "A Night." The fourth section considers the influence of "A Night" on sexology—in particular ideas about male homosexuality—and state policies toward the poor. The fifth section functions as an extended postscript in which I read several well-known works of social criticism and urban exploration from the 1870s to the 1930s against Greenwood's "A Night." By so doing, I show that the cultural logic underpinning representations of the very poor set in motion by "A Night" had all too real consequences for the way public officials and private individuals dealt with homelessness and homosexuality in modern Britain. Social and sexual politics became inseparable bedfellows in the history of "A Night" and its long afterlife in the nineteenth and twentieth centuries.

JAMES GREENWOOD AND LONDON IN 1866

James Greenwood was a prolific writer who produced a flood of articles and books between the 1860s and the turn of the century.[20] And yet, for a man whose thoughts circulated so widely in public, we know remarkably little about his life. The younger brother and sometime collaborator of the founding editor of the *Pall Mall Gazette*, Frederick Greenwood, James often presented himself to his readers as a "gentleman" reporter. He frequently exploited the contrast between his supposed status as a gentleman and the squalor of the scenes of his journalistic investigations. His gentility was a recent acquisition, more wishful pose than reality.[21] One of eleven children of a carriage upholsterer, he entered the world of letters through his work as an apprentice in a print shop and later as a freelance journalist.[22] At the time he wrote "A Night," he was an obscure thirty-five-year-old journalist and hack novelist. The newspaper editor, Edmund Yates, who under the nom de plume "The Flaneur" commented on Greenwood's exploits for the *Morning Star*, characterized the denizens of the Bohemian demi-monde of which Greenwood was a part as "young, gifted, and reckless; . . . they worked only by fits and starts, and never except under the pressure of necessity. . . . [T]hey had a thorough contempt for the dress, usages, and manners of ordinary middle-class civilization."[23]

Greenwood wrote extensively in many genres about crime, poverty and empire, but London's children especially engaged his sympathies. In the 1850s, he contributed frequently to the *Boy's Own Magazine*. At approximately the same time he wrote "A Night," he published the novel *The True History of a Little Ragamuffin*, which combined fiction with documentary reportage in examining the life of a London "street arab."[24] He followed up his casual ward workhouse sensation of 1866 with another commissioned exposé for the *Pall Mall Gazette* entitled the "Wrens of the Curragh"—about a community of female "Irish" prostitutes living in so-called nests made of "furze" and serving the sexual needs of the British army camp stationed in Newbridge, Ireland. Reminding his readers about the truthfulness of "A Night," Greenwood explained that he had once again spent a harrowing and "long night" mingling freely with the forlorn objects of his inquiry.[25] While the misery of the poor provided copy and hence a livelihood for Greenwood, he also participated in philanthropic work. In the 1890s he joined forces with John Kirk, the secretary of the Ragged School Union, to send slum children on country holidays. Although consistently engaged with social issues, he never developed a systematic program of reform. Had Greenwood died in 1900, at the height of his fame, he would undoubtedly have been hailed as a pioneering journalist and altruistic writer on social evils. But Greenwood was one of those minor Victorian celebrities who simply lived too long, his efforts long forgotten. His death in 1927 at the age of 96 went virtually unnoted by the London press, whose development he had so importantly encouraged.[26]

Greenwood's premise for "A Night" was simple: he would disguise himself in what he imagined were the clothes of an unemployed casual laborer and spend a single night in the workhouse in Princes Road, Lambeth. Lambeth, site of the archbishop of Canterbury's London residence on the south bank of the Thames, was also beset by chronic poverty.[27] Greenwood aimed to investigate the workings of the recently enacted Metropolitan Houseless Poor Act from the perspective of an inmate of a casual ward. Greenwood published the articles in three consecutive numbers, January 12, 13, and 15, without his name. Anonymity, far from deflecting attention away from the author, added to the playful air of mystery Greenwood cultivated. The *Birmingham Journal*, for example, wryly remarked that

> Who wrote the experiences of a casual in a Workhouse? has been almost as momentous a question during the week as "Who killed Cock Robin?" in the nursery tales. Mr. Oleby, Mr. Hollingshead, Mr. Halliday, Mr. Greenwood, Mr. Trollope, have been all named as probable authors . . . but it turns out it was written by Mr. Greenwood. Not the Mr. Greenwood, the Editor of the *Pall Mall*, but his brother. . . . For authority, it is said he doesn't deny it.[28]

What impelled Greenwood to undertake such a novel descent? Greenwood anticipated that readers would question his motives and felt compelled to justify his actions. Others had written about workhouses, he averred, but he alone, "with no motive but to learn and make known the truth, had ventured the experiment of passing a night in a workhouse, and trying what it actually is to be a 'casual.'"

Seeking "truth" may have played a part in Greenwood's plan, but he had other, far less disinterested motives as well. The scheme was concocted by his older brother, Frederick, who offered the assignment to James, "a rough diamond" who "did not by any means jump at the proposal" until offered the very substantial sum of "thirty pounds down and more if it turns out well."[29] While James had a large financial stake in the success of his venture, Frederick was under even greater pressure. By the beginning of 1866, the *Pall Mall Gazette* was in jeopardy of closing down on account of its meager circulation and revenues; "when to stop or go on became a question daily renewed," Frederick candidly recalled almost thirty years later.[30]

An array of specific and general circumstances made an incognito inquiry into the state of the casual ward of a workhouse attractive to Greenwood in January 1866. An unusually cold winter in 1865–66 exacted a high toll on the homeless poor, whose ranks were still swollen by the economic dislocations of the American Civil War and the ensuing unemployment caused by the Lancashire cotton famine. For many Britons, the cotton famine had revealed an admirably stoic and moral working class whose sufferings compelled redress.[31] The day the first installment of "A Night" appeared, January 12, the streets were blanketed by snow drifting three and four feet high. Under these conditions, even the most hardhearted Londoner would probably have felt some compassion for the homeless poor.

The winter of 1865–66 was also an opportune time to test the efficacy of the Metropolitan Houseless Poor Act, which had only a few months before been made into a permanent statute.[32] The act obliged guardians of the poor to provide food and lodging for all "destitute wayfarers, wanderers, and foundlings" regardless of their character and place of settlement.[33] It was a kind of bill of rights for vagrants, some of whom kept up with the latest enactments of the Poor Law and tenaciously invoked its clauses in their often brutal encounters with recalcitrant local officials. As Beatrice and Sidney Webb noted in their encyclopedic history of English poor-law policy, the act offered guardians of poor districts heavily populated by casuals a substantial bribe by "making . . . the cost of relief given in the casual wards a common charge upon the whole of London."[34] It was one of many attempts to more equitably share the burdens of caring for the poor across the entire metropolis. This was a matter of considerable importance as the last remnants of the resident urban gentry in parts of South and East London moved west and north or to the rapidly expanding ring of suburban "villadom." Just barely respectable ratepayers (residents whose taxes—"rates"—supported local government and service) in slum districts were much less able than wealthy Londoners in fashionable districts to shoulder the high cost of helping their impoverished neighbors in time of need.

Even before coming into effect, the act had been attacked severely from many quarters in terms all too familiar to students of poor-law reform. Vestrymen, elected agents of the most local form of government within London, tended to be small businessmen and tradesmen who zealously tried to curb the costs of assisting the poor within their community. They complained that the Houseless Poor Act interfered unduly in the affairs of overburdened rate payers and forced them to enlarge their accommodation for the homeless but did not provide them with adequate funds to do so. Others grumbled that the act left too much discretion in the hands of mean-spirited local guardians who could not be trusted to meet their obligations to the poor.[35] While champions of local government bemoaned the act's tendency to expand the power of central government, the president of the Poor Law Board and his inspectors felt that the act had not given them enough authority to ensure uniform compliance.[36] Its sponsors never pretended that it would solve the fundamental social and economic problems that produced vagrancy. Rather, by forcing poorhouses to make room for the homeless, the act aimed to clear the streets, doorways, and alleys of the very poor, whom many Londoners abhorred as an unsightly and foul-smelling public nuisance. The Greenwood brothers were determined to expose the iniquities of parochial treatment of the homeless poor, who had been so recently secreted from view by Parliament.[37]

Throughout the final months of 1865, mistreatment of casuals had become a regular feature of the London press. Sanitarians, poor-law reformers, and journalists closely monitored workhouse deaths caused by inhumane management and grossly inadequate medical and nursing provision. Ernest Hart's Lancet commission was only the most visible form taken by the campaign to reform workhouse infirmaries. In the late 1850s, a group of progressive women reformers led by Louisa Twining had already taken the initiative in demanding improved conditions in workhouses and in workhouse nursing by forming the Workhouse Visiting Society and its informative and forceful Journal of the Workhouse Visiting Society. In September 1866, Millicent N., a correspondent to the Victoria Magazine for Women made no attempt to conceal her anger that men were getting all the credit for discovering workhouse abuses for which women had earlier put forward "wise and careful" remedies.[38]

The two workhouse campaigns complemented one another: while Greenwood's articles about scandalous conditions in the casual ward attracted greater public notoriety, reform of workhouse medical provision engaged some well-established luminaries, such as Florence Nightingale, Charles Dickens, and John Stuart Mill.[39] Years later, Frederick Greenwood explicitly acknowledged his debt to Hart's initiative in providing inspiration for "A Night." Searching for a story that would draw attention to the Pall Mall Gazette, he began to ponder "some dreadful reports of investigation into certain infirmaries, which reports excited no public attention whatever, being printed in a medical journal. This recollection suggested a night in the casual ward of a London workhouse as a sort of knife that might accomplish several efficient bits of business at one stroke."[40] Only the week before Greenwood's "A Night" appeared, papers in the metropolis followed the inquiry into the death of a rheumatic elderly casual named Fellowes or Flowers (the press apparently could not decide or did not care what his actual surname was). Locked in an unlit ward of the Bethnal Green Workhouse, he had fallen from his bed in the middle of the night and had been left to die without benefit of medical treatment.[41]

It is also likely that the Greenwood brothers were influenced by Charles Dickens's "night walks" published in his *Uncommerical Traveller* and by his latest novel, *Our Mutual Friend*, which appeared in serial form in 1864 and 1865.[42] "A Night" bears striking resemblance to many aspects of *Our Mutual Friend*, especially in its use of cross-class incognito disguises and the confusion of altruistic, heteroerotic, and homoerotic impulses.[43] Dickens's journal, *All the Year Round*, published several articles about "A Night," and commentators frequently described "A Night" as Dickensian and invoked characters from various Dickens's novels in their responses to it.

The *Pall Mall Gazette* and the Greenwood brothers also benefited from the way in which London, by virtue of its unique status as the seat of parliament and as the financial capital of a global empire, magnified and transformed local issues into national and imperial ones.[44] If Manchester, with its filthy industrial landscape and strained relations between industrialists and laborers, was the shock-city of early Victorian Britain, London, with its dramatic contrasts between remarkable wealth and squalid poverty, increasingly preoccupied social commentators from mid-century onward. With the death in October 1865 of Lord Palmerston, the great Whig Prime Minister and inveterate opponent of parliamentary reform, the enfranchisement of a substantial number of laboring men seemed inevitable. Debates over the nature of franchise reform in 1866 and 1867 revolved around establishing the boundaries between one group of men deemed worthy of inclusion in the political nation—the respectable, independent working man living in a stable residence as head of household—and another deemed unworthy of the privileges of citizenship—the wayward "rough" and dependent pauper who flitted from one cheap lodging to another.[45] By 1867, the great Liberal reformer John Bright had declared the existence of a class he called "the residuum," whose exclusion from the rest of the male working class was essential for the nation's well being.[46] Controversies surrounding the democratization of the franchise contributed substantially to the overheated atmosphere with which London's elites received disclosures about the state's treatment of the poor. In writing and publishing "A Night," the Greenwood brothers hoped to cash in on widespread anxieties about the government of the metropolis, the conditions of workhouses, and parliamentary reform and, at the same time, expand the *Gazette's* readership and advance their own professional fortunes.

James Greenwood's claim that he was motivated solely by "truth" was but one of many misrepresentations concealed in "A Night." Greenwood also erased entirely from his text a young stockbroker called Bittlestone, who accompanied him on his night's errand.[47] Perhaps Greenwood felt that acknowledging Bittlestone would diminish the drama, danger, and heroism of his singular descent. Once "A Night" was published and critics began to scrutinize it for factual errors, it was impossible for Greenwood to mention Bittlestone without compromising his credibility. The crusading journalist W. T. Stead, writing about "A Night" in 1893, felt that there was nothing more to say about Bittlestone beyond the fact that "four eyes were better than two" in observing and writing up the results of their investigation.[48] I disagree. Restoring Greenwood's invisible male companion to "A Night" leads the reader to ask new questions about each scene: Where was Bittlestone? What did he see and what did he do? Because Bittlestone remains a silent witness and participant in Greenwood's escapades, the answers to these questions can be no more than speculations.

Bittlestone's oddly absent presence has come to embody for me all the other omissions, half-truths, and partially concealed messages contained in Greenwood's text. His relationship to Greenwood mirrors the way sexual themes are both unmistakably joined to and yet also entirely hidden by concern about poor relief and vagrancy in the metropolis. He is, at least in textual terms, so completely absorbed into Greenwood that he leaves no trace of his existence. At the same time, Bittlestone's pairing with Greenwood is just one of the many duplicitous doublings that structure "A Night," including Greenwood's double self as the journalist who writes about workhouse abominations and the gentleman disguised as a tramp who witnessed them. Greenwood's omission of Bittlestone from his narrative gives us good reason to believe that Greenwood's description of his incognito persona as a "sly and ruffianly figure" is also an apt description of Greenwood the philanthropic journalist and author of "A Night."

READING "A NIGHT IN A WORKHOUSE"

January 12, 1866

Exploiting the comic and ironic detachment of the third person singular, Greenwood opens the first installment of "A Night" with a description of his costume and his descent from his carriage to the dirty street.

He was dressed in what had once been a snuff-brown coat, but which had faded to the hue of bricks imperfectly baked. It was not strictly a ragged coat, though it had lost its cuffs—a bereavement which obliged the wearer's arms to project through the sleeves two long inelegant inches. The coat altogether was too small, and was only made to meet over the chest by means of a bit of twine. This wretched garment was surmounted by a birds eye pocket handkerchief of cotton, wisped about the throat hangman fashion; above all was a battered billy-cock hat, with a dissolute drooping brim. Between the neckerchief and the lowering brim of the hat appears part of a face, unshaven and not scrupulously clean.[49]

Greenwood's costume ostensibly signals his self-refashioning into one of the casual poor. However, his ease of transformation may have unintentionally reminded readers that clothing was not only an essential source of information about a person's social identity but also an unreliable one as well. After all, if Greenwood could pass for a casual, how could his readers know whether others were what they appeared to be? Such questions were consequential for Londoners who, lacking direct knowledge of so many of the people they encountered in their daily lives, nonetheless had to distinguish between the credit-worthy and the profligate, bona fide and false philanthropists, deserving and undeserving poor. When reformers discussed reorganizing charitable relief on a metropolitan-wide basis in the 1860s, they couched their arguments explicitly in terms of the need to curb imposture, importunity, and fraud.[50]

Greenwood's pleasure in the details of his costume underscores one of the many unacknowledged ironies of "A Night": he has gone to great lengths and expense to acquire a costume to impersonate someone who cannot afford decent clothes. The details ostensibly illustrate Greenwood's authority as an ethnographer of the poor by demonstrating that he already knows what a typical "casual" looks like and how he wears his clothes. The image he evokes of his own absurd appearance allows him to laugh with his elite readers at the expense of the ragged poor. As the tale unfolds, his readers learn that his "wretched garments" are in fact quite elegant by prevailing standards among his fellow inmates who, we must presume, are either "professional" or "actual" casuals in contrast to his own status as an "amateur" theatrical performer.[51]

Greenwood's experiment in disguise simultaneously reinforced and undermined the fundamentally mimetic goals of Victorian and Edwardian philanthropy. If philanthropy was supposed to encourage the poor to mimic their social betters without seeking to displace or become them, Greenwood's incognito "inverted" this framework by making a spectacle of a dandy pretending to be, but never quite becoming, a tramp. Greenwood and his readers allow themselves to enjoy the otherwise forbidden pleasures and dangers of pretending to "become" tramps, the lowest of the outcast poor; but just as Greenwood can and does return to the reassuring and familiar comfort of his home, so, too, "A Night" never calls into question the existing structures of power that subsidized both Greenwood's incognito descent and the fantasy of slumming in cross-class dress.[52] His adoption of masquerade as a tool of social investigation ironically echoes the use of drag by London's sodomites in the nineteenth century to advertise their sexuality and the widespread use of disguises by extortionists and undercover policemen from the 1830s onwards to entrap men on grounds of indecent assault.[53]

It is not clear precisely when Greenwood assumed or was given the pseudonym Amateur Casual in the days following the publication of his unsigned articles, but he continued to use it for many years as did other slum explorers.[54] The word "amateur" had deep resonance in Victorian culture. It carried with it connotations of a gentlemanly ideal of engagement in public life or in pursuit of an interest actuated by the pleasures of "love" as opposed to the money-grubbing imperatives of professionalism. Contemporaries celebrated local or parish government as a bastion of amateurism and as a distinctly English way of governing. Greenwood's use of the name Amateur Casual was disingenuous: it implied that he was literally a lover of casuals while at the time obfuscating the fact that he was a professional casual, if not an habitual one, in that he was paid for his masquerade.

"A Night" revolves around a series of overlapping and parallel tropes of dressing and undressing the body, hiding and exposing social evils, and saying and censoring the full truth. Its structure anticipates the emergence of the striptease as an erotic performance practice.[55] While its outcome is always heavily pre- and overdetermined, the narrative inflames its readers' desires for full disclosure by delaying or sometimes altogether refusing to expose the mysteries it has produced. In this respect, Greenwood participated in a tradition of writing about the city as mystery that had been popularized by Eugène Sue's Les Mystères de Paris in the 1840s, which spawned imitators throughout the European and trans-Atlantic world.[56] To heighten our sense of sharing in his dangerous exploits, Greenwood adopts the rhetorical strategy of doing what he says he cannot—or should not—do. For example, at one point he declares that "no language with which I am acquainted is capable of conveying an adequate conception of the spectacle I then encountered." The claim that his discovery cannot be represented was a familiar device often used by writers describing conditions of the poor, the insane, and other suffering people. It invited—in fact, it required—readers to represent for themselves indescribable horrors. The pretense that the scene is beyond representation is immediately belied by the following paragraphs, which offer ample evidence of Greenwood's ability to overcome this supposed limitation.

Greenwood makes literal the rhetorical striptease of "A Night" in one of its most memorable scenes. Adopting the alias Joshua Mason, he enters the workhouse. He is received by an older man called Daddy. Daddy is the benevolent pauper warder, an inmate of the poorhouse who superintends food distribution and sleeping arrangements in exchange for extra daily rations. Like a real father, Daddy lovingly tends his flock of dependents. Daddy orders the infantilized Joshua to "take off your clothes, tie 'em up in your han'sher" so that he can lock them away for safety. Joshua Mason/James Greenwood compliantly removes his coat and waistcoat, but Daddy insists "that ain't enough, I mean *everything*." Transformed into a frightened, deferential school boy, Joshua asks, "Not my shirt, sir, I suppose?" "Yes, shirt and all" Daddy insists. Greenwood disrobes not only for Daddy, but also for the "gentleman readers" of the *Gazette*.[57]

Greenwood's ritual stripping is followed by his plunge into the repulsive water of one of the "three great baths, each one containing a liquid so disgustingly like weak mutton broth." His "plunge" excited universal commentary and, more than any other episode in "A Night," earned him praise for heroic self-sacrifice. A writer for *Reynold's Newspaper* gave free play to his own imagination in fabricating "facts" about Greenwood's bath and the previous bathers. The "grey and greasy appearance of the water," he claimed, "was the result of the filth, floating and liquified, eliminated from the unclean carcases of miserable paupers."[58] In this nightmarish rewriting of Greenwood's "mutton broth," paupers' bodies become "carcases," their dirt almost excrement.

Why did Greenwood's account of the bath resonate so deeply with contemporaries? In part, the bath was noteworthy because Greenwood's language and staging of the scene are so vivid. The "weak mutton broth" color of the water ironically comments on the absence of all meat products from the daily diet of adult male casuals, which consisted of six ounces of bread and a pint of thin gruel.[59] More compellingly, the bath, like the workhouse itself, fails miserably to perform its task. Instead of cleansing Greenwood, the water fouls his body with the dirt of at least a dozen tramps who have entered the workhouse and the tub before him.[60] Greenwood's "desperate" plunge into the much-used basin of water produces a disconcerting intimacy between his naked gentlemanly body and those of the tramps who have left part of themselves—their dirt—in the water. Greenwood's description of the bathwater adumbrates an even more disorderly mingling of male bodies awaiting him in the sleeping shed of the casual ward and awaiting his readers as they consume his narrative. His entry into the mutton-broth bath signals his willingness to violate, at least for one night, bourgeois taboos concerning hygiene, the body, and modesty. It is a parodic baptism, not into a community of Christian brothers, but rather into an atavistic fraternity of casuals.

Bathing had been a cornerstone of sanitary reformers' public-health agenda in London at least since an 1844 meeting at the Mansion House (the official residence of the Lord Mayor of London). Reformers had attempted but failed to convince local governments and the laboring poor that frequent bathing was not merely a godly activity, but also an effective means of containing the spread of disease and pestilence. In 1850, the bishop of London headed the Committee for Promoting the Establishment of Baths and Wash Houses for the Labouring Classes, which lobbied for the erection of model public baths throughout London. A pamphlet published by the Manchester Statistical Society in 1854 made explicit an assumption underlying the movement: the filthy bodies and clothing of the poor harbored infectious diseases that led to fatal epidemics. The pamphlet contended that public baths had mitigated the extent and deadliness of the cholera outbreak of 1854 in London.[61]

In the autumn and winter of 1865 and 1866, Britons were preoccupied with a widespread and costly cattle plague even as they prepared themselves for the likelihood of another deadly visitation of cholera. And, according to Norman Longmate, some even believed that "the cattle plague was really an animal version of cholera." John Snow's studies of the early 1850s linking the spread of cholera to impure water supplies and linens fouled by the excrement of its victims did little to allay popular perceptions that workhouses (and not water) were themselves sites of deadly contagion. Many continued to believe that filth, squalor, and sexual excess in themselves produced and predisposed people to disease. The brief appearance of cholera in Britain in late September 1865 offered no hint of the devastation destined to follow in the summer of 1866, but it did stimulate renewed public interest in preventing the spread of the disease and heightened public sensitivity to the dangers of precisely the sorts of unsanitary conditions prevailing in the casual wards of workhouses. While the mandatory dip into the workhouse bath was intended to prevent the spread of disease, the filthy bathing conditions prevailing in the casual ward struck many as a breeding ground of pestilence.[62] Greenwood played upon these anxieties effectively in his description of the bath and by using images of infection and contagion throughout "A Night" to describe the effects of mingling decent men and boys with already depraved and degraded inmates.[63]

According to Frederick, it was another bath the next day, one not recounted by James in the text of "A Night," that brought to an end James's experience as a casual.

When they [James and Bittlestone] went in they were well disguised, but any close observer would have perceived they were got up for the occasion. After spending sixteen hours in the cold, squalor and obscene brutality of the casual ward they seemed absolutely to have become confirmed tramps and vagabonds. . . . It was not until they had gone home, had a bath, and were comfortably warmed and fed, that they could be induced to talk quietly about their experience.[64]

This second bath reverses the terrifying descent into the casual ward initiated by the first. It enables James to metamorphose once again, only this time he is transformed from a tramp back into a gentleman-journalist. Perhaps even more significantly, this bath allows him to reclaim his social identity and marks the beginning of the process whereby he translates "experience" into speech and hence into narrative. The two baths—one involuntary, punitive, and disgusting; the other voluntary and therapeutic—underscore the vastly different experiences and meanings of bathing for rich and poor Victorians. It helps to explain the resistance and hostility so many poor people showed toward the well-intentioned zeal of many proponents of baths as instruments of social hygiene. Just as most of the poor loathed porridge because it reminded them of workhouse food, so too the ritual of bathing smacked of the humiliating initiation rites into the discomforts of prisons, casual wards, and night refuges.[65] In *Pygmalion* (1913), George Bernard Shaw used this history to great satiric effect in the most famous bath scene in British literature. The coerced confiscation of an enraged Eliza Dolittle's clothes and her compulsory plunge into a bath initiate her transformation from a "draggle-tailed guttersnipe" into a "lady" who can pass for a duchess. Shaw, like Greenwood, was keenly attuned to the confusion of erotic and hygienic impulses. What upper-class Higgins insists is merely a matter of basic cleanliness, Eliza and Higgins's servant, Mrs. Pearce, construe as an immoral violation of her bodily privacy worthy of police intervention.[66]

As soon as Greenwood enters the casual-ward bath, he learns that Daddy never intended him to bathe. Apparently, Daddy has not been fooled by Greenwood's disguise. Greenwood reports that Daddy tells him that he is "a clean and decent sort of man." Reproducing the social distinctions of the world outside the workhouse, Daddy explains that the bath is only for "them filthy beggars . . . that want washing." The kindly Daddy then hands Greenwood a fresh towel and a blue striped shirt. Wearing only his shirt, Greenwood progresses into the makeshift sleeping shed where his "appalled vision" takes in a scene akin to Dante's *Inferno*. As Greenwood begins to make sense of the contorted jumble of naked limbs and torsos in the overcrowded and cold shed, he observes that "in not a few cases two gentlemen had clubbed beds and rugs and slept together. In one case (to be further mentioned presently) four gentlemen had so clubbed together."

Greenwood's word choices layer irony upon irony. The repeated epithet "gentlemen" to describe naked, impoverished men and boys captured in lewd postures reminds readers that they, like Greenwood and his unacknowledged companion, are the only real gentlemen. At the same time, Greenwood's and his readers' claims to respectability are compromised by their desire and willingness to enter, literally or imaginatively, into the contaminated space of the shed. While the word "clubbed" means "shared," it also evokes the cozy intimacies of the upper-class male world of public schools, colleges, and the social, literary, and political clubs of London.[67] Once again, Greenwood suggests a parallel between his readers and the casual poor that simultaneously distances and collapses the distances separating them.

Victorian readers were well acquainted with the moral and sexual dangers of crowding large numbers of poor people into confined spaces. Alarm about the mingling of sexes, generations, and naked bodies played an essential role in several major public health, workplace, and purity campaigns in the decades before the publication of "A Night." *The First Report of the Commissioners for Enquiring into the Employment and Conditions of Children in Mines and Manufactories* (1842) was an immediate sensation because of its lurid descriptions and accompanying illustrations of the obscene conditions surrounding the work of naked (or near-naked) men, women, and children in the depths of mines.[68] The report so effectively deployed its sexually charged written and visual rhetorics that Parliament passed the 1842 Regulation of Mines Act, which overrode prevailing prejudices against state interference in the free labor market and excluded women and children from work in mines. Fears about sex between men and women and between men and girls were also staples of housing reformers throughout the century in their attempts to abolish single-room cottages and tenements. Such dwellings inhabited by entire families, and often by male subtenants unrelated by ties of kinship, promoted not only the spread of contagious diseases, reformers insisted, but incest as well.[69] With his 1847 *Quarterly Review* article, the evangelical Tory reformer Lord Shaftesbury became the most outspoken champion of state-mandated inspection of mixed-sex common lodging houses, whose unregulated disorders made them "the deepest dens of vice, filth, and misery."[70]

These campaigns and the subsequent parliamentary legislation stemming from them assumed that physical closeness necessarily led to the sexual degradation and exploitation of girls and women by men. Greenwood radically reworked this tradition by suggesting that an all-male space and institution could also be a site of moral and sexual danger. There were scattered precedents for such arguments. For example, some laboring people in the 1830s lamented that the New Poor Law encouraged unnatural sex in place of procreative sexual relations by substituting boys for wives as the bedpartners of destitute men.[71] More spectacularly, parliamentary investigations in 1846–47 revealed the chronic and pervasive practice of sodomy in convict colonies at Norfolk Island and Moreton Bay, where prisoners were housed in conditions very similar to the casual ward. The vast barracks lacked lights and supervision, and many lacked even rudimentary boards to separate sleepers from one another.[72] Many elite men, for their part, were all too well aware of the intense emotional and physical bonds between boys and young men that bloomed in the hothouse atmosphere of all-male public schools and colleges.

While the men and boys are condemned to the workhouse for the sin of homelessness, "A Night" intimates that they are guilty of other "unspeakable" vices as well. Exploiting fully the dramatic possibilities of serial newspaper publication, Greenwood postpones speaking about these vices until the next installment because he has, quite literally, reached the bottom of the printed page of the newspaper. He assures his readers that what he has told "is true and faithful in every particular. I am telling a story which cannot all be told—some parts of it are far too shocking; but what I may tell has not a single touch of false colour in it."[73]

January 13, 1866

So swift was the impact of the first installment of "A Night" that by the next day, Greenwood's audience had grown far beyond the regular readers of the *Pall Mall Gazette*. The installment for January 13 opens briskly with Greenwood's realization that the commotion of his fellow inmates—who smoked and spat tobacco and boisterously swapped autobiographical vignettes—made sleep impossible. In a passage that must have tested the limits of permissible expression in the daily press of the 1860s, Greenwood ruminates: "For several minutes there was such a storm of oaths, threats, and taunts—such a deluge of foul words raged in the room—that I could not help thinking of the fate of Sodom; as, indeed, I did several times during the night." At first glance, Greenwood's allusion to Sodom need not necessarily carry with it sexual connotations; in the 1860s, Sodom represented vice and deviant behavior in many forms. But his coy aside that he could not help thinking about Sodom "several times during the night" deliberately provokes readers to ask why and raises expectations of more explicitly prurient disclosures.

In the next paragraph, Greenwood indirectly but unmistakably demonstrates why he thought of Sodom "during the night," and, by so doing, implicates himself in the erotics of "A Night." His musings on Sodom are immediately followed by the introduction of "Kay" or "K.," an androgynous "lanky boy of about fifteen" to whom Greenwood is deeply attracted.

> He was a very remarkable-looking lad, and his appearance pleased me much. Short as his hair was cropped, it still looked soft and silky; he had large blue eyes set wide apart, and a mouth that would have been faultless but for its great width; and his voice was as soft and sweet as any woman's. Lightly as a woman, too, he picked his way over the stones towards the place where the beds lay, carefully hugging his cap beneath his arm.

Kay's entrance allows Greenwood to escape briefly from the squalor of his surroundings and experience a moment of visual and visceral pleasure. By metaphorically feminizing Kay—Kay picks his way "lightly as a woman"—Greenwood makes him into a somewhat more acceptable object of male admiration and lust. But when Kay, in a "sweet" voice, asks "who'll give me part of his doss [bed] . . . who'll let me turn in with him," Greenwood "feared how it would be."

One may well ask: what is it that Greenwood fears and for whom? Ostensibly, Greenwood is fantasizing about the fearful fate the beautiful Kay will suffer by sharing his bed and body with a degraded brute. Several paragraphs later, Greenwood acknowledges his own fears as well.[74] The arrival of "great hulking ruffians, some with rugs and nothing else" precipitates what can be read as another moment of panic. "This was terrible news for me. Bad enough, in all conscience, was it to lie as I was lying; but the prospect of sharing my straw with some dirty scoundrel of the Kay breed was altogether unendurable." Kay, the erstwhile "remarkable-looking lad" is now a paradigmatic "dirty scoundrel."

Greenwood ends his contribution for January 13, 1866, with an erotically charged glimpse of Kay standing at the water pump "without a single rag to his back," illuminated by the pale light of the "frosty moon" coming through the "rent in the canvas" wall of the shed. Reiterating his theme that what he has written is accurate and true, Greenwood unconvincingly dons the mantel of the self-sacrificing martyr and attempts to deflect responsibility for the articles onto Mr. Editor: "I hope, Mr. Editor, that you will not think me too prodigal of these reminiscences" in writing about "an adventure which you persuaded me ('ah,! woeful when!') to undertake for the public good." Once again, the *Pall Mall Gazette* and Greenwood used the literal limits of the printed page to keep readers eager for more disclosures.

January 15, 1866

The final installment, published on January 15, is the longest but, in many respects, least interesting of the three. The bulk of it describes the process of getting dressed in the morning, eating breakfast, and performing the compulsory labor of turning the large cranks of the flour mill located in the shed that had just served as the dormitory the night before. The last two paragraphs of this final installment of "A Night" offer a suggestive condensation of the written and unwritten messages, both permissible and taboo, contained in the articles taken together. Declaring that "the moral of all this I leave to the world," Greenwood absolves himself of responsibility for interpreting the tale he has told and for the consequences of leading his readers into morally and sexually dangerous territories. He also enjoins readers not to be swayed by the more favorable assessment of Lambeth Workhouse offered by Mr. H. B. Farnall, the metropolitan inspector for the Poor Law Board, published by the *Daily News* that same day.

Greenwood's short last paragraph, addressed to Farnall, is an almost spiteful act of titillation: "One word in conclusion. I have some horrors for Mr. Farnall's private ear (should he like to learn about them) infinitely more revolting than anything that appears in these papers." Greenwood will only whisper the naked truths of his nocturnal adventures among men and boys into the "private ear" of another man. The last paragraph, then, recapitulates not only the transgressive erotics of "A Night" but also recalls the homosocial character of both the male casual ward and the *Pall Mall Gazette*'s aspiration to be a paper written by and for "gentlemen."

Farnall's report on the condition of the Lambeth Workhouse—duly entered onto the workhouse visitors' book on January 13, the day the second installment of "A Night" was published—offers a terse official alternative to Greenwood's. While he demanded that the guardians immediately take certain corrective measures, Farnall lent the support of the Poor Law Board to the guardians of the Lambeth poorhouse: "I have today inspected the wards provided for the houseless poor in this workhouse, and which I have some time since certified as good and sufficient wards, and which I still consider to be so."[75] As Farnall's phrase "I have *today*" [my emphasis] makes clear, he visited the workhouse during the day in his official capacity as a poor-law inspector. By contrast, Greenwood gathered the data for his report on workhouse conditions disguised as a casual during the "night." Juxtaposing Greenwood's and Farnall's "inspections" suggests that the Lambeth Workhouse and its inmates look very different under cover of night than in the glare of the day. Greenwood uses "night" both as a condition of darkness and as a specific time to stimulate his audience to read beyond the printed page, to produce their own texts out of the dark corners of their fantasies about themselves and the poor.

Both literally and as a ubiquitous trope of philanthropic slum narratives, night liberates the impoverished inhabitants and well-to-do explorers of the slums to redefine the seemingly immutable conventions of class, gender, and sexuality that govern day and their "official" daily lives.[76] The darkness of night and his imposture as a casual make possible the "true" revelations Greenwood offers readers, whereas the light of day and the sanctioned apparatus of state inspection can only produce concealment and hypocrisy. Greenwood provides readers with the disturbing discovery that the meanings and uses of urban space are mutable and depend on who occupies the space, at what time, and under what conditions.[77] The workhouse, ostensibly the epitome of the state's disciplinary authority over the lives of the poor, becomes in Greenwood's account of it a place of publicly subsidized disorder and male same-sex license.

My reading of "A Night" has emphasized its many homoerotic themes and images; however, the calculated ambiguities of Greenwood's prose make it easy to miss them if we so choose. Greenwood's brilliance lay in his ability to disclose just enough of what he claimed to have observed to excite in his readers a desire to know the whole truth about male casual wards. He understood the particular pleasures of the process of coyly disrobing, in not allowing his audience to stare too long or too closely at the naked body supposedly concealed beneath. This is especially true for "A Night" because we are not quite sure that its rhetorical performance depends on real men engaged in real sodomitical acts. We, like Greenwood's mid-Victorian readers, can never recover what actually happened in the Lambeth Casual Ward the night Greenwood visited. However, we can explain why Greenwood's contemporaries were so obsessed with trying to authenticate every detail of his narrative. What was at stake for them?

RESPONSES TO "A NIGHT IN A WORKHOUSE"

"A Night" was at once remarkably protean and sticky. Its shape seemed to change according to the needs of each person who tried to grab hold of it. It literally assumed many different forms as it moved from its site of original publication as a series of articles in the *Pall Mall Gazette*, to condensed reprints and summaries in other newspapers, to pamphlets and broadsides,[78] to multiple theatrical productions, and even to illustrative photographs. Contemporaries succeeded in attaching many issues to "A

Night," such as parliamentary reform and the bloody suppression of the Jamaican insurrection in Morant Bay, which had no obvious or necessary connection to it. It provoked passionate public and private responses among a wide range of constituencies: the staff and readers of the *Pall Mall Gazette*; other journalists and writers; the guardians and vestrymen of Lambeth; state officials, including the home secretary and the commissioner of the Metropolitan Police; inmates in workhouses and casual wards; and a vast public of affluent and poor, educated and uneducated readers. It triggered many imitators and led to a far-reaching investigation, conducted largely through the daily and periodical press, into Greenwood's truthfulness and into the workings of the poor law. Even the leaders of the workhouse infirmary movement tried to take advantage of the furor to renew their claims to public sympathy. Reassembling the textual chain set in motion by the publication of "A Night" and tracing its complex effects (historical and literary) make it possible to analyze the social, political, and sexual investments that powerfully informed the various ways in which Greenwood's contemporaries understood "A Night." It also underscores the ways in which social and sexual categories sometimes reinforced one another, while at other times the social all but eclipsed the sexual, erasing its traces as effectively as Greenwood concealed the existence of his companion Bittlestone.

Politicians and Journalists

Frederick, in his lead article "Casual Wards," published the day after the final installment of "A Night," left no doubt that the Amateur Casual had witnessed an orgiastic scene of sex between men and youths. "What was done was worse than what was said," Frederick insisted, "and what was said was abominable beyond description or decent imagination." The workhouse had been transformed into a male brothel, "a sort of chapel of ease to the Cities of the Plain [Sodom and Gomorrah] for the hideous enjoyment of those who are already bad, and the utter corruption of those who are obliged to hear what they cannot prevent."[79] Sounds replace sights, ears replace eyes as the sensory means by which the moral and physical contagion of the casual ward spreads ineluctably from those who *are* corrupt to those who necessarily *will be* corrupted. Frederick's emphasis on the relationship of hearing to the "hideous enjoyments" of "A Night" recalls James's own repeated claim that what he heard during the night was worse than what he saw. "The conversation was horrible," James explained, "the tales that were told more horrible still, and worse than either (though not *by any means* the most infamous things to be heard—I dare not even hint at them) was that song." Of course, James *has* hinted at "them." Far from repressing the memory of these "infamous" sounds—which can only be sounds of sex—James and Frederick encourage readers to imagine and perhaps enjoy them. A popular penny broadside put the matter more succinctly though less explicitly: "there's queer doings after dark" in the Lambeth Workhouse.[80]

One indignant correspondent to the *Gazette*, John Smeaton, the governor of the Combination Poor House, Hawick, was agitated by what Greenwood had written and what he suspected Greenwood had done during his "night" in the workhouse. Greenwood was an untrustworthy guide, Smeaton insisted, because he misrepresented his identity and profession to gain admission to the casual ward. More threateningly, he insinuated that Greenwood had moved beyond the position of observer, one who merely sees and hears, to become a participant, one who knows through touch and intimate proximity. "P.S.," he wrote, "How did your correspondent find out that 'K.'s' hair was soft and silky, and his eyes large and blue, in such a large shed lighted by only one solitary gas jet?"[81] Smeaton's postscript viciously parodies Greenwood's own, which he introduced with the phrase "one word in conclusion." Far more important than the mere "postscript" it pretends to introduce, Smeaton's closing remark emphatically does not bring closure to his argument. It opens up the possibility of interpreting "A Night" as a text that incriminates its author in the evening's "abominations."

The *Pall Mall Gazette*'s editors answered Smeaton's question exclusively on its most literal level. The author of "A Night" and K. were together, the newspaper explained, "from sunrise till eleven o'clock in the day" so there was ample daylight in which to observe K.'s physical appearance. The editors sidestepped Smeaton's explosive suggestion that the *Gazette*'s correspondent had found in K. enjoyable compensation for his night's discomfort. However, three years later, in an essay on female prostitution, James did offer some revealing general remarks about what motivated him to meddle with such "unsavoury business." His work was galvanized, not by a search for dark pleasures, but by a righteous sense of social obligation and duty. Silence, he explained, served as a prophylactic—the "'evil-doers' armour of impunity'"—which encouraged "monstrous evil" to flourish.[82] For the journalist-as-social-observer to remain silent about evils he has seen would make him an accessory to immoral acts. In this way, the slum explorer bears a heavy moral weight to expose and correct the abuses he has uncovered even at the risk of compromising his moral standing in the eyes of others.

The public responded to "A Night" with a mixture of incredulity, outrage, and admiration. Was it possible that such abuses actually existed in Lambeth and elsewhere in the metropolis? Journalists and officials, as well as the merely curious, rushed to answer this question by following in Greenwood's footsteps. The first of Greenwood's many imitators was none other than the home secretary, Sir George Grey, who was accompanied by Sir Richard Mayne, the commissioner of the Metropolitan Police, and several others. According to the *Tower Hamlets Express*, this impressive group of gentlemen paid an "unexpected visit at midnight to inspect the casual wards" at Poplar.[83] Dubbed the "ministerial midnight inspection" by pundits, the dignitaries expressed themselves "perfectly satisfied" by conditions in the Poplar Workhouse.[84] They had selected Poplar because six weeks earlier, its guardians had enlisted the Metropolitan Police to act as assistant relieving officers. All those seeking admission to Poplar's casual ward first had to apply for admission at the police station. Direct police involvement not only diminished the number of applicants at Poplar but also curbed disorderly behavior inside the ward and made it explicit that the casual poor were indistinguishable from the criminal and dangerous classes. Soon thereafter, the Poor Law Board urged guardians throughout London to adopt the Poplar model by employing police as relieving officers. Although humanitarian impulses to secure the dignity and welfare of homeless citizens may have originally motivated some supporters of the Houseless Poor Act, such generous intentions were now hopelessly entwined with the more urgent imperative to police this population. The poor themselves were outraged that Greenwood's masquerade as a casual and as their would-be champion resulted not in improvements in their conditions but in further indignities. As one sharp tongued homeless woman exclaimed six months after the publication of "A Night," "D—— that fellow that made a bother about the vagrants; he has only given us extra trouble" by forcing the homeless to endure humiliating delays and abuse at police stations[85] (figure 1.2).

Journalists, unwilling to be outdone by cabinet members in their daring search for the truth about workhouses, no longer confined themselves merely to the "scribbling department." Emboldened by Greenwood's success, they anticipated a more dignified and elevated role for themselves as "the most efficient teachers of the age" and pioneers in "the realms of practical and everyday philanthropy."[86] Descending into the haunts of poverty promised journalists social prestige and professional advancement. In the winter of 1866, "practical philanthropy" proved extremely profitable for editors who dispatched scores of reporters to undertake midnight visits to workhouses, night refuges, and tawdry lodging houses. Publication of "A Night" initiated an extended dialogue between the *Pall Mall Gazette* and the rest of the London newspaper world, including the *Observer*, *Daily News*, the *Saturday Review*, the *Spectator*, the *Morning Star*, the *Telegraph*, and above all the *Times*. The *Times*'s enthusiastic and swift approval of "A Night" conferred prestige and legitimacy on the *Gazette* and the Greenwood brothers. Its

PUNCH, OR THE LONDON CHARIVARI.—February 3, 1866.

THE NEW WORKHOUSE PORTER.

Master Prig. "BLEST IF THEY HASN'T PUT ON A BOBBY! PRETTY STATE WE'RE COMIN' TO, WITH
THEIR CENTRALISATION! LET'S CUT TO LAMBETH."

FIGURE 1.2.   *Punch*'s cartoon rightly pointed out that "A Night" had made
admission to the casual ward more complicated and intimidating for the truly
deserving who, like the mother and child depicted, were compelled to present
themselves to the police before gaining admittance to the workhouse. The
cartoon also suggests that the criminal element, whom the new regulations
intended to control, would merely find another workhouse with more lax
enforcement—in this case, Lambeth itself. (*Punch*, February 3, 1866.)

report about promiscuous arrangements in the Stepney Male Casual Ward rivalled Greenwood's series in its unsparing description of the moral, physical, and sexual dangers awaiting young and old, innocent and corrupt alike.[87]

Some few papers condemned the "pretentious" sensationalism of "A Night," foremost among them the *Observer*.[88] Yet disdain for the new style of journalism ushered in by Greenwood's story did not prevent the *Observer* from participating in the mania for workhouse sojourns. Promising that its reporters would "paint their pictures as they really exist,"[89] it launched an unremarkable four-part series of articles entitled "Midnight Visits to the Casual Wards of London."[90] In contrast to Greenwood's dramatic self-costuming as a tramp, the two reporters for the *Observer* were "attired in the ordinary winter garb . . . of the middle class."[91]

It is hardly surprising that politicians threw themselves into the controversy surrounding "A Night." At a time when the political rights of unenfranchised laboring people preoccupied Parliament, politicians could ill afford to ignore the social claims of the poor. The condition of the workingman's home, the air he breathed, the water he drank, and the poorhouse he may one day be compelled to enter were not just social questions but political ones as well in the tense months leading up to the passage of the Second Reform Bill.[92] The Greenwood brothers, especially the savvy Frederick, ensured that the press would take a leading role in thrusting social issues into the political arena. Although journalists did not create the abuses in metropolitan workhouses, they did invent them as a public scandal. The Greenwood brothers and the *Pall Mall Gazette* in particular, and the newspaper and periodical press in general, had a great deal at stake in insuring the longevity and intensity of the scandal surrounding "A Night." By constantly commenting on and referring to the inquiries undertaken by rival papers, journalists expanded their own social and political authority and helped to sell sordid facts as print commodities.[93] The workhouse casual-ward controversy anticipated many of the features we usually associate with the birth of the New Journalism of the 1880s and the ascendancy of the press as the Fourth Estate in public affairs and politics.[94]

Theatrical Imitators

The cycle of imitation begun by Greenwood's decision to disguise himself as a "casual" gathered its own momentum and quickly reached fantastic heights of absurdity. By mid-February 1866, Joseph Cave, proprietor of the Theatre Royal in Marylebone in West London, announced that he was opening a new "spirit stirring drama" set in the infamous sleeping shed of the Lambeth Casual Ward.[95] According to theater historian Jim Davis, Cave commissioned Colin Hazlewood to adapt Greenwood's articles for a production called *The Casual Ward*. In addition to his Marylebone venue, Cave staged the play at the Pavilion in Whitechapel and the Britannia Theatre in Hoxton, both located in densely populated slum districts. Another play, entitled "Nobody's Son or A Night in the Workhouse," was also based on Greenwood's articles and produced in East London at the Effingham Theatre. Tens of thousands of people from across the social spectrum must have seen Cave's and Hazlewood's production because it sustained runs ranging from four and a half to fourteen weeks.[96]

The play itself is entirely undistinguished. A piece of hack writing, it dramatizes the plight of Richard Glover, who has fallen from respectability by extending credit to false friends. Glover unexpectedly inherits a substantial estate from a distant relative in India, but his good fortune is imperiled by the aptly named swindler Graspleigh, who attempts to claim the fortune for himself. While the title page of the manuscript prompt copy claims that the play was "founded on the revelations of Workhouse treatment recently published in the Public press," the workhouse casual ward is little more than an opportunistic location for a scene. Following the conventions of working-class popular melodrama, honest plebian folk prevail over the unscrupulous collar-wearing petit-bourgeois scoundrels.

Davis's analysis of the manuscript of the Cave and Hazlewood play focuses on the ways in which the text was "subject to censorship in so far as sentiments that [were] excessively subversive or critical of the establishment [were] deleted."[97] He astutely notes several examples in which harsh denunciations of poor-law guardians and workhouse officials contained in Hazlewood's script were banned by the examiner of plays. The censorship was so successful that the examiner reported to the lord chamberlain that he heard nothing at the play that "any guardian or relieving officer could justly object to." However, Davis overlooks Hazlewood's and Cave's most significant act of censorship, one that they imposed on themselves: their decision to erase all traces of sexual "abominations" between males. According to the surviving notes of the stage director, F. C. Wilton, women were substituted for boys and men for the nonspeaking parts of the casual ward inmates. All the actors were clothed and very little effort was made to make the "ladies" appear to be men and boys.

> All the Ladies discovered in this scene filling the 6 beds in the back row of each side of the stage. Handkerchiefs tied round their heads. 3 beds discovered empty. . . . All the Ladies supposed to be dressed as boys . . . Barefooted—no

shoes . . . The ladies being hidden under the rugs need not go into male attire though they are supposed to be boys.[98]

The lead roles continued to be played by well-known male actors. For example, at the Britannia, Kay was played by Cecil Pitt, "known for his intimidating size." Casting Pitt obliterated the sexual ambiguity that had made the slender and androgynous Kay so attractive to Greenwood and the other male casual ward inmates. Perhaps the text of Hazlewood's play and the casting decisions were meant to encourage viewers who had previously read Greenwood's "A Night" to forget its homoerotic elements or to reimagine them along more acceptable male-female lines. Regardless of motivation, the theatrical productions of *The Casual Ward* not only muted condemnation of the workings of the poor law but also concealed the discoveries about sex so essential to Greenwood's political and social message.

In the weeks between the publication of "A Night" and its appearance on the stage, Greenwood's revelations played upon "the vitiated and morbid tastes of the lovers of 'sensation'" and prompted heretofore respectable men and women to play the part of workhouse casuals in their own private dramas.[99] Two such performances tickled the fancy of the press. The first involved an army accoutrement maker from Soho, Mr. David Greenhall, who entered the casual ward of St. James Workhouse at 9:15 p.m., ate some bread and gruel, and was shown his berth. During the course of a routine search, the workhouse superintendent discovered that Greenhall possessed 6s. 91/2d. in pocket money, in violation of workhouse rules prohibiting inmates from possessing any property or money. What Greenhall had undertaken as a lighthearted affair soon became a serious legal imbroglio. To make matters worse, the hapless Greenhall inadvertently revealed that he had slept the night before at Greenwich Workhouse. Insisting that his masquerade as a casual was merely a "drunken frolic," he handed the superintendent his card and demanded release from the casual ward. Instead, he was promptly given into police custody. The next day he stood before the magistrate of the Marlborough Police Court charged with obtaining poor relief under false pretenses. A contrite Greenhall was extremely fortunate that the magistrate agreed to discharge him with only a "severe caution."[100]

The second case was more ludicrous in its execution and more severe in its denouement. A boisterous, well-to-do woman ostentatiously took a cab to the Mile End Workhouse and demanded admission to its casual ward. When the porter refused to let her in, she said, "I can demand a lodging in the casual ward; you are only a gate-porter, and the orders, rules, and regulations of the Poor Law Board are to take in all who claim admission." Fearing a row, the porter admitted her to the female casual

ward only to find that she had illegally brought 17s. 17 1/2d. with her.
To the delight and amusement of the press and public, the magistrate at
the Thames Police Court, Mr. Paget, "rewarded" the woman's impu-
dence and ignorance of the details of the Houseless Poor Act with a
month's hard labor in prison.[101] Was her punishment less forgiving than
Greenhall's because she had the misfortune to face a less gentle magistrate? Or was she perhaps being punished not only for violating workhouse regulations but also for flouting accepted notions of female behavior? What a "lady" could and could not do troubled the medical doctor
J. H. Stallard, who insisted that the public had a right to hear the
women's side of the story and learn about the female casual ward. Claiming that a true lady (unlike a true gentleman) could never pass for a
tramp, Stallard hired a destitute but once respectable widow to penetrate
four different casual wards and report to him her harrowing findings.
Unlike the calculated titillation of "A Night," the widow's narrative is
singularly devoid of "hideous enjoyments." Instead, she underscores her
terror at the ubiquitous vermin and her belief that cholera was generated
every night in the Whitechapel Casual Ward.[102]

Vestrymen, Poor Law Principles, and Sodomy

If the cases of Greenhall and the ill-fated woman at the Mile End Workhouse provided comic relief for the general public, the unfolding drama
of "A Night" was no laughing matter for the workhouse officials and
vestrymen of Lambeth. In marked contrast to the self-serving solidarity
displayed by the Lambeth Board of Guardians in their closed weekly
meetings,[103] the public meetings of the Lambeth vestry were rancorous.
Mr. Stiff, representing the Third Ward, spoke for the overwhelming majority of his peers when he insisted that he was not disturbed by the
charges levelled by the Amateur Casual because he was confident that
"the Guardians had done their duty." The rector of Lambeth, Rev. Lingham, was even less apologetic. He had personally gone to inspect the
workhouse and casual wards and had been impressed by their "well ordered comforts." In vituperative language, he denounced the *Pall Mall
Gazette* articles as pernicious misrepresentations. Lingham's ill-tempered
remarks released a flood of anticlerical invective. An enraged correspondent to *Reynold's,* a paper renowned for its plebian radicalism, used the
occasion to denounce the clergy in general as "toadies of the rich," who
were "nothing better than a spiritual police by which the minds of the
oppressed millions are bludgeoned into cowardly submission to all sorts
of legalized cruelties." The writer declared that clergymen were "rev-
erend quack doctors" who administered "stupifying opiates to an infatu-
ated society reposing on a volcano."[104] Only two Lambeth vestrymen

dared to brave the anger of their colleagues and supported the findings of the Amateur Casual. Mr. France "had been to the workhouse and found everything as he had read it in the paper." Mr. Giles praised the *Gazette* and apologized for the conduct of the guardians. The author of "A Night" deserved "a testimonial from his country." It was only his heroic visit to the casual ward that rescued the poor from the horrors of the shed, and he urged his colleagues to show kindness to the "poor outcasts" in their midst.[105]

The London and provincial papers blasted Lambeth's "Bumbledom," Dickens's famous term for inept officials. The *Daily News* was particularly vexed that the vestrymen of Lambeth had "passed over" in complete silence "the dire moral disorder in the pump shed" while "the great anxiety of the Guardians was to prove that they had kept the filthiest of scoundrels warm and comfortable." The guardians "might have opened a public brothel in the parish," insisted the *Daily News*, "and maintained it out of the rates with less scandal than they have caused by tolerating in their ignorance the commission of nameless abominations in the parish workhouse." "What is really 'in its trial' now," the article concluded, "is the capacity of our local bodies for the duties of local government."[106] In the aftermath of the publication of "A Night," controlling the sexual conduct of male casuals became the touchstone of debate between supporters of local self-government in London and those who called for increased centralization.[107]

The public humiliation of Lambeth's workhouse officials and vestrymen was not yet over. In the fortnight following the publication of "A Night," reporters for *The Daily News* repeatedly inspected at night the Lambeth Workhouse and the licensed lodging house to which it sent excess casuals. To their amazement, they discovered that arrangements for casuals remained "as shamefully inefficient as before the recent exposure." The certified lodging house made a mockery of the beautifully ordered "show rooms" that the Lambeth guardians put on display for visitors. More than a dozen men and boys were packed into a tiny room holding six bedsteads.

> They were all perfectly naked, and had clustered together for the sake of animal heat, just as sleeping swine are seen to do. . . . The naked sleepers had rugs for covering, and on an adventurous visitor turning down one of these the brawny figures of three muscular tramps—bare as when they came into the world—were seen to be entwined together, an indistinguishable mass of naked flesh. Youths lay in the arms of men, men were enfolded in each other's embrace; there was neither fire, nor light nor supervision, and the weak and feeble were at the complete mercy of the strong and ruffianly. The air was laden with a pestilential stench.

Only the inmates' exhaustion saved the journalists from witnessing "any active or boisterous devilry."[108] The message of the *Daily News* was clear: official inspections, like "show" beds and "show" wards, are untrustworthy shams that mislead the public.

Workhouse controversies placed the president of the Poor Law Board, Charles Pelham Villiers, and his inspectors, especially H. B. Farnall, in an awkward and vulnerable position.[109] On the one hand, they were acutely embarrassed by revelations of workhouse abuses because they had ultimate responsibility for—and hence a substantial stake in preserving the reputation of—the institutions they regulated. On the other hand, press reports stirred up public opinion and put extreme pressure on local officials to comply fully with the demands of poor-law inspectors. In this respect, the press was an invaluable ally in the Poor Law Board's decades long struggle to increase its authority over intransigent and uncooperative local guardians and vestrymen. Furthermore, Villiers had himself taken a particularly keen interest in the problems associated with vagrancy and as early as 1863 had issued strongly worded minutes (administrative orders) demanding more humane conditions and competent administration of casual wards. Only two weeks before "A Night" appeared, the poor-law inspector Andrew Doyle submitted his massive and insightful study of vagrancy and casual wards to Villiers.[110] Villiers was no villain in the casual-ward scandal.

Even Edwin Chadwick, the sole surviving member of the original Poor Law Commission, entered the controversy to defend himself and the principles of the landmark 1834 New Poor Law. He and his fellow commissioners had long ago recognized and provided practical remedies to the problems supposedly "discovered" in the winter of 1865–66. The current scandals resulted entirely from "disorganization" and "maladministration" by officials who refused to implement the "established administrative principles" of consolidation and centralization of authority, aggregation of distinct classes of paupers, and their segregation into metropolitan-wide institutions.[111] For Chadwick, whose rationalizing initiatives had been repeatedly thwarted during his stormy career as a civil servant, the workhouse scandals of 1866 were merely local symptoms of a more global disease in the administration of the poor law.

A concerned correspondent to the Poor Law Board, John Wilson, was unwilling to mention sodomy as the most dangerous and contagious vice festering in the workhouses; but the remedies he proposed to the "evils in the casual wards" were more imaginative and more likely than Chadwick's to impede sex between men in the workhouse. Wilson suggested the construction of individual sleeping cubicles—6 feet high, 2–3 feet wide, and 8 feet deep—with a suspended hammock into which only one person could enter.[112] Needless to say, the high costs of implementing such a scheme and the harsh isolation it would have imposed on the poor guaranteed that the proposal garnered support from no one. It does however highlight just how difficult it was to design and administer all-male casual wards as spaces immune to sodomitical contamination.

It should come as no surprise that Chadwick and every other poor-law reformer and activist conspicuously ignored the role of sex in the work-house scandal. For Chadwick to acknowledge that workhouses could be made into male brothels would have made a mockery of the Malthusian and Benthamite principles of political economy underpinning the New Poor Law. At least in theory, poor-law officials could separate husbands from wives, the deserving from the undeserving poor, and the sick from the able bodied. But how could officials identify and separate sodomites from other men and boys? While that task defied even the classificatory genius of Chadwick, it was nonetheless essential to safeguarding the moral and physical health of the poor. As "A Night" suggested, sodomy was so contagious it threatened to corrupt even innocent bystanders compelled by circumstances to witness it. Chadwick simply could not stretch the logic of the New Poor Law, which intentionally herded men together into cramped and uncomfortable all-male spaces, to accommodate the moral and physical dangers revealed by "A Night." The sodomitical subtext of "A Night" threw into disarray the social scientific categories underpinning sanitary and poor-law reform. Had Chadwick noted the prevalence of sodomy in the casual ward, he would have been forced to admit the responsibility of poor-law policies and institutions for creating the very conditions that spawned such deviant populations. We can be quite sure that Malthus would have been appalled by the moral dilemma arising from the application of his principle of separating impoverished men and women to check the procreation of more paupers, but might not Bentham, whose philosophical radicalism inspired Chadwick and several other authors of the New Poor Law, allow himself a smile at the entire messy affair? After all, Bentham was not just the creator of Panopticon but also the author of a daring essay arguing that sex between men should not be a crime.[113]

Science, Sensation, and Charity Organizers

The debate that "A Night" galvanized about the relationship between central and local government cascaded into broader questions about charity organization, social citizenship, class relations, and parliamentary reform. Contemporaries in turn often connected these issues to one another. Greenwood's articles revealed not only the lack of uniformity among London casual wards, but also the failure of poor-law officials to coordinate their work with the vast and growing machinery of private benevolence in London. Mid-century economic prosperity followed by the cotton famine in Lancashire had encouraged the profuse expansion of philanthropies with no effective apparatus for regulating them and their clients. Many persons who were committed to the emerging science of charity organization wondered why such private charities should continue to exist when their functions had been absorbed by public authorities with the passage of the Houseless Poor Act.[114]

In the December 1866 issue of *Macmillan's Magazine*, the influential Anglican clergyman John Llewelyn Davies provided a thoughtful and wide-ranging analysis of the relationship of the poor law and private charity in light of the "great blots" "discovered in two departments of our workhouse system, in the treatment of vagrants and in the condition of the workhouse infirmaries." Davies' analysis merits close examination both because it was a constructive response to "A Night" and because so much of what he had to say soon became the dominant orthodoxy among those metropolitan social reformers who in 1869 would found the Society for Repressing Mendicity and Organizing Charity—better known as the Charity Organisation Society or COS.

In the intervening months between the publication of "A Night" and Davies' essay, a devastating cholera epidemic had wreaked havoc on London, particularly in the slums of the East End. The outpourings of public benevolence following "A Night" and the epidemic were at once heart-warming and discouraging for Davies. "Gentlemen and ladies," he observed, "have made it their business to journey from the West-end into the dreary tracts from which luxury and leisure have long fled, to offer sympathy and aid to the suffering."[115] He feared that their slumming and the "sympathy and aid" it produced would further pauperize the poor and reduce their capacity for self-respecting independence by increasing indiscriminate relief on the part of private agencies and encouraging officials to make the workhouses more comfortable. As much as his heart impelled him to "clothe the naked" and "feed the hungry," such indiscriminate philanthropy, which was favored by many Evangelicals, ultimately failed to meet his test of true Christianity. The key to reducing pauperism, he insisted, depended upon clearly separating, not amalgamating, the work of state-administered poor relief from that of private charity. The poor law should provide relief to "all distress caused immediately by vice or willful folly" (139). While poor-law officials needed to respect the human dignity of recipients of their relief, the vast majority was "the very dregs of the population . . . worthless and vicious" (132). Voluntary charity should serve those reduced to poverty by illness or by permanent disability (139). He called for the strict organization and coordination of all private charity as a means of checking "importunity and fraud" (133). Based on the principles first put forward by the Scottish divine Thomas Chalmers and the Elberfeld system in Germany, Davies called for the creation of a system of district visitors throughout London. These district visitors would carefully investigate and determine the worthiness of each applicant for relief and ensure that charities worked in concert with one another. "Unreflecting benevolence" (138) would give way to rational management. Davies believed that increased wages and the continuing growth in the dignity of the working classes provided the only hope for solutions, as opposed to amelioratives, to the problem of pauperism. Moving from the reorganization of charity to the Reform Bill, he concluded that if the agitation for the parliamentary franchise indicated "growing self-respect" and "a higher moral standard" among the working classes (142), it augured well for the nation's future.

Davies was far from isolated among reformers in London. His own ideas evolved in tandem with those of other leaders of charity organization, including the Anglican clergyman, William Henry Fremantle. Fremantle developed a system of dividing his Marylebone parish into small districts to which trained individual charity visitors were assigned. His early recruits included Octavia Hill, Henrietta Rowland (later Barnett), and his curate Samuel Barnett—all of whom were destined to play influential roles in the history of slumming and social welfare. These so-called district visitors coordinated the distribution of private charity, investigated the circumstances and history of individual applicants for relief, and upheld the deterrent principles of the Poor Law Amendment Act of 1834. Visitors investigated applicants for charitable relief using a standardized protocol, which in turn became part of a centralized system of data collection. In 1868 and 1869, men and women sharing Davies' and Fremantle's views convened a series of metropolitan-wide meetings resulting in the formation of the COS and the rapid expansion of its system of district offices and scientific charity.[116]

The COS's first major undertaking was its "Conference on Night Refuges" in the spring of 1870. Their choice of topic reflected the immense impact on the charitable public of Greenwood's disclosures. Sir Charles Trevelyan opened discussion at the conference and explained the object of the meeting and the events that had precipitated it. He acknowledged that the revelations of the Amateur Casual had led to "a great improvement" in the administration of casual wards.[117] Increased administrative effectiveness of casual wards under the terms of the Houseless Poor Act made it all the more vital to determine whether private charitable night refuges ought to continue to exist in the metropolis. Not surprisingly, Trevelyan and the other COS stalwarts in attendance felt strongly that most private night refuges competed with, instead of complemented, the casual wards of poor houses, and they called for them to be disbanded.

Vagrancy remained a major preoccupation of the early leaders of the Charity Organisation Society. Its first organizing secretary, C. J. Ribton-Turner, for example, devoted years of his life to researching and writing his encyclopedic *A History of Vagrants and Vagrancy and Beggars and Begging*.[118] The sober men and women who formed the COS shunned the sensational writing and investigative methods pioneered by Greenwood, but the public interest stimulated by "A Night" and its aftermath helped to set the stage for the COS to organize itself and advance its vision of the proper relationship between the state and private charity. In its protracted struggle to destroy the evangelical philanthropist Dr. Thomas Barnardo in 1877 (see chapter 2), the COS attempted to assert its paramount right to police the boundaries between scientific and sentimental charity, between true and false philanthropists and beggars alike.

Parliamentary Reform and Empire: Racializing the Tramp, Orientalizing the Slum Journalist

Many other commentators like Llewelyn Davies explicitly linked "A Night" to the Reform Bill, which promised to enfranchise at least some respectable, regularly employed working-class men. "If a Reform Bill be really passed, and the artisan influence make itself distinctly felt in the House of Commons," the *Pall Mall Gazette* asked, "what will be its action in respect to the proceedings of the guardians of the poor whose self-ishness had been exposed by "A Night?" The *Gazette* looked forward to the enfranchisement of the hardworking and intelligent artisan whose socioeconomic proximity to the poor and disdain for the indolence and "scoundrelism" of parochial officials and paupers alike promised to sweep away the incompetent "reign of Bumbledom" among poorhouse officials. The "better class of artisan would constitute a real aristocracy" to counteract the selfish influence of grocers, publicans, and shoemakers. These petit bourgeois citizens, who openly defied the Poor Law by refusing admission to casuals or not complying with minimal dietary requirements, abetted "crime and vice down to the lowest depths of animal degradation."[119]

"A Night" also provided ample fodder for commentary about the relationship between domestic and imperial affairs as well as between race and class anxieties. Greenwood's literary output in the 1860s suggests that the slums of London and exotic outposts of empire were interchangeable sites of adventure and heroism in his imagination. He wrote "A Night" in between the completion of his London slum novel, *The True History of a Little Ragamuffin*, and works such as *The Adventures of Reuben Davidger, Seventeen Years and Four Months Captive Among the Dyaks of Borneo*. He explicitly likened the casual ward inmates to "brutes" he had read about in "books of African travel," and he clearly was intrigued by what he called "curiosities of savage life" wherever he could find them. Despite his sympathy for the poor and his frank admission that he hankered after the strange freedoms of the lives he chronicled, he described the poorest of the poor as primitive vestiges of "savagery." In Greenwood's rhetoric, they lived outside civilization in "anachronistic space" in which the boundary between animals and humans seemed all too easily crossed.[120] The "bestial" sexuality of the men and boys in the casual ward was merely an extreme example of a more generalized phenomenon.[121]

Workhouse casuals occupied an unusual niche at the bottom of the Victorian social hierarchy in which racial, sexual, and class categories and norms converged. "Street arab" and "nomad" were widely used synonyms for the homeless. These terms were figures of speech, but they also drew upon the widely shared assumption that casuals were literally members of a savage race because they existed outside the seat of domesticating, moralizing, and civilizing influences: the home.

If the poor were rhetorically orientalized, so, too, were incognito social investigators, who followed in Greenwood's footsteps. Journalists and writers who imitated Greenwood's incognitos claimed that they were going "Haroun Al Raschid," in homage to the celebrated late-eighth-, early-ninth-century caliph who masqueraded as a poor man to better understand the needs of his subjects.[122] G. R. Sims, London's most famous slum journalist and a consummate master of disguises, recalled that male journalists fancied themselves members of a radical "Bohemian fraternity" bound by none of the conventions of respectable middle-class life.[123] Workhouse masters and tramps used precisely the same term to describe the values and way of life of vagrants, who, like journalists, felt a keen sense of solidarity with one another and apartness from the rest of society.[124] Just as Greenwood played fast and loose with the boundaries separating participants from observers in his sociological experiment, so, too, incognito journalists and tramps saw themselves as Bohemians who, in defiance of bourgeois respectability, made their living by appearing to *not* work. Sir Arthur Conan Doyle cleverly explored this ironic affinity in "The Man with the Twisted Lip," in which the lure of easy money leads the respectable slum journalist to become a professional tramp.[125]

Victorian anthropologists' fascination with the sexual practices of primitive peoples closely mirrored social reformers' own obsession with working-class sexual promiscuity as a root cause of overpopulation, demoralization, and poverty.[126] Given how widely both bourgeois and working-class people identified masculinity with economic independence and the male breadwinner, Greenwood and his readers were well prepared to discover that male workhouse casuals—who were by definition dependent and did not engage in manly labor—resembled other "savages" in their spectacular deviation from accepted norms of masculinity and sexuality. As Greenwood pithily remarked in his sardonic essay, "Mr. Bumble and His Enemy the Casual," any man entering the casual ward "consign[ed] his manhood and his long-cherished self respect . . . to the grave."[127]

While Greenwood and other writers deployed racial rhetoric in describing homeless tramps, contemporaries explicitly linked "A Night" to urgent issues of imperial rule. Throughout the winter of 1865 and 1866, articles about metropolitan workhouses and casual wards often shared the same page with disclosures about the British treatment of colored Jamaicans during and after the Morant Bay "insurrection." The free mulatto George William Gordon, an articulate critic of colonial misgovernment and the supposed leader of the insurrection, had been summarily executed in a military court rather than granted the rights of a freeborn Englishman to a full trial. Hundreds of other colored Jamaicans were victims of the brutality of the British army and its military courts. In January and February of 1866, Londoners began to assimilate the results of the official commission of inquiry into the ruthless way in which Sir George Grey's erstwhile protege, Governor Eyre, had suppressed the insurrection and the character of the justice meted out by hastily convened British military courts in its wake.[128] The *Pall Mall Gazette* denounced the distant miscarriage of justice by British officials in Jamaica as "not only an outrage on the rules of law, but on the plainest dictates of natural justice and common good sense."[129]

British conduct in Jamaica deeply divided champions of the rights and liberties of the working class in Britain and elicited some surprising comparisons to "A Night." The Christian newspaper the *Orb*, for example, combined antipathy toward those who condemned Governor Eyre with ardent criticism of parochial indifference to the poor. In an extended editorial, the *Orb* belittled what it took to be the self-righteous stance of the liberal humanitarian supporters of Jamaican liberties who met at London's famed Exeter Hall.

> Exeter-Hall will have its May meetings in due time and we shall be invited to extend our sympathies to the blessed niggers—we beg pardon—men and brothers of colour in the West Indies. . . . True to their duty, the Lambeth rector and guardians will assuredly be there. Their sympathies are surely very warm towards the inhabitants of the Polar circle or the Esquimaux. . . . The guardians of the London parishes will still set at defiance the law which would secure a night's shelter for the homeless, and the various Sodoms and pandemoniums of the metropolis will still flourish. . . . Still, Mr. Farnall will visit the

workhouses, and still, the show-wards and show-beds will be ready for him, kept scrupulously clean and all right.

Infuriated by the hypocrisy that led clergy to weep for the mistreatment of blacks abroad but to defend the degradation of the English poor at home, the writer concluded with the sarcastic observation that "verily, we are a Christian people."[130]

The *Orb*'s one-sided appropriation of the controversy surrounding "A Night" to chastise Exeter-Hall's liberal humanitarianism was but one of many examples of the diverse ways in which contemporaries chose to extract lessons from the casual-ward scandal that served their own particular agendas. To a remarkable extent, contemporaries were unable or unwilling to act upon Greenwood's claim that casual wards not only harbored dirty bodies but also the dirtiest and most unnatural form of male sexuality—sodomy. As the tidal wave of anxieties unleashed by "A Night" washed up on distant shores, its powerful source—the "hideous enjoyments" of the male casual ward—no longer seemed to matter.

Refusing to initiate a public debate about how to regulate sex between men, reformers and shapers of public policy returned to the much safer and more familiar terrain of workhouse infirmaries. All but eclipsed as an issue in January 1866, the workhouse infirmary campaign was ultimately the greatest public-policy beneficiary of "A Night." Under the aegis of Gathorne-Hardy's presidency of the Poor Law Board during the shortlived Conservative ministry that came to power in the summer of 1866, the movement made rapid gains. By February 1867, Gathorne-Hardy successfully introduced a measure to the House of Commons for "improving the management of sick and other poor in the metropolis."[131] The passage of the Metropolitan Poor Bill in March 1867 marked a quiet revolution in the way public authorities served the health-care needs of the London poor within their localities. It not only separated the healthy from the infirm but also established the Metropolitan Asylums Board to oversee the management of a fledgling system of state hospitals for the poor.

"Two-Days' Dream": The Characters of "A Night" as Instant Celebrities

From Greenwood's memorable cast of characters, readers selected heroes who spoke to their specific concerns, needs, and aspirations. Hoping to enhance their own standing, most members of the press lionized Greenwood. "Daddy," however, was the darling of the masses. Daddy was a workhouse pauper named Budge, who served as a warder in the casual ward in exchange for improved rations and sleeping quarters. Greenwood's whimsical depiction of Budge made him a celebrity. G. R. Sims recalled that "songs were composed in [Daddy's] honour, songs sentimental, comic, and serio-comic."[132] Daddy discharged himself from the workhouse and sat as a model for an "enterprising" photographer for five shillings, undoubtedly a princely sum for Daddy. Portraits of the blinking, almost dazed, old man sold briskly on the streets. A correspondent for the *Daily Telegraph* overheard women with "pretty eyes" and "pretty voices" wasting their money and their "benevolent feelings" on his photograph. "Half the sympathy evoked for 'Daddy,'" the paper noted acerbically, "might have rescued a dozen families in Bethnal-green." A chastened Daddy, his photographic windfall squandered, returned to the Lambeth Workhouse a few days later.[133] The magazine of humor and social satire, *Punch* relished the inversions and ironies of "A Night" and offered its own running commentary on the scandal in words and pictures. It naughtily imagined Daddy's disconsolate attempts to compose verse "heppigrams" to commemorate his ignominious return to the Lambeth Workhouse:

> Of Life's extremes each towards other stretches,
>   Till houseless wretchedness this comfort hath;
> That our C.P.'s (or casual pauper wretches)
>   Are all C.B.'s, Companions of the Bath.[134]

Daddy's flirtation with fame was not yet over; nor had photographs of Daddy slaked the public thirst for irrefutable evidence that the people and scenes depicted in "A Night" were "true" and "real." Several weeks after Daddy's return to the Lambeth Workhouse, Joseph Cave hired him (supposedly at the salary of £2 per week) to play himself at the Marylebone production of *A Casual Ward*. Though Daddy said almost nothing, he was "greeted with a warmth many practiced actors might envy" according to the reviewer for the *Era*.[135] Cave no doubt hoped to capitalize on the public's love affair with Daddy, or rather, its infatuation with Greenwood's depiction of him.

By making the "real" Daddy into a character in a stage melodrama, Cave satisfied, but also undercut, the urge to verify Greenwood's account that led contemporaries to want to see Daddy for themselves. On the one hand, Daddy's presence on stage made Greenwood's experiences authentic by allowing the audience to meet for themselves someone Greenwood had encountered in the workhouse. On the other hand, Daddy playing Daddy confounded those who aspired to clear-cut distinctions between fictions and facts, artifice and social reality. Such confusion was part and parcel of Greenwood's self-consciously theatrical decision to impersonate a tramp to learn the truth about the workhouse.

Cave's production and Greenwood's articles both contributed to that "mania for realities" that ironically encouraged Victorians across the social spectrum to understand the lives of the poor as an ongoing series of dramatic performances. If theatrical conventions enabled the rich to distance themselves from the brutal realities of metropolitan poverty even as they claimed to confront them, such conventions offered the poor not only the consolation of pathos and humor but a sense of themselves as heroic agents of their own destiny.[136]

Long after Budge, the "real" Daddy, had been entirely forgotten, Greenwood's Daddy remained an archetypal figure of kindness in the lore of the London slums and in music-hall ballads. In her naturalistic slum novel, *Captain Lobe*, written more than twenty years after "A Night," Margaret Harkness expected her readers to recognize immediately her allusion to Greenwood's story and to smile at the illustrious company Daddy now kept in East London:

> "Waxwork Cosmorama and Panorama, programme one penny!" shouted a little girl at the entrance, . . . "containing our most gracious Majesty Queen Victoria, Napoleon the Third, the Shah of Persia, Joan of Arc . . . kind Old Daddy of the Lambeth Casual Ward, made popular by a visit from a Lord, who, seeing the kindness of Old Daddy to the paupers, made him a present of a £5 pound note."[137]

Daddy's apotheosis as a wax figure in a slum novel constituted the final stage in the reproduction and commodificaton of his image for the financial benefit of others. Although the careworn old pauper had only been allowed to enjoy what *Punch* called "two-days' dream" of celebrity, his image became an enduring "spectacular reality" in Victorian culture.

Two other members of the dramatis personae of "A Night" briefly shared the spotlight with Greenwood and Daddy: one of K.'s adolescent companions, a boy named Punch, as well as a "respectable" man in the Lambeth Casual Ward whose philological musings on the word "kindle" had impressed Greenwood. A few days after Greenwood's visit, Punch had been expelled from the workhouse for destroying his regulation blue shirt—satirically called a "Lambeth silk" by inmates—and sent to prison for three weeks. A week later he surfaced at a supper for two hundred destitute boys hosted by the Boy's Refuge in Great Queen Street, Lincoln's Inn Fields. The idea for the supper, according to the secretary of the refuge, William Williams, owed entirely to Greenwood's "self-imposed penance" in spending a night in the workhouse. The ravenous boys, who had been recruited from casual wards, feasted on huge portions of roast beef, bread, coffee, and "large dishes of smoking plum pudding." They were then treated to hymns and a speech by Lord Shaftesbury then handed four pence to pay for a lodging house.[138] Twenty-four of the boys, including Punch, entered the refuge to be taught a trade and "helped on in the world." The secretary, Mr. Williams, noted with joy that after only a few days in the refuge, Punch had become an altogether different boy: "It would have made your heart right glad had you seen [Punch] . . . as I did this morning, with his flesh clean and wholesome. . . . There he was sitting on the shoemaker's seat, sewing away with a hearty good-will, contented and happy."[139] Williams' message was unmistakable. Left in the hands of poor-law guardians, boys like Punch would become criminals and moral reprobates. Only private Christian charity could remake them into healthy and productive workers.

The story of the discovery of Greenwood's "respectable man" owed much less to serendipity than to the ingenuity of J. C. Parkinson. Parkinson was a minor civil servant at Somerset House (home of the General Register Office and the Board of Inland Revenue) and sometime writer on social issues for various periodicals. During the two years preceding the publication of "A Night," Parkinson devoted much of his leisure time to investigating and reporting on abuses in the administration of the Houseless Poor Act and on conditions in workhouses. In an essay published in June 1865 in *Temple Bar*, he detailed a day he spent in the Marylebone Workhouse with a poor-law inspector, possibly H. B. Farnall. "Impelled alike by duty and inclination to peer below the surface of this mighty London," Parkinson entered "blind alleys and dark courts; . . . into dirty frowzy houses . . . where a stranger and an Englishman seldom penetrates." He had carefully studied "the abodes, haunts, ways, manners, foibles, tastes, and pleasures of the criminal classes; the lurking-place of the professional mendicant, and the home of the swindling letter-writer."[140] Although Parkinson had a vast and intimate knowledge of the casual poor, Greenwood's articles "revealed a depth of shameless mismanagement [he] had never fathomed" and made him anxious to learn "what the impression the horrors written of by the amateur had left upon the minds of habitual sleepers in workhouses."

If the novelty of "A Night" lay in Greenwood's masquerade as an "amateur" casual, Parkinson proposed an even more unprecedented scheme: to retell Greenwood's story from the point of view of a "real" casual. He published a brief advertisement in the *Times* on the morning of January 23, 1866, and asked workhouse masters to spread the word among their inmates that he was willing to pay a sovereign to every man who could prove that he was in the shed of the Lambeth Casual Ward on the night Greenwood's incognito visit.[141] After verifying the claims of each of his respondents, Parkinson entered into an extraordinary correspondence with a man he called the Real Casual, an educated draughtsman sucked into the vortex of poverty by illness and misfortune and whom Greenwood had identified as a "respectable man."

The Real Casual sent Parkinson a detailed treatise on the casual wards and charitable night refuges of London. He highlighted the extreme diversity of conditions among workhouses and widespread indifference to and violation of Poor Law Board regulations. Casuals not only spoke their own distinct language, they used casual wards as hubs in a thriving underground economy of information and goods.[142] The Real Casual and many of his fellow travellers were remarkably knowledgeable about their legal rights and quite vocal, if not always successful, in demanding them. Far from being passive recipients of public welfare, they actively claimed their rights and sought to manipulate the system to their advantage. They abhorred being made into a spectacle by workhouse guardians who "examined us all intently [during breakfast], like so many wild beasts in an exhibition."[143] Lying and dissimulation were not only commonplace, they were virtually mandated by the way in which public casual wards and private soup kitchens were run. The poor never gave their real names or occupations for fear of being identified and turned away as habitual applicants. The incentives to lie infuriated the Real Casual. "You get a basin of pea-soup and a quantity of bread-and-cheese [from soup kitchens]," he observed bitterly, "proportionate to the number of lies you tell." "If you say you are going out of town and have also a wife and children, perhaps a quartern loaf and a pound of cheese, may be your share—but if you tell the truth, and say you are going to stay in town to try and get employment, small, indeed, will be your quantity."[144] The moral of the Real Casual's story was quite clear to Parkinson, who consistently linked the results of his slumming to the formulation of social policy:

> We want uniformity of treatment in the refuges kept up by voluntary subscription, as well as in those prescribed by law; and this we shall never have until the central authority is strengthened, and some amicable understanding is established between the two. . . . Give London a uniform poor rate, and the rest follows; withhold it, and jobbing will be perpetuated, charity misplaced, and clamorous rogues lie and fatten, while the honest poor languish and starve.[145]

Politics and poor-law administration, not regulating sex, were the key issues for Parkinson.

The Real Casual did not dwell on what had happened on the night of January 8, 1866, in the Lambeth Casual Ward because Greenwood's narrative was, he acknowledged, almost wholly correct. In a letter he wrote to Parkinson on January 23, 1866, three days before the *Daily News* published its exposé of the certified lodging house, the Real Casual lamented that the Lambeth "lodging-house accommodation [to which he had been sent as an overflow casual] . . . was a great deal worse than the crank—in truth getting out of the frying-pan into the fire." Confirming the details of the sleeping arrangements that had appalled both Greenwood and the correspondent for the *Daily News*, he nonetheless took exception to Greenwood's suggestion that obscene words necessarily implied obscene acts between men. The Real Casual's description of a night he spent in the workhouse in Gray's Inn Road notably lacks Greenwood's sexualized treatment of a near identical scene in Lambeth.

> In a few minutes after supper is demolished, a pauper inmate conducts us, by the aid of a lanthorn, down some stone-stairs, and at the bottom puts us in a room, and closing the door after him, not forgetting to lock it, leaves us in darkness. . . . I was laid among two more on a mattress on the floor, with nothing to cover us but a piece of sacking. It was a cold night in the later part of November, and I never in all my life suffered more from cold. My two companions and myself were perfectly naked—not even our shirts on (no one who knows workhouses will ever sleep in them with their shirts on, for fear of catching certain insects); and as I laid in the middle between the two, you may judge my position was not very pleasant. I might have been a little warmer if I had chosen to cling up to my companions, as they wanted me; but I would sooner have borne more than I did than do so, for two dirtier or more repulsive men I never saw. Not a wink of sleep did I have that night.[146]

This account is much less transparent than it might appear at first glance. According to the Real Casual's own words, what made his "position" so unpleasant and prevented him from "clinging" to his bedfellows was aversion to intimacy with them *not* because they were men, but rather because they were repulsively dirty. This distinction opens up two different, though not necessarily incompatible, interpretations. On the one hand, it is possible that the Real Casual found nothing abhorrent about men sharing their bodies with one another. On the other hand, physical contact that a gentleman observer might choose to construe as sexual may well be merely an undesirable but sexless survival strategy from the perspective of a naked, freezing pauper. Whether acts *are* sexual rests not in the eye of the beholder, but rather in the minds of those involved. The queerness of "A Night" as a text and the casual ward as a space derive less from the putative intimate physical activities of the homeless men and boys, but more from the way in which some men— and not others—chose to interpret these activities.

In the final analysis, very poor men, women, and children like the Real Casual had the most at stake in the controversy surrounding "A Night," so it is worth asking what, if anything, they thought about it. Within a few days of its publication, the class "usually termed the 'lower'" was avidly reading and discussing "A Night." "We have seen it in the hands of ragged boys," one newspaper reported, "scarcely able to spell over its contents; we have seen it conned over by a group of persons looking not much unlike casuals themselves."[147] When the poor read "A Night," apparently many saw themselves—not Greenwood, Daddy or K.—as its beleaguered heroes.

Greenwood's articles spurred some to rebel against the indignities meted out to them by the workhouse and its officials. The *South London Journal* claimed that "A Night" had made casuals "saucier and more defiant than ever." The incidence of reported cases of workhouse inmates tearing up their clothes increased dramatically in the last two weeks of January as the casual poor themselves read, heard about, and discussed "A Night." For the destitute poor, "tearing" or "breaking" up their clothes was at once a pathetic gesture of defiance and a practical response to their situation. It allowed inmates to vent outrage over their treatment and forced officials to provide them with a new and valuable suit of clothes. Given the minute resources the poor law made available to workhouse inmates, tearing up was a perversely logical and effective way for paupers to claim some control over their own lives. When two eighteen-year-old women were sentenced to a month's hard labour for "tearing up" their clothes, they responded by singing "a requiem over their rent garments, 'Here we are, here we goes; we are the —— what tears up our clothes.'" Their performance inspired one observer to conclude that "the Houseless Poor Act has developed in such as these an exuberant vileness, which shocks us the more as it also classifies with them the honest destitute wayfarers."[148] Notice that it is the act which is blamed both for developing the "vileness" and for failing to adequately classify populations dependent on the state for food and shelter.

"A Night" stimulated officials to wonder how they could keep order in workhouses if inmates preferred prison to the casual ward. Such questions puzzled the lord mayor of London a few days after the publication of "A Night" as he attempted to decide how to punish a lad named William McIntosh. The boy had ripped up his workhouse clothes in front of the superintendent when he was told to dress in the morning. Alluding to "A Night," the lord mayor said that "if all we read be true the prisoner would be treated better in gaol than he is in the workhouse. . . . It was utterly useless to send [him] to prison." His hands tied, the lord mayor needed more time to find an appropriate punishment and remanded the boy to the custody of the workhouse.[149] It would be easy to dismiss the lord mayor's indecision as a trifling matter. In itself, the case of the boy McIntosh *was* inconsequential. But in such gestures of overt insubordination by the poor and in the paralysis of judgment they induced in the lord mayor, the British elite confronted the limits of their own authority, the undisguised hostility of the poor, and the circumscribed power of local and central government. What made "A Night" so terrifying was its depiction of a nightmarish world bereft of the coercive sanctions and effective instruments of state classification needed to control the real and imagined social, economic, and sexual forces of London's underclasses.

HOMELESSNESS AS HOMOSEXUALITY: SEXOLOGY, SOCIAL POLICY, AND THE 1898 VAGRANCY ACT

The publication of "A Night" had a volcanic impact on John Addington Symonds, the brilliant man of letters and scholar of Renaissance Italy. In spite of his own frank but as yet unconsummated passion for men, Symonds had married Catherine North in 1864 in an attempt to make himself into a "natural" man and gain the approval of his beloved father. Symonds was acutely aware of his own sexual love for men[150] and the strain of living a false "double" life which outwardly conformed to social convention sickened him.[151] In his autobiography, he elaborately set the stage for an impending crisis triggered by two episodes of metropolitan slumming. Overwhelmed by same-sex urges, he wandered through "the sordid streets between my home and Regent's Park." After encountering lewd phallic graffiti during his walk, his "vague and morbid craving of the previous years defined itself as a precise hunger after sensual pleasure, whereof I had not dreamed before save in repulsive visions of the night." In his diary, Symonds explicitly connected this disturbing stroll with an event that transpired several weeks later, in mid-January 1866: "I also read Greenwood's article 'The Amateur Casual' in an early number of the *Pall Mall Gazette*." "This brought," he explained, "the emotional tumour which was gathering within me to maturity. . . . Since then I have suffered incessantly from my moral trouble."[152]

Symonds's "repulsive visions of the night" merged into his experience reading Greenwood's dark narrative. Greenwood's articles pushed Symonds to go beyond a largely idealized and aestheticized love of "comrades" and fully satisfy his urgent need for physical sexual relations with men.[153] Symonds was so stimulated by Greenwood's erotic subtext that he believed his experience reading it altered the course of his sexual and conjugal life. A master of sublimation and self-censoring writing,[154] he seems to have had little difficulty deciphering Greenwood's homoerotic message and his apparent conflation of male same-sex desire with cross-class philanthropic social investigation. The *Gazette* articles inspired Symonds to write a long and passionate poem about cross-class love between men, "John Morden," which included a lengthy section entitled "Kay," in homage to Greenwood's depraved but beautiful slum youth. Symonds's appropriation and reworking of Greenwood's text does not, of course, prove that Greenwood shared Symonds's inclinations, but it does help to shed some light on the covert language necessarily deployed in discussions of same-sex desires. To his confidant, Henry Graham Dakyns, Symonds wrote a short, heretofore cryptic, letter: "As you cared for Kay, I send you the rest of John Morden. Please return him. It is an old moral put extravagantly."[155] The phrasing is intentionally ambiguous. Which "Kay" did Dakyns care for: Symonds's, Greenwood's, the real Kay and boys like him, or some combination of all three? To emphasize his sense of sharing Greenwood's discoveries and perhaps to remind Dakyns to read the *Pall Mall Gazette*, he indicated that his return address was simply "Pall Mall G."

For Symonds, benevolence was intimately wedded to eros. Symonds struggled to understand and justify his same-sex longings within an elevated moral and ethical framework that distinguished between different kinds of desires and between desire and sex acts.[156] He disdained as impure the exploitative cross-class liaisons pursued by many of his acquaintances, such as Lord Ronald Gower, who regularly went slumming in search of soldiers and laboring men willing to trade sex for cash.[157] His most satisfying relations were always with men of much lower social class whom he sought to educate and elevate through "Arcadian" love: "I've never been able to understand," he opined, "why people belonging to different strata in society—if they love each other—could not enter into comradeship."[158] Philanthropy was both figuratively and literally the "love of man" in Symonds's lexicon.

Symonds believed that if social conventions permitted free and full expression of the ideas prompted by his reading of the Amateur Casual, he would "have perhaps a subject there of transcendental ethics."[159] This subject was nothing less than the harmonizing of eros with altruism through cross-class brotherly love between men. In 1866, neither Symonds nor his contemporaries were prepared for such an undertaking. None of Greenwood's readers (including those attuned to "A Night"'s sexual themes) seems to have suggested that the inmates of the Lambeth Casual Ward were part of group of persons defined by their sexuality. Rather, their behavior illustrated the ways in which the exigencies of extreme poverty—the need for human warmth in the absence of proper clothing and heat—intersected with criminality, immorality, and official incompetence and parsimony. Contemporaries frequently used the term "blackguardism" as a convenient albeit imprecise shorthand that included the indecencies Greenwood claimed to have observed, ranging from blasphemy, swearing, thievery, to same-sex acts. Kay and his admirers may (or may not) have committed unspeakable "abominations," but it was their moral and economic status and undomiciled lives, and not their sexual identities, that defined them as a distinct class of persons: they were tramps or vagrants, not sodomites or mariannes.

In the vastly different world of the 1890s, Symonds's long deferred hope to take up his "subject of transcendental ethics" no longer seemed chimerical. In the three decades following the publication of "A Night," Britons had been forced to confront the existence of cross-class sex between men in London many times, albeit within the context of scandals. The metropolitan press had feasted on sensational disclosures during the arrest and trial of the cross-dressers, Boulton and Park (1870), the aristocratic habitués of the Cleveland Street brothel (1889), and, most spectacularly, Oscar Wilde.[160] With each of these sensations, Britons came closer to developing a vocabulary and an intellectual framework by which to understand the relationship between same-sex desires and behaviors on the one hand, and homosexual identity on the other. It was within this highly charged atmosphere that Symonds began to work with the young sexologist Havelock Ellis to write a psychological and historical analysis of "sexual inversion"—one of many terms developed by sexologists to refer to same-sex desire. Despite fundamental differences in their approach to the subject and their attitudes toward sexology as a science, Symonds and Ellis both sought to use their study as a battering ram to knock down the 1885 Labouchère amendment, which had made sexual contact between men subject to harsh criminal punishment.[161] Their study drew heavily on case histories written by "inverts" who attempted to make sense of their own sexual histories.[162] Symonds even contributed a loosely disguised fragment of his own sexual autobiography.[163] To avoid legal obstacles in Britain, Ellis and Symonds's work, *Sexual Inversion*, first appeared under joint authorship in German in 1896, three years after Symonds's death.

The figures of "Kay," the burly ruffians whose "doss" Kay shares, and the philanthropic gentlemen-observers seem to reappear, albeit in different guises, throughout the pages of *Sexual Inversion*. Many of the case studies submitted by their correspondents spoke about the ways in which class and race differences substituted for sexual difference as the axis of their desire. "M. N.," for example, noted the "peculiar predilection shown by inverts for youths of inferior social position."[164] While this "predilection" was undeniably sexual, it could also provide "the motive power for an enlarged philanthropic activity" in which "morality" has "become one with love."[165] Here was an ethics of male same-sex love perfectly calibrated to Symonds's values: a reimagining of the ennobling erotic ideals of the ancient world within the context of modern, class-divided, social life.

The widespread belief that unemployment unsexed a man may well have been an underlying assumption contributing to the ways in which Greenwood, his readers, and Ellis and Symonds chose to understand and represent the sexual practices of male vagabonds and casuals.[166] After all, because success as a breadwinner was one of the defining characteristics of manliness, failure to be gainfully employed signaled deviation from acceptable norms of masculinity. Ellis and Symonds claimed that "sexual inversion" was particularly widespread among tramps and criminals and devoted an entire appendix, "Homosexuality Among Tramps," to the topic.[167] The appendix was written by an American sexologist/criminologist, Josiah Flynt, who himself had "lived intimately with the vagabonds of both England and the United States" in the 1880s and early 1890s.[168] Most tramps, according to *Sexual Inversion*, were not aware of themselves as "real invert[s]." While homosexual practices were common "among lower races" and "among lower classes" (the authors felt no need to justify the way in which they blithely moved between "race" and "class"), few were true "homosexuals."[169] This exalted level of self-awareness, they contended, remained as yet largely the psychological achievement of men of genius and rank such as Symonds himself. By the turn of the century, the "hobo" had almost but not quite become the modern homosexual.[170]

The close identification between homelessness and sexual deviancy was soon to be codified into law by the British state, albeit in a manner utterly at odds with Symonds and Ellis's own political and ideological goals. With virtually no debate, Parliament passed an amendment to the 1824 Vagrancy Act in 1898.[171] While the main thrust of the 1898 amendment was to expand the state's capacity to imprison bullies or pimps who lived on the earnings of female prostitution, it soon became one of the twin pillars of the Victorian state's draconian regulation of all forms of sex between men.[172] According to the act, "every male person who in any public place persistently solicits or importunes for immoral purposes shall be deemed a rogue and a vagabond and may be dealt with accordingly." In practice, the law was applied only to men who "importuned" or "solicited" other men for sex.[173] In the absence of any explanations or justifications by members of Parliament, the law seems misguided if not absurd. What does sexual behavior have to do with the status of being a vagabond, a person without a home?

By equating disorderly sexual practices between men with vagabondage, the Vagrancy Act of 1898 and the way officials chose to enforce it clarified and attempted to stabilize the cultural logic implicit in "A Night" and more fully developed in the sexology of Ellis and Symonds, who were themselves inveterate opponents of all such forms of state regulation.[174] The extreme economic margin occupied by the tramp coincides with the space of extreme sexual marginality inhabited by the homosexual—at least in the eyes of the law and in the imagination of elite men whose parliamentary monopoly was just beginning to be challenged.

Some scholars have argued that during the three decades separating the

publication of "A Night" and *Sexual Inversion*, the sexological categories and lived social identities of both the "homosexual" and the "heterosexual" first came into existence.[175] Regardless of whether one accepts
such a position, the period between the 1860s and 1890s incontestably
constituted a watershed in the histories of sexualities, social welfare, and
representations of the poor in Great Britain. Greenwood's "A Night in a
Workhouse" and the public's responses to it are an important starting
point for rewriting these histories in a way that recognizes how deeply
they shaped one another. "A Night" mattered so much to its Victorian
readers because it both helped to create and drew upon widely held fantasies and anxieties about poor men and their sexuality.

POSTSCRIPT: LEGACIES OF "A NIGHT" ON
REPRESENTATIONS OF THE HOMELESS POOR

Recovering the sexual and social politics of "A Night in a Workhouse"
and readers' responses to them is more than an exercise in historical arche-
ology. Many others—men and women alike—self-consciously imitated
Greenwood in seeking to discover the truths of metropolitan poverty.
Greenwood routed their literal and imaginative footsteps along the path he
had blazed. While "A Night" participated in a well-established genre of
urban flaneurie,[176] it also initiated quite new and unconventional ways of
writing and thinking about slum dwellers and spaces. Today it opens up
new ways of thinking about the history of slumming and slum narratives
and offers opportunities to reconsider several canonical texts, each of
which bears distinct though heretofore unacknowledged traces of the influence of "A Night." I want to sketch out a tradition of writing about culture and society, poverty and sexuality which, using "A Night" as its point
of departure, includes Matthew Arnold's essays in social criticism written
between 1866 and 1871; Blanchard Jerrold and Gustave Doré's collaboration, *London: A Pilgrimage* (1872); Jack London's *People of the Abyss*
(1902), and George Orwell's *Down and Out in Paris and London* (1933),
arguably the most popular slumming narratives of the twentieth century.
Reading these well-known texts against "A Night" reorients our understanding of them by drawing attention to elements of each that might otherwise be overlooked.

At first glance, it seems improbable that the apostle of "sweetness and
light," Matthew Arnold, would have deigned to notice, much less comment on, Greenwood's playful and prurient exploration of the dark environs of the casual ward. But we must remember that many of Arnold's
now canonical prose masterworks of the 1860s were first written as occasional pieces, often in response to passing controversies of the same ilk

as "A Night." Most of his essays of social criticism initially appeared in the *Cornhill Magazine* and the *Pall Mall Gazette*, both published by his friend George Smith. Like James Greenwood, Arnold thrived on witty, barbed public exchanges with fellow correspondents. If the name Matthew Arnold today conjures up "high seriousness," he had a far different public persona in the 1860s. He was lampooned as an intellectual dandy who, along with Greenwood, affected an air of annoying "kid-gloved" gentility.[177]

Despite the sensationalism of "A Night," many of its themes were quintessentially Arnoldian: its carefully orchestrated encounter between an "exquisite" man of letters,[178] the gentleman-journalist, and the repulsive dirt and anarchic power of the poor; the tension between the intellectual narrowness and financial mean-spiritedness of parish authorities and the ineffectual pleadings of state officials. As an inspector of schools in a nation still lacking a national system of education, Arnold was all too painfully aware of the limited powers of the British state to interfere in local affairs.

Arnold was a regular reader of the *Pall Mall Gazette*, so it is likely that he followed "A Night in a Workhouse" as it appeared on January 12, 13, and 15, 1866. Surviving evidence suggests that "A Night" remained vivid in his imagination for at least the next five years. The first and the last of the essays and letters he wrote on social questions between 1866 and 1871, which were published as books under the titles *Culture and Anarchy* (1869) and *Friendship's Garland* (1871), pointedly refer to Greenwood's "A Night."[179] Arnold was reviewing proofs for his jeremiad "My Countryman" when "A Night" first appeared. In "My Countryman" (published in February 1866), Arnold rehearsed many of the key themes that he would later develop in "Anarchy and Authority" and "Culture and Its Enemies." For Arnold, the weakness of poor-law officials and the pettiness of vestry authorities disclosed by "A Night" and the condition of workhouse infirmaries were examples of what he famously called the "illiberalism of liberalism."[180] These were evidence of the failure of the British state and its ruling classes to educate and elevate the masses.[181] A month later, in the first of what proved to be a long series of satirical letters he published in the *Pall Mall Gazette* between 1866 and 1871, he alluded once again to the malign role of vestrymen in the casual ward scandal. In choosing to publish his letters in the paper that had been so recently made famous by "A Night," Arnold had reason to assume that his audience would necessarily read his contributions against the backdrop of James Greenwood's exposé. In his letters to the editor of the *Gazette*, Arnold criticized English values and state institutions from the perspective of a fictional German tourist named Arminius. When he decided to republish the letters in book form as *Friendship's*

Garland, he added a foreword, "Dedicatory Letter," to the volume. Authored by Arnold's fictional alter ego, "Matthew Arnold of Grub Street," the dedicatory letter paid lighthearted homage to the Greenwood brothers: "I love to think that the success of the 'Workhouse Casual' had disposed the Editor's heart to be friendly toward pariahs." Extending this comparison between himself as a "pariah" and a workhouse casual grateful for charity, Arnold's fictional persona archly observed that "my communication was affably accepted, and from that day to this the *Pall Mall Gazette*, whenever there is any mention in it of [my friend] Arminius, reaches me in Grub Street gratis."[182] Presumably, his delight in receiving the *Gazette* "gratis" underscored his putative penury and the high cost of the genteel newspaper.

Despite the jocular tone of the Arminius letters, *Friendship's Garland* and *Culture and Anarchy* articulated Arnold's longing for the British state to become the efficient organ of "right reason" for the nation. From Arnold's perspective, many events in 1866 boded ill for the realization of his goal, including the social and sexual dangers Greenwood brought to public attention.[183] Public outrage and anxiety over "A Night" contributed to the atmosphere of bourgeois panic with which Arnold and so many of his contemporaries greeted the news that a crowd of Reform Bill demonstrators, reputed to be East End camp followers, had toppled some railings in Hyde Park in the summer of 1866. In "A Night in a Workhouse" Greenwood reported that he was particularly tormented by an incident which parodically adumbrated events in Hyde Park several months later. A drunken man arrived in the Lambeth Casual Ward singing a music-hall tune about his desire to be a "swell a-roaming down Pall Mall, Or anywhere,—I don't much care, so I can be a swell." The couplet, which at first had "an intensely comical effect," grew more and more horrible for Greenwood as other casuals joined in to form a "bestial chorus." "A Night" ominously revealed that the corrosive spirit of anarchy and rowdyism was no mere phantom of Arnold's imagination but rather a fearful reality. For a gentlemen to go dressed incognito among the degraded poor was a heroic gesture and a daring novelty; for the poor themselves to invade one of the chief spaces of sociability and recreation of the West End elite, or to even sing about such trespass, was altogether a different matter.

In contrast to Arnold's depiction of the poor as brutalized, Blanchard Jerrold and Gustave Doré's treatment of them in *London: A Pilgrimage* (1872) was sympathetic, almost affectionate.[184] The English journalist and the French artist tended to focus more on the triumphs of the poor over adversity than on their spirit of rebellion. *London* combined Jerrold's breezy touristic narrative with Doré's lushly detailed, though not always accurate, illustrations to offer a panoramic view of the entire metropolis. The effect of the whole was to make a powerful argument about the simultaneous geographic and social isolation of groups from one another *and* their economic interconnections. Late one night as Jerrold took Doré to visit a night refuge in the slums, he explained to his companion that philanthropy in London was organized in such a way that "the relief of the multitude is connected with the pleasures and the Christian charity of the rich."[185] Jerrold was referring to the organization of charitable bazaars and other fund-raising events. His words also apply to the ways in which slumming was a source of "pleasure" and an act of "Christian charity" for the rich.

The written and visual texts of *London*, in particular Doré's pair of images entitled "Scripture Reader in a Night Refuge" and "A Bath at the Field Lane Refuge" have notable affinities with Greenwood's "A Night." I should emphasize that no direct evidence links "A Night" and *London*; however, the two works deploy strikingly similar fantasies about disguises, urban space, and relations between elite male social observers and male tramps. As the editor of *Lloyd's Weekly Newspaper* in 1866, Jerrold was well acquainted with "A Night."[186] Following Greenwood, Jerrold assured the readers of *London* that the only way for them to gain genuine insight into the lives of the London poor was to "adopt rough clothes" and go among them.[187] Doré, like Matthew Arnold and James Greenwood, had a penchant for masquerades and gladly dressed the part of a tramp when he visited the London netherworlds.[188] His costume, according to a witness, was "a triumph of vagabondage and Bill Sykes [from Dickens's *Oliver Twist*] style of significance."[189] By the time Jerrold and Doré embarked on their joint venture, a tour of the London slums was an essential part of the itinerary of any "thoughtful and serious observer."[190] In his biography of Doré, Jerrold recalled that the pathos and sad beauty of destitute Londoners riveted his French collaborator. Jerrold shared Doré's attraction to the "picturesque" lives of the poor, which "tempted" him to imagine and write about the "great city's life and movement."[191]

At least three versions of what Doré and Jerrold saw the night they visited the Field Lane Refuge near Smithfield in 1869 have survived: Jerrold's prose narrative, Doré's roughly sketched study of paupers bathing at the refuge, and the completed pair of images from the refuge published in *London*. The differences between these representations are more notable than their similarities. Jerrold's written narrative concisely recounts the sequence of events. Presumably referring to the recent creation of the Charity Organisation Society, Jerrold offers one of his many criticisms of recent schemes to organize charity along scientific lines when he praises "spontaneous charity to the houseless." He and Doré then watch a "crowd of tattered and tired out creatures" "being filtered into a refuge." The superintendent "distributes the regulation lump of bread to the guests, and they pass on, by way of the bath—rigorously enforced for obvious reasons—to the dormitories set out like barracks, and warmed with a stove, which is always the center of attraction. Here, when all are in bed, a Bible-reader reads, comforting, let us hope, many of the aching heads."[192]

The placement of Doré's two illustrations of this scene offers a different chronology. The large full-page image of the "Scripture Reader" (figure 1.3a comes two pages before the much smaller image "In the Bath," figure 1.3b). Thus the reader of the visual text first meets the male casuals in their thin nightshirts packed onto inclined sleeping boards and only later does one see them bathing. In the "Scripture Reader," the male casuals are haggard and skeletal. They resemble living corpses entombed in a windowless, cell-like dormitory. Many of the men clutch themselves, and the sinuous lines of the bedsheets seem to writhe like snakes. The source of warmth and comfort in Jerrold's account, the stove, is not visible in Doré's illustration. The Scripture Reader replaces the stove as the literal "center" of Doré's representation of the scene.

Many structural elements of Doré's design ought to reinforce the Reader's centrality. As the only standing figure, he also provides the illustration's most important vertical axis. His shadow dramatically doubles the horizontal lines of the pipes above and pulls the viewer's eye toward him at the apex of a triangle formed by two well-lit sets of bare feet at the extreme bottom right and left, the shadow, and the double railings of the barrack beds. Nonetheless, he is much less visually compelling than the sea of anonymous men ranged around him. Why? I suspect the answer lies in the way Doré intentionally undercuts the Reader's aspiration to control both the image and the souls of the inmates of the refuge. Whereas Jerrold held out the hope that the Reader could provide comfort to "many of the aching heads," Doré's image is less optimistic. Only one man appears to have the energy or the interest to sit up and, perhaps, listen to the Reader. The Reader's absorption in his text and his audience's indifference to him suggest the profound alienation of the poor from the church's spiritual ministry and redirect the viewer away from both the Reader and the "book" toward the men themselves.

Doré's "In the Bath" presumably depicts a group of five of these same men taking their mandatory dip into the "mutton broth" liquid of a communal bath. But unlike in "Scripture Reader," the casuals are naked, active, and mostly upright. The men have been transformed beyond recognition. In place of the emaciated figures in "Scripture Reader," the viewer confronts male bodies more closely approximating a neoclassical ideal than exhausted paupers staving off starvation, except for their torn flesh. The two central bathers are strikingly well-built, much like the "brawny men" whose belated entrance into the casual ward fascinated

SCRIPTURE READER IN A NIGHT REFUGE

a

b

FIGURE 1.3. From Gustave Doré and Blanchard Jerrold,
London, A Pilgrimage, 1872.

and frightened Greenwood. One, drawn frontally, contorts his body as if to show off his sculpted upper torso; powerful buttocks and back muscles are the most prominent feature of the other bather, depicted with his backside to the viewer. Doré's main concession to modesty is concealing the bathers' genitals from the viewer, although presumably not from the two inspectors/observers who monitor the paupers' ablutions. The two male inspectors ironically stand in for Doré and Jerrold, as well as for readers of *London*. They are reminders that the poor, even when they are bathing, are subject to the voyeuristic surveillance of their superiors.[193]

According to Jerrold's biography of Doré, Doré tended to take only hasty visual notes as he walked the streets. Doré bragged that he did not need to make detailed studies because his visual memory was almost photographic in its capacity to imprint precise images on the "collodion type" of his brain.[194] Fortunately, Jerrold reproduced many of Doré's unpublished preliminary studies for *London*, including one for "In the Bath." Doré most likely executed this hasty and impressionistic notebook sketch (figure 1.6) in situ during his visit to the Refuge with Jerrold. Doré's study depicts two bathers, both of whom are bent over and visible only from the side. Like the published illustration, the sketch relies on large metal pipes to give vertical and horizontal structure to the image. There is only one inspector, and he is drawn so abstractly that he could be mistaken for the dripping towel hanging on the wall which replaces him in the final illustration. It is impossible to explain why Doré reworked his original sketch into "In the Bath"; however, the changes he made between the two images do provide evidence about how Doré reimagined the scene. If Greenwood transformed himself from a gentleman to a casual by putting on clothes, Doré's sickly paupers become robust, if still degenerate, athletes simply by taking off their clothes. In Doré's iconography, figures clothed in rags speak to the misery and poverty of the poor; the naked bodies of poor men, by contrast, suggest an idealized admiration for their raw, primitive, and powerful masculinity.[195] Doré's visual images and Jerrold's written text recapitulate Greenwood's ambivalent representations of the male casuals he meets in the sleeping shed and whose bodies he first comes into contact with through the bathwater: they are simultaneously degenerate and strangely attractive.

Perhaps the two best-known works of urban tourism and slum exploration written in the twentieth century, Jack London's *People of the Abyss* and George Orwell's *Down and Out in Paris and London*, also participated, like *London: A Pilgrimage*, in the eroticization of male vagabondage that had been given such wide cultural currency by Greenwood. While neither author mentioned Greenwood, their works are deeply indebted to the tradition of slum writing he had inaugurated with

FIGURE 1.4. Image executed in 1869, but not published until 1891. (Blanchard Jerrold, *Life of Gustave Doré*.)

"A Night."[196] London and Orwell, like Greenwood, were perpetually crossing borders—between nations, classes, races, and ideologies. In these crossings, they found themselves and their subjects as writers. This was particularly true for Orwell. *Down and Out* was not only his first published book, it was also the first time he adopted the pen name George Orwell, by which he remains best known. In publishing *Down and Out,* Orwell literally became Orwell; he transformed himself from Eric Blair, a disaffected former member of the imperial civil service in Burma into the journalist, writer, and social critic.

London, the embodiment of robustly independent American manhood, and Orwell, the outcast "shabby genteel" socialist from the "lower upper-middle class," lived as what the Marxist literary critic Raymond Williams called "exiles" and "vagrants." Both authors condemned the structures of inequality in society and their consequences for the lives of individuals.[197] In his analysis of Orwell in *Culture and Society* (1958), Williams offered a powerful way to think about the meanings of "exile" and "vagrancy" in British culture. According to him, the exile asserted his (I use the word "his" because exiles and vagrants were both emphatically male for Williams) independence from settled ideas and ways of living, and as a result of doing so, he derived acute critical insights about society's shortcomings. While the "exile" and the "vagrant" stand outside the familiar comforts of home, "there is usually principle in exile . . . only relaxation in vagrancy." "The vagrant," Williams continued, "in literary terms is the 'reporter' . . . an observer, an intermediary" whose powers of observation surpass his understanding. The exile, by contrast, stringently applies his principles to the task of changing his world rather than merely recording its intractable dilemmas.[198] How can Williams help us understand Greenwood, London, and Orwell? How does placing Greenwood at the beginning of a tradition of slum writing shift our understanding of Williams's seminal analysis in *Culture and Society*?

Greenwood, London, and Orwell were literally reporters who lived at least part of their lives as vagrants—or disguised as vagrants. London's *People* began as an assignment to report on the impact on Londoners of the Boer War.[199] By the time he arrived in England, the American Press Association had cancelled his assignment and he was free to pursue the story closest to his heart. Disguised as a tramp, he decided to chronicle conditions in "this human hell-hole called London Town."[200] Like Greenwood before him, London made his slum "dives" and himself into news. Living among the poorest of the poor in London and Paris, Orwell staved off hunger by publishing nonfiction slum stories—which later became the kernels of *Down and Out*—in both French (*Le Progrès Civique*) and English journals (*Adelphi*).

While Orwell openly and frequently acknowledged the influence of Jack London and *People* on his work, both writers paid indirect—and presumably unintended—homage to Greenwood's homoerotic adventures by exploring the sexual oddness of slums.[201] At the time London wrote *People*, he was in the midst of maneuvering his way through complicated love affairs with women, only one of whom was his pregnant wife.[202] His incognito slumming gave him some respite from these pressures and allowed him to enter into the homosocial intimacies of "mateship" and "comradeship" among tramps. In the course of one memorable evening of research, he encountered a sailor who had entirely sworn off women who were, he insisted, too expensive and dangerous for him. The two got drunk, "talked as natural men should talk," and spent the night together in the same bed.[203] Reveling in the democratic familiarity his disguise made possible, London unashamedly extolled the physical beauty and attractiveness of his bedpartner in words that echoed Greenwood's admiration for Kay. London's mate could have been one of Doré's degenerately noble bathers comes to life. His "mouth and lips" were "sweet," London observed:

> His head was shapely, and so gracefully was it poised upon a perfect neck that I was not surprised by his body that night when he stripped for bed. I have seen many men strip, in gymnasium and training quarters, men of good blood and upbringing, but I have never seen one who stripped to better advantage than this young sot of two and twenty, this young god doomed to rack and ruin in four or five short years. (15)

London concluded his description by casting his mate's distaste for women within the framework of eugenics, not sexuality. His newly found friend, London predicted, will die "without posterity to receive the splendid heritage it was his to bequeath."[204] Throughout the passage, London deflects the very homoeroticism that he conjures. He accounts for his expertise in evaluating naked male beauty by referring to manly homosocial institutions: the gymnasium and the training quarters. He seems disingenuously confused by the discovery that some men, like his beautiful bedpartner, choose not to have sex with women.

Orwell's *Down and Out* is much more explicit than either Greenwood's or London's work in recognizing slums as "queer" spaces and slumming itself as a means to explore the homosexual subculture of interwar London. In fact, Orwell's depiction of homosexuality in the slums is so straightforward that it seems hardly possible that critics have said so little about it. Orwell retraces many of Greenwood's steps. He goes to the slums of Lambeth to purchase an outfit that closely resembles the one Greenwood had so lovingly described in "A Night."[205] As soon as he makes the purchase, he fears that the police might arrest him "as a vagabond." In light of the Vagrancy Act of 1898, with whose terms Orwell was familiar, his fear may also be interpreted as an anxiety that he will be taken into custody as a "homosexual." In any case, Orwell eventually makes his way to a casual ward of a workhouse where he, like Greenwood before him, stumbles upon an underworld inhabited by "fifty dirty, stark naked men elbowing each other in a room twenty feet square."[206] He even meets a pauper he calls "Old Daddy"—though this Daddy has none of the playful charm of Greenwood's original.[207] In place of Greenwood's mutton-broth bath, Orwell must clean himself in a tub "streaked" with the antique filth of other tramps and dry himself using one of the two "slimy roller towels" provided for all the men.[208] Each man is allowed to sleep with his special "mate" with "naked limbs constantly touching." Orwell finally makes explicit the homoerotic tensions that form a connecting thread of *Down and Out*: about midnight, his "mate" "began making homosexual attempts upon me—a nasty experience in a locked, pitch dark cell. . . . [The man then told him that] homosexuality is general among tramps of long standing."[209]

Unlike Greenwood and London, Orwell openly and often expressed his disgust for homosexuality. In his writing, he never enjoys the sight of a beautiful male body in the casual wards and lodging houses he frequents. Nakedness is utterly unsentimental. Orwell's world out of clothes reveals only the ravages of social and economic inequalities on the sagging muscles, hollow chests, and potbellies of the tramps.[210] He concludes his observations about the slums as queer spaces with an account of a "fashionably dressed" Old Etonian he meets in a common lodging house who, he speculates, went there "in search of the 'nancy boys.'" While Orwell tried to make *Down and Out* as literally true as possible, he confided to a friend that the elderly "poof" was not in fact an Etonian but a graduate of "some other well known school."[211] Why did Orwell make him into an Etonian, a graduate of Orwell's own elite public school? Was this merely a spiteful act by a schoolboy who could not resist sullying the reputation of his alma mater? Or was this yet another example of Orwell's ambivalent sense of identifying himself with the outcast men he encountered without every having truly to become one of them? After all, the elderly man implicates Orwell in his quest for sex by posing the rhetorical question: "Funny sort of place for you and me, eh?"[212] At the very least, the presence of the Old Etonian satirizes the ethos of service and philanthropic benevolence trumpeted by England's elite public schools—most established missions to the London poor in the 1880s—and reminds readers that public schools, like casual wards and Oxford colleges, remained hotbeds of homosociability and homosexual experimentation in interwar Britain.

The career of Tom Driberg, Orwell's not-so-shabby-genteel contemporary and a leading Labour Party politician, was in many respects quite similar to Orwell's in terms of their deep engagement with the lives of the working class and poor.[213] But Driberg was only too happy to conflate journalistic forays to see how the poor lived with his relentless pursuit of sex with working-class men. In one episode of his memoir, *Ruling Passions*, Driberg swaps clothes with a young male beggar in exchange for a night of sex. The next morning, he dons the tattered outfit and plays the part of street beggar. Later hauled into court on charges of indecently assaulting two homeless miners whom he had sheltered in his London flat, Driberg claimed that he was motivated by "philanthropy" and the pursuit of "useful copy" for a story he was writing about labor troubles. His lawyer even produced the newspaper article Driberg had written using the data he had collected from the men—as if the existence of the jour-nalistic artifact proved his client's innocence.[214]

Both Driberg and Orwell perpetuated the linkage in the elite male imagination between homelessness and homosexuality, though they did so for very different reasons. Only the Real Casual, the educated but im-poverished man in the Lambeth Casual Ward the night Greenwood had visited in January 1866, challenged the erotic framework that elite ob-servers had imposed on the physical intimacies they witnessed between male tramps. Recall that the Real Casual had suggested that men in the casual ward clung together to generate enough heat to endure a freezing night on cold stones. Survival, not sex, was at the heart of the matter for him. Six decades later, another "real casual," John Worby, wrote his own two-volume memoir chronicling his days and nights tramping across Britain and the United States. When the first volume, *The Other Half* (1937), appeared, it created a minor sensation, and Worby enjoyed celebrity as the man who spoke not *for* but *as* one of "the other half." Just as the Real Casual's narrative provides an important counterpoint to Greenwood's, so, too, do Worby's stories offer a disturbing companion to Orwell's tales of queer slumming in the 1930s. Orphaned at four and raised by foster parents for several years, Worby spent his adolescence moving from one harsh boys home to another until he fled to Canada as part of an emigration/farm work program. As soon as Worby escaped the clutches of institutional boy-welfare schemes, he was picked up by a handsome but "curious" and "queer" man named Reg who was driving a Ford coupé and who offered to feed and clothe him, keep him in pocket money, and give him a home. Presenting himself as a naïf, Worby elabo-rately stages his first homosexual encounter and details the feelings it stirred in him.

> When he kept endearing me with his words and caresses I began to get a queer sensation which I could not for all the world of me account for. It was a sort of soothing thrilling feeling which seemed to urge itself on as soon as he touched me. It seemed as if I didn't want him to take his hand off my thigh and when at last he did take it off I had a feeling of utter loneliness. I had never experi-enced anything like this before and the fact that I was with a man made it all the more difficult to explain. I wondered and marvelled that a man could talk and act so much like a woman. He kept asking me if I loved him and if I minded him feeling my leg muscles. He said he just loved to do it and hoped I would always be his. I told him I loved him even though I didn't know what it meant and if he liked to run his hands over me, well I didn't mind.

Worby's responses to Reg's lovemaking suggest that their encounter is one based on mutual sexual attraction and desire and not on the grotesque exploitation of a homeless boy by an older and economically secure man. Worby appears to conform precisely to the expectations of sexologists: he *is* Greenwood's Kay reincarnated, the beautiful and sexually promiscuous male tramp whom no reporter or photographer in the 1860s was ever able to find.

But Worby's "thrilling feelings" soon give way to outright disgust as he realizes that Reg wants to have sex with him. Once Worby figures out that adult men assume that homeless boys are "queer" and available for sex, he ruthlessly reverses the power dynamics by stealing money from Reg and returning to the road. The ostensibly vulnerable adolescent becomes an accomplished exploiter of adult male drag queens, fetishists, and homosexuals. Worby returns to England and makes his way to Trafalgar Square, where he joins the "boys" who teach him the inside tricks involved in conning older men—"mugs" or "steamers"—out of substantial sums of money without giving them the sex they think they have purchased. In contrast, when Worby is picked up by Avril, a very wealthy West End woman addicted to drugs who makes him her "companion" and "lover," he feels pity and tenderness for her. Because the older men he preys upon while posing as their prey are homosexuals, Worby believes they deserve to have their money stolen. Once he understands the game, Worby is all too happy to invoke the homophobic norms of his society in justifying his thievery. Avril's relationship to him is every bit as exploitative as Reg's, but because she wants him to pose as the husband of a wealthy woman, he gladly plays the part and guards her honor with zeal. Worby is genuinely invested in the role of husband and protector even as he understands its falseness.

Worby's memoirs provide powerful evidence that "queer" and "curious" men with economic resources in Britain and America did assume that adolescent tramps were "rough trade" willing to sell their bodies for a suit of clothes and some cash, but they also show just how canny Worby and the other Trafalgar Square "boys" were in manipulating elite preconceptions to their own advantage. Worby and the older queer men he met were willing participants in a complex sexual masquerade in which boy tramps and men alike were pathetically vulnerable to exploitation and ready exploiters of one another.[215] Unlike the Real Casual, who rejected Greenwood's eroticization of poverty, Worby only confirmed the "truth" that Greenwood had discovered: extreme poverty among men was itself a form of sexual deviance.

Placing "A Night" at the beginning of a tradition of writing about the poorest of the London poor (and as the first chapter of this book) makes visible the complex links between sexual and social politics in modern British history, literature, and culture. I am not arguing that this tradition is exclusively a queer one; far from it. But I am proposing that it is not nearly as straight or as straightforward as Williams and many others have supposed it was. If we follow the logic of "A Night," of Symonds's and Ellis's emerging sexological categories, and of the terms of the Vagrancy Act of 1898 defining the homosexual as vagrant, then we need to rethink the implications of Williams's concept of the social-critic-as-reporter as vagrant. The reporter writing about vagrancy; the reporter posing as a vagrant; the vagrant as homosexual; the reporter as homosexual: these sets of closely-associated terms generated by "A Night" and its many nineteenth- and twentieth-century legacies seem to proliferate, each opening up new lines of inquiry.

Chapter Two

DR. BARNARDO'S ARTISTIC FICTIONS:

PHOTOGRAPHY, SEXUALITY, AND THE

RAGGED CHILD

A S LONDONERS opened their newspapers to devour the latest disclosures about workhouse abominations in January and February of 1866, the *Times* asserted its dignity by declaring that it had "no sympathy with the professional philanthropy which makes a pet of everything depraved." Nonetheless, it could not resist challenging its readers and the investigative prowess of the so-called Amateur Casual (James Greenwood) of its junior rival the *Pall Mall Gazette* to "dare the horrors of the commonest of common lodging houses" which, the paper implied, would surpass workhouse casual wards as dens of vice and depravity.[1] A few weeks later, Thomas John Barnardo, the young Anglo-Irishman who would take up this unsavory challenge, first arrived in the metropolis to live and evangelize among the poor of East London. In homage to Greenwood's nom de plume as the Amateur Casual, Barnardo playfully called himself the Amateur Tramp several years later when he disguised himself in the rags of poverty to investigate lodging houses. He had left his native Dublin and its millenarian religious community of Plymouth Brethren determined to study medicine at the London Hospital in Whitechapel and then to devote his talents to serving God by joining Hudson Taylor's Inland Medical Mission to China. But the achingly desperate childhood poverty he daily encountered as he walked the congested streets and decaying alleyways surrounding the hospital utterly changed his plans and his life's vocation. He never made it farther east than East London, and some of his contemporaries questioned whether he had studied long and hard enough to deserve the title Doctor Barnardo, the name by which he still remains well known throughout Britain and the world. One of the Victorian age's best known philanthropists, he proved himself a master publicist, inveterate self-promoter, and controversialist. Even a century after his death, the romance of his life and the audacity of his philanthropic schemes still capture headlines, in part because the organization he founded remains one of the world's best-known child welfare agencies. As recently as 1995, BBC television aired a poignant six-hour series critically assessing Barnardo's life and the work of his organization from the 1860s onward. The *Independent* ran a Sunday magazine cover feature on his photographic archives.[2]

What accounts for such broad public interest in Barnardo's history? For many, the ubiquity of homeless people—the "street arabs" of Barnardo's day—visually confirms their suspicion that the post–World War II welfare state has failed and emboldens them to call for its abandonment. The supposed inefficacy of the state's interventions has led some to reexamine how Victorians dealt with the poorest of the poor and to look toward the revival of so-called Victorian values of self-reliance, minimal central government, and voluntarism (both secular and religious) as the cornerstones of contemporary social policy.[3] According to Gertrude Himmelfarb, the most influential and persuasive academic proponent of neo-Victorianism, the on-going crisis in welfare is a result of the demoralization of society.[4] The solution, she insisted, must be to recover those certitudes that united Victorians in their commitment to making morals central to all debates about welfare. In a *New York Times* op-ed piece in the midst of a political controversy in the United States Congress over the advantages of boys homes and orphanages, Himmelfarb pointed to Dr. Barnardo as an exemplary Victorian moralist and invited her readers to reconsider his methods of child rescue. Himmelfarb is far too learned and astute a scholar to romanticize the Victorians or Barnardo. In a *Wall Street Journal* article she published soon thereafter, she acknowledged that any assessment of the Victorian past would have to take into account the "social and sexual discriminations . . . the constraints and inhibitions" of the age. Nonetheless, she enjoined us "to relearn the [Victorian] language of virtue" which, she averred, was not tainted by the discriminatory contexts of its production, and "apply that language to social policy."[5]

In this chapter, I take up all of Professor Himmelfarb's suggestions. I concur with her that Barnardo *is* an exemplary Victorian moralist. I, too, believe we have much learn by studying his language of virtue. But unlike Himmelfarb, I do not believe that his language of virtue can be separated from the social and sexual contexts of its production and reception. I will show that Barnardo's written and visual language of morality was so compelling *because* it was embedded in "social and sexual discriminations . . . constraints and inhibitions" that it not only criticized but also reproduced. This chapter concerns the moral imagination and its implications for the history of private and public provision for the very poor. I suggest that this imagination divided Victorians as much as it united them; that it disturbed them more often than it offered them reassuring platitudes.

My analysis of Barnardo centers on the most painful but also the most pivotal episode in his career in the late summer of 1877. Eleven years before, he had arrived in the metropolis without friends or money to study medicine. He was a charismatic Anglo-Irish outsider in the genteel world of metropolitan philanthropy. His only obvious assets were his religious fervor, his gift for attracting slum children, and his knack for raising large sums of money for his benevolent schemes.[6] Diminutive but fiercely self-assertive, Barnardo felt drawn toward what James Greenwood called "our immense army of juvenile vagrants"—the more than one hundred thousand children who wandered the streets of London "destitute of proper guardianship, food, clothing, or employment." Where Greenwood indicted the "keen-witted, ready-penny commercial enterprise of the small-capital, business-minded portion of our vast community" for exploiting slum children and demanded state legislative intervention, Barnardo focused on saving their souls and on clothing and feeding their bodies.[7] He created an array of child rescue institutions, vocational training, and immigration schemes for boys and later girls that laid the foundations of the Barnardo's philanthropic empire in the century after his death. A talented organizer and demanding leader, Barnardo was not an obedient foot soldier in the evangelical army combating sin and poverty. He displayed an almost truculent disregard for authority. His incapacity to compromise with others and his unwillingness to accept the dictates of his superiors alienated fellow missionaries and workers at schools for "ragged" children during his first years in East London. Nonetheless, contributions flowed into his East End Juvenile Mission, best known simply as Dr. Barnardo's, and the institution grew rapidly in the early 1870s. At a time when most other reformers and philanthropists routinely established committees of trustees to oversee the proper use of the charitable funds they collected, Barnardo insisted on retaining exclusive control over the finances and direction of his institutions.

By the spring of 1877, Barnardo confronted a personal debacle that threatened to undo a decade of patient labors among the poor. Donations to his institutions dropped precipitously amidst vicious rumors impugning his integrity and probity. "Our night of trouble and tears, we feel certain, must soon be over," Barnardo consoled himself in June. "The light will surely penetrate and dispel the mists and shadows."[8] Throughout the summer months of 1877, a panel of three distinguished arbitrators, as well as Britain's larger philanthropic and Christian communities, scrutinized every aspect of his public and private life. The arbitration hearing had all the ingredients of a story that would have appealed deeply to Barnardo's theatrical imagination had he not been cast in the leading role in the unfolding drama. Scores of witnesses, rich and poor alike, paraded through the arbitration chamber at the Institution of Surveyors, Great George Street, Westminster, to testify for and against

Barnardo. He stood accused of a potent and sensational mix of charges which, if proved true, would necessarily have destroyed his good name and ended his work. These included misappropriating funds to enrich himself; physically abusing the children he rescued from the streets by cruel punishment and inadequate attention to their religious, dietary, and medical needs; falsely assuming the title of Doctor without completing his qualifying examinations; and engaging in immoral relations with a prostitute. Finally, Barnardo was charged with producing and distributing falsified photographs of his ragged children that purported to show them exactly as he found them but actually depicted them in artificially staged poses. Anxieties about photographic falsification were compounded by the nature of the images themselves, which some considered indecent and sexually provocative in displaying the bare limbs and bodies of the children through their ripped and torn garments.[9]

A transitory cabal of three groups of people led the assault on Barnardo's character and institutions. George Reynolds, an obscure evangelical Baptist minister, brought the controversy into public view by publishing and personally distributing his scathing pamphlet about Barnardo entitled *Dr. Barnardo's Homes Containing Startling Revelations*.[10] He was soon joined by other evangelical slum workers, foremost among them the bachelor-brewery-heir-turned-purity-crusader, Frederick Charrington. Scion of East London's wealthiest and most powerful family, Charrington believed he had an almost seigneurial right to act as the sole missionary among the poor who lived in the shadow of his family's great brewery in Mile End.[11] Once an admirer of Barnardo and a beneficiary of his public endorsement, Charrington felt that Barnardo's schemes threatened the success of his own religious and benevolent projects.[12] Perhaps the most eccentric star in London's philanthropic firmament, Charrington possessed an almost instinctive genius for choreographing bizarre and well-publicized incidents that drew attention to his self-sacrificing moral rectitude and the immorality of others.[13] Even his closest fellow workers found it difficult to accommodate his "hot tempered" and "unyielding" manner.[14]

Behind the scenes, Reynolds and Charrington were supported by the champions of scientific and secular approaches to poverty, the leaders of the Central Office of the Charity Organisation Society (COS), among them C. J. Ribton-Turner, Alsager Hay Hill, and Charles Loch.[15] As I argued in the previous chapter, the workhouse scandals of 1865–66, along with an immense increase in the scope and variety of evangelical charities founded in the 1860s, had greatly stimulated charity workers, civil servants, and philanthropists to organize themselves along more rational and scientific lines.[16] This movement culminated in the formation of the COS, which had begun its work in London only a few years after Bar-

nardo's arrival, and had quickly established district committees throughout London, whose activities were coordinated by a handful of paid professional agents at the Central Office. Without Barnardo's knowledge, the
COS had disapprovingly monitored his philanthropic activities—as well
as many other evangelical initiatives, such as soup kitchens and night
shelters—for three or four years before the beginning of the arbitration.[17]
The leaders and staff of the Central Office of the COS distrusted Barnardo's methods of relief, which they believed perpetuated pauperism
rather than deterred it.[18] In the eyes of the COS, Barnardo violated the
proper relationship established by the New Poor Law in 1834 between
the state, the free market, and the benevolent institutions of civil society.
By providing food and shelter for poor children, Barnardo undermined
the principles of the New Poor Law by freeing parents from choosing between either supporting themselves and their children through paid labor
or incarceration in workhouses. Finally, both Barnardo's evangelical rivals and the leaders of the Central Office of the COS were abetted by a
third group intent to sully Barnardo's name. A handful of working-class
employees at Barnardo's homes for ragged children, whom he had fired
for "gross misconduct" the year before, were secretly on the payroll of his
enemies and anxious to exact revenge on their former boss. They would
serve as star witnesses against Barnardo as they told their own versions of
the inner workings of Barnardo's institutions.

Dr. Barnardo's ordeal in the summer of 1877 was the culmination of
several years of misunderstandings and petty rivalries among a small circle of evangelical philanthropists, clergymen, and the poor in East London. As Gillian Wagner has shown, these local contexts and internecine
struggles explain a great deal about how and why specific charges were
leveled against Barnardo.[19] Personalities clearly did matter a great deal
throughout the controversy, both in setting it in motion and producing
an atmosphere of vicious recrimination. Barnardo, Charrington, and
Ribton-Turner (the COS leader in charge of the Barnardo case) were ambitious and determined men, each incapable of strategically backing
down from a position. While the record of their disputes forms a sadly
riveting tale, the arbitration's wider significance is only apparent within
the broader contexts in which it unfolded and which it so singularly illu-
minates: the histories of visual and literary representations of poor children, social welfare and voluntary philanthropy, metropolitan evangelicalism, and sexuality. Questions about the "truth" bind together these
seemingly disparate histories and form one connecting thread in my
analysis of them. At the most obvious level, the public needed to know
the truth about Dr. Barnardo and his accusers. The enmity between Barnardo and the Charity Organisation Society was one skirmish in the ongoing struggle between empathic and scientific, religious and secular, ap-

proaches to poverty and over who should control the vast apparatus of metropolitan charity. As the controversy moved toward arbitration, the question of how philanthropists determined who was truly poor was turned on its head. People demanded to know who was a true philanthropist and what constituted true charity. This proved no simple matter because its answer depended upon the widely differing ways in which Evangelicals, members of other Christian denominations, and secular-minded reformers understood the truth.

Doubts about Barnardo's personal truthfulness cannot be separated from anxieties about his sexuality, the sexual conduct of his staff, and the supposedly sexual character of some of his photographs. Barnardo's innovative use of photographs, what Reynolds decried as his "artistic fictions," led contemporaries to ask themselves the broader philosophical question of what was (and was not) a truthful, legitimate, and decent representation of the poor. How could unwary readers distinguish between the conventions of truthfulness that governed journalistic exposés such as Greenwood's "A Night in a Workhouse," philanthropic reports, and the vast didactic literature produced by Evangelicals? Were photographs of ragged children objective and scientific documents of human misery, or were they subjective images meant to appeal to emotion more than reason? Barnardo's use of photography also raised questions about truth in advertising: what were the boundaries separating the largely unregulated practice of commercial advertising and the documentation of social evils to raise money for benevolent schemes?

I tell the story of the arbitration, or perhaps more aptly explain why it happened and what it meant, from several different perspectives. First, I compare evangelical conceptions of truth and rationality with those of the COS to explain their conflict in terms of their differing notions about charity, welfare, and the role of the state. The next section explores those elements of the arbitration that threatened to, but never quite did, transform it into a major sexual scandal. The third section links together and mobilizes the arguments developed in the previous sections to analyze Barnardo's representations of ragged children. I offer close readings of a few of Barnardo's literary and visual texts to explain what Alan Tractenberg aptly described in 1974 as the "unsettling ambiguity" of Barnardo's photographic images of ragged children, which "approach yet fall just short of an unbearable revelation."[20] The fourth section uses the lens of the Barnardo controversy to interpret one of the best-known stories in Victorian history: the discovery and rescue of Joseph Merrick, the so-called Elephant Man. I argue that Merrick was a Barnardo-boy manqué and that his history can and should be read as an episode in evangelical philanthropy, child rescue, and photography. The conclusion serves as both coda and postscript. It simultaneously takes stock of my analysis of

Barnardo's story while using a few examples to underscore its usefulness in making sense of the histories of child welfare, photography, and sexuality in the twentieth century.

This chapter is in no sense intended to besmirch the name of one of the Victorian age's most luminous do-gooders. Dr. Barnardo did a tremendous amount of good for thousands of children, women, and men whose lives would have been much poorer but for his efforts. Even Charles Booth, not prone to hyperbole, commented that Barnardo's organization in the 1890s "was beyond question the greatest charitable institution in London, or, I suppose, in the world, and its success has been deserved. . . . [T]here are few charities in favour of which so much, and against which so little, can be said."[21] I have tried to keep such well-deserved judgments in mind. At the same time, my appreciation for Barnardo's achievements is tempered by a keen sense of their costs. Barnardo's history continues to capture the public's interest because so much more was at stake than his reputation and so much continues to be at stake in the way we think about and represent the poor.

FACTS, FICTIONS, AND EPISTEMOLOGIES OF WELFARE

The spectacle of evangelical slum workers accusing one another of lying, defrauding the public and engaging in immoral sexual relations exposed all Evangelicals to public ridicule. The Barnardo scandal unfolded at a particularly inopportune moment for Evangelicals. Resources for domestic mission work were largely diverted toward aiding the Christian victims of Turkish atrocities in the Balkans, while atheists such as Charles Bradlaugh and ritualist slum priests such as Father Lowder were making substantial inroads among the London poor.[22] Extremists and fundamentalists within evangelical ranks were eclipsing the influence of moderates, who had successfully mobilized large numbers of men and women to support their causes in the 1830s, '40s, and '50s. While William Gladstone's rhetoric and politics remained saturated by evangelical theological and social ideas, the political clout of Evangelicals as a loose but once formidable coalition was unmistakably in decline.[23] Perhaps most damningly, the arbitration confirmed the impression in the minds of some that Evangelicals were hypocrites, purveyors not of godly truths but of mere cant.

The concept of "cant" was closely bound up with questions of integrity, truthfulness, and religious enthusiasm. What "cant" meant—what it was, and was not—lay at the heart of the Barnardo affair. A founding father of the COS first demanded that the COS investigate Barnardo because one of Barnardo's fundraising performances "gave an impression that there was a good deal of cant mixed up with it and that Dr.

B. was a humbug."[24] A contributor to *Temple Bar* offered an acerbic portrait of the "representatives of cant": "Let a man imagine himself called to be champion of a religious principle or truth and there is no absurdity, no eccentricity, of which he will not be guilty, and the wilder the absurdities, the larger will be his band of disciples."[25] Barnardo's well-publicized midnight rambles in the back alleys of East London in search of homeless children and Charrington's dramatic storming of brothels to rescue girls from the hands of pimps certainly struck some contemporaries as absurdities hiding behind the name of religious truth.

What their critics decried as cant, many Evangelicals cherished as truth. Evangelicals believed in what Barnardo called the "saving knowledge of the truth."[26] It is a phrase that requires some elucidation because it had considerable implications for Barnardo's understanding of the truth and for his photographic practices; it also helps to explain what Evangelicals took to be appropriate and rational behavior in light of truth. Truth consisted of that which could lead a person to God's saving grace. For Evangelicals, from Wesley's followers in the eighteenth century to Barnardo, authentic religious experiences were signaled by a superfluity of emotion whose excesses threatened to overwhelm both the social and sexual order. The loving truths of God that pierced the heart of the believer existed in uneasy tension with the sober facts of reasoned experiences. For many Evangelicals, truth could be quite different from fact because facts, not animated by God's love, in themselves lacked the power to save (figure 2.1).[27]

This gap between truth and fact was exacerbated by Evangelicals' propensity to circulate narratives between fictional and nonfictional philanthropic writings—the same story might appear in a novel or a "true narrative" and then would appear verbatim later in a nonfictional article—and indicates a remarkable fluidity in the way they understood generic boundaries and conventions. Popular evangelical "novels," such as Anna Shipton's *Following Fully* (1872), were hybrid works combining elements of sermons and documentary reporting on social problems with narrative strategies derived from novels. "I cannot but regret," Shipton averred, "that fiction should in any way mingle in this brief narrative, which I have endeavoured to use as an illustration of following the Lord fully." She did not choose "imaginary characters or faultless models, but some whose mission has been accepted and blessed."[28] R. M. Ballantyne's novel *Dusty Diamonds Cut and Polished* (1884) offers a striking example of the license Evangelicals took with commonplace notions of fact and fiction in their determination to represent higher truths. *Dusty Diamonds* was one of many realistic novels written about the lives of street boys published from the 1860s onward that conveyed accurate and detailed information about London street life and child-rescue agencies.

"MY LORD KNOWETH THAT THE CHILDREN ARE TENDER."—*Gen.* xxiii. 13.
"FEED MY LAMBS."—*John* xxi. 15.

FIGURE 2.1.   Taken from the cover of Barnardo's ninth annual report, for 1874–75 (but released in January 1876), entitled *Rescue the Perishing*, this image joins together God's love with truth as the animating forces behind evangelical rescue work. The imperative for others to act on behalf of street waifs is accentuated by the passivity of the forlorn sleeping figure who clearly cannot act on her own behalf. Barnardo pioneered the use of photographs, but he remained devoted to graphic images long after it was technologically possible to reproduce printed words and photographs on the same page.

The plot was full of those surprising but also reassuringly predictable twists of fate that gave so much satisfaction to Victorian novelists and their readers. Ballantyne insisted that his tale was "founded on well authenticated facts" (figure 2.2),[29] but it went beyond distilling facts and recasting them as fictions intended to represent social and spiritual truths. Entire chapters of the novel paraphrased the published reports of various evangelical agencies, in particular the Ragged School Union and Annie Macpherson's Canadian Homes for London Wanderers. One of its many subplots was lifted almost verbatim from a case study in G. Holden Pike's nonfictional *Pity for the Perishing, The Power of the Bible in London*, also published in 1884. Pike's source, and perhaps also Ballantyne's, was a report by the venerable George Holland, founder of the George Yard Ragged School in Whitechapel.[30] Finally, the bulk of Pike's chapter on Barnardo in *Pity for the Perishing* reproduced, almost word for word and without attribution, a series of articles Barnardo wrote and pub-

FIGURE 2.2.   R. M. Ballantyne's novel *Dusty Diamonds Cut and Polished* (1884) drew heavily on nonfictional reports produced by various Evangelical child-rescue agencies. The novel and its frontispiece highlighted the power of Christian love to remake a homeless London street child (shown sleeping in a barrel with a drunken man strolling nearby) into a healthy agricultural laborer, who enjoys both his work and his new opportunities for invigorating play in the Canadian wilderness. In this way, Ballantyne supported emigration schemes as solutions to London poverty.

lished in *Night and Day* in 1877.[31] If the experience of finding the same story in a novel and in a philanthropic report made each narrative seem more authentic and true, it must also have destabilized expectations about the relationship of fact to fiction. This confusion was part of a much broader problem confronting readers in an age when many novelists, not just writers of evangelical tracts, drew on reports produced by social investigators whose authors, for their part, often deployed novelistic conventions in presenting their own "facts."[32]

Evangelicals' ideas about the saving power of truth went hand in hand with the logic underpinning both their conception of God's role in sustaining their enterprises and their unwaveringly inclusive ideas about who was worthy of charitable relief. Evangelicals often insisted that their successes resulted entirely from God's favor and redounded exclusively to His glory. Such convictions infuriated members of the COS Central Office, who believed it was irresponsible to rely on God's favor, as Barnardo claimed he did, instead of prudent financial planning when the lives of poor children depended on Barnardo's ability to raise money to feed and clothe them. For members of the COS, the words "NO DESTITUTE CHILD EVER REFUSED ADMISSION" emblazoned in large letters over Barnardo's Central Offices and Boys' Home in Stepney Causeway were a daily reminder of the evils of Christian charity untempered by scientific principles (figure 2.3). How could parents be made to fulfil their duties toward their children if they knew that, regardless of their behavior, their children would be cared for by Dr. Barnardo? To leaders of the COS, Barnardo's brand of evangelical philanthropy contradicted the laws of social relations that governed charity with the same immutable certainty with which the laws of the free market were meant to govern the economy.

What Evangelicals regarded as Christian duty, their critics condemned as indiscriminate relief. Scientific charity, according to the founders of the COS, was not inclusive but exclusive. Its task was to exclude as many people as possible from all forms of costly outdoor relief, which included cash, goods, and services offered to the poor outside the workhouse. Curtailing outdoor relief would force the poor to choose between self-help or incarceration in their local poorhouse under the stringent guidelines established by the New Poor Law of 1834. The COS aimed to work in concert with poor-law officials to reduce costs of local relief by coercing adults to undertake paid labor in the free market. Some leaders of the COS privately hoped that their well-publicized assault on Barnardo would convince Parliament to grant them sole statutory authority to regulate relations between private and public charity. From the perspective of the men who dominated the Central Office and Executive Committee of the COS, putting an end to Barnardo's work was crucial to the success of their future plans.

The essence of COS reforms consisted in perfecting technologies of information collection, surveillance, and investigation to produce accurate case records of each individual applicant for charity. These highly factual case records, based on systematic inquiry into the past and present lives of applicants and their families, were centralized to prevent enterprising

FIGURE 2.3.   This image of Barnardo's Central Office and Boys' Home in Stepney Causeway accentuated the solidity and orderliness of the institution. The
building is mostly detached from its actual surroundings in the slums except for
the locomotive on the elevated tracks, one person walking on the clean and
quiet street, and a woman leading a child up the front steps. (From T. J.
Barnardo, *"Something Attempted, Something Done!"* 1890.)

applicants from cajoling relief from one charity and then turning to another to get even more relief. Any evidence that suggested the applicant
was responsible for his or her destitution, such as intemperance and indolence, was grounds to deny charitable relief. Case records were the literal form into which the COS crammed the life stories of its clients.
Evangelicals preferred "true narratives" that underscored the interplay
of human error and sinfulness with divine omnipotence and moral redemption.[33] If past lapses in moral judgment, no matter how serious, did
not disqualify a person from receiving Jesus's redemptive love, why then
should such errors disqualify that person from receiving something so

much less valuable—charitable relief? Evangelical preachers, especially those recruited from the ranks of the poor, paraded past sins rather than concealed them. Their ability to overcome a vice-ridden past only amplified the wonders of God's saving grace in their lives while narrowing the distance separating them from their plebian audiences.

The COS and Barnardo seemed to have adhered to profoundly different visions of rationality because they sought such different outcomes from their charitable work. Evangelicals aimed to save souls by sharing the central truths of the Gospel. The conduct of their labors among the poor flowed logically out of these premises. Thus, it made perfect sense to expend effort to save a drunkard on his deathbed despite the unlikelihood of reaping earthly benefits. For the COS, in contrast, people who had demonstrated previous moral failings were simply too risky and unworthy an investment of scarce resources. Economic efficiency went hand in hand with moral rectitude.

Although the arbitration clarified the differences between the COS and Barnardo's brand of evangelical philanthropy, it also exaggerated them by obscuring their similarities. Evangelicals no more formed a rear guard opposed to all forms of "rational" charity than the COS was populated exclusively by secular and heartless reformers.[34] Lord Shaftesbury, for example, was the leading evangelical social reformer of the age and a supporter of Barnardo's work as well as an early vice-president of the COS. Barnardo himself was receptive to the application of social scientific principles to rescue work. Despite his claim to assist all who sought his help, Barnardo annually admitted less than one quarter of the applicants to his institutions. Those he did admit were subjected to a rigorous investigation into the root sources of their destitution. Sounding remarkably similar to members of the COS, Barnardo explained that "the story of every boy's and girl's life is established upon a basis of certitude once for all."[35] Barnardo also tried to keep up to date with the latest ideas about scientific charity. In 1876, he addressed the Social Science Congress about his work on "preventive homes" in East London, but, his performance must not have comforted his critics within the COS. It revealed the strain he felt in attempting to combine the statistical language of social science with the heart truths of his faith: analysis of statistics on juveniles in common lodging houses gave way to unabashed personal exhortation and self-promotion intended to stimulate the emotions of his audience.[36]

If Evangelicals had deep connections to political economy and the scientific practice of charity, many prominent early members of the COS, including the housing reformer Octavia Hill and Rev. Samuel Barnett, were committed to the value of religious thought and institutions. The diaries of Charles Stewart Loch, the COS's secretary from 1875 to 1913, show us a man of Christian faith and compassion who turned to 1. Corinthians, rather than to *Social Statistics*, in seeking guidance about the nature of true charity. He defined "practical charity" as "all acts of loving kindness" that "spring from sympathy, the suffering with those to whom the loving act is done." Loch's sensitivity to human frailty in his private meditations seems incompatible with his defense of the COS's refusal to assist those who had failed to live up to its standards of moral conduct. The daily work of running the Central Office of the COS was, he lamented,

> like a python winding around resolutions, enthusiasm, willing work, and suffocating them and after long months of sleepy digestion, passing out a few useless morsels—the hair and the hoofs—the vain relics of possible good,—the hair which will clothe none, hoof on which no creation will every walk or step.[37]

What is so striking about Loch's diary is his resistance to the seemingly logical imperatives of modern bureaucratic rationality with which his own work and that of the COS are so closely identified. Loch's ambivalent musings about his COS duties capture the dilemmas felt by many rank-and-file members of the COS, whose personal contacts with the poor as friendly visitors engaged their sympathies in ways that sometimes made it difficult for them to adhere to the scientific guidelines disseminated by the COS's Central Office. During the course of the Barnardo arbitration, more and more of the public came to share Loch's private doubts and condemned the COS for believing that "none but the strong-minded, the harsh, the suspicious, and the ultra-systematical, can be worthy dispensers of private or public benevolence."[38]

The Central Office of the COS was acutely aware that it had to contend not only with many external critics of its untrusting and ungenerous vision of relief, but also with the challenges posed by its own members, some of whom bridled under the restraints of COS principles and procedures.[39] Nothing demonstrates more vividly the diversity of principles and practices flourishing among local branches of the COS during its first years than the relationship between the Deptford office of the COS and the evangelical child rescue worker J.W.C. Fegan. In the 1870s James William Condell Fegan was the person whose background, religious and philanthropic interests, achievements, and methods most closely resembled Barnardo's. Born in Southampton in 1852 to a devout, middle-class Plymouth Brethren family of Irish extraction, he studied at the City of London School for four years before entering a firm of colonial brokers in the city in 1869.[40] Like Barnardo, he was initially interested in medicine but ultimately decided to pursue a "mercantile life,"[41] which was only brought to an end by his complete immersion in missionary work among ragged street children.[42] Like Barnardo, he assumed sole responsibility for all aspects of his children's home and also staged before-and-after photographs to encourage sympathy and charitable donations for his scheme.

Given the striking similarities between Barnardo and Fegan, why did he escape unscathed during the Barnardo arbitration? To begin with, he was a less influential figure than Barnardo, and his field of operations, Deptford, was less crowded with competing philanthropists and attracted less public notice than East London. He also was more inclined than Barnardo to acknowledge that prominent benefactors provided him with personal financial support. Most crucially, he, unlike Barnardo, had initiated his scheme *as a member of the COS* and with the financial support and oversight of other members of the Deptford COS. The Deptford COS, even after it had ceased to have formal links to Fegan, offered him staunch protection in response to inquiries made to the Central Office between 1875 and 1880.[43]

The warm ties between Fegan and his fellow evangelical workers within the Deptford branch of the COS suggests that friendships and personal connections could sometimes smooth over the differences in first principles that proved so intractable in Barnardo's case. Fegan's relationship with the Deptford COS also underlines the heterogeneity of COS practices among its various branches. COS branch offices asserted considerable freedom from the centralizing and homogenizing influence of the central committee. In fact, letters about Barnardo from district offices to the central committee during the years leading up to the arbitration amplify this. The Shoreditch COS had long urged the Central Office to investigate and denounce Barnardo.[44] In contrast, Ralph Ellis, secretary of the Bow and Bromley COS, was very favorably impressed by Barnardo's entire establishment and worked well with him until the "inquiry commenced."[45] In the tense weeks between the end of the arbitration and the announcement of the decision, the Kensington COS staged a small-scale insurrection against Ribton-Turner and the central committee for arrogating too many powers to themselves and falsely speaking in the name of the entire organization without first consulting the quasi-representative council.[46] Because existing histories of the COS have too often been written from the perspective of the central committee and its secretaries, they have uncritically accepted the central committee's rather exaggerated sense of its ability to control and impose uniformity on local branches. Fegan's relations with the Deptford COS in the 1870s as well as the responses of individual branches to Barnardo's troubles point to the need to rewrite the COS's history with an eye to the diversity of both its members' ideologies and the practices of local branches. It is fair to say that in attempting to discipline Barnardo, the Central Office of the

COS may well have hoped to tighten its control over its own members and local branches throughout the metropolis.

The imbroglio between Barnardo and the COS is not another chapter in the unconvincing story about the clash between secular modernity and religious conservatism in the nineteenth century. As we shall see, Barnardo's enthusiastic embrace of that most radically modern technology of representation—photography—disturbed his contemporaries more than anything else he did. It seems plausible that because so many of Barnardo's actual practices resembled those fact-finding procedures advocated by the COS, the COS felt all the more determined to convince the public that its fundamental principles were incompatible with Barnardo's. Barnardo's rift with Charrington and his battles with the COS serve as reminders that what people have in common can deepen their perception of differences rather than bring them together.

"The Very Wicked Woman" and "Sodomany" in Dr. Barnardo's Boys' Home

The conflict between Barnardo and the COS took place amidst a host of accusations and rumors about the sexual conduct of Barnardo, his staff, and the boys in his homes. Most of these rumors and accusations never entered into the public record of the case reported by the press, in large measure because only one of George Reynolds's several dozen charges submitted for arbitration against Barnardo was explicitly sexual. However, the surviving files of the COS on the arbitration contain explosive depositions and letters detailing supposed incidents of drunkenness, adultery, illegitimacy, blackmail, spying, and sodomy at Barnardo's homes. These files leave little doubt that all the parties directly involved in the case—including the local poor and many within the evangelical-philanthropic community—knew about these sensational charges. Rumors of sexual misconduct seeped into every aspect of the arbitration and help to explain the depth of passions the controversy unleashed. If the case against Barnardo arose from personal antagonisms among erstwhile friends and from differences about what constituted the truth and true charity, it also must be understood as a sex scandal manqué.

Under the caption "The Very Wicked Woman and Her Story" in his pamphlet *Startling Revelations*, Reynolds claimed that Barnardo had lodged, openly escorted home "arm-in-arm," and had immoral relations with a drunken prostitute, Mrs. Johnson.[47] Before the arbitration began, Barnardo had successfully demonstrated his innocence in this matter. Reynolds's own testimony during the arbitration suggests that while he maliciously continued to spread the accusation, he himself had long since ceased to believe it was true. In light of its wholly insubstantial basis, why did so many still seem willing to believe that Barnardo had consorted with a prostitute? Did its persistence reflect suspicions about the motives and sexual conduct of male Evangelicals engaged in slum philanthropy? Did it stem from the specificities of Barnardo's public and private image in East London? Or from peculiarities of his social and sexual status?

Surviving evidence suggests that all these factors may have contributed to the dogged persistence of the rumors. Religious enthusiasm had long been associated with sexual excess and disorder in nineteenth-century Britain.[48] Ambiguities in Barnardo's sexual persona in East London contributed to the confusing ways in which others perceived him. During his first years in East London, Barnardo's peers noted his utter lack of interest in women. His fellow medical students remembered Barnardo as a "queer fellow" and a "dark horse" who, unlike many other students, shunned the readily available pleasures of drink, music halls, and women in East London. They dismissed his religious enthusiasms as "eccentric," "extravagant," and "hypocritical."[49] But this initial image of Barnardo as the self-denying, celibate young man must be counterbalanced by the impression produced by his outward appearance and mannerisms by the time of the arbitration. He often dressed more like a dandy, that sexually ambiguous outlaw, than a *dévot*. For all their apparent differences, there were also powerful affinities between the ascetic male slum worker and the dandy as competing masculine personae in Victorian culture (a theme to which I will return in chapter 5). Each defied social conventions and yet remained, as James Eli Adams explains, "abjectly dependent on the recognition of the audience he professes to disdain."[50] The male slum worker may have eschewed the physical comforts of the dandaical life, but he found ample compensation in a world of physical sensation and exotic excitations.

Playing on the perception of Barnardo as dandy, Reynolds released and distributed a three-quarter-length photograph of him as a man about town suggestively holding a walking stick in ungloved hands (figure 2.4a). The stick, which cuts and protrudes beyond Barnardo's body just at his groin, is the focal point of the image. The portrait, which Barnardo decried as that "miserable photograph" and "wretched caricature," had been stolen from Barnardo's office by a disgruntled employee and given to his enemies.[51] Anticipating the central role contrasting photographs of child waifs would play during the arbitration, Barnardo quickly countered and circulated a half-length portrait showing him as a bespectacled, earnest do-gooder[52] (figure 2.4b). Unlike the purloined image, which depicted Barnardo in motion and echoed contemporary British and French images of the flâneur, the second portrait used its subject's stillness to suggest his trustworthiness; and, of course, the half-length portrait showed

a   b

FIGURE 2.4.   By the 1870s, photographic *cartes de visites* were a ubiquitous
feature of bourgeois sociability. Barnardo, always meticulous about his physical
appearance, was infuriated when the photo (figure 2.4a) was stolen from his
studio and displayed for sale in nearby shops next to a "carefully executed"
photograph of his archrival, Frederick Charrington. Charrington was a scion of
one of East London's wealthiest families, whose fortune derived from their
brewery. Barnardo countered by releasing a portrait of himself (figure 2.4b),
which conveyed the high seriousness of his Christian mission and was compatible with his standing as husband and trustworthy paterfamilias within his private home and within the homes he superintended for ragged children. (Images
courtesy of Barnardo's Photographic Archive.)

his body above, not below, the waist. This battle of competing *cartes de
visites* demonstrates just how canny Barnardo and his rivals were to the
power of photographs in conveying moral messages in visual form.

The debate over Barnardo's public sexual persona entered into the formal proceedings of the arbitration. Alfred Thesiger, Barnardo's gifted legal
counsel who took on the case at the behest of the evangelical lord chancel-
lor, Lord Cairns, offered his own explanation for rumors about Barnardo's
relations with women.[53] Thesiger insisted that it was normal for an able
and appealing young man like Barnardo to "attract the attention of young
females whilst engaged in work of this kind." While dismissing all the rumors as "entirely mythical," he was surprised there were not "more stories
about" since he expected sexuality to play a role in popular perceptions of
an evangelical slum worker's relations with his community.[54]

Barnardo was not the only member of his organization beset by rumors of sexual impropriety. Sometime in the early autumn of 1876, Barnardo fired his boys' beadle, Edward Fitzgerald, on grounds of habitual drunkenness and gross immorality. For years, he and Barnardo had roamed the backstreets and alleyways of London after midnight, with Fitzgerald leading the way with his bull's-eye lantern, in search of their nightly catch of street waifs (figure 2.5). Fitzgerald, a former policeman, used his knowledge of the criminal classes quite effectively in playing the role of a double agent for several months as he passed information and documents about Barnardo to his enemies.[55]

Fitzgerald's escapades came to an abrupt halt in the early autumn of 1876. On September 13, 1876, a Mrs. Andrews, the mother of several children in Barnardo's Boys' Home, sent Barnardo a letter. Mrs. Andrews claimed to have given birth to Fitzgerald's child out of wedlock the previous August. Her letter paints a shocking picture of Fitzgerald's duplicity. It is at once plaintive, desperate, and threatening. "For some time past," Mrs. Andrews wrote,

> He [Fitzgerald] has been corresponding with me as a single man and also promised me marriage which has resulted in the birth of a child. . . . I have neither seen nor heard from him since till [sic] last Saturday when I met him accidentally as he was going to Oliver Terrace [Barnardo's home and site of his first photographic studio] when he gave me half-a-crown and he told me he was coming to you to get some more money and he would send me some more money and he would send me some Monday, but I have neither seen nor heard from him since. I appeal to you as a Christian gentleman to ask your advice as I do not wish to take it into court as it would be such a slur on the Mission and he has threatened me if I take any proceedings against him he will make you turn my children out of the Home. He has taken me from a good home and all my friends have turned their back on me and I am at present in a state of starvation.[56]

Lacking leverage with Fitzgerald himself, Mrs. Andrews's only apparent power lay in threatening to destroy the reputation of the boys' home by exposing Fitzgerald's perfidious abuse of his authority. She portrays herself as an injured victim of male lust and chicanery and as a canny opportunist. Barnardo and his former servant Fitzgerald, already closely associated with one another as partners in their nocturnal adventures, now both stood accused of leading duplicitous lives and engaging in illicit sexual conduct.

During the two years leading up to the arbitration, Barnardo's detractors, especially Charrington and the leaders of the COS, sought out and paid money to Fitzgerald in exchange for information about Barnardo. The surviving evidence suggests that Fitzgerald was intoxicated by the sense that he had the power to preserve or destroy the reputations of em-

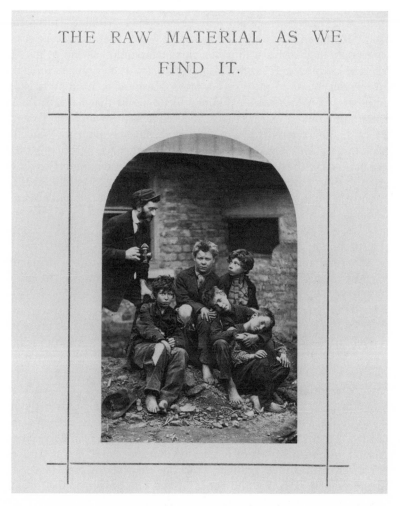

THE RAW MATERIAL AS WE
FIND IT.

FIGURE 2.5.   This photograph, "The Raw Material as We Find It," depicts not only a
group of homeless boys, but also the beadle, Edward Fitzgerald, Barnardo's erstwhile
assistant before he was fired for gross immorality. Since this photograph was clearly taken
during the daytime, the bull's-eye lantern in Fitzgerald's hand functions both as a reminder
that he usually rescued boys at night and as a metaphor for Barnardo's rescue work,
which brought the "light" of Christian teaching to the dark corners of the metropolis.
The arched shape of the photograph and the rubble scattered at the boys' feet suggest a
decayed ruin from the classical past, secreted in the back alleyways at the heart of the
British empire. The photograph also unintentionally captures a moment of loving
solidarity among the seated boys, whose bodies touch one another, and their separation
from the standing Fitzgerald. (Image courtesy of Barnardos Photographic Archive.)

inent men in public life. The day that Barnardo fired him, he told his replacement at the boys' home that he intended "ruining" his former master.[57] In the end, however, he learned a bitter lesson: once he served his purpose, each of his well-to-do patrons abandoned him to his fate. Fitzgerald disappears from the historian's view as a penniless inmate in the Lowndes Ward of the Consumption Hospital in Brompton in late November 1877. Fitzgerald explained to Reynolds that Barnardo's lieutenants had come to extract a deathbed confession from him. To entice Fitzgerald, they offered to admit his legitimate children into the Barnardo homes. "This was too much for me," Fitzgerald raged, "you ought to see me then with passion, the blood came from me nought I could not speak. . . . Just fancy the idea to have my children to exhibit them to every fool who gives him money." Frantic to communicate with his wife and family, his letter ended, "P.S. I should be grateful for a few stamps as I have not one penny in the world to get one."[58] What galled Fitzgerald the most about Barnardo's offer to "care" for his children was the prospect that they would become part of Barnardo's spectacular menagerie of ragamuffins and be forced to exhibit themselves to anyone willing to pay Barnardo's price.

Fitzgerald's letter begging Reynolds and Charrington to save his wife and six children from starvation is a chilling reminder that disgrace and loss of employment for a poor man could mean life or death for his family. Like Mrs. Andrews, whose bitter desperation he had caused and which he was forced to share, Fitzgerald refused to play the part of silently deferential member of the proletariat. Laboring men, women and children in the Barnardo arbitration emphatically *did* have strong voices as individuals, which they were quick to use in trying to get what they could from their "betters." They willingly stepped forward to criticize Barnardo and his methods of rescue. At the same time, it was Andrews and Fitzgerald and their families—and not their social superiors—who paid the highest price for the entire affair. The power of their voices, vividly captured in the pathetic letters that constitute the sole surviving record of their own words, could not offset the vulnerability of their precarious economic status.

A lengthy fragment of an unsigned report in the COS files, probably written by another dismissed employee, John Hancorne, offered intimate details about widespread drunkenness, criminality, insubordination, and sexual immorality inside the boys' home. According to this document, many of Barnardo's workers "used to be constantly" in a local pub where their public brawling brought disgrace on the home. They sometimes returned to the home drunk and locked up boys in dank and dark cellars for long periods. The boys, for their part, were in open rebellion. They smuggled in a loaded pistol, gun powder, caps, and a jimmy to

break into the superintendent's locked office. One boy was severely punished for bragging that he "used to have criminal intercourse" with the
gin-drinking schoolteacher, Mrs. Waller. This same boy was discovered
"in the fact of Sodomany" with another adolescent inmate. Only four
months later, the two boys were reunited in the home, where they "commenced the same game again." This time, in order to rid himself of the
boys, the governor of the home gave one of them a "good character" and
helped him get employment. The other boy, "age 17, died from the effect
of Bugery—a abscess in his fundement." As with so much else in the Barnardo arbitration, we will never know whether any of these charges were
true or malicious falsehoods. If they were fabrications, they were ingenious and plausible. Regardless of the document's veracity, it disturbingly
depicted Barnardo as amused and unperturbed by the sordid and immoral management of his institutions and contributed to the sexually
charged atmosphere surrounding the arbitration.[59]

In the midst of the arbitration controversy, Barnardo published a long
article in his periodical *Night and Day* that unintentionally echoed the
sexual and social insubordination recounted in the unsigned deposition.
Imitating James Greenwood's famous incognito descent into the sodomitical world of the Lambeth Casual Ward, Barnardo decided to disguise himself as a tramp and sleep among the poor in a common lodging
house for a single night.[60] "For once," Barnardo explains, he decided to
"lose [his] identity, and become one of the great class known as tramps."
Barnardo informs us that he was tempted to enter the doss house by a
"native" tour guide, Mick Farrel, "a little Irish lad who had often accompanied [him] on [his] nightly peregrinations."[61]

Barnardo anticipated that his readers might misconstrue his motives
and felt compelled to offer an elaborate justification for embarking on
his most memorable night of slumming. The plain style of his justification bears no resemblance to the melodramatic narrative that follows.

> No mere love of adventure led me to contemplate this visit. I had the following
> important objects in view:—First, to obtain by experience a truer and more
> exact knowledge of lodging-house accommodation and *habitués*; second, to
> influence in the early morning, any young people whom I might meet in the
> house, and whose mode of life would appear to be depraved or approaching
> the criminal; and third, to obtain an introduction into other houses through
> any chance acquaintance which might be formed during my visit to this one.
> In all this, the main desire of my life—*to save poor boys from the life of the
> streets, by bringing them into our Homes, and thereby under the sound influ-
> ences of the Gospel*—was, of course, uppermost in my mind.[62]

This apology excites rather than stifles readerly expectations of fantastic revelation—expectations that Barnardo does not disappoint. We

watch Barnardo enjoy the initial stages of his masquerade as he dons lousy clothes and blackens his face with mud and dust to prepare for the part he has chosen to play. Forcing himself to lie in a disgusting bed surrounded closely by thirty-three naked boys (including his companion, young Mick), he removes most of his own clothes and falls into a terrifying dream world. In his dream, the recipients of his benevolence, the ragged street boys, enact revenge against him by painfully penetrating his body.

> How long I slept I do not know—not, I think, more than an hour—when I awoke suddenly out of a horrible dream, in which I thought I had been discovered by my bedroom companions and denounced as a spy, in punishment for which they had each inflicted vengeance on me by pricking pins all over my body, and then rubbing in pepper. I appealed against their cruelty: I struggled, but in vain; and now the pins came to my face, and it seemed as though in my eyes and nose the pepper was pushed; smarting, burning, almost maddening me! Aiming a blow at my assailants, I rolled out of bed, and suddenly awoke from my uneasy slumbers, to find that there was horrible reality in the brief vision; for while I lay now quite wakeful in the bed . . . the sensations I had just experienced in my sleep were found to be no mere fancies . . . . my hand and arm . . . were covered with blotches and weals. . . . the sheet was almost brown with myriads of moving insects, which seemed to regard my bed and my body as their rightful property.[63]

As Barnardo's readers, we experience with him the disorienting obliteration of the boundaries between dream and reality, fantasy and fact. The story comes to a conclusion that inadvertently recalls the sexual confusion of the dream. "Reaching Mick's bed, I shook him lustily" and the two of them flee the doss-house for the relative safety of the dark street. When he returns home, he cannot recognize the face, swollen and distorted by bites, greeting him in the mirror. What began as an imposture as a tramp concludes with his literal metamorphosis into a freakish monster. Mimesis terrifyingly produces nemesis.[64]

Barnardo's narrative is both a richly self-revealing piece of evidence and one that must be interpreted with considerable caution. There can be no doubt, however, that it is a story Barnardo expected his readers to interpret and not merely accept on face value. Within protestant evangelical culture and within the body of Barnardo's own writings, dream narratives function as allegories about larger spiritual issues or troubles. If it seems certain that Barnardo intended the dream to be read as an allegory, we still must ask how he intended his readers to construe it. Why would he deliberately publish a narrative about disguise and masquerade in the midst of a controversy that centered around claims that Barnardo and his photographs were not what they appeared to be?

As with so many of the questions raised during and by the arbitration, we can be certain of very little. However, Barnardo's dream narrative can sustain several plausible interpretations. Barnardo probably expected his readers to applaud his willingness to sacrifice his personal well-being and safety for the benefit of ragged children. Evangelicals often emphasized the physical dangers they willingly confronted as they carried God's message to an all-too-often scornful world. Their ministry to the poor, unlike those of their Church of England rivals, often involved very direct physical contact—a literal touching of bodies and souls in rituals of prayer and conversion. On one memorable occasion, Barnardo's East London neighbors had jeered and jostled him, pinned him under a bar table, and danced on it until his ribs cracked. He may have hoped that his readers would see the merciless ingratitude of the boys in the dream as a veiled allusion to the way in which his selfless labors had been rewarded by devastating betrayals by fellow slum workers and employees. The story suggests that Barnardo feared that his benevolence had been misunderstood by the poor as merely another form of elite surveillance over their lives.

It is also possible to read the dream as a self-incriminating narrative that exposes the perversity of Barnardo's moral imagination. Barnardo's depiction of his experience during his night in the lodging house shockingly reverses his philanthropic project of remaking wild street waifs into productive workers by literally making him into a hideous beast. Its setting within an unlit, promiscuously overcrowded, unsupervised room full of naked boys combined with Barnardo's helplessness in the face of physical torture and penetration make it possible to read the dream as a dark sexual fantasy. According to Barnardo's own account, his body, like those of the ragged children sold into sex slavery every day in London, ceases to be his own. It becomes the "rightful property" first of the boys and then of vermin and insects.

Barnardo and his most zealous critics probably would not have understood, much less accepted, an interpretation of his dream so at odds with his purpose in recounting it. During the arbitration, none of his enemies attempted to introduce the story as evidence against him, although they were willing to stake key parts of their case on easily discredited rumors spread by disreputable men and women. Without anachronistically imposing contemporary ideas about dreams and sexuality on the past, we can say that Barnardo's carefully crafted narrative reveals his keen appreciation for the bodily and psychological excitations of slumming which made it possible for him to voyage into unrespectable corners of the metropolis and his own imagination.

What role did sex or rumors about sex play in the arbitration? First, none of the charges about sexual misconduct against Barnardo, his employees, or his boys were *proved* to be true. We do know that Barnardo found the claims against his employees sufficiently convincing to fire them and that there was and is no credible evidence that Barnardo committed any sexual improprieties. It is also clear that many *believed* that Barnardo's homes were sites of undifferentiated male lust and sexual danger for ragged children. Outwardly proclaiming social purity, Barnardo and his staff were, at least according to this version of events, "in truth" morally polluted sinners. Such views informed Barnardo's relationship with the local community in East London and with the COS and shaped the ways in which many of Barnardo's critics came to see his photographs of ragged children.

REPRESENTING THE RAGGED CHILD

In August 1877, Barnardo finally took the stand on his own behalf. Through astute examination and cross examination of dozens of witnesses, Barnardo's lawyer, Alfred Thesiger, had carefully laid out a compelling case demonstrating the deliberate malice of Barnardo's detractors and the benevolent intentions of his client. But all his efforts threatened to be undone when Barnardo refused to reveal the real name of the pseudonymous Clerical Junius, the author of several intemperate assaults on Barnardo's enemies published in various East London newspapers. Although his critics insisted that Barnardo's silence was tantamount to a confession that he himself was Clerical Junius, Barnardo protested that he was honoring his gentlemanly vow to protect the anonymity of his over-zealous supporter. Amidst confusion and frustration the arbitration ground to a halt and the arbitrators were left to decide whether, under the extraordinary circumstances, they could pass judgement on any of the headings submitted before them.

Piqued by Barnardo's obstinance, the arbitrators at first indicated their unwillingness to offer a ruling. Perhaps they recognized the disastrous consequences of a public trial for Evangelicals and their vast but uncoordinated system of charity; or perhaps they were convinced by Barnardo's lawyer that the matter of Clerical Junius bore no relation to most of the key issues of the arbitration. In any case, the arbitrators reconsidered their position and promised to prepare a judgment. From August until mid-October 1877, Barnardo awaited the arbitrators' decision in a state of near exhaustion and high tension while funds to provide food, shelter, and fuel for the children in his care dwindled to nothing. Then, on October 15, the arbitrators announced their award. To Barnardo's immense relief and the outrage of his antagonists, the arbitrators exonerated him of most of the substantive charges against him. The *Times* assured the public that Barnardo's homes were "real and valuable charities, worthy of public confidence and support."[65] The judgement was not, however, a complete victory. The arbitrators chastised him for producing "fictitious representations of destitution" for "the purposes of obtaining money." Throughout most of the award, the arbitrators' language was guarded and reserved; however, on this heading, their censure was unambiguous. "This use of artistic fiction," the arbitrators explained, "to represent actual facts is, in our opinion, not only morally wrong as thus employed, but might, in the absence of a very strict control, grow into a system of deception dangerous to the cause on behalf of which it is practised."[66] The press, including Henry Labouchère's *Truth* and Frederick Greenwood's *Pall Mall Gazette*, surpassed the arbitrators in the vehemence of their condemnation of Barnardo's photographic practices.[67]

Barnardo's "artistic fictions" consisted of a small number of photographs (probably less than a dozen of many hundreds taken) in which he and his staff had staged or arranged the clothing of the child being photographed to convey information that was not strictly speaking accurate. For example, he posed a boy with a shoeblack's box even though the boy had worked as a shoeblack only for a single day. In another case, the caption under the portrait of a child's head described her as "only a little waif taken from the street." In reality, her mother had threatened Barnardo that she would abandon her daughter to the street unless he admitted her to the home. Barnardo had not actually "taken" her from the streets, though he did save her from them. Most of Barnardo's so-called photographic deceptions hinged on such fine points of fact or verbal semantics.

Why did these seemingly inconsequential violations of literal truth elicit such excoriating condemnation? One explanation lies in the fact that Barnardo was not only an aggressive outsider in London's philanthropic circles, but also a daring innovator in his exploitation of photography's as yet untested and wholly unregulated possibilities as a marketing tool for philanthropy. The controversy over Barnardo's use of photographs was not merely another example of the dubious ethics of "truth" in advertising in the nineteenth century. Contemporaries expected philanthropists to use the materials they distributed to advertise their benevolent accomplishments, to stimulate donations, and to provide trustworthy information about the lives and conditions of the intended beneficiaries. Victorians were deeply invested in believing that Christian charity was a bulwark of integrity and honesty against the predatory machinations encouraged by their commodity culture and the free market. Some found Barnardo's photographic practices so dangerous because they threatened to undermine public confidence in the disinterested and truthful character not just of his own schemes but of philanthropy itself.

Beginning in December 1876, Barnardo issued a leaflet, attached to every packet of photographs he sold, that explained his "objects in photographing boys and girls." Photographs, he argued, served as instruments of memory, surveillance, and advertising.[68] He used before-and-after photographs, approximating *cartes de visites* in appearance, to demonstrate the transformative effects of his benevolence on children. These contrasting portraits mirrored the framework of evangelical conversion narratives whose power depended upon the stark contrast between an initial condition of abject sin and depravity and the joys of salvation in Jesus.[69]

Barnardo produced tens of thousands of these "contrasting" portraits of children which he sold or gave away to men, women, and children across the social spectrum (figure 2.6). He anticipated that his photographic "contrasts" would evoke different responses among the rich and poor. The rich, he hoped, would make generous donations to assist the work. Among the poor, Barnardo used the cards to publicize his work and to encourage in them a desire for moral and physical elevation. For example, in his chapbook *A City Waif: How I Fished for and Caught Her*, he told the story of his pursuit of the nearly naked Irish Cockney girl Bridget, whose raggedness foreshadowed the likelihood that she would become a prostitute. She was represented as both an innocent object of benevolence and as the potential object of male erotic desire.[70] Bridget had "no boots or stockings . . . no hat or bonnet covered the wild hair. . . . Her thin dress show[ed] great rents here and there."[71]

The climax of Barnardo's story about Bridget's reclamation was the moment when he held before her a cardboard photograph of a smiling well-dressed Barnardo girl hard at work.

> "Oh, my!" was the admiring exclamation that burst from Bridget's lips. "Ain't she smart."
>
> Having allowed a few minutes for examination of the picture, I asked, "Wouldn't you wish to be like her? Better, I should think, to be dressed in that way than to wear the things you have on," pointing to her ragged dress.
>
> "I should think it wor," she replied; "but I ain't got such luck, you see."
>
> "Nonsense," I rejoined.[72]

Bridget plays Galatea to Barnardo's Pygmalion, not however, in order to become his beloved, but instead to become a servant in another man's household.

The lucrative illicit market in Barnardo's photographs among the poor themselves suggests that they knew that photographs of ragged children were valuable commodities. In January 1877, for example, a street urchin

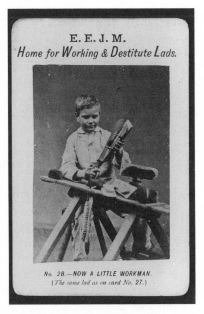

FIGURE 2.6.   Barnardo's photographic "contrasts" purported to illustrate the ways in which the loving regime at his homes transformed children from dangerous and costly threats to society into productive, self-supporting workers of the future. Evidence that several of these before-and-after images had been taken on the day the child was admitted into the home called into question both the trustworthiness of photographs as documents of social reality and of Barnardo's philanthropic methods and institutions. (Image courtesy of Barnardo's Photographic Archive.)

in Leeds had been caught pretending to be a Barnardo collecting agent. He had already cajoled 60 shillings from a credulous public by selling Barnardo photographs.[73] Some poor children also understood the economic benefits of making themselves appear as ragged as possible to gain sympathy and money from passers-by. One young boy, Stuttering Bob, manipulated his self-representation to conform to the ways in which he believed elites imagined and expected him to look. According to J.W.C. Fegan, who rescued Stuttering Bob from the street,

> the hoardings at the time, in London, were placarded with wood-cuts of a crossing-sweeper, advertising a play (one of Dickens' novels dramatised) called "Poor Jo." Bob dressed himself up so as to exactly represent "Poor Jo," and standing near the theatre as the audience came out with their feelings worked upon by "Poor Jo" on the stage, confronted them with a counterpart of the character, crouching down, shivering all over, and beseechingly whining,

"Pl-pl-please to re-re-rember poo-poo-poor Jo." Bob reaped a silver and cop-
per harvest for a while.[74]

The story of Stuttering Bob illustrates the way in which Dickens's representation of a single ragged child circulated between visual, written, and
spoken media. While Bob was a bona fide street urchin, he astutely masqueraded as the fictional Poor Jo, whom Dickens had modeled on the
lives of real children such as Bob. Representation and reality are intertwined in an amusing but confusing circle of mutual imitation. At approximately the same time Stuttering Bob offered his street performances, Barnardo's studio executed a "representative" photograph of a
crouched, tattered boy entitled "Lost," which clearly quoted O. G. Rejlander's widely admired photograph entitled "Poor Jo."[75]

Rejlander was the most prominent and controversial exponent of photography as a fine art in mid-Victorian Britain.[76] By the early 1860s he
had executed many celebrated photographic studies of children costumed to look like ragged street waifs, and he had gained international
fame when he exhibited his monumental photographic allegory, "The
Two Ways of Life, or Hope in Repentance" in 1857. Closely resembling
an immense neoclassical history painting, it was a composite photograph
printed from over thirty negatives that included several nude and semi-
nude figures. Anticipating Barnardo's own arguments defending his
posed photographs, Rejlander insisted that photographs and paintings
had equal claims to be "truthful" and "real," "both being but representative."[77] Many were not convinced. While "The Two Ways of Life" was
"intended to teach a high moral lesson" about female virtue and vice,
Photographic Notes observed that the Scottish Photographic Society had
demonstrated lamentable prudery in refusing to admit the photograph to
its exhibition. One critic exposed the hypocritical standards of delicacy
imposed on contemporary visual representations: "Anything which
bears with it the impress of antiquity, however lewd or indelicate, is idealized into classicism, whilst anything like an attempt to elucidate an
idea in the present moral age, is at once condemned as indelicate."[78]

Barnardo's photographic practices emphatically demonstrated that he
was well aware of contemporary debate about the moral standards used
to judge photographs and the confusion over whether they were objective documents of social reality or subjective works of art. This debate
concerned not only questions about the audiences for and uses of photographs, but also the thornier issue of the authenticity of photographs as
records of actual past events.[79] For Barnardo, the debate posed a false di-
chotomy since both ways of understanding and using photography
served his benevolent ends. He devised his own code to distinguish between photographs that purported to depict a particular individual with

documentary fidelity and "artistic" photographs that were "representative" or "typical" of entire classes of people. Photographs identifying specific people were similar to the case histories assembled by COS investigators (and Barnardo's own staff) about each applicant. They were attached to a case file as a visual record of the child's physical appearance at the time of admission. These identification portraits were accompanied by the subject's real initials.[80]

"Typical" or "representative" photographs closely resembled evangelical "true narratives" in that they represented higher truths transcending the details of any individual case. Typical photographs were accompanied not by the initials of a person, but by captions or titles such as "Rescue the Perishing" or "A Night's Catch" in order to suggest their function as visual parables. The staging of the images along with accompanying captions highlighted their similarity to nonphotographic forms of art, especially paintings, sketches, and engravings. As such, Barnardo believed that his "typical" photographs should be judged by the prevailing standards of truthfulness expected of works of art including social realist paintings and literature.[81]

To buttress his case, he pointed to the work of several well-known contemporaries, including the widely praised canvasses of the Welsh painter Bernard Samuel Marks.[82] Marks extolled the effectiveness of Barnardo's rescue work in his painting "100,000 Neglected and Destitute Children in London," shown in the Royal Academy in 1873. The painting, which consisted of contrasting portraits of Barnardo boys "before and after rescue training," was hailed by the critic for the *Art Journal* as a "remarkable memorandum" of Barnardo's "wholesome treatment" of ragged children.[83] Other social realist painters, foremost among them W. P. Frith, were also widely praised for their efforts to draw attention to the plight of poor children. Frith felt no need to conceal the fact that he hired street children as models and then ripped and arranged their clothing to achieve the artistic effect he sought.[84] Placed within this context, it is easy to sympathize with Barnardo's perplexity about the public furor unleashed by the way he occasionally dressed and undressed his ragged child models before photographing them. Barnardo believed that his "typical" photos, like other works of art, revealed essential truths about ragged children and their lives, if not always their literal conditions.

Barnardo's conception of the illustrative uses of photography approximated those of Charles Darwin, the leading man of science in Victorian Britain. In the early 1870s, Darwin had hoped to harness the supposedly objective, authenticating powers of photography to support his scientific theories. He built on a tradition as old as photography itself of using photography to serve the pursuit of scientific truth. William Henry Fox Talbot, Britain's preeminent pioneer of photography in the 1830s, had created many of his first images of plant leaves to serve as specimens for scientific study. At the same time, Darwin knew well that photographs could easily be manipulated to tell stories that were not quite as truthful as they appeared. In illustrating his 1872 study *The Expression of the Emotions in Man and Animals,* Darwin collaborated with none other than Oscar Gustave Rejlander, the acknowledged master of manipulating photographs to serve the needs of art, not science. The images Rejlander created for Darwin were clearly posed—in no sense were they the records of spontaneous expressions of emotion they purported to be. At least one was a photograph of an engraving drawn from a photograph to which important details had been added for effect. Darwin did not disclose these facts but instead labeled the image simply as a photograph—which, in a literal sense, it was. Darwin's illustrations were intended to reinforce the truthfulness of his hypotheses and to make his book more attractive and persuasive to readers; they were not supposed to memorialize particular past moments that actually had occurred. Understood in this way, Darwin's photographic practices were in harmony with Barnardo's. Both played upon viewers' assumptions that photographs presented objective facts while exploiting the possibilities of using photographs as "artistic fictions."[85] In other words, the boundaries between photography as science and as art, as a record of objective reality and its subjective manipulation, were far from clear in the 1870s. Debates about the proper and improper uses of photography closely mirrored struggles among charity workers, such as Barnardo and the COS, who sought to strike a balance between the conflicting demands of science and sentiment in the practice of philanthropy.

Rumors about sexual misconduct at Barnardo's institutions may well have encouraged some of his critics to suspect that his images of children were not only deceitful but indecent. Barnardo's public was well aware of the existence of a large underground market in pornographic photos of women and children. Invoking the 1857 Obscene Publications Act, the police conducted several well-publicized raids in the 1860s and '70s that yielded tens of thousands of obscene books, pamphlets, and photographs.[86]

Barnardo's photographs and his graphic images intentionally underscored the raggedness of the children's clothing (figure 2.7). Raggedness—ripped and torn clothing which exposed the bodies and extremities of children—was not only an effective visual marker of poverty but could also be a disturbingly erotic sign. C. L. Dodgson (Lewis Carroll), perhaps the foremost photographer of children in Victorian Britain and, like Barnardo, an expert in photographic masquerades, understood well the erotic power of the not-quite naked child and photographed Alice Liddell in artfully torn rags in 1858.[87] As Mario Perniola has argued,

Standing in the Waiting Hall hoping for Admission.

FIGURE 2.7.   The words "Drawn From Life" in the upper left corner emphasized that the image documented the physical appearance of real children whom
Barnardo had rescued. Barnardo's graphic images were even more effective than
his photographs in exploiting the visual iconography linking ragged clothing,
spiked hair, and bare feet with extreme poverty and endangered childhood.
Graphic images, unlike photographs, could also mobilize the visual language of
Victorian physiognomy, which equated the facial features of the poor with those
of primitive races. (*"Something Attempted, Something Done!"* 1890.)

"[I]n the figurative arts, eroticism appears as a relationship between clothing and nudity. Therefore it is conditional on the possibility of movement—transit—from one state to the other."[88] Barnardo's literary and visual representations of poor children dramatized several interdependent movements from "one state to another." They linked the erotic transit from naked to clothed, implicit in raggedness, to the physical and spiritual movement between indecency and decency, damnation and salvation, lost and found, homeless and domesticated.[89]

Two photographs examined during the arbitration offer compelling examples of the mingling of philanthropic and erotic rhetorics in Barnardo's language of virtue. Whether the images themselves *are* indecent is less important for the argument I propose than the apparent willingness of some to believe that they were. What makes an image "indecent" or "pornographic" is determined less by what is contained within its frame than in the historical circumstances of its creation and reception and the meanings that others found in it. Barnardo adorned the cover of his 1875 report, *Rescue the Perishing*, with a photograph of a boy named Samuel Reed. This photograph was the basis for the charge that "Dr. Barnardo makes a practice of stripping children of their proper clothing, cutting their clothes, and dressing them in rags, for the purpose of getting up fictitious and deceptive photographs."[90] Reed, a seaman on board the ship *Boscowen* in 1877, was asked to recall the events surrounding his admission to the home six years earlier. "The morning after I entered the Home I was taken by a boy named Brown to have my photograph taken." Barnardo led "[me] to an upper room, where he took out his pen-knife and tore my clothes to pieces. After he had disfigured me, I was then laid on the floor and my photograph was taken."[91] Soon thereafter, Reed was dressed in a new uniform, placed in a hammock, forced by Dr. Barnardo to affect an "unnatural" smile, and photographed to complete the pair of contrasting images.[92] Reed's testimony and his examination by Reynolds's lawyer, St. John Wontner, emphasized his status as the passive object of Barnardo's violent manipulations. Reed's coerced "smile" functions as an insidious sign that Barnardo's, not his own, desires have been gratified.

Wontner used even more explicitly charged language in his examination of Barnardo's photographer, Mr. Barnes. His questions to Barnes— "How was Reed deranged? How was he [Reed] altered?"—were suggestively ambiguous. On the literal level, Wontner wanted to know whether Reed's clothing had been changed, but the phrasing of the question reinforced Reynolds's published contention that the experience of being photographed by Barnardo had a "tendency to destroy the better feelings of the children"—to "alter" them in undesirable ways.[93] Wontner's interrogation strove to produce an impression of Reed as Barnardo's unwilling and violated child model.

Upon his admission to the home, Reed's clothes were torn and his limbs exposed for the benefit of the camera. Several years later, according to a published affidavit submitted to George Reynolds by John Hancorne, another employee dismissed for "gross impropriety," the boy had been forcibly stripped and flogged before the staff and other boys. Reynolds published Hancorne's account to expose and denounce Barnardo's scandalous abuse of his charges, but his text verges on reproducing the disturbing excitations of contemporary flagellant pornography.[94] It emphasizes the consequences of the inequality in power between the helpless boy, denied the right to speak in his own defense, and the Governor, Mr. Fielder, whom Reed addresses deferentially, but to no avail, with the phrase "Please, Sir."

> Mr. Fielder, the Governor of the Home, summoned all the masters up to the schoolroom during school-hours. He then offered a long prayer, which was followed by a lecture, after which he called Reed to the front. He came.
>
> Fielder.—"Reed, take off your clothes."
> Read [sic].—"Allow me one word, please Sir."
> Fielder.—"Not a word. Take off your clothes."
> Reed.—"Please, Sir, I should like to say one word first."
> Fielder, addressing those who stood by.—"Take his clothes off."
> The lad was seized by the throat, when a terrible scene ensued. After a time the lad was laid on his back insensible.
> This I declare to be true. I was an eye-witness to the whole of what is stated above.
> Signed, John Hancorne, 34, Bower-street, Commercial-road, London.[95]

Karen Halttunen's analysis of what she calls the "pornography of pain" in humanitarian appeals in the late eighteenth and nineteenth centuries provides insights into understanding Hancorne's affidavit and Reynolds' decision to reproduce it verbatim in his pamphlet. Halttunen shows how the sympathy provoked by the sight of suffering and its representation emphasized the "moral dangers of watching cruelty" and contained an erotic charge. "The humanitarian sensibility," she concludes, "fostered an imaginative cultural underground of the illicit and forbidden . . . at the center of which was a flogging scene."[96]

Barnardo's photographs of ragged children amplified "the moral dangers of watching cruelty" by making the suffering person they depicted appear more unique, specific, and physically real than nonphotographic representations. For most of Barnardo's contemporaries, the "realism" of photography narrowed the gap between representation and reality and thereby further intensified the ambivalent intimacy that philanthropic appeals strove to foster between their readers and the objects of benevolence.

Reynolds's published account of Reed's experiences as a Barnardo boy compresses the temporal distance separating the moment Reed was photographed from his flogging by narrating them one immediately after the other and thereby encourages readers to see the two events as successive scenes in a single, obscene drama.[97] The flogging episode recapitulates, albeit in a sadistic key, the initial scene of disfigurement, dressing and undressing at the photographic studio. Flogging, the epitome of the "pornography of pain" in the nineteenth-century imagination, becomes an almost inevitable culmination of the violations Reed suffered from the moment Barnardo photographed him. Contrary to the wishful message proclaimed by the photographic "contrasts," we see Reed degraded, not uplifted, by the Christian benevolence of Barnardo's institutions.

Barnardo's version of the events surrounding Reed's photograph and his treatment at the home were dramatically different. He successfully discredited claims that Reed, or any other boys, were subjected to abusive punishments.[98] To justify ripping Reed's clothes, he relied on his arguments about the artistic nature of his "representative" photographs, which in turn were compatible with evangelical distinctions between "truth" and "fact." He acknowledged tearing Reed's clothing, but only because Reed's original clothes were so tattered and verminous that they had to be immediately destroyed upon his arrival at the home.[99] Actions that Barnardo's antagonists chose to depict as the promiscuous derangement of a helpless young boy's clothing, Barnardo described as an inadequate attempt to re-create for the benefit of the camera the horrible "truth" of Reed's degraded condition.

If the threat of indecency surrounded the case of Reed, anxieties about child prostitution and miscegenation lurked just beneath the surface of the investigation into Barnardo's photograph of three naked black children entitled "Out of the Depths." Barnardo wrote a lengthy and moving account of the circumstances surrounding his discovery of the children, Eleanor, Annie, and John, and their virtuous widowed mother, Elizabeth Williams. Barnardo introduced their story as a "narrative of the rescue of three mulatto children."[100] His deliberate choice of the word "mulatto" drew upon widely held cultural assumptions about race and sex relations between African and British populations in the British Caribbean. Barnardo's readers would have assumed that these children (or, as we later learn, their father) were the product not of a legitimate marriage, but of exploitative sexual relations between a white man and a black woman. Barnardo's representation of the children as mulattos recalls this presumably immoral union.

By entitling his photograph "Out of the Depths," Barnardo must have expected some viewers to link the image to a controversial novel by that exact title published in 1860. The novel, an evangelical recasting of *Moll Flanders*, purported to be the autobiography of a servant girl who descends into prostitution only to be rescued by a handsome young clergyman. Its climax and most shocking passage eerily adumbrated one of the central issues raised not only by the Barnardo Arbitration but also by public discussion of William Gladstone's celebrated midnight rescue work on the streets of London: did men, whom society praised for their Christian work rescuing the fallen, clandestinely engage in immoral sexual acts? The passage details the clergyman's entrance into the young woman's bedchamber, ostensibly to have sex with her. When he attempts to assure her that he has not come to "do you the great wrong you may expect" because he is married and a clergyman, she replies cavalierly, "Oh, bless you! Clergymen and married men come here quite as often as others." While the novel leaves no doubt about the purity of its hero, it nonetheless did intimate that other men were not what they appeared to be.[101]

As Barnardo's written narrative accompanying the photograph unfolds, we learn that their mother, Mrs. Williams, is a hardworking Christian "negress," tragically widowed when her husband was mauled by a shark in the waters of the Caribbean. Barnardo watches her monotonously "stitch, stitch, stitch" sack after sack to keep herself alive and is stunned to discover three utterly naked children concealed among the heaps of sacks. Mrs. Williams acknowledged that her "great struggle was to keep them from the street. 'Any way and any how,' she said to us with streaming eyes, 'away from sin and wickedness!'" The distant miscegenation on the fringes of empire threatens to be reenacted on the streets of the Christian metropolis in the 1870s. To save them from this seemingly inevitable fate, Barnardo intervenes: "I have a Home for such; I will take them."[102]

The penultimate paragraph of the leaflet contained Barnardo's version of how he photographed and rescued them.

> That was conclusive, and they came; or rather we took them, wrapped up by the kindly hands of the landlady and their own mother in some of the sacks with which they had been invested. Off the next morning we carried them in a cab, and in the studio of our photographer laid them and their sacks down in a heap, much as they had been the day before in their mother's dingy room; and thus, in a few brief seconds, preserved for future years a picture of the state in which we found them. Then, away again to the Girls' Home in a cab, which waited at the door. How glad they were for the delightful luxury of a warm bath and clean clothing and . . . some warm soup . . . given by the matron to each.

If Barnardo can be believed (and this was of course a key question throughout the arbitration), only the loving hands of females (their mother, the landlady, and the matron) touched or saw the naked bodies of the children.[103]

The photograph "Out of the Depths" works with and against Barnardo's written text (figure 2.8). It ostensibly corroborates Barnardo's narrative by proving that three naked black children (of remarkably indeterminate age and sex) covered only by burlap sacks actually did exist. It makes literal the ubiquitous Victorian trope that the very poor constituted a separate and distinctly bestial race who both were and were not British.[104] But the photograph also raises questions about the narrative and draws attention to gaps in the sequence of events as Barnardo recounted them.

If, as Barnardo tells us, the children were not photographed until the next day, then surely the photograph is evidence that someone must have stripped them once again. But who? St. John Wontner relentlessly pursued the answer to this question during his interrogation of Barnardo's photographer, George Collins. To St. John Wontner's question "Who took the partial clothes off?" Collins replied evasively "I don't remember any clothes being taken off, I simply did the mechanical part. . . . [T]hey were arranged. I believe Dr. Barnardo posed them, or if not positively posed by him he was present." Collins' convenient lapse in memory consigned the precise conditions surrounding the moment of disrobing to his listeners' imaginations.[105]

The photograph itself unintentionally represented this second "undressing," which was arguably more disturbing than their original nakedness. The harsh lighting that oddly whitens the children's faces (and hence makes them appear to be more mulatto-like) and the backdrop of the photograph indicate that this undressing took place not in the shadows of their slum room before their mother but in the glare of a well-lit photographic studio in the presence of male strangers. The literary text shows Barnardo fulfilling his Christian duty by clothing the naked; the photograph reverses this trajectory by memorializing a disturbingly voyeuristic moment of undressing. Reading the photographic text in relationship to Barnardo's written narrative initiates a dialogue between them that challenges the reassuring closure of the written story alone.

Joseph Merrick and the Monstrosity of Poverty

Barnardo's photographs of the Williams children were potent reminders to good Christians of the obligations of empire. Distant acts on far away

FIGURE 2.8.   Barnardo, unlike most others engaged in slum rescue work in Victorian London, consistently included images of people of African descent along with children with various physical disabilities in his annual reports, books, and pamphlets, to underscore the inclusiveness of his work. Discussion of this photograph, "Out of the Depths," and the various stories surrounding the tribulations of Mrs. Williams and her three children arguably marked the emotional climax of the arbitration hearing, and, according to press reports, elicited tears of sympathy and offers of cash assistance from listeners. (Image courtesy of Barnardo's Photographic Archive.)

shores—the violent death of the children's father in the shark-infested waters of the Caribbean—imposed urgent burdens on those living in ease at the heart of the empire. Less than a decade later, Londoners confronted another set of shocking photographic and textual images of a desperately poor youth called Joseph Merrick. His life, like those of the Williams children, collapsed the distances separating home and empire, East and West London, rich and poor, the bestial and the civilized, science and sentiment. Born in dire poverty in Leicester, Merrick was Victorian Britain's most celebrated beneficiary of metropolitan charity by the time he died in 1890 in carefully appointed rooms in London Hospital, the institution from which Barnardo had begun his own career. To his contemporaries and to the wider public today, he remains best known as the Elephant Man, so named because of his grotesque deformities.

A vast amount has already been written about Merrick. We arguably know more about him than any other pauper in late Victorian Britain as he shuttled between freak shows, poorhouses, and poorhouse infirmaries.[106] His life and death seem to invite reflection about universal struggles between good and evil; about inner beauty locked within outward ugliness; and about the triumph of the human spirit over extreme adversity. Those who have resisted the urge to transform him into the stuff of parables have focused on his freakishness to unlock Victorian and post-Victorian attitudes about deformity.[107] Others have diligently searched archives and tracked his movements in an attempt to reconstruct his "real" life and disentangle it from the myths that enveloped it during his lifetime.

I do not have anything to add to the facts of Merrick's life or to his complex posthumous life in Anglo-American culture in the twentieth century. Instead, I propose that we think about him as a severely disabled, ragged young person rescued from the slums of Whitechapel and cared for by a group of philanthropic medical doctors, many with close links to evangelical charity in the metropolis. I want to pursue the ways in which photographic and written accounts of Merrick participated in traditions of slum narratives, metropolitan philanthropy, and spectacular representations of the poor, particularly those pioneered by Dr. Barnardo.

At the height of the mania for slumming in 1884, an ambitious and talented young medical doctor named Frederick Treves learned that a freak of nature, a so-called Elephant Man, was on public display not far from where he worked at London Hospital. London Hospital had long been distinguished as an institution in which medical care and philanthropy were closely joined. Not only did it serve the poorest of the London poor, it was headquarters for a variety of philanthropic schemes such as the East London branch of the University Extension movement, which brought distinguished scholars to teach classes to laboring men and women. Treves himself was closely involved with a variety of evangelical schemes to succor the bodies and spirits of poor boys and attracted athletic young medical students who shared his social concerns. At the time Treves assumed responsibility for Merrick's care in 1886, he had two students particularly distinguished by their commitment to missionary and medical work among the "rough lads" of Whitechapel: Wilfred Grenfell, destined to achieve international renown as the Labrador

Doctor, and his housemate, Denis Halsted. Grenfell, whose father had served as chaplain of London Hospital in 1885, was an evangelical embodiment of muscular Christianity—a lover of sports, nature, God, male comradeship, and the poor. Treves, Grenfell, and Halsted formed Merrick's inner circle of medical caretakers. When not tending to Merrick and their other hospital duties, Grenfell and Halsted devoted themselves to their club for poor boys located in the sparely furnished first floor of their home close by the hospital. The other residents of their unconventional household (Grenfell called it a "queer beehive") included a Brahmin from India, a converted Jew, and an Afro-Caribbean man they met while he was preaching in East London's largest park, Victoria Park.[108] Halsted and Grenfell, like their university-educated neighbors living in colonies of philanthropic gentlemen in settlement houses, regularly took groups of Cockney boys on trips to the seaside for therapeutic encounters with nature and to practice the manly and moral "simple life" they espoused.[109] Treves himself took Merrick on one such country holiday, although not as part of a larger group.

Treves probably heard rumors about the freak show from his students, many of whom (unlike the puritanical Grenfell) took advantages of the peculiar pleasures that East London offered gentlemen. Sir John Bland-Sutton, during his medical student days at London Hospital, recalled that on one of his frequent Saturday night visits to the Mile End Road "to see dwarfs, giants, fat-women, and monstrosities," he first spied Merrick, whose "thick and pendulous" skin hung in folds resembling the hide of an elephant.[110] For the price of a shilling, the freak-show proprietor granted Treves a private view of the "creature" in an abandoned storefront. In contrast to Bland-Sutton's frank avowal of the delights of urban flâneurie, Treves insisted that the pursuit of scientific knowledge was his sole motive. Nonetheless, his description of the encounter (written with great rhetorical brilliance in 1922) is unabashedly voyeuristic: we peek through red curtains and threadbare pants before glimpsing Merrick's naked limbs faintly illuminated by the blue light of a gas jet in the darkened room.

At first, Merrick seems no different from hundreds of youths rescued by Dr. Barnardo: "[H]e was naked to the waist, his feet were bare, he wore a pair of threadbare trousers that had once belonged to some fat gentleman's dress suit." However, Treves's language quickly positions Merrick as an exotic "creature" within a fantastic imperial bestiary, all too similar to the animals the London Zoo regularly sent to Treves for dissection. His description explodes with metaphoric excess—as if the sheer accumulation of analogies can recapture the horror of seeing Merrick for the first time. Merrick defies taxonomic categories and hovers between sexes, races, and species. He is a "creature," "a perverted version of a human being," an "elemental" and "primitive being," "a monstrous figure as hideous as an Indian idol," "a block of gnarled wood" with a hand resembling "a fin or paddle," and a "lizard" with a dewlap suspended from his neck.[111] Merrick's sexuality figures prominently in Treves's account. One arm, Treves explains, was a "delicately shaped limb covered with fine skin and provided with a beautiful hand which any woman might have envied." But as Treves's photographs of Merrick's naked body (which circulated in a widely read medical journal) make clear, his penis was his other "normal" and unambiguously manly limb. Apparently, Merrick's attraction to the opposite sex was unimpaired: "[H]is bodily deformity had left unmarred the instincts and feelings of his years. . . . He would liked to have been a lover." Treves happily played the role of procurer for Merrick, one of the many services he performed in demonstrating the power of cross-class friendship to cultivate humanity in even the most outcast of the bestial poor. "I asked a friend of mine," Treves recalled, "a young and pretty widow, if she thought she could enter Merrick's room with a smile, wish him good morning, and shake him by the hand."[112] While the Jack the Ripper murders made Whitechapel the epicenter of elite fantasies about sexual and social disorder, Merrick's rooms constituted a site that was exotically horrible but reassuringly safe and domesticated. Merrick cherished the company of the endless stream of charitable lady visitors—including Alexandra, Princess of Wales—who put his rooms at London Hospital on the map as East London's most popular philanthropic destination.

Like the Barnardo boy named Reed, Merrick was photographed upon his admission as a permanent resident to London Hospital and later photographed again in his Sunday best, visual proof of the transformative benevolence of those who cared for him.[113] In Treves's telling of the Elephant Man's story, Merrick was an ideal recipient of elite philanthropy. Gratefully deferential, Merrick was the quintessential "mimic man" who wanted nothing more than to imitate the manners of a "dandy and a young man about town." According to Treves, Merrick's desire to no longer merely "mimic" but become a normal man led to his death.

> He often said to me that he wished he could lie down to sleep "like other people" [who did not have to support massive heads]. I think on this last night he must, with some determination, have made the experiment. The pillow was soft, and the head, when placed on it, must have fallen backwards and caused a dislocation of the neck. Thus it came about that his death was due to the desire that had dominated his life—the pathetic but hopeless desire to be "like other people."[114]

Mimesis once again produces nemesis. Treves's account of the life and death of Joseph Merrick draws upon the political economy of the Victorian moral imagination. Twain's pauper may look just like the prince but he neither can nor wants to become him; the black spots of Kipling's leopard, like the black skin of Kipling's Ethiopian, once gained, can never be washed away; Treves' Elephant Man can never quite become a swell; the London poor can never truly escape the mark of their poverty, no matter how much they wish to be real ladies and gentlemen.[115] Treves discretely did not reveal the ultimate fate of Merrick's corpse: his grotesque form was preserved in a body cast, his tissues were sampled, his flesh removed, and his bones boiled down for display as a skeleton.[116] The philanthropic and evangelical doctors at London Hospital put aside the claims of friendship and common humanity and asserted their traditional right to use the body of an outcast, impoverished man to serve the needs of science. It was an ending feared and reviled by the Victorian poor, for whom a proper burial was often the only luxury earned by a lifetime of hard labor. At once an object of scientific study, evangelical benevolence, and prurient curiosity, Merrick was, I have suggested, a sort of Barnardo-boy manqué, albeit one who thanked his rescuers rather than testified against them.

Conclusion

The aftermath of the Barnardo arbitration left a deep mark on each of the individuals, organizations, and movements involved in it and raised important issues about competing notions of truth, social welfare, and representation. The COS was profoundly affected by the avalanche of criticisms it received for its unsuccessful and vindictive pursuit of Barnardo.[117] Lloyd's Weekly pugnaciously suggested that the time had come for a "searching investigation of the COS" whose "unfeeling inquisitions" "tortured" poor folks and "closed the giver's hand to many a deserving human creature."[118] The COS's mishandling of the arbitration dashed its hope that Parliament would grant it exclusive legal control over the organization of charity and allow it to regulate the relationship between the state and private charity.[119] The president of the COS chose to resign (though not because anyone held him personally responsible for the Barnardo fiasco), and his handpicked organising secretary, who had orchestrated the COS's campaign against Barnardo, was ousted in a series of extraordinary COS council meetings.[120]

Evangelical charity, including Barnardo's ambitious ventures, continued to flourish in the 1880s to an extent inadequately recognized by historians blinkered by their search for the secular origins of the twentieth-century welfare state. As a result of the arbitration, Barnardo claimed he would not take any more "representative" photographs of his children.[121]

He did continue to amass his archive of admission photographs which, according to John Tagg, marked an important moment in the harnessing of photography as a tool of surveillance of the poor in the nineteenth century.[122] This analysis leads toward rather different, though not contradictory, conclusions. Just as the COS was determined to destroy Barnardo, or at least contain the scope of his philanthropic methods, so, too, the arbitration and the response of the press revealed deep concern to discipline and regulate the "legitimate"—in terms of morality, sexuality, and veracity—uses of photography as an emerging technology to represent the poor.

Reformers from the late-18th century onward had recognized the power of images of poor children to stir the sympathies of the public and stimulate generous donations to humanitarian causes.[123] Barnardo worked within and transformed the rich legacy of representations of ragged children he inherited: the forlorn but prophetic waifs of Dickens's novels and the spirited shoeblacks of Lord Shaftesbury's famous brigades. Barnardo's "representative" photographs, sketches, and narratives were all part of his apparatus to arouse public sympathy and activity on behalf of street children.

If arousal is the essence of eros, it also was essential to the sympathy Barnardo strove to stimulate with his daring philanthropic appeals. The tension between sexual innocence and sexual experience lay at the heart of the urgent sympathy he evoked in his images of ragged girls. Anticipating W. T. Stead's *Maiden Tribute* tactics of the mid-1880s,[124] Barnardo conveyed a keen sense of the imminent sexual dangers awaiting what he called "the not yet fallen" ragged street girls he saved.[125] By representing them as sexually vulnerable and available, he attempted to reproduce for his audiences the dangers awaiting ragged girls without incriminating himself as a purveyor of such images. On the one hand, he needed to show his audience that poor girls *were* sexual commodities within the predatory economy of prostitution. By so doing, he forced his contemporaries to see female children as sexual beings, albeit not by choice but rather as victims of adult male lust.[126] On the other hand, Barnardo conjured up images of ragged girls as objects of male sexual desire in order to censure and condemn such desires as un-Christian and exploitative and redirect them toward benevolent ends (figures 2.9a,b).

What part, if any, sexuality played in the sympathy Barnardo excited in his representations of ragged boys was neither explicit nor intentional. Barnardo and most other child welfare advocates claimed that boys schooled on the streets would become criminals unless they were subjected to rigorous but loving institutional discipline. Despite the existence of a lucrative "rough trade" in boy prostitutes and soldiers in Victorian London, Barnardo never acknowledged that life on the streets

a

b

FIGURE 2.9. Victorian elites viewed poor children as dangerous threats to the social order and also simultaneously as sentimental objects of unspoiled and innocent humanity. In marked contrast to Barnardo's use of ragged clothes and exposed limbs to suggest sexual danger, Mrs. H. M. Stanley (Dorothy Tennant), wife of the famed explorer, highlighted the ways in which the joys of childhood were undiminished by poverty. Most of the images she included in her book *London Street Arabs* (1890) showed children at play (figure 2.9b) or with their mothers or enjoying the attentions of a "Lady Bountiful" (figure 2.9a).

posed sexual dangers for boys as well as girls. However, rumors about sexual misconduct in Barnardo's boys' home and the character of the questions posed by St. John Wontner to Barnardo's photographic staff darkly hinted that his photographs of ragged boys were evidence of "unnatural" passions and behaviors.[127]

Just as the photographs incited and contained their sexual message, so, too, they criticized and took advantage of the relationship of the state and the free market to ragged children and their welfare. The images graphically demonstrated the inadequacy of the free market to satisfy the minimal needs of children and the state's refusal to remedy this shocking neglect. To protect ragged children from selling their bodies on the streets of London, Barnardo distributed and sold images of them and used these images as marketing tools. In this way, he foreshadowed the rise of philanthropy as big business and the philanthropist as entrepreneur. Barnardo's use of his photographs collapsed the distinction between morality and marketing. The images served as advertisements for his work and as condensed visual parables about imperiled childhood innocence. If, as Viviana Zelizer has argued, Victorian children became increasingly "priceless," Barnardo nonetheless understood how to use their images to "make capital" for his philanthropic enterprises.[128]

In the decades following the arbitration, ragged children and representations of them proved even more formidable adversaries for the COS than did Barnardo himself. Time and again, the COS opposed private and public schemes to provide goods and services for poor children on the grounds that such benevolence undermined parental responsibility. Aware of its growing isolation and unpopularity, the COS denounced "indiscriminate" relief for children in ever more strident tones by the turn of the century. In vain it opposed those landmark state-welfare measures on behalf of poor children—the medical inspection of school children and the feeding of necessitous school children—which proved the entering wedge for so much interventionist social welfare legislation during the Edwardian years.

The leaders of the COS and other champions of liberal economic and social theories about citizenship and the state were singularly ill-equipped to respond to their critics who contended that because children were not autonomous, rational citizens, they could not be held responsible for their poverty. Children were by definition dependent, not independent; lacking the capacity to make free choices, they necessarily operated within a framework of adult compulsion. Barnardo's photographic images of ragged children called attention to children's blameless dependence in order to condemn the workings of the poor law and galvanize the sympathy of adults. But as his enemies during the arbitration tried to prove, his photographs also unwittingly bore witness to the extent to which his child models were subject to the coercive authority of even those who, like Barnardo, claimed to act in their best interests. In this way, Barnardo's "artistic fictions" are ambivalent monuments both to the ubiquity of ragged children in the urban landscape and their centrality in the Victorian moral imagination. The power of images of ragged children in promoting private benevolence and public welfare policies paradoxically relied upon the utter powerlessness of street children themselves to make claims on the state and civil society. Barnardo's very success in making visual images of his ragged children such unforgettable markers of poverty undercut the dynamic of benevolent transformation at the very heart of his mission. The Barnardo boy or girl became fixed in the British cultural imagination as a synonym for the ragged child, trapped forever in the spectacular and iconic poverty of torn clothes, bare feet, and unkempt hair. While his plaintive "before" pictures leave an indelible mental imprint, the "after" images of neatly clad children engaged in industrious labor are easily forgotten.

Images of ragged children have continued to play an important role in the way we think about poverty in the century since Barnardo's death. When I open up a magazine and confront the dirty face and tattered clothes of a child appealing to me to "save" her or him by contributing a few dollars (or pounds) each month, I cannot help but recall the words of the boy Reed and the beadle Fitzgerald and see the haunting images of the Williams children and Joseph Merrick. We are not supposed to know that these images have a long and problematic history. If we did, we would surely understand that such philanthropic schemes may have done good work for tens of thousands of individual children but have done little to address the deeper structural problems that produce new generations of child waifs who, like Barnardo's children, will be photographed in their pathetic rags. Worse yet, some may even suspect that giving money to Barnardo's over the years has made it just a bit easier for generations of compassionate men and women to avoid demanding more fundamental changes in our approach to childhood poverty.[129]

Just as this chapter situates Dr. Barnardo's "artistic fictions" at the confluence of several historical and discursive streams in nineteenth-century culture and society, we can detect its visual traces and hear echoes of its protagonists' voices in the ongoing work of Barnardo's today and in the history of one of the most notable and innovative child welfare organizations founded in the twentieth century: Save the Children. Comparing the current discursive and photographic practices of these two justly celebrated private charities throws into sharp relief the urgency of the questions raised—but not resolved—by the 1877 arbitration.

In 1994 Barnardo's launched its Streets and Lanes Project with the explicit aim of protecting girls and young women abused through prostitution. Barnardo's sought to provide services for victims of sexual abuse while shifting the discursive terrain in which debates about sexual abuse were and are embedded. As Carole Howlett, deputy assistant commissioner of the Metropolitan Police explains, "we no longer talk about 'child prostitutes, pimps and punters.' . . . Instead we say children abused through prostitution, abusing adults and child-sex offenders." Thanks to Barnardo's efforts, the police "no longer view [children] as young criminals but rather as victims of sexual abuse and thus in need of protection."[130] Barnardo's has unmistakably shed the framework of fallenness and criminality that were so integral to its Victorian founder's conception of the moral status of the children he rescued. In its place, Barnardo's has embraced a philosophy which seeks to ensure that the voices of victims are heard and their needs made paramount.

If Barnardo's approach to child poverty has been transformed almost beyond recognition over the past 130 years, its techniques for calling attention to the plight of neglected children and to itself have not. In the year 2000, Barnardo's embarked upon a campaign to promote its programs to protect the child victims of homelessness by depicting a baby, sitting in its own feces, injecting heroin. Buoyed by the publicity generated by this image (much of it highly critical), Barnardo's ventured into even more provocative and dangerous territory in 2002 with its multimedia Stolen Childhood campaign. The photographic images accompanying this campaign, like those produced by Dr. Barnardo himself in the 1870s, are unabashedly confrontational. Shot in a starkly documentary-realist idiom, they position us as voyeurs, witnesses to scenes of child sexual abuse as they are about to unfold. These images intentionally mimic the visual conventions of kiddie porn widely available on the Internet, even as the accompanying written texts allow us to hear abused children explain their entrapment in sexual slavery through Internet chat rooms and pornographic photographs of them sold over the Internet. The power of these images resides partly in their refusal to show us sex acts (which we would register as pornography) and partly in the way they cause us to imagine these sex acts for ourselves. The tawdry banality of the settings—a urinal in a public men's room, a sparely furnished bedroom—only highlight the grotesque monstrosity of the half-visible, partially unclothed but anonymous adult, male, sex abusers, one of whom is conspicuously wearing his wedding ring (figure 2.10b).

Perhaps what is most shocking about these images is the way in which they intentionally undermine their own claims to be wholly faithful to reality: the face of each of the child victims has been digitally aged, their right to be children literally stolen from them. In other words, Barnardo's has resurrected its founder's conviction that the deepest truths about society's most vulnerable members can be represented most powerfully

through "artistic fictions" which compel viewers simultaneously to acknowledge and to take action against child abuse. And like Dr. Barnardo
himself, the leaders of Barnardo's today have chosen to exploit the possibilities of new technologies of the "real" to capture the public's attention
and financial support. "We must ensure that our relatively small budget
overachieves by cutting through the media clutter," explains Barnardo's
employee Rachel Knott. "The adverts need to grab attention."[131] As part
of its effort to outlaw the sexual commodification of real children's bodies, Barnardo's continues to raise money by producing eroticized—and
falsified—images of them[132] (figures 2.10a,b).

In the past two decades, the approach of Save the Children to both its
own history and to its current photographic policies has diverged dramatically from Barnardo's. Save the Children was founded in the immediate
aftermath of World War I, when a group of highly educated women and
men decided to apply their deep knowledge of childhood poverty in England to the problems facing children worldwide. Led by Eglantyne Jebb,
a graduate of Lady Margaret Hall, Oxford, the founders of Save the Children very quickly adopted sensational and innovative techniques reminiscent of Barnardo's to promote the fledgling agency and its causes. One of
its leaders, Ernest Hamilton, purchased double-column advertising space
in major newspapers which he filled with "crude 'line' drawings of ago-
nised, screaming women clutching to their breasts ghastly skeletons of
children whom the British public were urged to save from otherwise certain death." By 1921, Save the Children decided to harness not only photography but also film to serve its philanthropic needs and produced riveting visual images of child victims of famine in Bolshevik Russia.[133] For
the next six decades, Save the Children regularly circulated images of
scantily clad and undernourished people, especially girls and women of
color, to support its growing international network of benevolence.

Not until the late 1980s did Save the Children self-critically reckon
with the ethical implications of its use of images of the poor and vulnerable. Do photographic subjects have rights and if so, what are they?
How can depictions of the poor acknowledge their dignity and humanity? What are the boundaries between sympathy and sexuality, truth and
fiction in photographs of poor children? The *Save the Children Fund
Image Guidelines* attempted to answer these questions by making clear
"the connection between images and how they influence the way people
are perceived and treated . . . [by] show[ing] the link between images,
principles and practice, and attitudes to racial, cultural, and sexual differences." The ten guidelines it offers, accompanied by examples of
"good" and "bad" photographic practices drawn from its own archives,
emphasize the dignity of the poor, their ability to act for themselves, the
diverse forms and causes of poverty, and the essentially collaborative

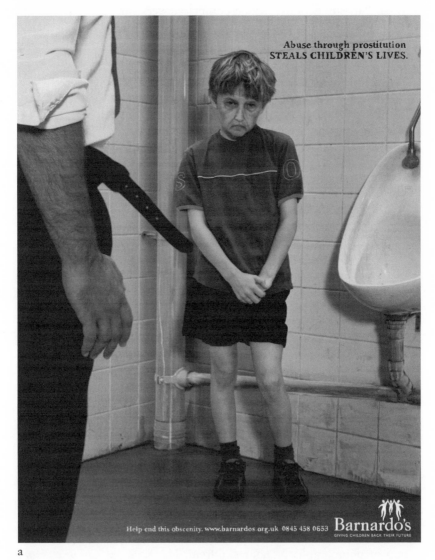

Abuse through prostitution
STEALS CHILDREN'S LIVES.

Help end this obscenity. www.barnardos.org.uk 0845 458 0653   Barnardo's
GIVING CHILDREN BACK THEIR FUTURE

a

FIGURE 2.10.   Barnardo's most recent campaign against childhood sexual
abuse in 2002, like its predecessors in the nineteenth century, has generated
tremendous controversy and also achieved impressive results. The faces of the

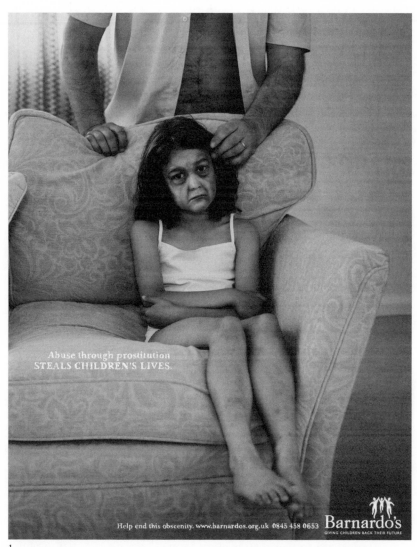

Abuse through prostitution
STEALS CHILDREN'S LIVES.

Help end this obscenity. www.barnardos.org.uk 0845 458 0653 Barnardo's
GIVING CHILDREN BACK THEIR FUTURE

b

children have been digitally aged to underscore that their rights to be children have been "stolen" from them by sexually exploitative adults. (Photographs from Barnardo's Stolen Childhood Campaign, 2002. Courtesy of Barnardo's.)

character of all efforts to assist those in need. Within this self-conscious ethical framework, sensationalism, even harnessed to serve a worthy cause, is incompatible with human dignity (figure 2.11). Perhaps most importantly, at least from my perspective, the guidelines do not aspire to be the final word on the subject: "since language and imagery are living and evolving all the time, it is hoped that the guidelines will encourage healthy debate."[134]

This chapter has sought to recapture at least some of the "healthy debate" stirred up by Barnardo's rescue work in Victorian East London. Contemporaries found in Barnardo and his institutions an unsettling convergence of roles that they wanted to believe were mutually exclusive. Barnardo and his staff were agents of child rescue *and* accused of child abuse. They advocated social purity in public *and* were rumored to engage in gross sexual misconduct in private. With good reason, the public wanted to know which of these characterizations was the truth.

Despite mountains of evidence, the whole truth about Dr. Barnardo remains infuriatingly opaque. We will never know the answers to all the questions raised about him during the arbitration. From his first days as a medical student in London, Barnardo impressed some of his peers as the consummate hypocrite. They were mistaken. The concept of hypocrisy tells us surprisingly little about Barnardo, and I suspect, about the earnest Victorian world he has come to exemplify. Sharing with his fellow Evangelicals an acute sense of the pervasiveness of human sinfulness, Barnardo never for a moment imagined that he himself was free from sin. His wife Syrie offered a particularly insightful assessment of him. She believed that an immense "desire he could not suppress" lay at the very heart of that "forcing house of his white hot passion to save the souls and care for the bodies of ragged children."[135] To suggest, as I have, that erotic desires mingled with religious and philanthropic impulses in the language of virtue Barnardo deployed on behalf of poor children neither diminishes his achievements nor impugns his integrity. Victorian reformers and philanthropists understood that what made the "morality" they proclaimed so powerful was in part its capacity to inflame and contain the unruly possibilities and passions of the "imagination" to which it was so intimately bound. In Barnardo's "artistic fictions," the ragged child constituted the point where evangelical, philanthropic, and sexualized gazes converged and made visible the erotics of benevolence in Victorian London.

images are everybody's business

These guidelines cover all forms of communication which aim to describe or represent the work of Save the Children, internally and externally.

They include:

● advertising on television, radio, poster sites or in cinemas, newspapers, magazines and direct mail

● publicity through press releases, internal publications, books, education packs, reports, slideshows, videos, displays, exhibitions, public gatherings, talks, seminars, fundraising events and promotions, work with corporate partners, speeches

Everyone involved in promoting Save the Children should follow these guidelines - staff, volunteers, committee members, project partners, corporate sponsors, advertising agencies, photographic agencies, photographers, illustrators and other commissioned freelances.

The guidelines carry the full authority of Save the Children's Council and directors, who take overall responsibility for applying them within their own departments. Each department is responsible for ensuring that the guidelines are reflected in its working practices. Individual members of staff should make sure that the guidelines are included in work plans. Don't forget to incorporate them into any brief or contract with outside agencies or corporate sponsors. Explain why they are important, and make sure that the finished work reflects these principles. When in doubt, check with your line manager or departmental director.

Photographs by:
Ian Berry/Magnum Photos, Martine Franck/Magnum Photos, Ben Gibson, Mike Goldwater, Jenny Matthews/Network, Caroline Penn, Eli Reed/Magnum Photos, Sebastiao Salgado/Magnum Photos, Ferdinando Scianna/ Magnum Photos, Liba Taylor, Penny Tweedie, Wendy Wallace, Mike Wells.

FIGURE 2.11.   Save the Children Fund Image Guidelines, c. 1995. (Courtesy of Save the Children.)

Chapter Three

———∞∞∞———

THE AMERICAN GIRL IN LONDON:
GENDER, JOURNALISM, AND SOCIAL
INVESTIGATION IN THE LATE
VICTORIAN METROPOLIS

IN NOVEMBER 1893, a young American woman called Elizabeth Banks—without wealth, social connections, or conspicuous beauty—had overnight taken London by storm. To be more accurate, she adroitly had placed herself at the eye of a storm of her own creation. According to George R. Sims, Banks was "the charming lady journalist, who has made the biggest score out of the disguise business since the days of the Amateur Casual" nearly three decades earlier. This was exceptionally high praise coming from Sims, arguably London's most accomplished master of cross-class masquerades, who was renowned for his empathic evocations of the London poor. The female journalist for the *Pall Mall Gazette* who signed her column "Autolycus" declared that Miss Elizabeth Banks, the "American Girl in London," was the "heroine of the town." Banks had masqueraded "courageously" as a servant and insinuated herself into the very fabric of a proper English home. In a series of articles published in the *Weekly Sun*, she laid bare to Londoners the unhappy relations between upstairs and downstairs, between mistresses and their housemaids. "Her strange, wild, and curious adventures," Autolycus begrudgingly acknowledged, were "the common theme of conversation in thousands of English homes." In the months ahead, Banks cashed in on the success of her articles on domestic service by publishing accounts of herself disguised as a flower girl, crossing sweeper, laundress, dressmaker, strawberry picker, and American heiress in search of introductions into English aristocratic society. While Banks's highly theatrical investigative reporting captured the public's attention, she had not won its uncritical admiration. Some insisted that her superficial treatment of the servant problem demonstrated not only her incompetence as a journalist but her failings as a woman. Without apology, Banks had amused her readers with incidents that revealed her ignorance about how to wash floors and clean candlesticks. Echoing the complaints of many readers of the *Weekly Sun*, Autolycus indignantly wondered whether "there actually breathe[s] a woman in whom the domestic instinct is so dead as this?"[1] Only a week later, Autolycus moved from ambivalent remarks about Miss Banks to a short summary of the debate over "what is unwomanly" then raging in the press.[2]

Autolycus's message was unmistakable. Banks's cross-class masquerades and her articles about them were "unwomanly." But beyond that, English lady journalists feared that Banks's introduction of what they called American style women's reporting to the London press might jeopardize their own precarious standing within the overwhelmingly male profession of journalism. Mary Billington, who made her name writing for the *Echo* and the *Daily Graphic*, rather wishfully and erroneously insisted in 1896 that "English lady journalists have not so far descended to any of the vulgar sensationalism and semi-detective business which has discredited the American reporteresses in too many instances." "Happily our editorial methods and our own instincts as gentlewomen," she concluded, "do not lead us to try being barmaids, or going out with costermongers on a bank holiday for the purpose of 'getting copy.'"[3] Three years later, however, Billington tacitly acknowledged the triumph of the new style of female journalism Banks had brought with her to London by disavowing the fad for "those startling undertakings" by women reporters which involved the "possession of some dramatic faculties and much make-up."[4]

Within little more than a year after her arrival in England in late 1892, Banks had propelled herself from an editorial position on the *Baltimore Morning Herald* into one of London's best-known journalists. She had become a celebrity who not only gathered news but was herself newsworthy. But how did she do this? Why was the public so anxiously fascinated with Banks's social investigations into female labor and their perpetrator? How can we make sense of the complex and seemingly contradictory ways in which English "lady" journalists like Autolycus and Billington responded to Banks's practices and persona as an "American girl" and journalist? Banks, unlike the original Amateur Casual (James Greenwood) and socialist women slum explorers and journalists such as Margaret Harkness, notably shied away from acknowledging the sexual dimensions of her subject. Why is there no sex in Banks's social reporting and in her writings about herself? The answers to these questions necessarily begin with Banks herself, who has left behind copious published traces of her "adventures" on three continents. But they also lead us away from Banks' personal history toward several important issues in the late-Victorian Anglo-American world: the emergence of journalism as a profession for women and the gendered character of the press; middle-class women's appropriation of the largely masculine tradition of cross-class incognito social exploration into the lives and labors

of the London poor; and fin-de-siècle debates about national character
and the status of women in the United States and Britain. The rise of the
female undercover reporter in the slums coincided not only with the
mania for slumming in late-Victorian London but with the emergence of
the New Woman both as a subject of fiction and as a way to talk about
newly emerging constructions of femininity. Were women journalists,
like the growing army of female social workers and slum explorers,
themselves a species of New Women? What part did women investigative
journalists play in broader public debates about the sexual and social
politics of London poverty and female labor? These panoramic themes as
well as Banks's individual role in their articulation are my subject.

Journalism as Autobiography, Autobiography as Fiction

Near the end of Banks's disarmingly shrewd memoir, *The Autobiography
of a "Newspaper Girl"* (1902), she informs us that "up to the present I
have been engaged mostly in writing about myself, and have, perforce,
been my own 'heroine,' till finally I decided to write this, my journalistic
autobiography."[5] At first glance, this is a damning admission. After all,
her reputation rested on her supposedly factual exposés of conditions of
female labor in London and later New York, not on her work as a mem-
oirist. Banks's elaborate descriptions of her costumed escapades accompanied by flattering studio portraits of her in disguise vied with the actual contents of her revelations for her readers' attention (figures 3.1a
and b). By the 1890s, photographers often accompanied reporters on
their slum investigations. But their job was usually to capture the spectacular raggedness of the poor, a form of portraiture developed by Dr.
Barnardo with his staged portraits of street children in the 1870s. Some
journalists used the camera as Jacob Riis had in New York City to convey the squalor and physical decay of slum environments, in particular
tenement housing. Riis's photographs powerfully advanced his arguments about municipal politics and social hygiene in New York and documented the effects of capitalist pursuit of profit unchecked by regard for
human need. Banks, by contrast, used the camera to show us only Banks
herself. She literally embodies the social problems she explores in her
journalism by standing in for real servants, laundresses, and flower girls.
We are never supposed to imagine that she actually *is* one of these girls.
These photographs neither document the social realities of laboring
women's lives nor capture Banks in the midst of performing her cross-
class impersonations.[6] As studio portraits, the photographs of Banks
bear no weight as evidence that Banks ever engaged in the labors she described in her newspaper exposés. Unlike the photographs the American

writer Jack London staged to illustrate his descent into the "abyss" of London a few years later, Banks's photographs do not even provide us a glimpse of real city streets, refuges, or workplaces as the backdrop for her impersonations. They are clearly a show, got up for the purpose of selling her literary work.[7] We are meant to be charmed and intrigued by Banks' portraits, not outraged by them or called to action.

Banks was a master of disguise not only in her journalism but also in her voluminous writings about herself and her closest relationships. They are a rich but unreliable source of information for her biographer.[8] What she chooses to tell us about herself cannot be taken at face value because her disclosures invariably serve to advance the particular argument she is making at any given moment.[9] They sometimes contradict previously published statements and at other times appear to be patently false.[10] Despite her craving for fame, Banks seemed determined to preserve for herself the exclusive right to tell her life story and to frustrate the historian's attempt to tell a different one. "I earnestly request," she wrote in her will, "my Executors to remove all inscriptions from my jewelry and to destroy all private papers and photographs."[11] Only a small number of her letters survive despite the large number of well-known people with whom she had frequent, though not close, contact.[12] We do have a vast array of articles she wrote that spanned her entire adult life and were published in newspapers and periodicals ranging from the *Oshkosh Northwestern Gazette* in Wisconsin, the *New York Times*, and *London Times*, to the *Anglo-American Times* and the *Referee*. While Banks was in no sense a typical or representative woman, she incessantly wrote her life story using the cultural materials that lay close at hand. In studying how Banks constructed her life against the backdrop of her journalistic slumming, we stand to learn a great deal about her world.

Taking into account Banks's unreliability, I have still been able to piece together the general contours of her career. Born in New Jersey (in either 1865 or 1870), she was adopted at a young age by her childless aunt and uncle, who owned and worked a farm in Wisconsin that they ran on experimental but unprofitable principles of modern agriculture. Her biological and adopted parents remain nameless in her autobiographies, although she calls the latter "Uncle Josiah and Aunt Rebecca" in a witty *Anglo-American Times* article describing her departure from Wisconsin.[13] Her supposed incompetence as a London housemaid—her inability to properly wash floors and clean candlesticks—was yet another pose she assumed to elicit commentary. As a member of her family's servantless household, she became quite proficient in most areas of domestic economy. Despite their financial hardships, her aunt and uncle saved carefully for her higher education. In Banks's account of her childhood, a bracing spirit of independence and self-help went hand in hand with strong com-

a

"I FELT MEEK AND LOWLY."

FIGURE 3.1.　Banks's flattering photographs of herself in various incognitos focus entirely on Banks herself. They provide no commentary on or glimpse of the lives of and conditions of labor for London's working girls. Instead, they contribute to Banks's determination to make her personal responses to working

munity support and an unquestioned assumption that girls had a right to higher education. Banks lived more than forty years of her life in England (in or near London), but in her imagination she returned over and over to her Wisconsin childhood in seeking out those sources of her own independent spirit and of the "American girl" as a distinct national type.

After graduating from Milwaukee-Downer College, she embarked on two years of journalism for Western papers in St. Paul, Minnesota, before accepting the post of personal secretary to John Hicks, proprietor of the *Oshkosh Northwestern Weekly* and U.S. Envoy Extraordinary and Minister Plenipotentiary to Peru. The weekly letters she published under the pseudonym Celia in the *Oshkosh Northwestern* from November

b   " ELIZABETH BARROWS," HOUSEMAID.

class life—and her femininity—into the chief commodity she sold in print to her readers. (From Elizabeth Banks, *Campaigns of Curiosity, Journalistic Adventures of an American Girl in London*, London, 1894.)

1889 until June 1890 provide a fairly detailed glimpse into her activities in Peru. Unwilling to be fettered by conventions governing the movements of foreigners, she passed for a native by donning the national dress of Peruvian women, the manta, and roamed the streets of Lima. She soon discovered that "robed in that garment" she might be mistaken for a "Peruvian girl who dared to be unconventional and go out alone," thus suffering the insults of Peruvian gentlemen. Banks, for all her bravado, was quite anxious to avoid casual encounters with men on the street. Years later, when the editor of one of New York's leading yellow newspapers asked her to be picked up as a prostitute on Broadway to show that the existing laws put respectable women at risk of being confused for their fallen sisters, she flatly refused.[14] Unlike most male and some female investigative journalists in London and New York, Banks expressed no interest in exploring the sexual underworlds of the metropolis. As she explained to her literary agent, she would not "under any consideration" or for any amount of money write about the "'seamy side' of a woman's journalistic life."[15] Banks's unwillingness to investigate sexuality in her journalism was matched by her refusal to reveal anything to her readers about her own affective life. If she had any romances, no traces of them have survived.

In Banks's experiences in Peru as a "girl diplomat" and her reports about them, we can find some of the roots of her later journalism in London and New York in the 1890s. In addition to her fondness for imposture, she also demonstrated a deep interest in exploring spaces, customs, and identities different from her own. Her observations about Peruvian social, religious, racial, and political structures spurred Banks to reflect upon what became an enduring preoccupation for her and for so many other American writers: defining what it meant to be an American. She left Peru in July 1890 and returned to the United States where she worked briefly in New York City before moving to the *Baltimore Morning Herald*. It was here that she became convinced that women journalists should not be treated the same as men and that women had distinct voices as journalists and specifically female tasks to perform for newspapers and their readers. Somehow, over the course of the next year, she accumulated four hundred dollars which she took with her as she embarked upon what she thought would be a trip of a few weeks to London in 1892. During the next four years, Banks made herself into a transatlantic celebrity through her witty and daring incognito investigations into the lives of laboring girls in London—exploits I will analyze closely later in this chapter.

Banks returned to the United States in 1896 during the heat of the presidential campaign pitting William McKinley against William Jennings Bryan. Her arrival in New York was a media event, and she was greeted by scores of journalists. The *New York Daily Tribune*, for example, devoted half of its "The Only Woman's Page" to an illustrated story about Banks entitled "She Is an American. The Wee Mite of a Woman Who Interviewed Li Hung Chang [a leading Chinese minister]." Several months later, William Randolph Hearst's *American Woman's Home Journal* devoted the entire cover page of its "Special Commencement Number" to photographs with captions of Banks.[16] Ishbel Ross, one of the leading women reporters in New York in the 1920s, described Banks's invasion of Park Row "in a new Knox hat and a tailor-made suit of the latest cut. She carried camphor and smelling salts, an alligator card case and an ivory-handled umbrella with which she waved office boys out of her way."[17] Banks deftly manipulated interviewers to include a description of her dress and physical appearance as part of her strategy to make sure her public knew that she was an attractive and feminine woman. An interview she gave a woman journalist in London two years before her triumphant return to New York allows us to see how Banks accomplished this. "Now, do you think I look the bouncing, outrageous sort of person," Banks disingenuously asked the interviewer, "which some people make me out to be?" Her question immediately set the agenda for the story the reporter offered the public by making newsworthy her appearance and behavior. Not surprisingly, the article began with a flattering description of Banks as "a slight, sensitive, delicate-looking girl . . . dressed in a dark blue gown prettily trimmed with cream lace."[18]

Why was Banks so intent to control her public image? Two answers come to mind. First, Banks was an unmarried woman who lived outside the supports and constraints of male authority and family. She was not a wife or widow, mother or daughter. "Spinster," with its connotations of dependence, redundancy, and old maidishness, was the most readily available category into which contemporaries could have placed her. Banks's resolve to be fashionably feminine and charming signaled her emphatic rejection of spinsterhood. She preferred to construct a new sort of female image, one which balanced her compulsive need to be "different from everybody else" with her determination to be an exemplary lady in her personal demeanor. "I am 'queer'" she breezily declared in an 1893 article describing her harmonious domestic menagerie in London of Dinah, her African-American servant, and her beloved poodle, Judge, for whom she reserved her deepest affections (figure 3.2).[19] Second, Banks understood that the contrast between her petite stature and the daring physical demands of her reporting was a key ingredient in her commercial success. Most of her social investigations end with a description of the "heroine" literally restored to a feminine position—prostrate in her cozy bed.[20] In Banks's astute gender performances, her every disruption of genteel feminine norms such as engaging in hard labor required a compensatory gesture of exaggeratedly feminine weakness.

Banks may have been the American Girl in London but for the next few years she reinvented herself as yet another sort of outsider with an insider's eye for social details: she styled herself the All-British Woman or the English Woman in New York. Once again, she took on the task of explaining England and America to one another. While she served as a New York correspondent for several London papers, the bulk of her energies went into the pursuit of sensational copy as a "special rate" writer of commissioned pieces for New York's leading yellow newspapers. To her delight, she reported that she often earned over $150 per week—putting her at the highest echelons of the profession. Banks catalogued her jour-

FIGURE 3.2.   This double portrait of Banks and her poodle, Judge, served as frontispiece to Banks's *The Autobiography of a "Newspaper Girl"* (1902) and accurately reflected Judge's prominence as the object of Banks's deepest affections in her telling of her life story. Banks translated her "dog love" into public service during World War I when she wrote a series of well-publicized and immensely popular stories about heroic dogs. She donated the proceeds from the sale of these books to help war animals and babies. She also used the stories to encourage Americans to join the war effort in support of Britain.

nalistic slumming in New York, much of which she published under the title "How I Live on Three Dollars a Day": "I worked among the Polish and Russian Jews in the sweat shops, writing up the lives they led and the life I led among them. I picked over refuse with the ragpickers; made artificial flowers for the adornment of the hats of the working girls."[21] For the first time in her life as a journalist impersonating the poor, she appeared to stop posing and allowed herself to feel deep empathy with their struggles and vulnerability. But as always, she focused on the impact of her slumming on her own subjectivity.

> As the days and the weeks went on I could even feel myself growing, growing in grace, growing in charity, putting aside such narrow creeds and prejudices as had been a part of my up-bringing. . . . Life! Life! Seething life was all about

me. The life of a great city, its riches, its poverty, its sin, its virtue, its sorrows, its joyousness—there it was, and I was in it. This life was no longer like a panorama spread out for me to look at simply, to smile or weep over and then to turn away my eyes from beholding it. I entered it and, while I studied, became a part of it, learning how akin was all humanity, after all, and how large a place had environment and circumstance in the making of character and the molding of destiny.[22]

Apparently her newly discovered kinship with "all humanity" did not diminish her enthusiasm for passing harsh judgments. We get a sense of just how opinionated Banks was when she embarked on her first explicitly political work in New York in 1896. While debates about the silver standard, monetary policy, and their implications for the distribution of wealth in America captured the headlines in the 1896 presidential election, gender also played a role at the grassroots level and in the campaign rhetoric. If Republicans blasted populist women as unwomanly "harpies" in an unholy alliance with William Jennings Bryan's pro-silver forces,[23] Republican women also entered the political fray. Banks, an ardent supporter of McKinley's economic policies, combined her reporting about the living conditions of New York's vast population of aliens with her efforts to recruit votes among them for the Republican party. Her account of her work as an electioneering woman in New York opened with a harsh condemnation of suffragists: "In this paper I do not propose to treat of the Anglo-American female suffragist, who votes where she can, grumbles where she cannot, and, robed in garments as unique as they are ugly, proclaims, in strident attitude from a public platform, her desire, while she emphasises her unfitness to take part in national affairs. Of none of her I write."

By contrast, Banks then sang of the Republican Girls whose ranks she joined. In a bit of shameless self-flattery, she described the Republican Girl as a "dainty specimen of femininity, who does not want to vote, and would not if she could" but who canvasses to get votes for the man she supports. Keenly aware of Anglo-American suffrage rhetoric claiming that women, given the vote, would domesticate and moralize politics, Banks countered by extolling the more "truly feminine and womanly" strategies deployed by the Republican Girls. They stormed the slum kitchens of immigrant women laden with armfuls of potatoes and apples, which they used as props to demonstrate to the alien women how much more food they could purchase for their money if McKinley rather than Bryan were elected. Banks and her fellow Republican girls would then accidentally leave the provisions behind to enhance the family diet and swell the electoral rolls of the Republican party.[24] What Banks did not mention is that the Republican Girls' strategy in their "missionary work on the East side" of New York closely resembled her own journalistic methods in London. As the *New York Sun* reported, the members of the Women's Republican Association looked like "a lot of tramps" as they set out for the slum tenements, divested of their jewels, cash, and fine clothes. It is easy to understand not only why Banks felt so comfortable in their company, but why New York Democrats complained that the Republican Girls had feminized old-fashioned bribery rather than infusing public life with private morality.[25]

In one of Banks's first essays written in London but for an American readership, she avowed that she had "always fondly imagined that I belonged to that class of women known as the 'emancipated.'"[26] How can we reconcile this claim with her barbed description of Anglo-American suffragists? We need to keep in mind that as late as the 1890s, support for female emancipation did not always mean advocating woman suffrage.[27] In Britain, some of the most prominent champions of women's higher education and participation in local government and social reform, such as the intrepid ethnographer and explorer Mary Kingsley and the famed novelist Mary Ward, were outspoken opponents of suffrage; they feared that women would lose their ability to bring their distinctly female moral authority to the public if they were implicated in the self-serving and bellicose policies of the imperial Parliament in Westminster. All suffragists were by definition emancipated women. Not all emancipated women were suffragists, though the gap between the two narrowed considerably in the next fifteen years as the campaign for the vote became the paramount social and political issue among women. In her articles about conditions inside London's laundries, Banks went out of her way to lash out against the New Woman, for whom smoking cigarettes, riding bicycles, and adopting rational dress were emblems of freedom.[28] "Despite the fact that I live in the days of the 'new womanhood,' which demands stiff shirts, high collars, neckties, and waistcoats as proofs of complete 'emancipation,'" Banks explained, "I still hold to the belief that boiled shirts are, or should be, a man's exclusive property, and I can readily understand his objection to the 'new woman' who, in her fierce clamour for what she calls her 'rights,' will not stop to consider the wrongs she is inflicting on the opposite sex, and, not content with having, in some professions, deprived man of his means of livelihood, would now take away from him his very clothes."[29]

Banks's need to caricature New Women and suffragists and her determination to enter into politics in a way that she deemed "feminine" and "womanly" recall the central question to which she returned time and again in her writings during the 1890s: Was the profession of journalism compatible with her own vision of femininity? To answer this question, we need to put aside Banks's personal history for the moment and consider the emergence of journalism as a profession for women and the relationship between gender and journalism in the 1880s and '90s.

GENDER AND JOURNALISM

In the eighteenth and early nineteenth centuries, only a handful of women earned their livings as journalists in the United States and Britain, and few magazines and journals targetted women as readers. Most of those that did address women were part of the vast print apparatus of didactic evangelical uplift.[30] At mid-century Bessie Rayner Parkes and Barbara Smith Bodichon launched first the *English Woman's Journal* (1858–1864), and later the *Englishwoman's Review*, as a mouthpiece for their radical views. But their wealth and unconventional lives— Smith Bodichon was the illegitimate daughter of an MP (Member of Parliament) and conducted an affair with the editor of the *Westminster Review*—disqualified them as models for future women journalists in Britain.[31] The journalistic enterprises of Samuel and Isabella Beeton in the 1850s and '60s provided a much more popular and commercially oriented alternative to the *English Woman's Journal* and marked a significant expansion of female readers beyond committed sex-radicals and Evangelicals. The Beetons' *Englishwoman's Domestic Magazine* enjoined its middle-class female readers to see themselves as "active hands" that stitched and sewed; as "loving hearts" that tended family and cared for the poor; and as "erotic surfaces" which wore (or hoped to wear) the latest fashions to capture the attention of men.[32] The magazine encouraged women to create and preserve the private inner sanctum of the home, uncorrupted by the crass materialism of the age. At the same time, it was their task to fill their homes with commodities that would reflect their taste and social status.

While the Beetons' magazines and newspapers employed women in a variety of positions, it was only in the 1870s in America and the 1880s in Britain that the female journalist began to emerge as a significant member of the press. A variety of factors, some internal to the history of the press and others more broadly linked to changing roles for educated women, galvanized this expansion in the ranks of women journalists. The single most important stimulus was the explosion in the number and variety of magazines and newspapers targeting women.[33] By the 1890s, virtually all newspapers intended for general readers included sections and regular columns written by and for women.[34] Contemporaries also believed that the growing prominence of the interview as a technique for gathering news, while first popularized by men in the 1880s,[35] favored women who "naturally" possessed an abundance of precisely those traits so essential to the successful interviewer: a gift for provoking conversation larded with salient gossip, tact, charm, an eye for the details of dress and speech, and personal diplomacy.[36] British women journalists' determination to make newsrooms more open to members of their sex led by the mid-1890s to their admission to heretofore all male professional societies as well as the creation of exclusively female organizations designed to advance their professional aspirations.[37] Newly founded single-sex clubs, such as the Writers Club and the Pioneer and Women's clubs, provided institutional settings where women could earnestly debate pressing social and political issues among themselves while providing informal networks of mutual aid, advice, and introductions to young women seeking work in journalism.[38]

Aspiring female journalists at the end of the century also benefited from the general broadening of women's opportunities to engage in paid work of all sorts, ranging from medicine and nursing to social work, education, and typewriting.[39] As an anonymous reviewer of Lady Jeune's *Ladies at Work* (1893) commented in the *Spectator*, "the number of societies, leagues and bands of workers, started and managed by women shows that a great wave of energy is sweeping over the feminine world; and it is another sign of the times that women are boldly adopting professions or trades who, a generation ago, would have sat meekly at home, fading away to a colourless old age among poverty-stricken surroundings because it was thought impossible for a so-called 'lady' to soil her fingers by earning money."[40]

If various factors spurred women to seek jobs as journalists, the workplace culture of the metropolitan press, as well as its formal and informal institutional structure, continued to constrain them. In the 1860s and '70s, many male journalists in London moved in a bohemian demimonde on the fringes of polite society into which no upstanding woman would willingly enter. Leading editors and journalists like G. A. Sala, Douglas Jerrold, G. R. Sims, Edmund Yates, and James Greenwood saw themselves as members of a penurious but rakish brotherhood. While they mocked the stiff formality and stifling conventionality of London's all-male clubland—those inner sanctums of prestige, power, and wealth in Victorian Britain—they deliberately cultivated eccentric masculine personae and eventually established their own private clubs, such as the Savage, the Eccentric, and the Press Club. Theirs was an intensely and intentionally homosocial world in which independent, educated women had no role.[41]

Following the passage of the Forster Education Act mandating universal education (1870) and the Third Reform Bill enfranchising substantial numbers of laboring men (1884), the press wielded ever more political power in the 1880s and '90s by providing news to an increasingly democratized and literate electorate. Press lords regularly recruited talent from the best and brightest young male college graduates to serve as editors, reporters, and special correspondents. The consolidation of the economic and political power of the press may have been accompanied by the increasing respectability of many of its practitioners, but editorial offices more often than not remained bastions of an aggressive, rough-and-tumble masculinity. William Beveridge's path from all-male Balliol College Oxford, to the leading all-male settlement house in the slums of London, Toynbee Hall, to his position as a leader writer for the *Morning Post* was a logical progression for an ambitious young man on the make. Beveridge secured his positions through the dense network of institutional and personal affiliations linking together elite men—and the professions of journalism, law, medicine, the church, the universities, the civil service, and Parliament—in late-Victorian London.[42] He used his career in journalism to enhance his credentials as an academic social scientist and as a leading social welfare bureaucrat. Women in Britain were at best relegated to the fringes of these interlocking worlds. The structure and hierarchy of newsrooms further disadvantaged women. The lowest positions—jobs such as messengers—offered points of entry into the profession for those lacking influence and personal connections but were monopolized entirely by boys and young men.[43]

The backlash against women's growing prominence in the press was swift. The female journalist was just one of many figures in the fin-de-siècle landscape around whom a host of anxieties about gender, sexuality, degeneration, social disorder, and national identity clustered.[44] In Britain, the evangelical writer G. Holden Pike believed that journalism compelled women to "assume a bold mien" and to lose their "feminine graces" by encroaching on the province of men.[45] XYZ, an anonymous and apparently male writer for *Author*, argued that the practice of journalism unsexed a woman by compelling her to form "promiscuous acquaintances" with strange men and placing "her natural impulses of reserve and unaggressiveness in the background." The cumulative impact of female journalists was as far-reaching as it was disturbing: their influence explained the "hysterical and emasculate attitude taken up in some quarters on certain social and other questions."[46] The "unsexed" woman journalist was the janus-face of the effeminate male contributor to journals such as the *Chameleon*, the *Yellow Book* and the *Savoy*, which self-consciously experimented with representing new ideas about masculinity.[47]

Women journalists' responses to these attacks revealed their ambivalence about the gender disorder of their age and their part in its promotion. They actively defended their honor and denied that journalism was incompatible with true femininity and the cultivation of domestic graces.[48] When English women journalists wrote about the female colleagues they admired, they invariably domesticated them by describing their "womanly" appearance, manners, or taste. So in one article, "Leading Lady Journalists," we learn that the editress of the *Sunday Times*, Mrs. Frederick Beer, has "beautiful drawing rooms" and that Mrs. Humphrey, the first woman's columnist in England, is the "sweetest voiced and most graciously mannered of Irish women."[49]

The transformation of the "social" with its myriad incidents of daily life into "news" created employment opportunities and endless subjects for women journalists. By the 1890s, many persons believed that women's journalistic domain rightly consisted of the "chronicling of fashions; the recording of social functions in which celebrities and pretty dress have their part, at weddings and bazaars; the discussion of philanthropic subjects; the special interests of the factory, labouring, and toiling classes of the sex; and such topics as the education of the young, cookery, furniture, and nursing."[50] The range of women's subjects, from the frivolity of a society wedding to the hardships of laboring women's lives reflected the elasticity of Victorian separate-spheres ideology.[51] Philanthropy stood side by side with dress and cookery as arenas of feminine duty and accomplishment and as fit subjects for women journalists. All were part of the realm of the "social" to which women were expected to contribute their peculiar gifts.[52] Throughout her journalistic career, Banks proved herself the consummate chronicler of the social. In the articles she wrote as London correspondent for the *Chicago Evening Post*, she blithely moved from utterly trivial banter about the pink frock she wore to theatre to serious discussion of the public-health threat posed by tainted meat.[53]

British women journalists tried to balance their desire to glamorize the dangers of their profession, so crucial to their commercial success, with an equally urgent need to be seen as feminine women.[54] Arguably the most powerful impressario of New Journalism in London, William T. Stead insisted that the "chief foe that women have to contend with in journalism is their own conventionality." But he also insisted that "if a girl means to be a journalist she ought to be a journalist out and out, and not try to be a journalist up to nine o'clock and Miss Nancy after nine." He believed that "no editor in his senses wants either mannish women or womanish men on his staff."[55] Women journalists (and men as well), Stead insisted, had to conform to rigid sexual and gender norms while simultaneously casting off their own conventionality. Throughout her years in London, Banks strove to achieve this elusive balance between being a conventional woman and an unconventional journalist. Perhaps this explains why Stead himself was so sympathetic to her and offered her hospitality in his country home.[56] Subjected to so much criticism by English women journalists for her "horrible," "unwomanly," and "demoralizing" antics, Banks seemed to believe in the 1890s that the only way she could secure her status as a "womanly woman" was by belittling advanced women or suffragists as unwomanly.[57]

The controversies surrounding Banks's *Campaigns of Curiosity* and the emergence of the woman journalist suggest that the press not only provided a space to debate relations between the sexes and the acceptable boundaries of male and female behavior but also actively promoted such controversies to enhance its own cultural, political, and economic authority.[58] Readers and journalists alike initiated endless circles of references to each other's published views and by so doing created a world in print that transformed the terms in which men and women came to know themselves. This was the world of journalism in late Victorian London—with its limitations and opportunities—into which Banks entered and by which we can make sense of her contributions to it.

AN "AMERICAN GIRL" IMPERSONATING LONDON'S LABORING WOMEN

Throughout her life, Banks used disguises to explore not only her own identity as a woman but larger issues about gender, class, and nationality in England and America. While these themes are the explicit subject of her last novel, *School for John and Mary* (1924), and second autobiography, *The Remaking of an American* (1928), they permeate all her writings and significantly shaped how others responded to her. Banks was so successful and controversial—the two were clearly connected in her case—because her incognitos called into question what it meant to be rich and poor, a woman and a journalist, an English Lady and an American Girl. So far, I have located Banks's struggles to understand herself as a womanly woman and as journalist within fin-de-siècle discussions about women's relationship to public life and their entry into the profession of journalism. In this section, I will shift attention to several other debates to which Banks contributed: the legitimate (and illegitimate) uses of cross-class incognitos by women reporters and slum explorers; the status of the home as the cradle of social values and as a site of class conflict between mistresses and their maids; investigations conducted by female sociologists, political activists, and journalists into women's labor in the metropolis; and, finally, the American Girl and the English Lady as distinct national types.

Gender and Domesticity in Banks's Maidservant Masquerade

The same penchant for self-invention that impelled Banks to be photographed in costumes and to write two autobiographies sustained her work as an investigative journalist.[59] To understand the lives of working girls, she left the ostensibly detached and safe position of observer to share their work with them. "You can only understand the lives they [the poor] lead by becoming one of them," she explained to Marion Leslie in 1894, the interviewer sent by *Young Woman* to introduce the "real" Elizabeth Banks to girl readers in London.[60] Banks had become one of them the year before with the publication of her "Cap and Apron" series in the *Weekly Sun* from October to December 1893. She passed herself off as a household servant and offered an insider's perspective on that inexhaustible topic of conversation among the well-to-do: the servant problem. She set out to discover why the spirited but threadbare girls and young women she had met during a day of slumming in south London expressed universal contempt for domestic service. Was domestic service compatible with English love of liberty? Banks wondered.

Banks was not the first educated, respectable woman in London to don the clothes of poverty and see for herself how the other half lived.[61] There were several precedents in late-Victorian Anglo-America upon which she might have drawn. The American journalist, Annie Wakeman had launched her career in London in 1883 by writing "some clever articles on the seamy side of East End working, and other class life."[62] In the September 1888 issue of the *Nineteenth Century*, Beatrice Potter published her "Pages of a Workgirl's Diary," a vivid record of her experiences masquerading as a trouser fitter and Jewess in a sweated workshop in East London. The daughter of a wealthy capitalist, Potter was closely connected by ties of kinship and friendship to many of the leading intellectuals, social reformers, and politicians of the day. Hired by her cousin Charles Booth to assist him in researching and writing the first volume of his monumental *Life and Labour of the People in London*, she decided to supplement her statistical knowledge about Jewish sweated labor with first-hand impressions. Booth himself had indulged in similar incognito fact-finding and had even let a workman's flat in East London as his base of operations for his sociological inquiries. Unlike the more rigorously scientific account of labor practices in the East End tailoring trade that she had published one month earlier in the same periodical, Potter's essay about her incognito slumming highlighted the humanity of the workgirls and their overseer. Just as Potter ultimately preferred social scientific analysis to social work, so, too, she later dismissed her incognito investigations as a "lark." Such "romantic adventures . . . would have been of no value at all," Potter (who was now Mrs. Sidney Webb) told Sarah Tooley, the journalist from *Young Woman* sent to interview her, "without the more solid work of investigation."[63] But at the time Potter disguised herself, the distinctions between "romance" and the "solid work of investigation" were far from settled in her own mind. "For Webb,"

Deborah Nord has argued convincingly, "the project of disguise was more than sound methodology; it was also a form of psychological experiment. Through it she could reconstruct her relationship to the working class and examine her own class identity. She could also express parts of her personality that customarily lay dormant or were hidden."[64]

Banks may have been familiar with Potter's exploits,[65] but it is much more likely that she modeled herself after the outrageous journalistic campaigns undertaken by female reporters in New York in the 1880s and '90s—the so called stunt girls and sob sisters. Nellie Bly (Elizabeth Cochrane) was an international celebrity who followed up her masquerade as madwoman confined to Blackwell Island Insane Asylum (1887) by pretending to be an unwed mother in search of a baby farmer. So great was her renown that various women successfully masqueraded as Bly herself in swindling a gullible public desperate to know the "real" woman behind her many masks. Following the publication of Bly's articles in the *World*, other young women—including Viola Roseboro, Fannie Merrill, and, somewhat later, Nell Nelson—began to publish stories detailing their own horrible masquerades.[66] Banks was quick to exploit the gap between the very different conditions prevailing in London and New York for women journalists and to serve as a well-paid intermediary between them. "In England women journalists are something of an experiment," she observed. "In the United States they are a firmly established institution" whose copy was the "best, cleverest and most thorough." She explained the disparity in female journalists' status in terms of the differing conceptions of womanliness prevailing on either side of the Atlantic, in particular American women's "longing to be in the world of men, to become part and parcel of the great bustle of our large cities."[67]

If Banks's news stories in London seem staid compared to the sensational fare standard in New York by the early 1890s, we need to remember that English readers judged her *Campaigns of Curiosity* in relation to their own attitudes about money and philanthropy and according to the conventions of men's and women's incognito social investigation they knew best. The *Pall Mall Gazette*'s Autolycus unfavorably compared Banks not to American journalists such as Nellie Bly, but rather to James Greenwood and Beatrice Potter. Nor was she the only one to make this comparison. Several readers of Banks's first major success as a costumed chronicler of laboring life, her "Cap and Apron" series, likened her articles to those published by the Amateur Casual (James Greenwood) in the *Pall Mall Gazette* in January 1866. According to a sympathetic reviewer for the *Ladies Pictorial*, Banks had finally opened up for English women the style of journalism pioneered by Greenwood as an "amateur casual."[68]

How did Banks's journalistic practices compare to those of the original amateur casual, James Greenwood, and other leading undercover reporters? Greenwood was a man with a carefully crafted persona as a dandaical rake who enjoyed the privileges of walking the city streets in pursuit of its visual pleasures and erotic sensations. In the 1860s and '70s, only prostitutes had similar freedoms to roam the streets, and they did so as fetishized objects of male lust, not as seekers after their own pleasures. Male journalists like Greenwood, G. R. Sims and W. T. Stead shocked readers by making them witnesses to the scenes of depravity that were described in their articles. While Greenwood purportedly stumbled into a sodomitical fraternity of tramps, Sims used disguise to penetrate one-room slum tenements where, he suggested darkly, incest flourished. Stead played the part of a "bully" (pimp) so well in acquiring a young virgin to sell into white slavery that he was sentenced to jail for violating the very laws he sought to reform.

Banks's incognito investigations, by contrast, revealed no appalling sexual or social abuses demanding reform.[69] The master's seduction of the female servant may have been the foundational plot of the novel as a literary genre and an ubiquitous and disastrous fact of life for tens of thousands of Victorian laboring women. However, no hint of this social evil made its way into Banks's witty "Cap and Apron" series, which launched her rapid ascent in London's journalistic marketplace in 1893. Men, sex, and titillation are conspicuously absent. Why? I suspect that Banks believed that discussing sex and putting herself in sexual danger were incompatible with the delicate balance she sought to maintain between her fairly conservative vision of womanliness, the gender ambiguities of the vocation of the female journalist, and her desire for fame and fortune. Banks rightly recognized that the mainstream commercial press and its readers—her targeted audience—would not have tolerated a young, unmarried female journalist penetrating the metropolis's sexual secrets.

In place of sex, Banks's "Cap and Apron" series probed the dynamics of class and gender. Banks offered readers a mostly female world beset by petty squabbles and misunderstandings between mistresses and their servants and among servants. The first unsuspecting home that Banks infiltrated provided abundant evidence of the degrading conditions servants endured. The physical demands of carrying buckets full of hot soapy water up steep flights of stairs were incompatible with womanliness, Banks insisted. The sheer multitude of tasks and hours of labor were entirely unreasonable; servants were subjected to the vagaries of their mistresses' schedules, which often required them to stay up late into the night while awakening early the next morning to begin their daily chores. Servants were denied the comforts of a wholesome meal and a few hours of privacy. Such revelations briefly provoked the gratitude of servants across the metropolis and the wrath of their mistresses, but Banks did not bask long in the role of champion of the oppressed. After quitting her first position as a housemaid, she began to record her experiences working in a much more benevolent household. In the second half of her "Cap and Apron" series, she detailed the way servants shirked their assigned duties and took advantage of their mistresses' generosity to line their own pockets or fill their stomachs with extra portions of food and drink. Far from leading servants to a promised land of fair pay for fair labor, Banks now appeared to have betrayed the trust of her fellow workers. Banks's ostensible reversal of her sympathies on the servant question invited readers to think less about social questions and more about Banks herself as an embodiment of them.

Apparently, the educated and able women members of the Pioneer Club in London believed that Banks's two weeks disguised as a housemaid made her an expert on the subject and invited her to address them on the servant problem. They were also curious to discover what had motivated her sensational journalism. Banks wrote at least three different accounts of her reception by the Pioneer women. The first appeared in the preface to her book *Campaigns of Curiosity*, a collection of previously published newspaper and magazine articles describing her incognito investigations. Perhaps hoping to win some favorable reviews, she thanked "the women journalists of London, . . . especially . . . the members of the Pioneer and Writers' Clubs" for their kindly feelings towards her."[70] However, only a few weeks later, she confided to an interviewer that "addressing the Pioneer Club" took more out of her than any of her campaigns. The prospect of speaking to the clubwomen was so daunting that "when I got to my feet I was so weak that I should have dropped if the President had not supported me. I am not an 'advanced woman,' you know." In this ingenious and compact version of the encounter, Banks presents herself as a helpless young girl and raises the possibility that at least some members of her audience were members of that fearful species of humanity, "advanced women."[71]

In her *Autobiography*, published in 1902, Banks assumed the privilege of dramatic license by recalling—or inventing—a lengthy dialogue between herself and a Pioneer Club member, a woman writer, to explain the events of that memorable evening. The conversation hinges on the opposition between hypocrisy and honesty, self-interest and altruism, the pursuit of money and the pursuit of social good.

At that meeting a woman writer came over to me and said:—

"Now, tell me exactly, what was your aim and object—your serious one, I mean,—in going out to service and writing about it? It is a question we are all asking."

"I did it for copy," I answered; "to earn my living, you know. I knew it was a subject that would interest everybody."

I shall never forget the shocked expression on that woman's face nor fail to remember her exclamation of surprise and disgust, as she replied:—

"Copy! You mean to confess you had no philanthropic aim, that you did it for mercenary reasons, merely to earn your living?"

"Yes," I returned, looking her squarely in the face, "I'm not a hypocrite and won't pose as a reformer."

"Oh! I really never thought any journalist would sink to such a level, or make such a confession, even if it were true! I must say I have never written anything except with the object of benefiting somebody by it."

"Perhaps you have an income aside from your writing, which I have not," I answered." (95–96)

The indignant rhetoric that Banks attributed to her interlocutor suggests that more was at stake in this conversation than merely Banks's reputation as a journalist. From that evening onward, Banks claimed that some looked upon her "as a sort of journalistic pariah, outcast from the circles of the truly good and worthy female writers for the press."[72] Issues of class, gender, and national identity simmer powerfully just below the surface of this exchange. Banks positioned herself outside the middle-class comfort of an English lady by underscoring that she had no income other than what she earned through her writing. She insisted upon conceptualizing herself as a woman worker—much like the subjects of her investigations. At the same time, English lady journalists placed her outside the acceptable boundaries of bourgeois femininity. Banks, unlike other male and female investigative journalists in London, did not offer her readers the comfort of vicarious benevolence. Her refusal to "pose as a reformer" was a subtle but unmistakable criticism of the thousands of well-to-do men and women in London who, she implied, were posing as reformers and philanthropists. Banks's phrase touched a sensitive nerve in Victorian society: as the Barnardo arbitration of 1877 had revealed, there was a world of difference between posing as a reformer and being one.

Many of the *Weekly Sun's* readers, like the members of the Pioneer Club, were infuriated by Banks's frankly self-interested approach to journalism. In the first batch of letters the editor of the *Weekly Sun* published after four parts of the "Cap and Apron" series had appeared, Miss Heather Bagon of Lewisham blasted Banks's falsehoods and exaggerations and offered her own far reaching critique of gender and economic injustices in London. Bagon was appalled that Banks should profit by writing about the labors of hardworking girls: "In conclusion, let me say that I am enthusiastic enough to look forward to a time when every man will earn enough to keep his girls at home, and instead of their being set out to clean other people's houses and being bossed by professional philanthropists, who climb to public notoriety and power over their backs, and make money out of their miseries, they will stay at home and clean and decorate their own mothers' homes."[73]

Banks's lengthy reply to Bagon's charges makes clear the extent of her break with British traditions of "philanthropic" journalism (male and female alike) and became the occasion for articulating her views about slumming, domesticity, and her ideal of relations between men and women. "I wish to disclaim all pretensions to being a philanthropist, professional or otherwise," Banks declared. She refused to exalt the role of journalist as social crusader. "I am only a journalist, and I admit that a curiosity to see how the other half lives sometimes leads me to slum and investigate the condition of the poor and outcast of my own sex." She readily acknowledged that she had sold stories about the hardships of the poor, but only to keep herself alive. "I have sometimes thought it not inconsistent to go slumming with a reporter's notebook in one hand and a loaf of bread in the other." What distinguishes Banks's remark is *not* the fact that she sold her tales of slumming to support herself—after all, Greenwood was willing to enter the casual ward only because he had received a £30 advance payment from his own brother—but rather her willingness to be so open about her motives. She is the only person I encountered in researching this book who unashamedly used the word "slumming" to describe her own activities in London.

Banks also felt compelled to clarify for Bagon and her readers her views on the education of girls and domesticity. Girls, Banks contended, should be instructed only in those arts and sciences for which they were individually well suited. The mere fact of being female was no reason in itself to teach a girl to clean and decorate a home. On the other hand, Banks concluded that service could provide a safe and respectable alternative to factory labor for some girls. Banks anticipated the time when "a girl reaching a certain age shall be treated with the same consideration as her brother." "Then a man taking a wife," she concluded, "will regard her in the light of a partner with a distinct right to have the same aims and ambitions as himself, and not as a mere housekeeper and multiplier of the human race."[74]

It is hard to believe that the author of these boldly egalitarian words was the same "girl" who would soon express her disdain for "new womanhood" during her subsequent campaign disguised as a laundress. A correspondent from Dublin, E.L.S., angrily chided Banks for being an "emancipated woman" whose views of maternity "are not less gross than are those of costermonger or a corner boy." Banks was contributing to the society-wide "inversion of wise nature's laws," E.L.S. claimed, by "showing an open preference for any and every employment where [women] will mix most with men."[75] While some readers condemned Banks as a gender radical, others felt she had not gone far enough in criticizing the larger social and cultural structures that compelled one class of women—servants—to live under the tyranny of another—their mistresses. Arthur Chitty of Finsbury Park claimed that Banks had badly misunderstood the justifiable class animosity prevailing between servants and mistresses. Chitty reminded readers that servant girls were subjected to the whim of a "thousand and one jumped-up nobodies who keep servants to wait on them hand and foot." Certainly readers of the *Weekly Sun*, which included both mistresses and their female servants, would have had ample opportunity to be exposed to radical perspectives such as Chitty's. At the time the paper ran Banks's story, it also published in serial form the autobiography of the free thinking Fabian socialist Annie Besant, who had used her own inflammatory reporting for the *Link* to organize and unionize London's matchgirls in 1888, and William Tirebuck's *A Wage of Sin, The Story of a Miners' Lock Out*, a loosely fictionalized account of events transpiring during the recent "coal war."[76]

Readers' critical responses to Banks's articles and the *Weekly Sun's* readiness to print large numbers of them in its aptly named correspondence column, "The Voice of the People," illustrate that the mass press of the 1890s could and did provide a genuinely demotic—and perhaps even democratic—forum for debating social questions. An elaborate system of personal employment references called "characters," without which a servant would rarely be hired, ensured that most maids deferred to their mistresses in their daily lives. But within the pages of the letters to the editor of the *Weekly Sun*, they debated various aspects of Banks's articles with mistresses on terms of genuine equality. Some critics of the New Journalism, such as J. A. Hobson, bemoaned its exaltation of commodity capitalism and its mindless jingoism as proof of its essentially conservative impact on society. British elites across the political spectrum condemned the mediocrity and vulgarity of the New Journalism as but one of the many dangers of democracy. These criticisms certainly carried significant weight. However, Banks's journalism is a striking example of how the popular press of the 1890s and early twentieth century importantly promoted intense debates about shifting gender and sexual norms and expanded the class and gender composition of those engaged in public discussion on political and social issues.[77]

Banks had embarked on her "Cap and Apron" series with no intention of stirring up political debate. At this point in her career, she had evinced neither knowledge nor interest in politics per se. But in offering an insider's perspective on the grievances mistresses and female servants harbored against one another, she had hit upon a subject that her readers insisted was fundamentally about class and gender and bourgeois life and its discontents. It was one thing to go disguised into the slums of London and reveal abominations in Lambeth or Whitechapel to an appalled public. What Banks had done was in its own way more threatening if less daring. She had hinted—and her correspondents had amplified—that the animosities and injustices in British society as a whole were reproduced within the bourgeois home, the very space that Victorians desperately wished to believe was a queenly haven from the struggles of the masculine world. Far from domesticating politics by bringing the values of the home into the public realm, Banks's campaign proved for some readers that the home was itself a class-polarized site of strife between women.

Women Journalists Investigate Women's Labor in London

One reader of Banks's "Cap and Apron" series insisted that Banks had failed to grasp the broadest and most consequential meaning of her own findings. She signed her letter "Another Woman Journalist" and explained that she "lived for several years on a common staircase in a densely populated quarter of East London." She blasted the "present capitalist system of unlimited industrial competition," which pressed "far more hardly on women than on men." She, for one, was confident that domestic service was a "badge of slavery" and that working girls throughout London were beginning to develop a vocabulary that would allow them to articulate their grievances.[78]

Who penned this sharp-edged retort? Only a handful of women in London could have written it and all of them were part of a loosely connected group of gender and political radicals in the 1880s who made the reading room of the British Museum into their second home: Eleanor Marx (Aveling), Amy Levy, Olive Schreiner, Clementina Black, and Margaret Harkness among them. By 1893, Levy had committed suicide and it seems improbable that either Marx or Schreiner would have described herself as a journalist. The most likely author is either the female trade unionist, Clementina Black, or the sometime socialist and Salvationist Margaret Harkness. Black and Harkness, like Banks herself, were unmarried, educated women who depended upon their journalism and novel-writing to help support themselves. But in marked contrast to Banks, these women were less preoccupied with their own earnings than in fighting for social and economic justice for their working-class sisters. We can more fully appreciate Banks's contributions to late Victorian debates over women's work in the metropolis by comparing them, first with Black's and then with Harkness's own slum journalism and social investigations.[79]

Black was born into the professional middle class, but family misfortunes denied her many of its material and psychological comforts. The ill health of her solicitor father and the death of her mother left Black saddled with a large family and compelled her to contribute to her own maintenance as a teacher and, later, as a writer. Living in London with two of her sisters in the early 1880s, Black combined fiction writing with immersion in the history, sociology, and economics of women's labor.[80] Such knowledge served her well in her frequent conversations with Karl Marx's ailing wife and daughter in London and provided the empirical foundations for her writings and political activism as a leader of the Women's Protective and Provident League (eventually renamed the Women's Trade Union League).[81] In March 1893, just six months before Banks embarked on her "Cap and Apron" series, Black adopted the "point of view of the servant" and wrote "The Dislike to Domestic Service," an essay in the *Nineteenth Century*, a highly respected periodical that Banks certainly read once she moved to London and to which she later contributed.[82] Black emphasized the moral and sexual dangers of removing laboring girls and young women from their families and isolating them from their peers. "There are too many households," she warned, "in which an unprotected girl is liable to temptation and insults from which she would be safe in most factories and workshops." Most of the girls she met at homes and refuges for fallen women had once been servants, she grimly reported.[83] Black returned to the evils of domestic service at the International Congress of Women a few years later, where she characterized it as a vestige of feudalism, as tyrannical as it was inefficient.[84] While Black never called herself a socialist, she located her account of domestic service—and each of the other female industries about which she wrote—within an overarching framework of relations between labor and capital.

The studies of female labor that Black published in socially progressive, specialized venues such as the *Economic Journal* were, not surprisingly, much more sociologically precise and politically engaged than the articles Banks wrote for mass consumption in the popular press.[85] But the demands of editors and the expectations of readers cannot explain why Banks and Black took such different approaches in their respective contributions about women and work to the same middle-brow periodical, the *English Illustrated Magazine*. Banks and Black wrote their articles in informal prose interlaced with first-person authorial asides ("I trust" or "I had been told") that were closely identified with the confidential and friendly "voice" adopted by so many women journalists. Banks, like Black, incorporated the methods and some of the language of sociology into her journalism. However, Banks's article in the *English Illustrated Magazine* on her experiences disguised as a crossing sweeper provides very little information about the trade beyond sweeps' belief in their right to protect their territory from competitors. Instead, we learn a great deal about Banks's feelings: "People walked on my crossing, but nobody offered me payment. . . . I began to despise them, and in my heart, I called them paupers, to patronise my crossing and not be willing to pay for the privilege."[86] Banks limited her intervention into the sweeping trade by criticizing the ineffectiveness of the system of licensing sweeps (at a cost to the sweep of 5 shillings per year) and by reminding Londoners that sweeps deserved payment for their labors.

Black's *English Illustrated Magazine* essay "Match-Box Making at Home" combined personal observations about her encounters with working women with rigorous analysis of statistical information. Her piece offers a detailed picture of each stage of the labor process and a careful accounting of the time and cost involved in making matchboxes. What begins as a description of a "pretty enough spectacle" of women cheerfully and nimbly assembling matchboxes turns subtly but unmistakably into condemnation of a system that pays the most efficient worker only 1 shilling 3½ pence for fifteen hours of labor a day. Black's rhetoric is measured, her tone friendly and polite; however, she used her article to summarize the tempestuous history of labor relations in the industry and drive home to readers the radical demand that sweated homeworkers join ranks with their unionized sisters working in factories.[87]

While Banks's treatment of crossing sweeps was lighthearted and lightweight, she sometimes ventured into more substantive and politically charged terrain. Well aware that twenty to thirty thousand men and women had gathered in Hyde Park to demand state regulation of the laundry industry just the year before her arrival in London,[88] Banks disguised herself as a laundress to provide an insider's exposé of the industry. Playing the part of both lady customer and woman worker, she literally followed her own clothes from her home to their destination at a large East London steam laundry. The articles she wrote about her experiences as a laundress come closer than anything else she ever wrote to the sociological rigor characteristic of Black's writings on female labor. Banks noted distinctions in the levels of skill and wages among different workers. Ironers occupied the upper rung of the hierarchy, earning up to 3 shillings, 6 pence per day, while the girls who put towels and linens into the ironing machine received the lowest wages of 3 to 6 shillings per week. She reported that girls and women at the laundry were fully and intelligently engaged in the debate over the Factory Act.[89] Banks also encouraged readers to question their own preconceptions about relations between labor and capital by praising and criticizing in equal measure both workers and managers. She had gone to the laundry expecting to meet girls and women who were "the most wicked of their sex" (159), but instead she found diligent, respectable, and friendly workers only too willing to lend a hand in teaching her their trade. Banks's admiration for the owner's relentless hard work and amiable relations with her workers did not mute Banks's criticisms of conditions prevailing at the laundry: the failure to fence off dangerous equipment such as the hydroextractor and the absence of any system to ventilate foul smelling steam. The laundry may have endangered the health of the women workers but, Banks concluded, it posed absolutely no threat to its customers.

Banks acknowledged the political stakes involved in women's work in the laundry, but she did so to make her copy more attractive to editors. Banks, unlike Black, refused to play a partisan role in the debate over regulating laundries. In her articles, workplace hazards at the laundry matter a great deal less than her readiness to place herself in harm's way in pursuit of a story. She repeatedly underscored that she was far too feminine and delicate to succeed at the arduous physical tasks required of her: after only three hours labor "I was so tired, I could hardly stand," she confided to her readers. "I had several times burned my fingers and once nearly fallen against the stove."[90] The frisson produced by reading Banks's incognito slumming adventures in the laundry derived entirely from the way she forced her readers to imagine their author—a petite, young, lady journalist—engaged in distinctly unladylike occupations.

Like Banks and Black, Harkness wrote extensively on the status of servants, matchbox makers, and factory girls in her slum novels of the 1880s and in her contributions to a sprawling series on young men's and young women's work published by the progressive Christian paper, the *British Weekly* in 1887 and 1888.[91] The editors of the series insisted that "we shall have nothing for the lover of the prurient—no directory to hell—nothing but what may be read in any family." However, it is not clear precisely what sort of family the editors had in mind because roving special commissioners escorted readers into "dingy, dirty, promiscuous gambling, dancing and betting" clubs and reprinted desperate letters written by neurasthenic men and hapless masturbators victimized by blackmailers.[92] Harkness's relationship to the *British Weekly*'s series is a complicated one, all the more because we know so little about it. We know with certainty that she contributed to the first series, "Tempted London: Young Men" and edited the second series, "Toilers in London: or, Inquiries Concerning Female Labour in the Metropolis." She also served as one of the many "commissioners" hired to gather social facts and interview men and women about the wide range of social, sexual, and economic issues covered in the series. Vexed that Charles Booth had not selected her to serve as one of his lady assistants in compiling the first volumes of his social survey of East London, Harkness found in the *British Weekly* an alternative way to support herself though the work of observing and representing the city.[93] She also found a vast storehouse of empirical data and human dramas, which she wove freely into her fictions.

Just as Banks took great liberties with facts in her writings, so, too, Harkness flagrantly dissolved the boundaries between journalistic facts and novelistic fictions. She incorporated not only many of the themes but lifted entire vignettes from the columns of the *British Weekly* series which she placed verbatim into her slum novels published under the nom de plume, John Law: *Out of Work*, *City Girl*, and *Captain Lobe*. Readers of the *British Weekly* sometimes encountered the same stories twice—first as a nonfictional piece of investigative journalism in *Tempted London*, and then, a few weeks later, as an installment of Harkness's novel about the slum work of the Salvation Army, *Captain Lobe*, which was itself serialized in the *British Weekly*. Harkness, like Black, aided Annie Besant in the industrial dispute between matchgirls and their employer, Bryant and May, in the summer of 1888.[94] In the weeks leading up to the resolution of the strike in mid-July 1888, the *British Weekly* ran an impressive set of unsigned articles, most likely written by Harkness, analyzing the structure and economics of the match trade and its impact on women workers. In the very same issue in which the *British Weekly* reported the triumph of the matchgirls, Harkness celebrated the solidarity of unskilled women workers by taking readers of her novel *Captain Lobe* on a sympathetic tour of a squalid room doubling as home and workshop of a family of sweated matchbox workers.[95]

The rebellious and disaffected daughter of a cash-strapped country rector, Harkness's grip on economic security and social respectability was even more tenuous than Banks's and Black's.[96] Forever trying on and taking off new religious and political beliefs (Salvationism, trade unionism, socialism) and subject to "morbid" and "hysterical" musings,[97] she was an outspoken, unsettled, and unsettling figure in the philanthropic landscape of late Victorian London. Harkness confessed in 1875 that she did not "thoroughly understand" "love or passion between the sexes" which "must exist in such different degrees in different constitutions." She loathed the "idea of marriage" for herself and preferred instead to eke out a precarious livelihood as an unmarried nurse, journalist, and novelist.[98] While Harkness evinced little interest in sex in her private life, she argued that it was a volcanic albeit sinister force shaping the daily ebb and flow of the metropolis.[99] The *British Weekly* articles, taken together, demonstrated how the constant influx of youths from the countryside into the anonymous city combined with the absence of social networks once provided by churches, kin, and friends led directly to sexual degradation and despair. Harkness's novel *Out of Work* retold the same story in human terms by tracing the inexorable path to death by starvation of the Christlike carpenter Jos Coney, who journeys from the countryside to London. In both her journalism and novels, the minotaur-like metropolis consumed young men and women drawn to it by the glittering but illusory promise of high wages, steady work, and new sorts of personal freedom. Hunger, unregulated sexuality, and sin are the by-products of capitalism unchecked by Christian principles in Harkness's bleak vision of the city.

While Banks altogether disclaimed philanthropy in her journalistic slumming, Harkness advanced a withering critique of it. In Harkness's writings, the philanthropic impulse is symptomatic of underlying psychosexual pathology, an unnatural "disease of caring about the sorrows of the world."[100] Men's altruism is merely a convenient cover for the expression of illicit erotic desires. Each of the case studies of women's work in the *British Weekly* series demonstrated that low wages led great numbers of laboring women to exit respectable society through the "door of escape" always open to members of their vulnerable sex and class: prostitution.[101] Drawing on critiques of male impurity so effectively publicized by Josephine Butler in her campaigns for the repeal of the Contagious Diseases Act,[102] Harkness revealed the hypocrisy of bourgeois gentlemen, whom she portrays as either sexual predators or gender dissidents. Her bitter 1887 slum novel, *City Girl*, revolves around the seduction of a beautiful East End Catholic girl, Nelly Ambrose, by a West End philanthropist, Arthur Grant, treasurer of a nearby hospital for poor women and children. Grant's callous sexual exploitation of Nelly is matched by the way her employers, owners of a sweatshop, ruthlessly exploit her labor.[103]

The *British Weekly* and Banks both investigated the wages and conditions of labor of watercress girls and flower girls—beside prostitutes, the most ubiquitous class of unchaperoned women workers walking London's street until the 1880s. Charitable agencies had directed their missionary gaze to flower and watercress girls in London at least since the 1850s in part because, as Carolyn Steedman argues, "the connection between flower and cress selling and prostitution was very easily made."[104] The *British Weekly*'s female commissioner found no romance but lots of squalor in flower girls' struggles to survive. The commissioner took her readers into a flower girl's sordid room whose sole furnishing consisted of "a four-post bedstead on which was a filthy mattress and an old torn blanket" and a "dirty yellow apron" stretched across the cracked glass of the window. After elaborating on the nuances of procuring, cleaning, and marketing flowers and watercress, the commissioner concluded that for every flower girl who "rises in life high enough to possess a [lucrative] whelk business, ten sink under the demoralizing influence of street-life" and turn to vice.[105]

Banks was drawn to impersonate a flower girl because of the incongruity between the beauty and innocence of the wares the girls sold—their flowers—and their own unkempt and vicious appearances. Like the *British Weekly* commissioner, Banks recounted the system used by the girls to procure their wares from Covent Garden as well as their hours of labor, their expenses, and income. But whereas the *British Weekly* used its detailed account of the lives of particular flower girls to force readers to confront their physical misery and moral danger, Banks used her exposé to suggest new and more fetching ways for the girls to arrange their wares in their baskets. While Banks observed that many of the flower girls she met had lost "all semblance of womanly modesty" and indulged in "obscene and profane talk," she did not directly connect their demoralized condition to her conclusion that no flower girl could honestly earn more than eighteen shillings a week.

Banks astutely recognized that debates over protective labor legislation, the rapid influx of sweated immigrant labor, and the growth of women's trade unionism had stimulated the British public's appetite for stories about women's labor in London. For radical and socialist women such as Black, Harkness, and their mutual friend Annie Besant, publishing the results of their inquiries was an effective instrument for exposing and also mobilizing protest against the endemic abuses of capitalism, in particular the ruthless commodification of women's labor. Banks, in contrast, participated fully in late Victorian commodity culture and transformed her own slumming into print so that she could sell it. Banks skillfully mimicked the form—though a good bit less of the substance—of the discipline of empirical sociology as practiced by that pioneering cohort of women experts on female labor including Black and Beatrice Potter. But Banks's interest in women's work and her analysis of it were always subordinated to her needs as a popular woman journalist. In notable contrast to Black and Harkness, she avoided political controversy and refused to acknowledge the interconnection between prostitution, the structure of women's wages, and the labor market. Banks presented her findings largely through descriptions of what she herself did, felt, and saw in her various assumed roles. Her method of collecting data and her style in presenting it combined to produce an intensely personal sociology in which the self and the social are purposely intermingled.

The American Girl versus the English Lady

Banks's motives for her journalistic slumming—producing copy to sell to newspapers and magazines—confirmed what many Londoners already suspected. Americans put money before morals. Rudyard Kipling, in an essay he published in the *Times* of London in December 1892, condemned the "indecent restlessness" of American society, its ostentation, and its obsessive worship of "Baal of the Dollars." American women were "worn out" and "go to pieces very readily." (Presumably, Kipling believed he had rescued his own American wife, Carrie Balestier, from such an unappealing fate.) American men, Kipling snidely observed, sacrificed their gentility to the single-minded pursuit of business. More damningly, they allowed their wives to form the rank and file of the "the pauper labour of America." Unlike English ladies, who commanded armies of sixteen-pound-a-year-household servants, American women performed their own household chores.[106]

A few days later, the *Times* published Banks's vigorous defense of American national character and American women under the caption, "An American Girl's Reply to Mr.Kipling." It was an auspicious debut for an unknown American which touched in passing upon many of the themes she would develop in depth in the months and years ahead.[107] In her series, "The Almighty Dollar in London Society," published in the conservative and clubby *St. James's Gazette* between January 10 and 16, 1894, Banks responded to Kipling's denigration of American materialism thirteen months earlier. She brilliantly exposed the hypocrisy of English men and women who professed disdain for American money while scheming to get some of it for themselves. Posing as an American heiress, Banks advertised in the papers for a "chaperone of highest social position" to "introduce her into the BEST ENGLISH SOCIETY." More than eighty ladies and gentlemen replied, each demanding a substantial payment for his or her services. As one of the *Gazette*'s headlines emphasized, Banks had shown "the market value of high social position." Given the prominent attention society-page editors paid to matches between such American heiresses as Jennie Jerome and Consuela Vanderbilt with cash-poor English nobles and the growing fear that American women were outpacing English ladies in making attractive marriages with the cream of English masculine society, few readers would have had difficulty appreciating the extent of the American Girl's triumph. Banks's *Campaigns* were at least partly an extension of her debate with Kipling over national identity as expressed through ideas about class and gender in England and America. She had challenged one of the most cherished and deeply institutionalized beliefs about English life: that class position could not crudely be equated with wealth because its essence lay out of reach of the marketplace in the world of long-inculcated cultural norms and social behaviors.

Banks's "mercenary" approach to journalism and her refusal to disguise herself as a philanthropist were hallmarks of her persona as the

American Girl in London. They suggested that the American Girl was as brazenly "almighty" as the American Dollar. Why were her efforts linked in the English imagination to the particular traits of the American Girl?

Some English commentators attributed Banks's wild behavior as a journalist to the promiscuous freedoms of the American Girl so brilliantly depicted by Henry James's eponymous Daisy Miller. Banks's readers had quickly discerned from her use of colloquialisms that the authoress of the "Cap and Apron" series was an American. The day after the *St. James's Gazette* published the final installment of "The Almighty Dollar in London Society," one of the paper's regular columnists compared the freedoms of English and American women. The author ruefully remarked that "some of us were under the impression that the English girl had got about as far along the plank of freedom as was desirable" until American journalists in New York had begun to complain about the suffocating system of chaperonage in England.[108] In particular, English observers complained that the "untrammelled" freedom of American college girls was producing a generation of hysterics and anorexics who pursued their own selfish desires in defiance of the biological obligations of their sex.[109] Gertrude Atherton put the question quite simply to readers of Annie Swan's *The Woman at Home*: "How far has the (suppositious) American girl influenced the English girl of the present generation?" Her answer: the revolt of the modern English girl may well be the consequence of "the invasion of the American maiden, both in fact and in fiction."[110] Just as several English "lady" journalists criticized Banks for introducing American style female journalism to London and degrading the moral tone of the English press, so, too, some feared the consequences of the Americanization of the English Lady by the American Girl.

This fear was compounded by several factors. First, many already shared Matthew Arnold's view that New Journalism was itself a "featherbrained" American import intended to pander to the degraded tastes of the newly enfranchised democracy.[111] Second, Londoners daily confronted unmistakable evidence that at least parts of the metropolis had fallen under the sway of erstwhile colonial subjects and other outsiders: Jews, Indians, Africans, Italians, Australians, and Americans.[112] Banks's reversal of the prerogatives of empire—her descents among the London poor disguised as one of them—was part and parcel of the larger threat of the Americanization of London and metropolitan culture in the late nineteenth century. In an article Banks contributed to *Living London*, which was edited by her friend, G. R. Sims, she detailed the visible signs of this process. Buoyed by a population of American expatriates exceeding twenty thousand and many more tourists, London merchants, hoteliers, restaurateurs, and even bankers vied for the American trade. Billboards and advertisements welcomed American customers. American flags festooned whole blocks of Piccadilly and Regent Street. Restaurants served Boston-style pork and beans while English shops were jammed full with American-made consumer goods and recipes. All of these things were materials signs of America's growing economic and military might, which made it such an attractive outlet for British capital investment while also portending Britain's relative decline as the paramount world power in the years ahead. Without a trace of irony, Banks noted that "with its good points and its bad ones," American journalism had become a permanent part of the London press. "Some papers being 'run' on the American plan, it of course, follows that the importation of American journalists has become a necessity, so all along Fleet Street American journalists can be seen at any hour of the day, and almost any hour of the night as well, flying hither and thither." Banks, with uncharacteristic modesty, offers no hint of the part she played in this transformation of the English press.[113]

The American Girl did have plenty of English defenders and admirers, and not only among the growing community of Anglo-American suffragists and women's activists. If Kipling had belittled the American woman as a nervous drudge, others admired her self-sufficiency and mental quickness. Mrs. H. R. Haweis, wife of a slum clergyman and music aesthete and herself a pioneer in interior decoration, contributed a story to the *Young Woman* in January 1894 extolling the virtue of the American girl as a "bright, self-helpful creature . . . well educated, but not a prude."[114] Discussion of the virtues and vices of American and English women briefly became the subject of a heated and amusing transatlantic debate in the early autumn of 1896 spurred on by London and New York journalists quick to recognize a good story. The initial salvo in this entirely press-created furore was fired by an American woman in London who insisted on the superiority of English men over American, and American women over their English counterparts. A wittily vituperative essay by an Australian man published in the October 1896 number of the *Contemporary Review* provided a common point of reference for readers on both sides of the Atlantic and throughout the empire. The author contended that the status of women in any given nation or civilization was the most accurate barometer of its well-being. American women were lamentably deficient in "self-sacrifice, devotion, trustfulness, gentleness, tenderness, delicacy, a high sense of duty, singleness of purpose." As "the most finished product of the democratic principle" in action, they were "the most unconsciously selfish beings on the face of the earth," obsessed with claiming rights and disavowing their duties.[115] Needless to say, such outrageous remarks provided abundant material for the proliferation of dissenting and assenting views in the metropolitan presses of New York and London. The *New York Sun*, playing on the inflammatory rhetoric of imperialism, ran a headline announcing that the whole world had declared "War On American Women."[116]

Here was a print controversy as perfectly tailored to Banks as the stylish suits she favored. Her published contributions to this debate reflected her ambivalence about her status as the American Girl in London, which in turn mirrored her surprisingly critical assessment of the American-style investigative journalism she herself had championed. Forever putting on disguises, she found herself constantly reevaluating English and American gender ideologies and social values. At the outset of the controversy, Banks found an unlikely champion of the American Girl in the great Chinese minister, Li Hung Chang, famous for his suppression of the Taeping Rebellion and his cooperation with Britain's greatest imperial martyr, "Chinese" Gordon. During the minister's highly publicized diplomatic visit to London (and shortly thereafter to the United States) in the summer and autumn of 1896, Banks had secured the first interview with him by brazenly camping outside his residence during the breakfast hour. She had demanded that Li Hung Chang weigh in on the international question of utmost importance: the relative merits of American and English womanhood. The "wily Chinaman" (the phrase is Banks's) had obliged by declaring "the most beautiful and clever women in all the world are the American women." Needless to say, Banks basked not only in the glory of his praise for American women but in her headline-grabbing scoop. By the time she had arrived in New York a few weeks later, she herself captured headlines as the "wee mite" of an American woman who had dared to interview Li Hung Chang.[117]

For the next few weeks, Banks gladly stepped forward as New York's chief expert on Anglo-American gender politics. Playing the part of cultural interpreter and intermediary she had mastered during her previous four years in London, Banks offered comparisons between the sexes of each nation. English women were not up to date but she envied the "sweet, low, well modulated tone" of their voices and their unobtrusive skills as hostesses. English women lacked the independence, vivacity, originality, and conversational daring of American women; they put their husbands before their children, whom they left to nurses to raise; they not only had chaperons but appeared to need them.[118] English men possessed calm and "Old World courteousness and devoted much less of their daily lives to pursuing wealth compared to American men. But their attractiveness was marred by their blatant favoritism of sons over daughters. American men took pride in educating their daughters.[119] Banks praised the extensive network of women's colleges in America, many of which allowed girls from poor families to perform domestic work and housekeeping in exchange for tuition. Banks herself had spent four hours a day polishing silver and china during her years as a student while mingling on the basis of perfect equality with her wealthier peers. In England, only a girl with some means could afford to go to Cambridge women's colleges such as Girton and Newnham, unless, by dint of exceptional intellectual prowess, she won a highly competitive scholarship. The manual labor Banks performed at college was incompatible with what it meant to be young lady in England. For Banks, the differences between the two systems threw into sharp relief the benefits of American democracy and the limitations of the English class system in shaping the character of women in the two countries.[120]

However, Banks also found much to criticize about the American Girl. In an article introducing her as the American Girl two years before the Anglo-American war of the sexes, Banks had played the part of the English critic. "I can always tell an American girl here [in London] directly I see her. . . . She is louder, and talks more; her bump of reverence is not so large as an English girl's." "I admire the quietude and modesty of your girls very much," she continued, "but they might be all the better for a little of our smartness."[121] During her years in New York, she wrote many articles under the byline "The Englishwoman in New York." She clearly enjoyed the perverse symmetry of the situation. When she returned to London in 1898 after two years as a yellow journalist in New York, she concluded without a hint of irony that England was "blessed" not to have a yellow press.[122]

The entire splendidly silly debate illustrates just how central a role the metropolitan press in Britain and America played in encouraging men and women to think aloud about gender issues. There were literally dozens of other such controversies on topics relating to marriage, "revolting daughters," "what is unwomanly," and "what is unmanly." Newspapers were as deeply invested in "newness" as they were in "news." Enterprising editors like W. T. Stead and reporters like Banks soon figured out that "newness" was "news" and that both could be fabricated rather than found. In a lengthy 1897 review essay on recent works of British literature as expressions of the "psychology of feminism," Hugh Stutfield noted that some believed fin-de-siècle decadence was merely "journalistic froth—just as the New Woman was said to be solely a creation of the comic newspapers." Whatever their origins, Stutfield was sure that social facts could no longer be separated from journalistic and literary fictions. The "morbid" propensity of modern writers of novels, magazines, and newspapers to wash "domestic dirty linen" in public had widened "the breach between men and women."[123] By making gender into the subject of public debate, editors and their staffs of men and women reporters made it difficult for readers to assume that what it meant to be a man or a woman was simply a preordained fact of nature. No one understood better the cash value of debating gender in print than Banks, who coupled her gender anxieties as a woman reporter with debates about American and English national character. These two issues recurred over and over as the underlying subject of each of her investigations into "how the other half lives."

Banks returned to the subject of the college girl in her most provocative and poignant incognito, one requiring neither make up nor costume. In 1899, she decided to investigate the policies of women's colleges in England and the United States toward mulatto women by pretending (at least in writing) to be one with light hair, blue eyes, and fair skin. Banks's fictive applicant concluded each letter with a confession that she was stained by a small amount of the blood of the African race. Her reason for writing, she explained to each college administrator, was to seek not only a place alongside the other girls in the classroom but in the dormitory as well.[124]

Banks had puzzled over race matters for many years before undertaking this inquiry. In Peru, she had been amazed by the depth and extent of racial mixing between people of African, Indian, Spanish, and Chinese descent. Miscegenation produced a wide array of racial types whose skin ranged from "alabaster to ebony."[125] As a reporter in Baltimore, she had disliked the unchivalrous attitudes of black men to white women, which violated her deeply engrained sense of how all men should treat all women. She had rejoiced when a white Southerner had thrashed a black man who had not yielded his seat to her on a crowded omnibus. Her African-American cook Dinah rivaled her poodle, Judge, as the most significant character (beside herself) in her *Autobiography*. Dinah remains a one-dimensional foil to her mistress, who never allows her to escape from prevailing white American stereotypes of African-Americans. Dinah's singing is melodious but unthinking; she is intensely loyal but stupid. Banks's portrait of Dinah and their relationship with one another is affectionately condescending and deeply racist.

What did Banks learn about Britain and America in the course of her literary imposture as a mulatto woman? To her astonishment she discovered that no college in America whose population was predominantly white would permit her to live among the other girl students as an equal. Even Oberlin College, renowned for its progressive views on race and gender, directed her to a boardinghouse run by a "a refined, Christian mulatto woman." English colleges, by contrast, happily offered her an equal place among its white girl students.[126] In Banks's analysis, race throws into doubt the opposition between the American Girl and the English Lady, between freedom and equality in America and "caste" or class in England.

The results of Banks's literary impersonation as a mulatto woman might suggest that she had decided to fight for the rights of Black American women. Such was not the case. Her discussion of the mulatto college girl was hidden in the midst of a much longer article entitled "The American Negro and His Place." Banks wrote the article to refute the charges of "a young coloured woman, a Miss Ida Wells" and to convince Britons that their sympathy for Southern blacks was misplaced. She openly defended lynching which, she claimed, "is seldom appealed to except in regard to questions that are more fitly settled at the point of a shot-gun than in the courts, notwithstanding the sensational reports that are continually being telegraphed to England." She compared the hypocritical but empty posturing of Northerners who envisioned no place for the Negro in their midst, to the admirable honesty of the Southerner. Alone among Americans, the Southerner really "understands the negro and likes him in his place." The article ended with a gloomy prediction that has often seemed all too true for much of the history of twentieth-century Britain: should the Negro come in large numbers to Britain, there "would be found no 'place' for him."[127]

Perhaps we should not be surprised that thirteen years after writing these words we encounter Banks strolling the streets of London jammed between two stiff boards advertising an upcoming women's suffrage meeting and blithely concurring with a friend that lynching was a shameful blot on American history. Her moving autobiography *The Remaking of an American* published in 1928, chronicled her path toward a whole-hearted embrace of American democracy which, she argued, compelled her to accept the core beliefs of the women's suffrage movement. By 1908 she had become an active member of the Women Writers' Suffrage Association,[128] and from 1911 onward, introduced feminist themes to the *Referee* as Enid, the sole female columnist for the paper. Remarkably, her second autobiography left no traces of her earlier deprecation of suffrage and the "advanced woman" and her idiosyncratic but virulent racism.

Banks's transatlantic peregrinations may have been motivated by an inner restlessness, but they were also crucial to her journalistic and financial successes. Her need to move across literal and figurative boundaries and social identities suggests that rather than attempting to resolve the tensions between rich and poor, women workers and their employers, American freedom and English order, she made a profession of writing about them. Banks always defined herself as an outsider whose gifts of disguise and mimicry allowed her to penetrate the secrets of her host locales—Lima, London, and New York; upper-middle-class households,

East London laundries, slum tenements in New York. As an outsider, she claimed to be able to see, describe, and satirize those habits of thought and conventions of behavior that people living within a society took for granted as natural. At the time Banks first ventured to England, women journalists in New York had considerably more license than their London counterparts to move through metropolitan space and report on what they saw and did. Whatever the social and political reality, both Britons and Americans described American women as more independent and emancipated than English women. New Yorkers openly celebrated their culture of commerce and the possibilities for social mobility that it supposedly offered newcomers whereas ambitious Londoners aspired to wedding the capitalist pursuit of profit with the deferential ethos and social exclusivity of the gentleman and gentle lady. All of these factors seem to suggest that as a free-spirited independent woman lacking money and social connections, Banks ought to have remained in New York where she would have been at home. But Banks abandoned the familiar comforts of home as a site of female domesticity and self-definition. From the moment she arrived in Britain, she exploited clichéed perceptions of difference between New York and London, America and England. She constructed her public persona as the paradigmatic American Girl whose defiance of English social and gender conventions could always be explained—and partially excused—in terms of her "American-ness." Similarly, her pose as an English woman in New York allowed her to put on foreign spectacles in her native land and see it through the eyes of an outsider.[129]

CONCLUSION

An anonymous reviewer of Banks's *Autobiography of a Newspaper Girl* for the *Nation* claimed that "the future historian of nineteenth century journalism will obtain more light from the story of Miss Banks's career than from many more pretentious volumes, especially through the contrasts it presents between the pursuit of this profession in London and New York."[130] While I concur with this assessment, I have demonstrated that Banks's career sheds light on a great deal more than the history of metropolitan journalism. Two things stand out most vividly about Banks's cross-class masquerades and the persona she crafted in her journalistic slumming. First, in marked contrast to James Greenwood's "A Night in a Workhouse," gender not only trumps sex but erases any trace of it in Banks's urban reporting. Banks style was playful but never coy or titillating. To preserve her public image as a feminine and respectable woman, Banks kept sex out of the stories she wrote about herself and her experiences among the poor. Her reticence about sex, I have argued, re-flected the contradictory tensions "lady" journalists negotiated in their daily lives as they moved through urban space in pursuit of copy, worked within male-dominated editorial offices, and courted wide readerships in the popular press. I have also suggested that the particularities of Banks's biography as an unmarried woman lacking familial support account in part for the notable absence of an erotic dimension in the articles she wrote about her incognito slumming. When she first arrived in London the early 1890s, she consciously chose not to identity herself with the community of independent, educated "spinsters," whose immersion in the dirt, sexual dangers, and pleasures of urban life forms the subject of my next chapter. Her "novelty" and that of the "news" she generated de-pended on her self-chosen role as an intermediary between the unwom-anly and the feminine, the subversive and the decorous, hidden abuses and surface appearances.

In writing and rewriting her life story in every text she authored, Banks transformed the instabilities of gender itself into a print commod-ity which she sold to editors and readers on both sides of the Atlantic. Banks understood that editors valued the services of lady journalists be-cause they produced copy for consumption by the widening audience of male and female readers in late Victorian London. Banks owed part of her success to the clever way she marketed herself and her anxieties about reconciling her womanhood with her journalism. To put this in more general terms, the debate about women journalists conducted in print ultimately benefited the business interests of newspapers and their "reporteresses" because it produced more copy and provided free adver-tising for the goods they sold to the public. At a time when the great re-tail palaces of London and New York strove to be the secular cathedrals of the age, women journalists like Banks and her rival, Autolycus of the *Pall Mall Gazette,* played the part of high priestesses. Autolycus's col-umn, appropriately named "The Wares of Autolycus," guided readers as they navigated the crowded marketplaces of the metropolis. While Clementina Black and Margaret Harkness also helped to support them-selves by selling their literary representations of women's work and slum life to magazines and newspapers, they positioned themselves as critics rather than celebrants, of commodity capitalism. And, in contrast to Banks, neither woman aspired to being a "lady" journalist. Banks's jour-nalism effectively linked together and sold her first-hand explorations of social questions whose interest lay less in their revelation of social abuses than in their witty depiction of the dilemmas of bourgeois femininity at the fin-de-siècle.

Second, Banks vehemently refused to cloak her reporting under the mantle of altruism. The *Pall Mall Gazette* reviewer of Banks's *Cam-*

paigns of Curiosity complained that her methods were "quite a question of literary ethics" and asked, "Is it not a flagrant case of the misdemeanour of obtaining *copy* [my emphasis] under false pretences."[131] The key word here is "copy." Most Victorians happily applauded the good deeds of philanthropists, sociologists, and even journalists who braved the horrors of workhouses and common lodging houses as a way to express Christian love, to uplift the fallen, to rectify an abuse, or acquire sociological knowledge. Banks did none of these things. She rejected utterly not only the philosophical premises of James Hinton, who insisted that eros abetted altruism, but also the reformers' and philanthropists' justification for their supposedly self-denying efforts on behalf of the poor. She unashamedly announced to all who would listen that her costumed adventures among London's laboring poor were motivated by her need to sell the fruits of her literary labors on the most favorable terms she could negotiate. In acknowledging the self-interested nature of her slumming, Banks forced Londoners to think about their determined disavowal of slumming as a social practice.

Banks's reinvention of herself from a snide critic of women's suffrage into an active suffragist in the first decade of the twentieth century was a sign of the growing acceptability of suffrage as a mainstream position among women in Britain and America before World War I. This in turn reflected the movement's success in controlling public representations of their supporters as womanly and sane, rather than mannish and hysterical.[132] Banks and many other woman journalists in London probably would not have recognized their own contributions to that sea change in perceptions about what women could—and could not—do that importantly laid the foundations for the expansion of the movement's rank and file. Banks was part of a much larger group of educated women in the 1880s and '90s whose economic and social aspirations led them to challenge existing restrictions on women in a wide range of traditional and newly emerging professions without consciously seeking to advance the political emancipation of their sex. Such women have largely failed to attract the interest of scholars precisely because they do not fit neatly into a heroic narrative about women's struggle for full citizenship.

It is easy to sympathize with Banks's desire in 1928 to rewrite her past, but we would be mistaken to play the part of her accomplice. Her career in the 1890s as an expatriate American in London and as an American woman passing for an English lady in New York captures an important albeit anxious moment in the histories of slumming, urban social reporting, and the women's movement. She forged her identity as a female journalist within the interstices of debates about poverty and urban life, the vices and virtues of the New Journalism, the New Woman, and the American Girl. Her *Campaigns of Curiosity* laid the foundations for other colonial women and men like the Anglo-Indian Olive Christian Malvery and the American Jack London to undertake similar incognito social investigations into the lives of the metropolitan laboring poor in the early twentieth century.[133] Banks's idiosyncratic history also sets the stage for the next chapter, which probes the politics and erotics of elite women's experiences in and narratives about the slums of London.

PART TWO

CROSS-CLASS SISTERHOOD AND

BROTHERHOOD IN THE SLUMS

Chapter Four

THE POLITICS AND EROTICS OF DIRT:

CROSS-CLASS SISTERHOOD IN THE SLUMS

> ... the silver teapot was placed on the table, and virgins
> and spinsters with hands that had staunched the sores of
> Bermondsey and Hoxton carefully measured out one, two,
> three, four spoonfuls of tea.
> —Virginia Woolf, *The Years*

"THE SLUM," George Orwell explained in the opening pages of *Down and Out in Paris and London* (1933), with its "dirt and its queer lives," was "first an object lesson in poverty, and then the background of my experiences." Orwell's influential account marked the culmination of a long history of Victorian and Edwardian social reporting in Britain that imagined the slums of London not only as sites of physical and social disorder—"dirt"—but as spaces hospitable to "queer" lives and "queer" sexual desires. If Orwell can be trusted, only men go slumming. They alone have sexual needs and can satisfy them. Women seem to enter his story merely so that men can sexually and physically exploit them.[1]

Orwell is surely right that slums were "queer" spaces in the imagination of many elite men in Britain from the mid-nineteenth century onwards, but his vision of slumming as an exclusively male enterprise cannot withstand scrutiny. Well-to-do women, like their male counterparts, were deeply attracted to the sights and sounds of metropolitan poverty and found in slumming a means to expand their social authority over the poor.[2] Many, like the social investigator Beatrice Potter, felt "a certain weird romance" in and for the slums. Others experienced a frisson of fear and excitement as they moved about the streets of London shopping, visiting the poor, or, like the charismatic and bohemian socialite Margot Tennant [Asquith], doing both.[3] Some women also felt a certain "queer" romance in and for the slums. In the name of caring for their down-trodden sisters in the slums, these women not only did battle with the dirt of city life, but in so doing found ways to express their own desires for closeness with one another and with laboring girls and women.

Orwell's insight connecting dirt with "queer lives" is the starting point for my investigation of the politics and erotics of dirt in the lives of philanthropic women. Throughout this chapter, I have bracketed the word "queer" in quotation marks to emphasize that it is drawn from the text I am citing. For Orwell, the phrase "queer lives" refers to homosexual men, though it also includes many other nonhomosexual men whose oddness placed them outside the conventional framework of bourgeois masculinity. Wary of anachronism, historians have rightly been careful not to impose later meanings of words such as "queer" on men and women in the past. But this caution should not prevent us from recognizing that the word "queer" from the 1880s onward did begin to accumulate a long chain of connotative meanings, some of which were associated with male and female same-sex desire.[4]

Part one focuses on elite women's representations of dirt in their accounts of their sisterly labors in the slums. I treat dirt not only as physical matter but also as a pervasive trope in women's writings about the slums and themselves. Their abhorrence and fascination with dirt, I argue, tell us a great deal about their vision of sisterhood and their own aspirations to engage in useful public work. I examine the ways in which these women invested the dirt of poverty with powerful political, cultural, and sexual meanings. What were the implications of their vision of dirt for the sorts of social politics and policies they advocated? How did they attempt to strike a balance between loving their working-class sisters and controlling them? The second part examines the links between "dirt" and the "queer lives" of elite women in the slums and considers the erotic valences of dirt and dirty spaces for women. While cultural anthropologists assure us that we normally think of dirt as destructive, this chapter explores the ways in which the dirt of slum life became a source of creativity in the lives of well-to-do female charity workers and philanthropists.[5] Women's writings about their slum labors along with novels about sisterhood, slum philanthropy, and same-sex desire serve as sources for analyzing the attractions of slum work for middle-class women seeking ways to create communities of loving solidarity with like-minded women and with the poor.

CROSS-CLASS SISTERHOOD AND THE POLITICS OF DIRT

Victorians across the political spectrum unanimously decried the messy squalor and moral degradation of urban life and vied with another to evoke the fascinatingly repulsive smells, sounds, and sights of the city. Some, like the famous sanitary and educational reformer of the 1830s and '40s, J. P. Kay, literally exhausted themselves in finding words adequate to represent the disgusting scenes they encountered.[6] Such descriptions were no mere flights of fancy or figures of speech, though they sometimes were both. Even the most salubrious commercial precincts of Victorian cities were dirty places, and the mere act of crossing a street in London without benefit of a sweeper leading the way inevitably left its mark on the shoes and clothing of the walker. If dirt was a ubiquitous fact of urban life, commentators increasingly identified the slums of East London after the cholera epidemic of 1866 with every form of literal and figurative impurity: contaminated water and fallen women; insect- and incest-riddled one-room tenements; rag pickers and rag wearers. Four decades later, the intrepid slum explorer Mary Higgs put the matter quite simply: "London acts as a kind of national cesspool."[7] But London did more than serve as a receptacle for the nation's refuse; it was also a prodigious producer of it. The dust heap that dominates the landscape of Dickens's *Our Mutual Friend* was a metaphor for the wastage of capitalism, both human and inanimate. But dust heaps were also actual sites within the metropolis, attended by men, women, and children whose scant "wealth" was refuse itself. The Thames, Britain's foremost imperial waterway, was a source of wealth and waste. Its bottom was regularly dredged by mudlarks, whose picturesque garb and extreme filthiness enthralled Arthur Munby, the age's foremost connoisseur of dirt and collector of photographic images of begrimed women. A sometime poet, civil servant, and instructor at the Working Men's College, Munby carried his obsession with dirt to the point of secretly marrying his maid of all work, Hannah Cullwick.[8]

Dirt was emphatically political in nineteenth-century Britain. Abetted by the rapid growth of the sciences of social statistics and hygiene, a host of men and women—politicians, civil servants, clergymen, doctors, and male and female philanthropists—turned to state and local government and private initiatives to contain and combat dirt. Traditional histories of public health, protective labor legislation, housing and slum clearance, the medical inspection of school children and the provision of rate-funded school baths celebrate the gradual but inexorable victory of the bureaucratic forces of order over the chaos produced by unregulated industrial capitalism and urbanization. While men such as J. P. Kay, Edwin Chadwick, and John Simon dominate these histories, scholars in recent years have increasingly recognized the key roles played by women, largely in the voluntary sector, including Mary Carpenter, Florence Nightingale, Ellen Ranyard, and Margaret McMillan.

Dirt and its politics were gendered from the outset of the campaigns to eradicate it. Benthamite men in the early Victorian years controlled many of the most influential positions within the central government, and domestic ideals powerfully informed their vision of how best to purify the social body.[9] The second generation of social welfare administrators, however, had no choice but to cooperate with and rely upon the labors of well-to-do women, who mobilized themselves into a growing army of social housekeepers intent on both purifying the city and asserting their ability to control slum spaces and dwellers. These women justified their initiatives by invoking the separate-spheres ideology and the writings of one of its most renowned, albeit unconventional exponents, John Ruskin. In Ruskin's oft-reprinted essay on women's public and private roles in society, "Of Queen's Gardens," in *Sesame and Lilies*, he contended that the proper sphere of women extends beyond the home into the surrounding public spaces of civic life. "Generally, we are under an impression that a man's duties are public, and a woman's private. But this is not altogether so," Ruskin explained. Woman's duties expanded "without her gates" to "assist in the ordering, in the comforting, and in the beautiful adornment of the state."[10] Ruskin's words inspired future generations of civic-minded women, especially middle-class spinsters, to take up public work, but they also confirmed the social reality that during the preceding decades women had already made substantial contributions to the multifaceted movements for social and moral hygiene. In the 1840s and '50s, the Ladies Sanitary Society in Manchester, Angela Burdett-Coutts's work on behalf of prostitutes and ragged children, and Louisa Twining's famous Workhouse Visiting Society were in the vanguard of this movement founded on the belief that well-to-do women had the right and obligation to minister to their downtrodden sisters and children.

While elite women's freedom to explore the lives of their poor sisters continued to expand in the 1860s, they were still constrained by expectations of what a lady could and could not do. For example, in the aftermath of James Greenwood's incognito descent into the men's casual wards in January 1866, the sanitary and poor-law reformer J. H. Stallard decided to mount similar inquiries into the condition of women's casual wards. But he contended that unlike gentlemen, with their chameleon-like abilities, no true lady could successfully disguise herself as a tramp and associate with the poor "on the footing of equality" needed to disclose the truth about workhouse conditions. Through every spoken and unspoken gesture, she would immediately reveal her essential gentility: "no rags would disguise her character, no acting conceal her disgust." Undaunted, Stallard hired "Ellen Stanley," a once respectable widow, impoverished through no fault of her own, who "purposefully went out as dirty as [she] could" to gain admission to the casual wards of London's workhouses.[11]

Despite her long experience of poverty, even Ellen Stanley was unprepared for the filthy sights, sounds, and language of the ward. The earthen floor of the water closet overflowed and oozed with excrement because the impure water and food caused mass diarrhea among the female inmates; women tore off and ripped up their rags in agony from the incessant bites of vermin. And Stanley silently prayed that the great banking-heiress-turned-philanthropist, Angela Burdett-Coutts, would "hear the groans of the women and the wailing of the children" and relieve the misery of her "sisters" (49).

Stanley's incognito exploration may have been inspired by Greenwood's, but the story she told was far different from his and underscores how class and gender shaped slum investigators' representations of the bodies of the poor. In contrast to Greenwood's coy staging of his descent into the casual ward with its revelation of sodomitical orgies, Stanley's narrative is utterly devoid of titillating pleasures. Where Greenwood lingers over his description of the bodies of the beautiful youths he encounters, Stanley feels horrified empathy for the nude, lice-infested female bodies she sees. Sex only enters her story as the potential and real threat of male sexual assault on all the female inmates, whose abject poverty both defines them as sexually available and disqualifies them from the protection of the police.[12] It is hardly surprising that Ellen Stanley, a poor woman, felt no attraction to dirt. She lived far too close to dirt to romanticize it; her very survival and self-respect depended upon the daily struggle to keep her body and clothes clean.

Two decades later, a handful of well-to-do women dared to imitate Greenwood and Stanley and disguised themselves in the rags of poverty to see for themselves how the poor lived.[13] What made this possible? The broadening of social and educational opportunities for bourgeois women with the creation of women's colleges; the extension of local government franchise to propertied women; the rise of women journalists and female professions emerging out of the social hygiene movements of mid-century; and the appearance of the New Woman in fiction—all these developments contributed to elite women's newfound freedom to move through urban space.[14]

For upper- and middle-class women raised in homes with armies of domestic servants—cooks, parlour maids, charring girls—immersing themselves in the dirtiness of the slums was a literal and symbolic act of independence and adventure.[15] In December 1883, *Punch*, that most sensitive and merciless barometer of shifting social fashions, lampooned slumming and women's self-serving investment in it. While the cartoon implicated both men and women in its satire, it focused on women's fantasies about slums as sites of dangerous pleasures. As a party of upper-class women surrounded by formally attired servants beats a hasty retreat from a social gathering, the hostess asks incredulously why her guests are wearing hooded, full-length mackintoshes. "Lord Archibald is going to take us to dear little slum he's found out near the Minories—such a fearful place! Fourteen poor things sleeping in one bed, and no window!—and the Mackintoshes are to keep out infection, you know, and hide one's diamonds, and all that!" Despite Lord Archibald's role as sherpa in the slums, women bear the brunt of the cartoon's charge that slumming was insensitive and sensation-seeking. The mackintoshes they wear are quite literally bodyguards, meant to protect elite women's bodies from being taken over by the infectious filth of East London. At the same time, the cartoon makes clear that these women crave the very dangers they fear. Why else would they choose to go slumming?

Such images were far from mere fancy. When Katherine Symonds, daughter of the famed man of letters John Addington Symonds, resolved to "undertake help at Toynbee Hall" in 1898 her mother "was afraid that I should pick up some infectious disease, and cancelled the plan." Undaunted, Symonds did eventually work at the Charity Organisation Society's Whitechapel office, not far from the famed university settlement.[16] *Punch*'s visual satire mocked upper-class responses to contemporary revelations about the plight of "Outcast London" even as it buttressed men's claims that they were better suited than women to understand and solve the problems of metropolitan poverty.[17] Regardless of whether women went slumming merely for an evening or devoted themselves to a lifetime of friendly visiting in the slums, all women engaged in slum philanthropy had to contend with public perceptions of them as voyeuristic and self-interested.

The writings of prominent women social welfare advocates suggest that *Punch* all too accurately captured the importance of spectacular filth in their initial attraction to slumming. Dirt was not only a visible sign of poverty but a marker of a sexualized "primitive" to which highly cultivated single women were drawn. For Mary Higgs, the middle-class widow of a Manchester clergyman, the homeless poor she met while disguised as a tramp were literally vestiges of an uncivilized past, individuals "permanently stranded on lower levels of evolution." But Higgs also insisted that "wise social legislation" could "quicken evolution" and reclaim individuals from their state of moral and physical dereliction.[18]

Higgs's incognito inquiry into female tramp life demonstrated first, that dirt could and did control poor women's economic fortunes, and second, that the economics of dirt were closely bound up with laboring women's sexual vulnerability. Higgs observed that official regulations governing London's casual wards mandated the confiscation of inmates' clothing, making it impossible for paupers to wash or mend them. Each time a woman resorted to the casual ward (or cheap lodging house), she left it a dirtier, shabbier person and hence less eligible for paid employment. In this way, workhouse regulations trapped female inmates in a vicious downward cycle whose logical endpoint was prostitution.[19] Higgs lamented that dirty bodies and clothes literally soiled not only individual women's lives but the nation itself.

The authority of middle-class women like Higgs to enter the squalid and dangerous precincts of the poor was predicated on their own irreproachable personal morality. At the same time, these women understood well that the power of their slum narratives, and thus their ability to establish their credentials as experts, derived at least partly from their willingness to pollute their own bodies in the name of protecting the imperiled purity of their outcast sisters. The prostitute, as the embodiment of all that was dirty in Victorian culture, functioned simultaneously as the female slum worker's doppelganger and her opposite. Compelled to put on "other [tramps'] dirty nightgowns," Higgs could "hardly describe [her] feeling of personal contamination" as vermin claimed possession of her body. Throughout her night in the casual ward, Higgs also grappled with the terrifying prospect that the male pauper employed by the casual ward would make good his threat and force her to have sex with him. Higgs's revulsion at donning the lousy clothes of female tramps only heightened her sense of sisterly solidarity with them.

Dirt, Higgs argued, was a literal and figurative marker of a woman's economic and sexual status; the two cannot be disentangled in either Higgs's analysis of the horrors of female tramp wards or in her slumming narrative. As a result of her incognito slumming, Higgs suffered a devastating hemorrhage brought on by the harsh treatment in the tramp wards. But she also effectively transformed her nightmarish experiences into political capital as she vigorously campaigned to reform conditions in female casual wards and municipal lodging houses. Publication of her studies of female tramp life in leading periodicals and books instantly made her into a celebrated expert on social problems and gave her access to influential male policy makers. With evident pride, she informed skeptical male members of the Departmental Committee on Vagrancy that her exposé of female casual wards and her analysis of female vagrancy had been "sent to every woman guardian and to the chairman of every board of guardians throughout the country."[20]

The socialist-feminist Muriel Lester, like Mary Higgs, recalled the origins of her love for the poor in her horrified curiosity about the dirty spaces and faces she glimpsed from her first-class train carriage as she sped from her country home through the slums of East London en route to the pleasures of the West End. Lester structured her autobiography to make her childhood encounters with the "sight and smell" of poverty into a kind of primal trauma that shaped her future life choices. Asked to attend a party of East End factory girls, she accepted the invitation as a pleasant diversion from her pampered and idle life but soon found herself "addicted" to East End visiting. She "longed" to enter the interiors of the factory girl's lives and homes and to master the outlook, patterns of speech, and secrets of the denizens of her adopted neighborhood, whose lives she endowed with romantic glamour. Years later, Lester insisted that "love for the people" not "duty" motivated her work for the poor. She "hated the very word [duty]," whose coldness was at odds with the joy she brought to her labors.[21]

Lester's day-to-day work in the slums propelled her toward the self-critical realization that her investment in the "dirtiness" of the poor, which was so crucial to her social awakening, was incompatible with the deeper life of sisterhood and brotherhood she sought. She joyfully recalled that the night before she and her sister Doris opened a teetotal pub and club for their neighbors in Bow, they cleaned and scrubbed the rooms themselves. For an educated daughter of the well-to-do, the mere act of doing hard cleaning—and not in telling others how or where to clean—constituted an assault on prevailing class and gender norms even after World War I. Many of the Lesters' poor neighbors were delighted by such maverick ideas and practices, which provided the foundation for deep and enduring relationships. One East Londoner warmly recalled that the Lesters' modest settlement house "played such a large part in my mother's life and in my own upbringing virtually from the cradle."[22]

The nurse, journalist, social investigator, and member of the London School Board, Honnor Morten, abandoned the comforts of her lovely home for a room in a "terrible street in the slums" where she "lived . . . as the people lived, for weeks and months, scrubbing, washing, cooking, marketing and all the rest, and going about all day nursing the sick poor." As she explained to an admiring interviewer sent by the *Young Woman* in 1900, "if you really want to know how the poor live, you must live as they do, but not only for a week or ten days."[23] Such a vision of cross-class sisterhood remained shocking—and newsworthy—well into the 1920s. The London papers sent a reporter and photographer to capture Rosa Waugh Hobhouse, daughter of the founder of the SPCC (Society for the Prevention of Cruelty to Children), "cleaning the windows in her workman's dwelling at Hoxton."[24] Hobhouse understood the symbolic importance of her gesture, which was calculated to draw attention to her radical social and political agenda. Her decision to live a life of voluntary poverty, which included cleaning her own house, stood within but also criticized a long tradition of cross-class sisterhood in the slums. Along with her husband, Stephen Hobhouse, and her friends Muriel Lester and Mary Hughes (daughter of the famous Christian socialist author of *Tom Brown's Schooldays*, Thomas Hughes), she refused to pretend that the poverty they had chosen for themselves was in any way the same as the involuntary poverty of their neighbors. At the same time, Mary Hughes adopted a life of such intense material self-denial that she was often mistaken for one of the tramps she sheltered at her famous Dewdrop Inn.

Through their work as housing reformers and rent collectors, friendly, school board and health visitors, settlement workers and members of religious sisterhoods, elite women saw themselves as altruistic social housekeepers who devoted themselves to bringing order and cleanliness to the lives of their poor sisters. Some of them believed that they had forged genuine friendships with their poor sisters—sharing in one another's cares by mobilizing the bonds of womanhood to overcome the barriers of class distance.[25] The well-to-do women who joined the Browning Settlement in south London asserted that they had created "a Christian sisterhood, with its weekday sacraments of maternity boxes, benevolent funds, and coal." Their Pleasant Sunday Afternoons drew well over a thousand working women, which helped promote "an atmosphere of simple cordial sisterliness, obliterating distinctions of class and caste and drawing together all grades and types of women in a common bond of mutual help and sympathy."[26] E. Asten Pope, a longtime resident and clubleader at the settlement, recalled with humor and humility how two working-class women took her under their wing and taught her the rudiments of bread baking.

> "I'll come along and put you in t'way of it, Tuesday afternoon, two o'clock."
> "How much flour shall I get," I [Pope] asked. "Never you bother about flour nor nothing else; I'll bring all as you'll want. You've got a yeller mug, haven't yer. Well, then, just go to t'stores and tell Jackson to give yer one of them yeller mugs at eight pence."

Pope ended her story by comically portraying her own ineptness in burning her hand on the oven door. Her telling of the story emphasizes that all three women believed that Pope, as a woman, ought to know how to bake bread. While it underscores the reciprocal character of their relationships, Pope's use of dialect reminds readers of the class differences dividing the women. Sisterhood is neither sameness nor equality. Just as Pope taught her working-class sisters how to save their pennies, they had skills to offer Pope. It is the poor women who share their hard-earned flour with Pope. The implicit message in Pope's anecdote was that the home and its concerns provided the common ground upon which rich and poor women alike could construct their friendships.[27]

However, sisterhood was at best a fragile enterprise in a world in which one group of women was destined always to clean the dirt created by another. Even self-denying philanthropic spinsters in the slums, such as the sisters Muriel and Stella Wragge, hired local women to cook and scrub for them, whose labors they affectionately—and also guiltily—celebrated in their memoirs.[28] A recent graduate in chemistry of Lady Margaret Hall, Oxford, Alice Lucy Hodson lived in a colony of educated single women in South London in the 1890s that employed several women to look after them. Desperate to sanitize her filthy surroundings, she mused that "it would be nice to walk about with a sponge, a can of water, and towel hung round the waist." But she dismissed as "obviously impossible" her fantasy of becoming a maid of all work for her neighbors and confessed that "the only thing is to go dirty, and take the top layer off whenever you have a chance." Confronted by the indescribable sight of a much-used sheet and blanket on an unmade bed in a tenement she was visiting, she had to check her desire to "send a charwoman to thoroughly clean up the house."[29] Hodson only partially understood the absurd inadequacy of such a solution, which violated the implicit political economy of dirt in women's lives. Women's relationship to the circulation and removal of dirt was fundamentally determined by class. It was the prerogative of elite women to define what dirt was—and was not—and to dictate how, where, and when their social inferiors should remove it.[30] It would have been much more sensible for Hodson to find paid charring work for the impoverished tenement dwellers she had visited rather than wishing she could send a charwoman to clean up their filth.

Hodson was unsure how to make sense of her ambivalence about "going dirty" and the meanings of dirt itself. She could not square her desire to preserve her own bodily purity with the imminent threat of bodily pollution she both abhorred and found so compelling. "I cannot exaggerate the pleasures of bathing," she admitted, after "tramping all day through London mud, in and out of dirty houses, after climbing dark and unspeakably dirty stairs, and shaking black and sticky little hands." "The dirt is so trying," she confessed in language that revealed an almost sexualized fear of invasion, "nothing is ever really clean, for dust, fog, and smuts are continually depositing themselves, not only on obvious and convenient places, but even the innermost recesses of your being." The sheer physicality of Hodson's description, her emphasis on actual dirt ("black and sticky hands," "dust, fog, and smuts") in inconvenient "places," gives her phrase "the innermost recesses of [my] being" an unavoidably literal connotation. The most private but unnamable spaces of her body, not just her carpets and windows, have been soiled by her contact with the "indescribable" dirt produced by the private lives of the poor. Apparently, no amount of hot water can get her clean.

In Hodson's prose, dirt marks the uncertain boundary between sisterly sympathy and class-based surveillance; it is deployed to fulfill the more general task of policing "the boundaries between 'normal' sexuality and 'dirty sexuality,' 'normal' work and 'dirty' work."[31] Hodson's cleaning rituals, far from firming up boundaries and meanings, throw social and sexual categories into disarray. Was the dirtiness of the poor and their homes symptomatic of a moral indecency so fundamental to their nature that even the hottest bath could not cleanse them? Or was their dirt, like Hodson's own, merely the unavoidable surface deposit of their contaminated environment, which concealed but could not diminish their innate goodness? Hodson's account of her life and work in south London perceptively raised these questions, but she herself was incapable of fully answering them. She made no attempt to reconcile her belief that no decent adult could "get a place in such a mess" with her epiphany that universal humanity lay just "under the dirt" of slum children.[32] Even as she sought to forge sisterly bonds with poor women and children, she could not free herself from a worldview shaped by her own lifelong dependence on the hard labor of domestic servants—a class of women and girls for whom deference and subordination were facts of life.

Nor should we castigate Hodson for being particularly obtuse or insensitive. In their work among the poor, well-to-do women often turned to the only model of cross-class relationship they knew firsthand: the intimate inequalities of their relationships with domestic servants. Several widely respected philanthropists such as Henrietta Barnett and Mrs. Nassau Senior, joint founders of the Metropolitan Association for Befriending Young Servants (MABYS) sought to remake unruly street girls and fallen women into domestic servants and thereby solve two problems at once. They would befriend and rescue the young women and girls from their (supposedly) otherwise inevitable descent into prostitution while simultaneously satisfying the insatiable middle-class demand for reliable household staff. In MABYS's vision of its mission, impoverished young women could save themselves from sexual degradation by forming friendships with philanthropic elite woman, subjecting themselves to the tutelage of mistresses, and devoting themselves to cleansing the domestic dirt of bourgeois households. The leaders of MABYS and many societies established to rescue "fallen" women believed that they could transform their clients from sources of sexual dirtiness to footsoldiers in the battle to order bourgeois homes.[33] It was no accident that benevolent agencies such as the Magdalen Asylums and Barnardo's Villages for Girls regularly trained many of their female charges to work in laundries. MABYS's optimistic leaders contended not only that inequalities between servants and their mistresses were perfectly compatible with sisterly love and affection, but also that servant girls "want to feel somebody above, yet with them." "It is wholesomely humbling to wonder how, amongst such dirt and din, outward and inward, these [servant] girls have grown up as tolerably pure as they have," proclaimed a lady worker for MABYS.[34]

At least some poor women found ways to manipulate elite women's preoccupation with dirt to extract the resources they needed to survive. In this, as in so many other matters, the district nurse Martha Jane Loane listened carefully to the poor women, men, and children she visited and recorded their thoughts.[35] One of Loane's Cockney informants and clients, Mrs. Stevens, was a mother of six and was married to an enfeebled husband who was often out of work. Charity was a business and job for Mrs. Stevens as much as it was for the lady visitors and settlement house workers who inspected her home. Stevens explained to Loane that she always kept an untidy house to ensure the flow of charity. She never put up curtains and she let strips of paper hang off the walls. Before a charity visitor arrived, she dumped coal and rags in the corner and dropped stale cabbage leaves to create a fetid atmosphere. No one, she averred, ever bothered to ask about *her* family's earnings. The spectacle of her family's poverty spoke for itself. In a poignant and stunning moment of revelation, Stevens elucidated the tragic-comic consequences of elite (mis)representations of poverty: "[R]ich people all think if you're too dirty to touch with a forty-foot pole you must be poor, and there's no end to what they'll give you, but if you're clean and decent—no matter what it costs you—you're lucky people who don't want nothing from nobody. The poor is to them what a theatre is to me,—if they haven't made my blood run cold, and if I haven't used up my hankicher, I don't feel I've had my money's worth."[36]

According to Stevens, the poor were sometimes willing accomplices in satisfying lady slum explorers' self-defeating preconceptions about how poor people ought to look and the public's appetite for witnessing spectacles of poverty and philanthropic benevolence.[37] We must assume that Loane, as the middle-class woman writer who attributed these words to Stevens and chose to include them in her book, was herself sympathetic to Stevens's critique. Ironically, poor women unwilling to abet middle-class preconceptions about their dirtiness sometimes paid dearly for their display of virtuous cleanliness. Lucy Rebecca Payne Williamson's son, "Father Joe" Williamson recalled that his mother often starved herself rather than allow either her home or her children's bodies and clothes to be dirty. As a consequence, when press magnate Alfred Harmsworth donated hundreds of pairs of shoes for distribution among children in the Williamson's neighborhood, "no Williamson child got a pair." "Our clothes were patched and repaired," Joe bitterly observed, "but we were not poor because we were clean!"[38]

Other laboring women directly challenged—rather than opportunistically manipulating as Mrs. Stevens did—the political economy of "dirt" underpinning the social welfare initiatives of elite women. One such woman was Mrs. H., a charwoman from Poplar and the friend of the Anglican social worker Maude Royden. Few well-to-do women achieved

Royden's depth of understanding of the intertwined and often antagonistic politics of dirt and cross-class sisterhood. Royden was at the forefront of many of the most progressive movements of her day including feminism, socialism, peace activism, and the campaign to expand women's sacramental functions within the Church of England. In her unpublished memoir, *Bid Me Discourse*, Royden remembered one afternoon when she and Mrs. H. left Poplar to visit the Baby Week Exhibition in Central London. "We were gazing at an exhibit of two rooms," she recalled.

> One was clean and tidy, the other dirty and in disorder. The first was a model of the sort of room in which babies could be reared, and the other a model of one in which they could not. Some "ladies," who were looking on, discussed the exhibits in words which suggested that all working people's rooms were piggeries. Mrs. H., filled with indignation, began to argue with them. They, cowardly, took to flight. Mrs. H., in ringing tones then hurled after them this unforgettable reply: "an 'ow clean would you be if I didn't clean yer?"

The shared domestic concerns of mothercraft and cleanliness, upon which the ideology of cross-class sisterhood theoretically rested, exposed rather than helped to resolve the fundamental conflicts separating rich and poor women from one another.[39] With the sort of humility that characterized Royden's ministry to the poor, she pondered the lesson that Mrs. H. had taught her and hence also made explicit why she chose to include this vignette in her own memoir. "Never since then have I been able to look with any complacency at my own (moderately) clean hands without reflecting on Mrs. H's toilworn and misshapen ones—worn with the toil which I was able to pass on to her because I was a little richer."[40]

Royden's politics are literally written on and express themselves through the body. She can only grasp the full meaning of her "moderately clean hands" in relation to Mrs. H's disfigured hands. The purity of the upper-class lady's body depends upon the dirtiness of the laboring female body—a relationship predicated on gender, class, and sexual hierarchies that Royden rejected. For Royden, true sisterhood entailed much more than sympathy and benevolence. It required an acknowledgement of the injustices of the distribution of wealth and power between rich and poor, men and women.

The politics of dirt propelled Royden, Lester, and like-minded women toward socialist feminism and ultimately to a broadly global sense of social justice. Gandhi's articles in his paper *Young India* helped Lester see that the "same principles we nobodies had been trying to live out" in England were of a piece with much broader struggles for justice "on a world stage." One of London's most visible pacifist critics of the First World War, Lester ultimately allied herself personally and politically with Gandhi and his nonviolent campaign for Indian independence. Lester followed in the footsteps of generations of women reformers such as Edith Langridge, the charismatic founder of the Oxford Mission Sisterhood of the Epiphany in India, who began their careers working in the slums of London within communities of educated women but ultimately extended their work to far flung sites of empire.[41] Lester relinquished control over the day-to-day operations of Kingsley Hall, the social welfare center that she and her sister Doris had founded, to travel to India where she met and worked with Gandhi. It was to Kingsley Hall in Bow that Gandhi retreated during his famous visit to England in 1930 on behalf of Indian independence. As Lester, widely called England's Jane Addams by the press in the United States, toured the world from the 1930s onwards bringing her message of reconciliation of races, classes and nations, she remained clear that "the farther I traveled, the more devoted I became to the East End [of London]."[42]

The radicalism of women like Royden, Lester, and their circle (including such notable feminists as Charlotte Despard[43]) grew out of their ability to connect the grimy particularities of laboring women's daily struggles with the systemic economic and social forces lying outside the control of individual women.[44] Nowhere is this more apparent than in Anna Martin's brilliant observations about poor women's battles with dirt, which she derived from her analysis of the intermeshing of their class and gender subordination to men.[45] Martin and her devoted friend and collaborator, Laura Robinson, moved from the large girls' school they headed in Capetown, South Africa, to the dockside neighborhoods of south London in 1898 to live together and work with the Women's Branch of the Wesleyan Methodist Bermondsey Settlement House.[46] Martin, like Alice Hodson, was struck by the unmade beds she frequently encountered during her visits to the homes of poor women. But where Hodson saw indecency, Martin recognized resourcefulness and logic. "The homemakers of the mean streets are not to be judged by middle-class standards," she explained. "Take, for instance, the question of order and cleanliness. Not to have beds made till 8 o'clock in the evening would reasonably be considered to show bad management in the case of a rich woman; to have them made earlier would sometimes show lack of organising power in the case of a poor one."[47]

Laboring women's double responsibilities as wage earners and as unpaid housekeepers forced them to leave their homes too early in the morning to do cleaning much before 8 at night, long after lady visitors like Hodson would have come to criticize their untidy houses. Martin believed that the only just solution was to mandate across all industries a "living or minimum wage" and allow laboring women to choose for themselves whether they worked both inside and outside the home.[48] Other female social workers in the 1890s and early 1900s, including the socialist Margaret McMillan, demanded state-funded welfare programs and policies, such as medical inspection and services for poor school-children.[49]

It would be a mistake, however, to suggest that female social workers' and reformers' encounters with dirt inevitably led them toward socialist and radical feminist critiques of economic and gender injustices. Prominent women social reformers such as Octavia Hill and Helen Bosanquet remained staunchly hostile to any expansion in the state's provision of goods and services for poor children which, they believed, would undercut parental responsibility.[50] For Hill, the dirty homes of the poor emphatically did not demonstrate the structural defects of capitalism that required the intervention of the state. Rather, the negligence of slum landlords and their unchristian refusal to recognize their social obligations exacerbated working-class women's feckless mismanagement of their households to produce hotbeds of immorality. Hill's solutions reflected her deeply held individualistic assumptions about dirt and sisterhood. First, she sought to convince landlords that a fair rate of return on their investment was compatible with the provision of decent housing for the poor. Second, she looked to armies of lady rent collectors, who combed womanly tact with rigorous training in the principles of scientific charity and home economics, to guide their poor sisters to use their resources more efficiently.

Not surprisingly, laboring women resented the intrusive authority female social workers had over their lives. Carolyn Steedman, in her biography/autobiography, *Landscape for a Good Woman*, captured the ambivalent meanings that such encounters, with their long history in Victorian and Edwardian London, continued to bear in her mother's and her own life in the mid-twentieth century. As a "dumpy retreating health visitor" left their bare apartment in 1951, Steedman and her mother were left to reckon with the visitor's harsh judgment that their "house isn't fit for a baby." The shame of that moment burned itself into Steedman's consciousness and continued to divide her from the bourgeois women whose world she now inhabits: "I read a woman's book, meet such a woman at a party (a woman now, like me) and think quite deliberately as we talk: we are divided: a hundred years ago I'd have been cleaning your shoes. I know this and you don't."[51]

Past and present, dirt and sisterhood, sameness and difference, rage and desire collide in Steedman's *Landscape*, producing intimate but also painful encounters between "sisters," creating new wounds even before old ones can begin to heal.

The political and sexual economy of dirt loomed large not only in the imaginations of elite women slum workers, but also in their analysis of poverty and in the charities and reforms they spearheaded. The dirtiness of slum life played a significant role in motivating elite women to see for themselves how the poor lived and in shaping their political agendas. For some, slumming was merely an evening's titillation, fodder for conversations at fashionable dinner parties. But for many others, their encounters with dirt stimulated an abiding desire to clean up the city, to gain deeper empathy for their poor sisters, and to live in loving communities with like-minded women.

"There will be something the matter with the ladies"

Elite women's willingness to "go dirty" (to recall Hodson's phrase) made it possible for them to flout bourgeois class and gender expectations even as they acted as missionaries bringing bourgeois values and culture to the working poor. It also created a space in which they could explore their own same-sex and opposite-sex feelings and identities. "Going dirty" sometimes gave rise to "dirty" desires in elite women, especially middle-class spinsters, who paradoxically claimed the right to enter slum districts because of their own presumptive status as sexless agents of moral and social purity. As cultural anthropologists have argued, "dirt" is "matter out of order" by which societies define the sacred and the profane, the clean and the unclean. Elite women's attempts to control dirt were accompanied by the perception that their lives as independent females contributed to the disordering of gender and sexual hierarchies and expectations.[52] Finding a way to live inside this tension, to negotiate its contradictions, was crucial for spinster reformers.

Edith Sing, an avid supporter of settlement houses for educated single women in slum neighborhoods, recalled a friend's reaction to her explanation of the object and methods underlying the movement. "But there will be," Sing's friend supposed, "*something* the matter with the ladies!"[53] In both fictional and nonfictional accounts, elite women's desire to live among the poor was often characterized as a kind of madness, just as their need to bring order to the slums was assumed to be a symptom of some disorder within them. What was the "*something* the matter with the ladies" who went slumming?

The doyenne of aristocratic slum philanthropy, Maude Althea Stanley, was one of those who took a dim view of most women's motives for helping the poor. She unfavorably contrasted men's noble "vocation" for visiting the poor with the hope harbored by some "idle" and bored women "to find in the homes of the poor a cure for what is called 'a disappointment.'"[54] Was Stanley correct to think that living or working in slum neighborhoods functioned as a philanthropic sublimation for unmet sexual and romantic needs? Some evidence, at least, supports such a view. The New Woman novelist Olive Schreiner moved to the East End in June 1887 to complete her work on a novel about life among the poor.[55] But to her closest friends, she revealed her deeper motives: the East End for Schreiner represented a space free from the tribulations of West End romance that threatened to overtake her. She wrote the homosexual socialist Edward Carpenter that she prayed for the death in her of "all that longs or wishes for anything."[56] For Schreiner, living in East London constituted a form of sexual renunciation—just as her unfinished project to write a novel about slum life was a substitute for her unfinished romance with the eugenicist Karl Pearson.[57] We find in Beatrice Potter's career in East London a similar elision between slumming, social analysis, and sexual discontent. Potter turned to work as a lady rent collector in Whitechapel to satisfy her need to "play a part in the world," to collect raw sociological data about social questions, and to escape from the torments of her feelings for the dashing political maverick Joseph Chamberlain, feelings that she identified with her "lower nature."[58] In March of 1885, as her perverse involvement with Chamberlain continued to preoccupy her, she noted in her diary that "all is chaos at present." However, in words that might more aptly have been used to describe her tangled affairs with Chamberlain, she described her experiences in East London as "a certain weird romance, with neither beginning nor end, visiting amongst these people in their dingy homes."[59] Her perceptions of East London invariably reflected her ambivalence about her sexual and professional status. Would she choose the role of wife or spinster, socialite or sociologist? The cultural link forged in late Victorian London between "disappointment" and slumming achieved the status of conventional wisdom in the decades ahead. In Barbara Pym's subtle evocation of the long shadow cast by Victorian manners and morals in the twentieth century, *Excellent Women*, two devout spinsters concurred that "people often do strange things"—by which they meant engaging in good works in East London—"when they've had a disappointment."[60]

If freedom from opposite-sex entanglements and a desire to exercise power attracted single women like Potter to the slums, their experiences sometimes confounded their expectations. When women directed their inspectorial gaze on laboring people, they were astonished and unnerved to learn that their sexual status was the subject of lively commentary among their clients. While Potter and her close friends Ella Pycroft and Margaret Harkness reveled in their "glorified spinsterhood," the residents of model housing in the Katherine Buildings, the focus of their collective efforts in East London, speculated boldly about the sexual availability and activities of the "odd women" in their midst. One East Londoner, Mr. Price, who lived in the adjacent Brunswick Buildings, took a fancy to Pycroft and shyly asked her out to dinner. Perhaps self-defensively, Pycroft minimized the threat he posed to her mission as a single woman and to her status as elite observer by trivializing his interest in her. As if to remind herself that her relationship to Price was that of ethnographic investigator and not potential lover, she concluded her thoughts about the incident with a dismissive aside: "These East End manners are too amusing."[61] She was even more unnerved when she learned that her neighbors detected a budding romance between her and a gentleman coworker, Maurice Paul. Pycroft, who spent her days inspecting the homes of the poor, resented speculation about her private life by her East End sisters because she felt it might interfere with her work. She claimed to be amused by the Cockneys' inability to appreciate the pure and altruistic—not sexual—motives that underpinned her womanly philanthropy.

Philanthropic projects like Pycroft's, Potter's, and Harkness's, which had been undertaken to build cross-class friendships and to dissipate sexual desire, could and did veer precipitously into all sorts and conditions of opposite-sex romance. Only two months after firmly rejecting Price's offer and reaffirming her commitment to spinsterhood, Pycroft was stunned to learn that her clients had understood her situation far better than she. Mr. Paul had fallen deeply in love with her: "I suppose I was a great donkey not to have seen long ago what other people saw—but I didn't. . . . If I had not thought of him as a boy I should have seen quickly enough—but he was very odd and unlike other men."[62] Two years later, still determined to sacrifice none of her life's work in the slums, Pycroft embarked on an ill-fated engagement with Paul. If female social observers exoticized the landscapes of the slums, Pycroft's story reminds us that working people in turn wondered about the romantic and sexual lives of the elite women who came to live among them.[63]

Plenty of philanthropic women did find romance with their male counterparts in the slums, especially those connected to Methodist and Congregationalist networks of benevolence, which actively encouraged male and female workers to marry and raise families in their adopted slum communities. There was nothing "dirty" about sexual attraction between men and women whose love, stimulated by the shared desire to help the poor, consummated in marriage. "There is a law of Settlement philosophy which we have often laid down in these pages," proclaimed the editor of the *Monthly Record* of the Wesleyan Methodist Bermondsey Settlement in October 1903. "Marriage is no deadly drug, but a healthy tonic; the duties of settlement membership are widened, the outlook is broader, the work is stronger."[64] In the previous five years, many of the settlement's key workers, male and female, had found their mates working together in the mean streets of south London. Grace Hannam began her distinguished career of social service with the West London

Mission in the early 1890s where she was known as Sister Grace, but she soon moved to the Women's Branch of the Bermondsey Settlement. She found herself drawn irresistibly toward the children "who sit eternally on the curbstones and in the gutters of our tenement house districts."[65] In marked contrast with the largely all-female, day-to-day life at Anglican women's settlements such as St. Hilda's and St. Margaret's, Grace and other members of the women's branch of Bermondsey Settlement were in constant and close contact with their male counterparts. No one was surprised when Sister Grace consented to marry the witty and fun-loving Dr. Charles W. Kimmins in July 1898. After all, Kimmins, the London County Council's leading child psychologist, had worked for years at the settlement and had assisted Grace in running her pioneering programs for crippled children. Their wedding was a great public event for both branches of the settlement house (male and female) and the neighborhood; it was not only a ritual joining of two lives, but a symbolic enactment of the settlement's ideals about class and gender relations.

> The Warden [of Bermondsey Settlement, Rev. John Scott Lidgett] performed the ceremony, Mr. Borland was at the organ, children from the Guild of Play [founded by Sister Grace] formed the choir, both floor and gallery was so crowded by the cripples and children who so warmly love "Sister Grace" that friends from a distance had some difficulty in finding seats at all. The very front row was reserved for some of the members of the Guild of the Brave Poor Things [another organization founded by Sister Grace], and when Dr. Kimmins—who was apparently quite too happy to keep still—came in some twenty minutes before time to help in getting people to their places, he had to shake hands with every one of them.[66]

Their marriage demonstrated that Sister Grace's romantic attraction to the unwashed children of the gutter was compatible with her "healthy" attraction to a single male fellow worker. While commentators could not pathologize such love affairs as symptoms of decadence, some, like the socialist H. M. Hyndman, cynically dismissed women's slum philanthropy as a mere pretext used by bourgeois women to snare suitable husbands.[67]

Bermondsey Settlement may have welcomed marriages among co-workers, but the tone of life at its women's branch was set by educated single women, such as its head, Mary Simmons, its treasurer Alice Barlow, and lifelong same-sex partners, Laura Robinson and Anna Martin. These women evinced little interest in matrimony for themselves. For them and for so many other educated women, social welfare institutions in the slums of London were safe havens outside the confines of marriage and male authority where they could most fully realize their aspirations. When Laura Robinson died suddenly in 1907, the settlement celebrated not only her achievements as an educator and social worker among girls, but also her "close and abiding friendship with Miss Martin." "Here, in congenial association with the Warden [John Scott Lidgett], with whom her relations steadily deepened into friendship, and with her closest friend [Anna Martin] as fellow worker, we are glad to feel she found the opportunity she desired and at the same time, helpful comrades and the freedom needed by her original personality and vigorous mind." Mary Simmons, the author of the obituary, also noted that "here too began my own eleven years' intimate personal friendship with her—but of that I do not write."[68]

Simmons's moving tribute depicts a community of single women who openly shared their admiration for spinsterdom, for social reform and social hygiene, and for each other. As several scholars have shown, women's social welfare institutions such as settlement houses and missions incorporated many of the intimate, domestic rituals of girls' schools and women's colleges—nightly cocoa, "gaudies," intense female friendships—into the fabric of their day-to-day lives in the slums. Surrounded by dirt, these women, like Florence Nightingale's nurses before them, were determined at all costs to guard the reputations of their institutions and themselves from any charge of impurity and unwomanliness.[69] Emmeline Pethick-Lawrence, fearing that marriage "would close all doors to deliverance" from her "limited little world," found precisely the liberation she needed by joining the West London Mission and living with like-minded women in a community "to carry out the subversive principles of social sharing."[70]

While philanthropic men who lived in the slums were praised for sacrificing their personal and financial ambitions, men often attacked women for enjoying precisely the freedoms that Pethick-Lawrence celebrated. One enraged clergyman condemned women's settlements as a recrudescence of the medieval "barbarities" of sexual celibacy. Woman seeks "some demonstrative way of expressing her new-found liberty; and, as all the sweet domesticities of life—husband, children and the loving care of them—are closely associated in her mind with the fetters of her slavery" she naturally "eschews the banalities of home, shirk[s] its responsibilities" while gaining "glory of a mild kind" for her benevolence.[71] Because so many of these women were graduates of women's colleges, commentators likewise criticized them for being hard, mannish, and unfeminine. These stereotypes were so powerful and widespread that they passed for truth among some philanthropic spinsters themselves. When Winifred Locket returned to London from a six months visit to Ceylon, she reluctantly agreed to take temporary charge of a branch of the Charity Organisation Society in North Lambeth. The organizing secretary of the COS, Charles Loch, suggested she lodge at the nearby Lady Margaret Hall Settlement. "I think I rather expected to find a somewhat rigid community of hard featured women," Locket recalled years later, "who combined hard living with high thinking." She was delighted with what she did find there—"a fellowship of work and sympathy and prayer"[72]—and stayed for thirty years.

Contemporaries were uncomfortable with the rise of same-sex communities of independent women—including celibate Anglican sisterhoods—who lived and worked outside the institutional, sexual, and psychological borders controlled by men. But the widely accepted ideal of women's "passionlessness," in combination with their supposedly inherent tendency to "selflessness," protected women from the charge of homoerotic license, which was leveled at their male counterparts. It also left them unable to articulate their thoughts about their own sexuality. "The inability to think about sexuality in terms other than sin," Martha Vicinus concludes, "inhibited both women and men from a deeper consideration of the motivations of their behavior, their own and that of those they sought to help."[73] At the same time, philanthropic institutions did support a remarkable number of lifelong partnerships between women. Some spinster slum workers were literally sisters, such as Margaret and Rachel McMillan or Anna and Fanny Tillyard. The Tillyard sisters lived and worked in Canning Town as part of the women's branch of Mansfield House, a university settlement house established along municipal and Christian socialist lines by the Methodist Percy Alden. They created a health clinic/hospital for women and children that was staffed entirely by women doctors and nurses. Anna felt that her nursing work allowed her to "penetrate the hidden recesses of the struggling life of these darkened homes . . . to alleviate the inevitable suffering and gloom."[74] But just as importantly, the Canning Town Women's Settlement gave them a place where they could engage in satisfying and productive work and live together with other single women. The lifelong partnerships of prominent spinster slum reformers and activists such as Anna Martin and Laura Robinson, Eleanor Rathbone and Elizabeth Macadam, Esther Roper and Eva Gore-Booth provided an alternative, non-kin model of passionate sisterhood.

But what was the nature of these non-kin sisterly loves? Where along a continuum of romantic friendship and sexual love should we place them? Historians of cross-class brotherhood and slumming have a range of sexually explicit sources (diaries, letters, transcripts and newspaper accounts of sex trials) that make clear that some elite men translated love for their working-class brothers into physical sex as well as into spiritual and cultural elevation.[75] But, with their female counterparts, we simply do not have comparable historical sources by which to assess the intimate workings of their relationships. What are we to make of this absence in the archive? It is partly the product of the systematic destruction

of sources. For example, it seems likely that Eleanor Rathbone's first biographer, Mary Danvers Stocks, destroyed any correspondence between
Rathbone and Macadam that revealed the character of their intimate life
with one another.[76] But it may also be a simpler matter. It seems very
likely that most elite women's physical relationships conformed to their
own rigorous standards of sexual purity. Sex acts that never happened,
like sources that never existed, cannot be recovered, no matter how diligently historians may search.[77]

The nature of surviving sources suggests that we can gain deeper insights by examining what role, if any, same-sex desire—not same-sex
acts—may have played in structuring the moral imaginations of elite
women engaged in slum philanthropy. We also need to begin to see that
the apparent eschewal of sex (however we may construe "sex" as physical acts) cannot be equated with the absence of sexuality. For many unmarried philanthropic women (like the celibate religious and philanthropic men I will discuss in chapter 5), celibacy constituted a reasoned
and deliberate choice about how to express their sexuality, as well as a
logical extension of their fetishized obsession with cleanliness in their
work in the slums. Sexual purity, along with education and class status,
entitled them to live in the slums apart from men and the conventions of
middle-class femininity as experts in child welfare, social hygiene, charity
visiting, and district nursing.[78] Understood in this way, the burdens of
preserving their own purity while regulating the "dirt" of the urban poor
cannot be divorced from their emancipatory consequences in their lives
and for future generations of women.

"Nasty Books": Dirty Bodies, Dirty Desires in Women's Slum Novels

Novels constitute one rich set of sources that historians can use in reconstructing the sexual dynamics of women's romances with the slums and
with one another in late Victorian London.[79] As with all sources, they
pose particular challenges and offer particular opportunities. I claim neither that these fictions transparently represent social reality nor that they
offer the concealed "truth" about the motives underpinning cross-class
benevolence. But novels do constitute attempts by their authors to organize self-consciously what they saw, thought, and read about the world
of slum philanthropy they knew quite well. The ways they chose to make
sense of this world—the discursive resources they mobilized as writers of
fiction—drew upon already available ways of conceptualizing slums,
dirt, and cross-class relationships. They also offered new possibilities for
thinking about slumming and the novel as a literary form. Novels regis-

ter not just what can be said, but also what cannot be said, and sometimes, what cannot be fully understood by contemporaries. Novels can give us access to cultural attitudes—and fantasies—about urban dirt and female sexual desire, which may allow us to reread and put greater pressure on our traditional historical sources.

Many female reformers believed that novels could and did powerfully shape women's perceptions of the poor and their moral sensibility. Some frankly acknowledged that reading novels about slumming had sparked their own curiosity about how the poor lived.[80] They saw novels as a way to prompt middle-class girl and women readers to feel obligations to the poor and to act on them. Muriel Lester believed that "the forceful imagery of Olive Schreiner's book *Dreams* awoke thousands of people to feel shame rather than pride in possession of riches," which in turn led many to go out "to the ends of the earth with a passion for friendship in their hearts."[81]

Two novels, Vernon Lee's *Miss Brown* (1884) and Mrs. L. T. Meade's *A Princess of the Gutter* (1896) offer particularly fertile opportunities for exploring the relationship between female sexual subjectivity, the regulation and representation of dirt, and philanthropy. Lee and Meade make an unlikely pairing. Lee's given name was Violet Paget. She was a paradigmatic figure of fin-de-siècle sexual dissidence who adopted the masculine nom de plume Vernon Lee not only as a writer but also in her private life in the late 1870s and '80s. Her companion of her final years described her as a "homosexual" (a term Lee never used to describe herself) who rejected physical intimacy and "never faced up to sexual facts."[82] Mrs. L. T. Meade, by contrast, was a pillar of respectability, a wife and mother, a staunch Evangelical, and the age's most prolific author of wholesome books for girls and young women.

Both women were deeply attuned to their self-presentations as women, to their public performances of gender. John Singer Sargent's 1881 portrait of Violet Paget (she was still called this by many in her circle at the time) and surviving photographs of her from 1912 capture her determination to look and act the part of Vernon Lee—that is, a male bohemian intellectual. Bespectacled, having short cropped hair and stylishly mannish clothing, Lee flaunts her deviation from norms of female beauty (figure 4.1). Meade zealously protected and shaped her public image. As two photographs taken for an article in a popular women's magazine illustrate, she projected a reassuring image of bourgeois respectability, feminine charm, domestic comfort, and maternal solicitude. She literally embodies Ruskin's Queen in the Garden as she takes her tea surrounded by her two children and their fancy pet dog. The Persian carpet covering the lawn pays homage to Meade's ability (or rather to the labors of her invisible servants) to extend her domestic dominion to nature itself (fig-

FIGURE 4.1.   Photograph of Vernon Lee, c. 1912. (Courtesy of Colby College Special Collections, Waterville, Maine.)

ures 4.2a and b). Comparing the lives and fictions of Lee and Meade makes it possible to explore a wide range of representations of female sexual and philanthropic subjectivities that calls into question the stark contrasts their portraits immediately suggest.

Lee burst upon the English literary and artistic scene in the early 1880s after a peripatetic childhood on the continent. Of Scottish, French, Welsh, and putative Russian origins, Lee's family had made its fortune in the eighteenth century with Jamaican sugar—and the blood of African slaves, a fact that haunted her life and fiction.[83] She is perhaps best remembered today as Henry James's "Tiger Lady," whose brightly burning green eyes, acid tongue, and insights into human passions (including James's own) terrified and attracted him. In 1893 Henry James confided to his brother William, that she is "as dangerous and uncanny as she is intelligent which is saying a great deal."[84] A virtuosic woman of letters and inveterate lover of women, she had quickly insinuated herself into highbrow and high-minded literary and artistic circles in London and Oxford. In the months leading up to writing *Miss Brown*, she was a regular guest of the bohemian socialist and pre-Raphaelite set that gathered

a   L. T. Meade.

From a photograph by]   [Bradshaw, Newgate Street, E.C.

b   In the Garden.

FIGURE 4.2. These photographs of Mrs. Meade are designed to remind readers that Meade was not only a literary celebrity but also a devoted mother and womanly woman. In marked contrast to the androgynously bohemian garb Lee favored, Mrs. Meade's blouse in figure 4.2a is all feminine ribbons and flounces. In figure 4.2b, "In the Garden," Mrs. Meade quite literally plays the part of Ruskin's "Queen" in her garden, surrounded by her two children, a tea pot, and gorgeous flowers. (From *Sunday Magazine*, vol. 30, 1894. Courtesy of Carnegie Library of Pittsburgh.)

at William and Jane Morris's Hammersmith home. She mingled freely and frequently with sexually dissident literati such as Frances Power Cobbe, John Addington Symonds, Mark André Raffalovich, and Walter Pater. Though she was never intimate with "the wonderful Oscar Wilde," they sometimes found themselves at the same social gatherings, and Lee invariably recorded her barbed impressions of his "lyrico-sarcastic maudlin cultschah" conversation.[85] Her letters of the 1880s and '90s constitute a de facto guidebook to the intersecting and overlapping worlds of metropolitan philanthropy, political radicalism, and bohemian sexuality. She attended meetings of groups ranging from the Salvation Army, the Fabian Society, and the Fellowship of the New Life, to the Socialist League, the Social Democratic Federation, and exiled Russian Nihilists. Her circle of female acquaintances included the radical Jewish novelist and poet, Amy Levy; the social scientist and expert in women's labor, Clementina Black; the foremost woman journalist and critic of the New Woman, Eliza Lynn Linton; the idealistic Leeds socialist, Emily Ford; and the uncompromising founder of the Women's University Settlement in the slums of south London, Alice Gruner.

As the mania for slumming gathered momentum and merged with aesthetic projects devoted to the cultural elevation of the masses, Lee found in slumming a subject well suited to her temper and keen eye for "those melancholy little psychological dramas which go on, unseen to the world, in a man's soul."[86] While she herself did not go slumming until the mid-1880s, Lee's descriptions of slum philanthropy were based on the impressions of her intimate and constant female companion of these years, Mary Robinson, who helped to run a club for working-class girls that was affiliated with the Working Men's College. The result of her musings about the philanthropic and aesthetic worlds to which she had so recently been welcomed was her sprawling three-volume novel, *Miss Brown*, published in 1884 to exceptionally hostile public and private reviews.[87] It was these reviews which prompted Lee to seek understanding and, perhaps, some solace, in autobiographical reflection.

In one of the two fragments from her voluminous diaries (written in 1883–34) that she could not bear to destroy, Vernon Lee agonized over the relationship between the pure and the impure, the dirty and the clean, the moral and the immoral—in the world and within herself. Such oppositions, lavishly staged and forever collapsing into one another in her writings, consumed Lee, who pondered the "slightly demoralized moralizings" of the past and present.[88] As she confessed in an 1884 essay, "we"—by which she presumably meant her readers and herself—feel an "imperious necessity" to gaze upon some "horrible evil" made all the more horrible because of "the still fouler intermeshing of evil with good."[89] History taught, Lee insisted, that "meanness . . . lurks in noble things" and "nobility . . . lurks in mean ones."[90] Written at a moment in history when Londoners claimed to be shocked by the foul intermeshing of evil with good within the metropolis, Lee's fictions, histories, and art criticism rejected a simplistic division of humanity into an enlightened and benevolent elite and an unwashed and immoral underclass. The social and psychological portrait she painted was bold and unnerving in its embrace of moral ambiguities, which were, she argued, symptoms of mongrelized sexual, racial, and national identities.

Here are some excerpts from Lee's 1884 diary fragment. Lee took advantage of the freedom from formal conventions of syntax and logical argument offered by diary writing to produce a text that reads like an interior monologue careening from self-confidence to self-doubt and self-loathing back to self-justification. She begins by lamenting the limits of the novel as a literary genre.

> I will show fight . . . when it came home to me that the anonymous reviewer in the *Spectator* was not alone in accusing me of having written . . . a "nasty book." I will show fight, argue, prove that I am in the right, that the restrictions placed upon the novel in England are absurd, that my novel is legitimate and praiseworthy.

It is impossible to say with certainty what connotative meanings Lee attached to the word "nasty." The Christian socialist Charles Kingsley had immortalized its association with shoddiness and exploited labor in his 1850 pamphlet *Cheap Clothes and Nasty*; but in the 1890s, one of Havelock Ellis's informants for his study of lesbianism used the word "nasty" repeatedly to describe her own homosexual practices.[91]

Lee's resolve to fight immediately yields to uncertainty as she wonders whether merely by representing immorality—albeit to condemn it—she has unwittingly reproduced it.

> I am accused of having, in simplicity of heart, written with a view to moralise the world, an immoral book; accused of having done more mischief by setting my readers' imaginations hunting up evil than I could possibly do good by calling upon their sympathies to hate that mischief; accused, in short, of doing in a minor degree the very things for which I execrate Zola or Maupassant.

Having located herself within and against the literary tradition of corrupting and sensational French naturalism, she then turns inward and offers an interpretation of her novel as a mirror of her diseased self. Her repeated use of the word "morbid"—a proto-psychological word often (though not exclusively) denoting same-sex desire—invokes the language of sexual dissidence.

> What if I had myself a morbid imagination made more morbid by a hundred accidents of training and reading. . . . Am I not perhaps mistaking the call of the beast for the call of God; may there not, at the bottom of this seemingly

scientific, philanthropic, idealising, decidedly noble looking nature of mine, be something base, dangerous, disgraceful, that is cozening me.[92]

A year later, the Irish novelist and playwright of sensation George Moore added grievous insult to injury. He attempted (without Lee's permission) to include excerpts from *Miss Brown* in an anthology of "the most improper" writings that, unlike his own, had escaped the ever-vigilant censors at Mudie's famous circulating library. Lee met Moore over dinner at the home of the parents of her beloved Mary Robinson; Mary set Moore straight and succeeded in removing *Miss Brown* entirely from Moore's "dirty collection."[93]

What had Lee written in *Miss Brown* to provoke such passionate self-doubts and strong reactions from reviewers? *Miss Brown* centers on a wealthy effeminate poet-painter Walter Hamlin, who falls in love with an idealized image of womanhood he projects onto Anne Brown, a sullenly beautiful nursemaid of Italian and Scottish descent. As Lee was writing *Miss Brown*, she was still reeling from the death of a beautiful real-life Anne, Anne Meyer, for whom she had an idealized but unconsummated passion. "It is sad," she wrote in her diary, "to have to admit to myself that had she [Anne] lived we might perhaps have not got much nearer to one another, never perhaps to that point of seeing, of being able to touch and embrace the whole personality."[94] Hamlin is the novel's antihero who, like the name and persona of Vernon Lee, functions as Lee's male double. Hamlin is no gentleman seducer of servant girls. He is described as an "aesthete" and "a queer creature . . . [not] in the matter of wrists and waistcoats, but in the matter of women" (3: 201). Sexual queerness and aestheticism remain inextricably linked in Hamlin, as they do more generally in the novel. Anne Brown is repelled by her benefactor's lack of manly passion, fortitude, and vigor. Hamlin's artistic genius is marred by "emasculating vices"—"longings after untold shameful things"—inherited from his immoral West Indian slaveholding ancestors (2: 52, 88). Hamlin's apparent benevolence, his Pygmalion-like project of cultural elevation, is doubly self-incriminating. On the one hand, it appears to be motivated by his selfish desire to transform Miss Brown into a suitable wife and object of perfect beauty. On the other, his lack of physical desire for her combined with the insistent reminders of his feminine appearance suggest that one of Hamlin's secret vices is not merely effeminacy but sexual inversion. Anne alone can rescue Hamlin, "this womanish fine gentleman" from his own decadent, self-destructive inclinations (1: 177).

The slums of East London appear in *Miss Brown* as an almost obligatory site of elite female benevolence. But oddly, they are the place which produces the only clean and healthy romance in the novel between one of

Anne's benevolent female friends, Marjory Leigh, and a sweetly sincere High Church slum priest, Harry Collett, who "had renounced a good living . . . in order to become a curate in the East End of London"(2: 156). The narrator's description of their courtship anticipates Ella Pycroft's romance with Maurice Paul a few years later: both parties were "perfectly unaware" of their own intense flirtations, which were disguised by their earnest discussions of "charity reorganisation" and "ventilation" (2: 158). Philanthropic slumming in London is a sexed activity in *Miss Brown*, but one which conforms to normative expectations of opposite-sex romance and morality.

The foulest physical spaces we encounter in the novel are not where we would most expect them—East London—but the derelict one-room country cottages owned by Walter Hamlin. In this respect, Lee challenged social workers' persistent identification of the sunlight, water, and dirt of country life as a necessary and purifying antidote to urban squalor. We can be quite sure that the armies of female settlement house workers across London spearheading the annual excursions of the Children's Country Holiday Fund (founded by Henrietta and Samuel Barnett) had no intention of sending their charges to stay in one-room cottages. Mirrors of their negligent and impure owner, Hamlin's cottages are hotbeds of filth and sexual perversion, beset by incest rather than inversion. Anne describes the cottages as "abominations" whose "sordid, filthy reality" literally nauseates her (2: 164). Dirt and "unnatural" sex are cause and consequence of one another. She desperately tries to convince Walter to rebuild the cottages into physically and morally clean dwellings. Despite her elevation to the status of a lady, she continues to play the part of the nursemaid in her determination to clean up other people's dirt. But to Anne's horror, Walter prefers to aestheticize the dirt and vices of his poor tenants by immortalizing them in his poetry rather than taking philanthropic action (2: 204). Like a latter-day Baudelaire, Hamlin insists that that "there is something very grand and tragic in this sin flowering like evil grasses in that marsh" (2: 213). Anne's disgust with Walter's "fleshly" aestheticism makes her long to plunge into and clean dirt. She yearns to return to her former life as a maid with "the tattered furniture and ill-swept rooms, the dirty and noisy kitchen with the haunting smell of sink; the dull routine of washing and ironing and mending, of dressing and undressing the refractory children" (2: 218). But recognizing the impossibility of such a return, she instead sets her sights on the dirt of East London, first vicariously through books and then directly by undertaking "ghastly rounds in the slums." Her cynical but practical cousin, Richard Brown, insists that she, like Hamlin, has merely transformed the squalor of the poor into an aesthetic experience worthy of Pater. The "very wise" get "as many moments of thrilling impression as possible" out of art and song, and "the less wise out of vice or out of philanthropy," he snidely informs Anne (2: 227).

While Hamlin's strange cross-class romance for Anne forms the core of the plot, it can barely contain the novel's "erotic counterplotting" which, Terry Castle has argued, is a hallmark of lesbian fiction.[95] Erotic counterplots swirl around Anne, whose beauty is hyperbolically sexualized while she paradoxically remains "a mere sexless creature" (2: 249) who wants nothing more than to flee men altogether and become a student at a women's college. Anne is a racially and sexually "unaccountable mixed type." The narrator and other characters persistently liken her complexion to that of a Jewess or Ethiopian, and her figure to one of "Michaelangelo's women"—that is to say, she possesses an essentially male body masquerading in a woman's.[96] While Hamlin's transgressive sexuality is debased and corrupting, Anne's sexual ambiguity, her status as a woman "born to have been a man," is part of her womanly purity. In spite of and because of her purity, Anne inspires the sexual passions of several men and women. The novel typologizes a range of same-sex longings among women which range from a violent schoolgirl crush (3: 238) to the unrequited love of an educated spinster friend (2: 137) to the sapphic and vampiric attentions of the sexually omnivorous Sacha Elaguine, who successfully seduces Walter and attempts to consume Anne.[97]

After almost one thousand pages *Miss Brown* lurches to an improbable and unsatisfying end. Anne abandons her aspiration to enter into a community of independent women and devotes herself to rescuing her would-be rescuer, Hamlin, as his wife. In some sense, Anne acts precisely the way a woman is supposed to: she annihilates her own desires to care for a man by marrying him. But this misbegotten union, far from resolving the novel's many plots and arguments, merely underscores that two of the pillars of bourgeois respectability, marriage and philanthropy, are not what they appear to be. Both are implicated in perverse same- and opposite-sex romances, which are literally and figuratively unclean and which often collapse into one another. Hamlin's seemingly benevolent desire to save Anne from her life as a maid is counterbalanced by his "mysterious temptations of unspeakable things, beckoning his nobler nature into the mud."[98] Perhaps even more significantly, Anne explicitly connects marriage to Hamlin with the embodiment of soiled femininity: she likens "loveless" marriage to a "mere legalised form of prostitution." "To become, therefore, the wife of Hamlin," Anne reasons to herself, "was an intolerable self-degradation—nay, a pollution" (3: 280). The dirtiness of Anne's marriage is magnified by her awareness that in marrying Hamlin she would "become the wife of Sacha's lover" and thereby be contaminated by Sacha's perverse sexual appetites. When Anne finally does yield to Hamlin and consent to be his wife and be touched by him,

"It seemed to Anne as if she felt again the throttling arms of Sacha Elaguine about her neck, her convulsive kiss on her face, the cloud of her drowsily scented hair stifling her. She drew back, and loosened his grasp with her strong hands" (3: 298). As Kathy Psomiades astutely points out, the "climactic moment of heterosexual union is displaced by yet another experience of the arms, the kiss, the drowsily scented hair of Sacha Elaguine"—that is, a sexually perverse and aggressive woman.[99]

Miss Brown's ending, far from signaling Lee's capitulation to the conventions of the novel and her acceptance of bourgeois values, seems to adopt a rhetorical strategy often deployed by male sexual dissidents in the late nineteenth century. It neither inverts nor rejects dominant social and sexual norms. Instead, the ending appears to sanction and reproduce these norms while allowing those readers who have understood the novel's many "queer" romances to enjoy its subversion of them.[100] Or does it? After all, as Lee's anguished diary entries reveal, she believed that she was emphatically not merely "posing" as a moralist but that she was one. Male aesthetes and sexual dissidents like Oscar Wilde intentionally mobilized a coded language of same-sex eroticism in their writing and hoped that those who were meant to break the code would. Lee's novel, unlike Wilde's literary productions, is a tirade *against* the sins of aestheticism, which she identifies not only with sexual perversion but with the indifferent refusal of aesthetes like Hamlin to clean up the poor. Unlike Wilde's delight in word play in his plays and prose, there is nothing intentionally parodic about *Miss Brown*'s bitter satire. Just as Dr. Barnardo's photographs of ragged children simultaneously incited and condemned viewers' desire to see "street arabs" as erotic objects (see chapter 2), so, too, Lee thrusts her readers into a world of proliferating and titillating perversions that she then demands that we abhor. But Lee's attempt to pathologize dirt and dirty desires cannot escape from her own obsessive attraction to and fascination with both. Her stance as a conventional moralist, signaled by her resort to marriage as the novel's resolution, is utterly unconvincing. Anne's and Walter's marriage threatens to corrode from within rather than buttress the institution of marriage and the ideological apparatus of cross-class benevolence.

The more that Lee appears to reject the impurities and sexualities she depicts, the more vehemently her readers and critics (then and now) have insisted that these sexualities express her deepest, albeit unmentionable, desires. Such an interpretation uncomfortably insists that Lee's "no's," motivated by her sincere quest for personal and social purity, are really "yes's." But we need to be careful in coercing Lee's assent to become for readers today what she resolutely chose not to be in her own lifetime. In *Miss Brown* and in the conduct of her private life, Lee ultimately eschewed lesbian sexual liberation even as she was a central participant in the emerging lesbian subculture of late Victorian and Edwardian London. Like the spinster do-gooders who populated London's settlement houses and countless charitable committees, Lee preferred to express her sexuality through celibacy and emotional intimacy with other women and to express her concern for the poor through fetishizing physical and moral cleanliness. In the years after she published the novel, Lee herself sought out, and apparently found, "thrilling" impressions in the London slums.[101] She and the female companion who replaced Mary Robinson in her affections, Kit Anstruther Thomson, spent the night at an outpost of glorified spinsterdom, the Canning Town Women's Settlement. The surrounding slums—"almost pitch dark & inconceivably grimy and foul"— enraptured her with their exotic mingling of people laboring amid the pathetic chaos of the dockyards.[102]

The expatriate American novelist Henry James seems to have understood *Miss Brown* and its ending all too well, though it certainly brought him very little pleasure. There was far too much at stake for James personally, since Lee had dedicated "for good luck" her first novel to "kind Mr. James who is most sweet and encouraging."[103] When he read *Miss Brown*, his response was anything but kind or encouraging. To a friend, he confided that the novel was "painfully disagreeable in tone . . . a rather deplorable mistake to be repented of."[104] To Lee, he was somewhat more diplomatic though quite critical. Anne's marriage to Walter Hamlin, he explained to Lee, struck him as "false, really unimaginable." James, who preferred to delicately suggest but never articulate the sexual demons haunting him and his fictional creations, criticized Lee for having "impregnated" her characters "too much with the sexual, the basely erotic preoccupation." He urged her to write another novel, one less hotly moral so that she would seem "less immoral" to her readers.[105] While Miss Lee did not return to the novel as a literary form for many years, James heeded his own advice. His next two novels, *The Bostonians* and *The Princess Casamassima* attempted to demonstrate to Lee and the world just how a great novelist ought to treat passionate friendships between high-minded spinsters and the sublimated erotics of the "passion" for "charity" prevailing on both sides of the Atlantic in 1885. In particular, James's eponymous Princess liked seeing "dirty hands," and "queer types and exploring out-of-the-way social corners" and "took romantic fancies to vagabonds of either sex." She situated herself at the apex of an unstable homoerotic love triangle with two radical artisans, the manly Paul Muniment and the androgynously effeminate Hyacinth Robinson, who appears to love Paul at least as much as the Princess herself. Hyancinth's suicide at the novel's end, apparently galvanized by his failure as a political anarchist, seems just as likely to mark a moment of despairing recognition of his own sexually anarchic desires for Paul.[106]

Read in this way, *The Princess* bears distinct traces of James's attempt to reckon with Lee's influence over him and to rewrite *Miss Brown* in a way that satisfied his literary and moral sensibility.[107]

A decade later, Mrs. L. T. Meade wrote *A Princess of the Gutter*, a novel about an heiress who, like James's and Lee's heroines, is fascinated by the spectacle of urban poverty and decides to live among the poor. Raised in the comforts of the Anglo-Irish clerical elite in Cork, Meade had made her way to London as a young woman determined to earn her living through her pen in defiance of her father. Her financial and literary success was swift and remarkable. From the late 1870s until her death in 1914, she produced over 250 books while editing a journal for girls and young women, *Atalanta*, and contributing countless articles to periodicals such as the evangelical *Sunday Magazine*. Meade and the female journalists who came to interview her went out of their way to emphasize her gracious womanliness and maternal involvement in the rearing of her children. Meade insisted that she put "domestic claims" before "those of the publisher or public." An interviewer for the *Sunday Magazine* underscored that her study, the space within her home she used to pursue her career, reflected "womanly attention," not professional ambition and independence.[108] An interviewer sent by the *Young Woman* gushed that "a healthy tone pervades all her works, and her pictures of English home life in particular are the best of their kind." "Her personality is like her writings," the interviewer continued, "bright, fresh, vivacious."[109]

At the same time, Meade was much less conventional than such portraits would suggest.[110] Her professional schedule left little time to attend to her own household. With a full-time staff of two or three female secretaries, who took dictation and typed for her, Meade toiled at her editorial office in the city until seven each night; she returned to the comforts of her suburban villa in Dulwich and, after dinner, "spent every evening correcting proofs."[111] She was an active member of the Pioneer Club in London, which attracted New Women, like Mona Caird, who were eager to discuss the "various movements for women's social, educational and political advancement."[112] Even more tellingly, Mrs. L. T. Meade was not really Mrs. Meade at all. Her maiden name was Elizabeth (Lucy) Thomasina Meade; in 1879 she married the solicitor, Alfred Toulmin Smith. She was thus either Miss Meade or Mrs. Smith. "L. T. Meade" and "Mrs. L. T. Meade," the names she used for interviews and on the title pages of her books, were noms de plume, suggesting her unwillingness to disappear entirely into the identity of Mrs. Alfred Smith.[113]

Meade's novels reflected her extensive firsthand knowledge about educated spinsters and their philanthropic enterprises in London. She wrote a series of essays about women's colleges for *Strand Magazine* in the early 1890s. She was deeply involved in evangelical philanthropy in London and actively supported Benjamin Waugh and the Society for the Prevention of Cruelty to Children from its inception in 1884.[114] From her first major success, *Scamp and I, A Story of City By-Ways* (1876), Meade was fascinated by the plight of poor girls and boys and the middle-class spinsters who sought to rescue them.[115] Unlike most of her novels, which Meade insisted did not portray specific individuals, Meade attempted in *A Princess of the Gutter* "to make this picture of life amongst our great unclassed as faithful as possible" and sketched one of its protagonists "from a living original" (preface, iii). The book made claims to document not just general truths but particular facts about East London.

Meade's engagement with philanthropy was matched by her strong views about the moral obligations of the novelist and the power of her novels in shaping the imaginations and aspirations of her readers. Girls needed books that reflected and molded their "inner lives." In marked contrast to Vernon Lee's ambiguous moral universe, Meade saw the world in terms of a clear-cut struggle between good and evil in which good must and always did prevail. Naughtiness, high spirits, frankness, compassion, and independence were qualities Meade gladly sanctioned in her fictional creations and in her readers. She abhorred duplicity, slyness, and vindictiveness.[116] Her views on novels—and women novelists—were equally vehement and straightforward. She denounced social-realist and sensational novels for circulating "microbes thrown off from disease." Reading itself could become a form of slumming, one every bit as capable of infecting the reader in the privacy of her home as a descent into the actual filth of a slum tenement. The modern woman writer bore an especially heavy burden of guilt. "In her hands there is no delicacy, no reverence, only a tearing aside of the curtain of reserve and decency. . . . I do think the hour has come for every right-minded mother in England to raise her voice in protest against this horror in our midst."[117]

These may have been Meade's guiding principles, but *A Princess of the Gutter* strayed extremely far from them in its depiction of women's sisterly love for one another.[118] The book is an examination of the connections between women's desire to wash away the dirt of slum life and their queer lives as sisters in the slums. It chronicles the social awakening of a recent girl graduate of Girton College, Cambridge, Joan Prinsep, who inherits a fortune derived from dilapidated slum tenement properties. Like so many nonfictional narratives written by female reformers, *Princess* depicts how Joan's conscience is pricked by her sensory impressions of the slums: "The broken windows were stopped up with rags, the floors were grimy with dirt, and vermin swarmed all over the horrible place" (73). She literally places her "clean soft hand" upon the bodies of the unclean people she meets (71), but the intimate contact almost causes her to faint

(75). Joan's initial expedition, like those of real-life female slum explorers such as Alice Hodson and Mary Higgs, ends with a hot bath, which purifies her and also serves as a kind of baptism into her new life as a servant of the poor (77). She soon moves into one of London's most notorious slum districts, the Old Nichol (called Jacob's Court in the novel), the scene of the real life philanthropic labors of the celebrated Anglican slum priest Father Jay, who was immortalized by Arthur Morrison's *Child of the Jago* (1896) less than a year after *Princess* was published.

A reviewer of *Princess* for *Literary World* praised it as worthy of Sir Walter Besant, the most commercially successful slum novelist and philanthropic journalist of his generation. However, in marked contrast to Besant's best-selling *All Sorts and Conditions of Men* (1882), which featured a wealthy brewery heiress who devotes herself to the East London poor only to find love there with a West End male philanthropist, Meade's heroine has no romantic interest in men or marriage. While spinsters' nonfictional slum narratives often included an amusing scene in which working-class girls wonder why their lady friends have neither a male suitor nor a husband, no one in Meade's novel even mentions the possibility that Joan would be romantically involved with a man.[119] Nor is this surprising since from the outset we learn that Joan has a surfeit of the "masculine element" in her (14).

Meade, unlike Lee in *Miss Brown* and James in *Princess Casamassima*, relegates marriage and opposite-sex romance to the margins of her girl-centered narrative. The central love story of the novel revolves around Joan and a charismatic "rough gel" from the neighborhood, Martha Mace.[120] Joan is immediately drawn to Martha who, like Bernard Shaw's Eliza Doolittle, is "so deliciously low—so horribly dirty." Joan is no condescending Henry Higgins, however, and Martha proves much more affectionate than Eliza. We first see Martha through Joan's admiring eyes.

> The girl stood now at the entrance door. Her hair was in steel curlers. She wore an untidy cotton blouse and an old skirt made of some drab material, which was partly out at the gathers, and streamed in a short, dirty train behind. She was a well-made buxom-looking girl, but her face was covered with smuts, and grimy from want of washing. . . . Will you come and see me this evening? . . . I have come here to make friends with girls like you. (121)

Joan's philanthropic, and, I would argue, romantic, interest in Martha depend on her outward dirtiness. Joan wants to make friends with a living representative of a sociological category—dirty girls like Martha—so that she can enjoy the spiritual reward of converting their minds, bodies, and souls. But Joan also glimpses beneath Martha's "smuts," detects her strength and beauty, and resolves to be "like a sister" to Martha and her "mate" Lucy Ashe (123). Joan couches her physical attraction to Martha in religious language: "God meant you to be beautiful. . . . God gave you a beautiful face and a grand figure" (143).

By deploying religious and familial rhetoric—sister, daughter, mother—Meade, in her fictional Joan, and other elite women slum reformers, in their nonfiction, distanced themselves from the unspeakable and perhaps unimaginable relationship of lover or spouse.[121] But the working-class girls in *Princess*, Martha and Lucy, are much less inhibited in how they define their "mateship": "[I]t's as good as bein' married in some ways, an' with none o' the troubles" (127). Beatrice Potter's "morbid" and "hysterical" cousin Margaret Harkness had encountered "mateship" in the 1880s while living and working in East London as a nurse, journalist, and novelist. In her own "nasty book" novel about the Salvation Army and sexual anarchy, *Captain Lobe* (1887), Harkness's "man-hating proletarian labor mistress" rebukes two factory girl "mates" who passionately kiss on the job.[122] Invoking this working-class slang, the aristocratic Anglo-Catholic slum priest James Adderley sincerely hoped that Muriel Wragge "had a 'Mate' to live with" when she returned to Hoxton as head of a local social welfare organization, the Maurice Hostel.[123]

A close observer of girls' schools and women's colleges, Meade was familiar with the school girl "crush" or "rave," which she helped popularize through novels such as *A Sweet Girl Graduate* (1891). Joan's and Martha's relationship conforms to some of the literary and erotic conventions of the "rave" as sensitively analyzed by Martha Vicinus: a passionately admiring love between an older and better-educated female teacher and a younger girl on the verge of womanhood. Vernon Lee's private life was dominated by a string of such relationships, in which she played the parts of both the "ravee" and the "raved." But the hallmark of these relationships, the enhancing of desire through the preservation of emotional and physical distance, is notably absent.[124] This is all the more remarkable because Joan and Martha are divided by age and authority as well as by an immense class distance.

The novel's emotional climax and the resolution of the adventure element of the narrative occurs in a prison cell at the Old Bailey, where Martha awaits execution for murdering the one sexually aggressive male in the novel, Lucy's wayward husband, Michael Lee. Joan knows intuitively and rightly that Martha could not have committed such a violent and immoral act and, like a latter-day Elizabeth Fry, visits her in prison to say farewell. The description of the scene, told from Joan's perspective, bursts the conventions of controlled passionate longing of previous encounters.[125] It is frankly erotic. In contrast to Lee's overheated rhetoric about immoral longings in *Miss Brown*, the narrator offers no apologies and betrays no anxieties. As soon as Joan enters, Martha takes Joan's hands, and bending down began to kiss them. I put my arms round her neck, however, and then she kissed my lips again and again, as if she were starving, and I had given her a full and satisfying meal. The door was locked behind us; the female warder in attendance withdrew to the most distant part of the cell, where she sat with her back to us, stooping over some needlework. (295/6).

This kiss bears no resemblance to the many other kisses of friendship women exchange with one another in the novel. Working-class Martha initiates their lovemaking, but Joan has "given her a full and satisfying meal." The freest expression of their spiritual and physical love is enacted deep within a prison cell in the institution that signified the policing and disciplinary authority of London, the Old Bailey. While the female warder discreetly turns her back to do womanly work, Meade's readers are given an unobstructed view of Martha and Joan and their words and actions. The imperative to use cross-class sisterhood as a means of purifying society leads Joan and Martha into physical intimacies that surpass the boundaries of romantic friendship. Had the homosexual socialist Edward Carpenter read *Princess*, he would have had no difficulty explaining Joan's relationship with Martha. Carpenter insisted that many of the world's "philanthropists of the best kind" (male and female) as well as the leaders of the movement for the emancipation of women were inspired by same-sex love, what he called the "uranian temperament" or the "homogenic passion among the female sex." "It is hardly needful in these days when social questions loom so large upon us," Carpenter explained, "to emphasise the importance of a bond which by the most passionate and lasting compulsion may draw members of the different classes together, and (as it often seems to do) none the less strongly because they are members of different classes."[126] As Carpenter developed a language by which to explain same-sex love from the 1880s onwards, he believed he had found one group of exemplary "urnings" (homosexuals) in the cohort of educated women committed to serving the poor and emancipating their sex.[127]

Princess offered its readers a deceptively radical ending. Absolved of guilt for a crime she did not commit, Martha is released from prison and free to assist in Joan's philanthropic enterprises. At the conclusion of the novel, Joan is happily ensconced in a small community of loving women she has constructed for herself: her faithful housekeeper, Mrs. Keys; her artistic and bohemian cousin Anne, who flees the demands of bourgeois femininity in the West End to join Joan; and of course, the various "rough gels," including Martha, who come to Joan's clubs, parties, and teas. Men and marriage have no part to play in Meade's unambiguously happy ending. In contrast to E. M. Forster's involuntary deferral of his fantasy of loving cross-race friendship between men in *A Passage to*

India—"not now, not yet"—Meade imagines an all-female arcadia in the slums of London. She, unlike Forster in *Maurice*, felt no need to postpone publication of her novel and exile her main characters to a distant greenwood. They lay claim to the very heart of the empire. Unlike New Women novels about slumming, such as Mrs. Humphry Ward's *Marcella*, Meade's heroine is not punished for violating gendered norms. In part, Joan has no price to pay for her unconventional life choices because Meade works so effectively to make the outcomes of the intertwined plots of romance and benevolence seem natural and inevitable. By so doing, she minimized the likelihood that her readers would scrutinize the implications of her novel's ending.

Meade was able to exploit the privileges that came with her socially central position as wife, mother, and author of "wholesome" girl novels in producing a text unashamed of its own explicitly homoerotic and subversive content. The unmarried, woman-loving Vernon Lee, by contrast, keenly felt the need to censure her own homoerotic impulses. She unreasonably expected her readers to wade into the morass of ambiguities depicted by her novel and emerge with a heightened commitment to traditional morality. Her ending, Anne and Walter's marriage, is all the more disturbing precisely because it is so bizarrely—or perhaps more aptly, "queerly"—conventional. On the other hand, for all of *Miss Brown*'s artistic and intellectual limitations, Lee at least tried to grapple with the dilemmas of self-aware (albeit crippling) adult female same-sex desire. These incompletely realized attempts make Lee's work more provocative and weighty than Meade's more open but less ambitious depiction of sisterly romance in and with the slums. Meade explored same-sex female love within the parameters of a well-established genre of schoolgirl fiction whose model of cross-age female friendships depended upon the willful ignorance of the very sexual desires the novel conjures. We are meant to know just enough about what is going on in the novel not to ask any uncomfortable questions.[128]

How did Meade's contemporaries respond to *Princess*? Did they condemn Meade for writing a "nasty book" masquerading as a morality tale? Far from it. One reviewer called it a "refined and fascinating tale of London" life; another, less enthusiastically, described it as "a novel with a purpose, . . . to show what good can be done in the East End of London if you devote your time, energy, and fortune to the task of elevating the masses" but confessed that "we cannot say we found the record of her [Joan's] doings very interesting reading."[129] What accounts for reviewers' failure to notice the homoerotics of dirtiness, which, I have argued, informed Meade's depiction of women's slum benevolence? First, Meade herself would have strenuously objected to my interpretation of her text—not simply because I have taken so seriously a popular novel written in haste, but because "nastiness" had no place in her vision of her writings. Sally Mitchell, writing about Meade's treatment of gender (not sexuality) argues that "it may indeed by Meade's very failure to pursue the implications of her plots and to look head-on at what she writes that allow her to introduce daring material."[130] Second, in the years following the publication of *Miss Brown*, the public had grown accustomed to ever more sensational and sexually charged writing, fiction and nonfiction. *Princess* makes pale reading compared to W. T. Stead's "Maiden Tribute" series. While all of Britain was intensely preoccupied with the dangers of male same-sex desires and friendships in the aftermath of the Wilde trial in 1895, lesbianism remained mostly hidden from public view by the beliefs in female moral superiority and "passionlessness" that buttressed domesticity. Finally, readers often find in books what they expect and want. As a reviewer for the *Saturday Review* commented, Meade was renowned for her attractive images of "healthy and innocent girlhood."[131] Readers' assumptions about Mrs. Meade's novels may well have precluded their noticing anything queer about her story. I feel certain that the anonymous "Momma," who on Valentine's Day, 1898, gave her daughter Mattie McMorris the copy I now own of *Princess*, had no intention of encouraging her daughter to "hunt up evil"—*Miss Brown*'s pernicious effect on some of its readers a decade before.

Meade and Lee were both self-conscious about their relationships to the novel as a literary form. Recall that Meade blasted social-realist and sensational novels as "microbes of disease," sources of contagion and pollution. Her stance on developments within the recent history of novels written by women was decidedly reactionary. She disassociated herself from such women writers and put herself forward as a wholesome and purifying alternative. Lee's standing in the world of letters was altogether different from Meade's. Her novel *Miss Brown* and her many essays on aesthetics contributed importantly to the emergence of literary decadence. In her 1884 diary entry, she attributed attacks on *Miss Brown* to the limits imposed on the novel as a form of literary expression. She alluded to this theme in a brief note she affixed to the diary manuscript in 1920. "What a pity," she scribbled, "I didn't put off writing Miss Brown thirty years!" In the aftermath of the much more frankly erotic and homoerotic literature produced in interwar Britain, we can understand Lee's lament.[132] But it also powerfully serves as a reminder that novels such as *Miss Brown* and *Princess* not only interpreted late Victorian perceptions of slum benevolence but also anticipated later sexual and social facts and fictions and thereby helped to make them possible as well. It should come as no surprise that Virginia Woolf paid fleeting homage to Vernon Lee and her contributions to aesthetics in *A Room of One's Own*.[133]

CONCLUSION: "WHITE GLOVES" AND "DIRTY HOXTON PENNIES"

What was the *something* the matter with the ladies who went slumming? This question needs to be put somewhat differently. There was no one thing "the matter," but rather a variety of "disorders" that elite women, despite their own best efforts, could not succeed in purging from how they thought about themselves and how contemporaries chose to represent them. The novels I have discussed suggest that elite women's desires for same-sex intimacy with one another and with their poor sisters were "pure" but "dirty" at the same time. Same-sex love, fueled by but seemingly incompatible with a Christian sense of mission, was an important though elusive dimension of their gospel of social housekeeping in late Victorian London. Novels offered readers an encoded (and hence in some ways still private) way to talk about managing society's dirt. With their public probing of private feelings and longings, they also offered women a safe space in which to examine the motivations of fictional—not real-life—characters. One of the problems that bedeviled Lee was the fact that too many of her friends and acquaintances believed that they saw themselves portrayed in *Miss Brown*. Lee's penchant for incorporating her friends into her stories collapsed the protective distance between life and fiction and ultimately alienated even people like Henry James, who genuinely admired her intellectual prowess. The late Victorian world tolerated a great deal of "sisterly" affection; but only in a novel like *Princess* could women passionately and hungrily kiss one another on the lips without compromising their status as sexless and pure workers on behalf of the poor.

Female social workers, charity organizers, and settlement house residents along with journalists, writers, and novelists, like Lee and Meade, powerfully reshaped gender relations, sexual subjectivities, and social welfare in late Victorian and Edwardian Britain. Not all of them chose to don the mantle of "feminism" when it emerged as an organized political and social movement at the turn of the century; even fewer identified themselves as lesbians, although sexologists increasingly popularized and attempted to stabilize what that term meant in the 1890s. But their self-fashioning of a wide range of subversive femininities—from Lee's mannish but "prudish" bohemianism to Meade's respectable New Womanliness—was closely bound up with their passionate attachments to other women and to their various projects to cleanse not just the streets but the private interior spaces of the London slums.

Dirt, sex, cross-class sisterhood, and female emancipation were all too clearly—and lamentably—joined together according to Roy Devereux the pen name of Mrs. Roy Pember-Devereux. In her 1896 study, *The Ascent of Woman*, she offered a sweeping assessment of the history of women and their long "ascent" toward greater self-expression. Published as part of a series called Eve's Library, *The Ascent of Woman* adopted an idiosyncratic though "modern" stance on social and sexual issues. Devereux called for easier divorce, not because she thought marriage was inherently unfair for women, but to preserve it from fanatics like Mona Caird who sought its total abolition. Whereas bonds of true fellowship had long joined man to man, history had shown that women more often than not stood divided against one another. But the present age, Devereux claimed in a chapter entitled "The Sisterhood of Woman," marked a distinctly new phase in women's relations with one another. In words that uncannily echo Vernon Lee's tortured diary entries of 1883–84, Devereux asked whether woman's interest in members of her own sex "is due to an impulse of morbid curiosity or to a genuine human sympathy." "Genuine human sympathy" would presumably uplift the fallen whereas "morbid curiosity" sullies what once had been clean.[134]

> It is certain that an increasing number of women who are morally stainless give evidence of an extraordinary absorption in the character and condition of those whose lives are notoriously and avowedly vicious. Formerly, the barrier which separated the virtuous among women from the fallen was absolutely definite and impassable. On the principle that to touch pitch is to be inevitably defiled, those within the fold held no communication with the outcast, whose very existence they were expected to ignore. Of late, however, the pharisaical passing-by on the other side has been replaced by an abnormal attraction towards the gutter. (58)

In this remarkable passage, boundaries seem to exist only to be violated. Moral opposites of the same sex (the virtuous and the fallen) promiscuously embrace, each literally blackened by contact with the other.

Devereux was quite sure that these "abnormal" attractions were symptoms of a deep and widespread social pathology among the present generation of women. She rejected outright those who saw in the mania for cross-class sisterhood in the slums "the germ of a brave humanitarianism, the inauguration of a new and fervent charity that presages an era of feminine fellowship and amity." Against such roseate views, she offered her own cynically perceptive assessment of the modern woman, many of whom were spinster-do-gooders: "To my mind it has no such [humanitarian] significance, but is simply a form of hysteria based upon a morbid appetite for coquetting with sin, so characteristic of the modern woman. . . . Her inveterate habit of throwing dust in her eyes no doubt obscures the underlying motive of her devotion to what is called 'rescue work.'" (59)

Devereux's psychosexual vocabulary intimates that the "modern woman's" illness is rooted in her deviant sexuality, whose source in turn she traced to the effects of "modern art and literature." Women, Devereux contended, had "caught the taint of . . . devotion to sordid actuality" through their contact with the "sham realism" everywhere prevailing in artistic and literary circles. "It is not too much to say that all the most repulsive characteristics of the emancipated woman have sprung from the cult of the gutter with which she has saturated her spirit." (64) Literary representations of the slums—"nasty books" like Lee's *Miss Brown* and Meade's *A Princess of the Gutter*—produce, rather than merely reflect, the "cult of the gutter," whose high priestesses are none other than flesh and blood "glorified spinsters," "new women," and other varieties of independent women social reformers in the slums. In Devereux's reactionary analysis of fin-de-siècle social and sexual politics, the gutter is both an obsessive subject of literary and artistic representation and a site of politicization for women demanding new rights for themselves.

By the first decade of the twentieth century, suffrage took center stage as the single most important issue around which activist women mobilized. The growing influence of Edwardian feminists depended at least in part on their ability to distance themselves from the sorts of psychosexual pathology upon which Devereux drew. With considerable success, suffrage campaigners represented themselves as healthy, "womanly women," the physical and moral antithesis of the hysterical, mannish spinster beloved of *Punch* and anti-suffragists.[135]

Women social reformers romances with dirt had several significant consequences for the history of social welfare in the twentieth century. Women across the political spectrum forged a distinctly urban vision of the fledgling profession of social work that joined theoretical with practical knowledge of poverty.[136] The Training Course for Women Workers, the precursor of the School of Sociology (the first in Britain) at the London School of Economics, was at the outset jointly sponsored by the Women's University Settlement and the Charity Organization Society in 1896. Course readings and lectures emphasized the wide range of structural forces producing dirt and disorder in working-class households through academic study of political economy and government blue books about housing and poor relief. The course included academic training in case management, domestic economy, and social and personal hygiene for their elite female students, who were expected to confront and correct the improvident behaviors of laboring women.[137] Anna Martin lampooned the clumsy interventions of middle-class women schooled in such programs. "A whole college of domestic-economy lecturers" knew less about how to run a working-class household, she insisted, than her untutored south London friend, Mrs. T.[138]

By the first decade of the twentieth century, two hierarchies were becoming rapidly entrenched. Men came to control sociology as an academic discipline while women dominated the supposedly more practical fields of social work and home economics. In other words, women were expected to do the dirty work of entering into the homes of the poor as social workers while men enjoyed the prestige and pristineness of practicing sociology as abstract brain work.[139] At the same time, female social workers asserted their expertise and authority on behalf of, but also *over*, working-class families. The emergence of social work as a heavily feminized profession was built on the assumption that working-class women and their families were clients to be investigated and instructed. Such unequal relationships between women pained the pioneering suffragist and feminist, Elizabeth Wolstenholme Elmy. In 1898, she ruminated upon the irony that "women's position of slavery" led so many to seek "rather power to coerce others than to free themselves."[140]

As Edwardian policy makers embraced collectivist visions of social welfare and called for increased state intervention in the lives of poor women and children, female social workers across the political spectrum remained committed to humanizing welfare through direct knowledge of and friendships with the poor. Their tasks were to serve as the bridge between the supposedly impersonal, male-controlled welfare bureaucracies and the homes of the poor and to gather information about the habits and eligibility of the poor for welfare benefits. The increasing institutionalization of female friendly visiting as an essential component of early-twentieth century social welfare legislation, such as the Education (Feeding of Necessitous School Children) Act of 1906 and the Medical Inspection of School Children of 1907, grew out of women's attempts in late Victorian London to know and sympathize with their poor sisters.[141] Some official committees of female visitors to the poor, such as the Care Committees created by the London County Council, literally co-opted their members from preexisting private committees of philanthropic (mostly female) workers. These acts redefined the status of the "army of workers dealing with the life of the child" by making them the official agents of public welfare.[142] Activities that began as forms of charitable slumming now became essential components of the state's apparatus to care for poor citizens. But transforming philanthropic women's legal relationship to local government did not change the cultural values they brought to their work among the poor. It was the women of the Care Committees, not male civil servants, who knocked on the doors of the local poor to talk with mothers about helping them meet the basic needs of their children: getting glasses for nearsightedness, medical treatment for adenoids, and free breakfasts for the undernourished. But lady visitors knew that friendship with poor women should not get in the way of passing judgments about their moral fitness and eligibility to receive benefits. We will never reach an accurate accounting of whether elite women's acts of loving sympathy to their poor sisters outnumbered those of petty tyranny. We are much better off acknowledging that gender solidarity *and* class difference shaped in ways both profound and subtle the daily encounters between female friendly visitors and their poor clients and the sources by which we can reconstruct them.

"Rolling in the muck," Aldous Huxley explained, "is not the best way of getting clean."[143] This may pass for an incontrovertible truth among parents of young children, but history suggests that many well-to-do Victorian and Edwardian women believed that "going dirty" was the only way to get society clean. In so doing, they built dense networks of female benevolence that allowed them unprecedented freedoms to move through urban space and to deepen the passionate friendships of their schoolgirl and college years. They used their freedom to construct an impressive array of private-sector programs and institutions for the London poor, some of which later served as models for male state welfare experts. The erotics of dirt underwrote elite women's social welfare initiatives and their deepest wish for true sisterhood with each other and their poor sisters. Such fantasies provide important insights into the Victorians' moral imagination and their discursive structuring of class relations and sexuality. However, they cannot whitewash the thorny social realities of their unequal relationships with laboring women. Dirt and sisterhood drew women together. It also profoundly divided them from one another and produced markedly differing visions of women's emancipation, social welfare, and social policy well into the twentieth century.

Nothing captures more poignantly the ambivalent implications of dirt and cross-class sisterhood than a story Muriel Wragge included in her recollections of her fifty years of social work in Hoxton, the easternmost of East London's slums. A titled aristocratic woman, Lady A., travelled weekly from her posh West End home to Hoxton to help out Wragge and the other educated single women who lived together at the Maurice Hostel. Lady A. had lost a family member to tuberculosis and felt special sympathy for the suffering of others. One of her duties was to count the pence the settlement women collected from their various club members' weekly fee. "She was a little spoilt, though much loved by everyone," Wragge acknowledged.

> I see her sitting at the table, erect and amazed as she gazed at the pile of dirty Hoxton pennies. She turns, and from a bag draws out a pair of white gloves and puts them on; there is a little silver too, and one coin catches in her sleeve and rolls away: "The money is wrong," she says severely, "I'm short of 6d." The assembled company gets onto its knees and scrambles on the floor; at last

a 6d is produced and held up. "Now I think it will balance." I say, "Well that was your fault!" She replies with great dignity, "I should not expect to find 6d on the floor."[144]

The "dirty Hoxton pennies" and Lady A's "white gloves" are almost too perfect as evidence. It is difficult not to imagine the dirty hands and bodies somewhere, someplace, that must have produced the wealth allowing Lady A. the leisure and the luxury of her weekly philanthropic errand in the slums. Surely, Wragge's story can have only one interpretation: Lady A. went slumming but never entered into meaningful relationships with the poor women and children of Hoxton whom she came to serve. Even their pennies are untouchably dirty. While such an interpretation may be true, it is not the only one Wragge's gentle narrative—and the arguments of this chapter—authorize. It misses out on at least two things: first, the genuine affection Lady A. inspired among the women of Hoxton. Second, the fact that she went to Hoxton at all, week after week, to provide distinctly unglamorous services and skills that were crucial to the functioning of one of East London's most effective grassroots social service agencies in the late nineteenth and twentieth centuries. Lady A. may have been an old-fashioned snob whose vision of the world was blinkered by her class privilege, but that does not give us license either to belittle her commitment or to sneer at her small contribution to bettering the lives of the poor of Hoxton.

Chapter Five

~∞~

THE "NEW MAN" IN THE SLUMS:
RELIGION, MASCULINITY, AND THE MEN'S
SETTLEMENT HOUSE MOVEMENT

CLUTCHING IN HIS hand the newly published exposé of over-crowding and immorality in the slums, "The Bitter Cry of Out-cast London," Rev. Montagu Butler enjoined his Oxford audience in October 1883 to "love the brotherhood." In a stark reversal of the social roles dictated by unrestricted competition, Butler claimed that the strong must live and work for the weak, "the rich for the poor, the educated for the ignorant." Butler was no revolutionary, but he clearly felt the dangers of civil discord pressing around him as laboring men clamored for the right to vote, higher wages, and better living conditions. He abhorred those who ignorantly idolized but did not understand the meanings of "liberty, equality, and fraternity." The task of interpreting these words and applying them to "complicated social problems" should naturally fall to Oxford men who "have learned the fair beauty of brotherhood and comradeship" in their youth.[1] Fraternity needed to be wrested out of its familiar place in the French Revolution's trinity and put to work to serve a domesticated English vision of comradeship across class lines.

Male reformers in late Victorian England sought to balance their faith in the healing power of brotherhood with a sober grasp of the deep resentment that the poor harbored against the rich. They returned time and again to the vexed history of the fraternal twins of Genesis, Esau and Jacob, as an allegory for class estrangement. If commentators invoked the loving ties of brotherhood to accentuate the bonds of kinship and obligation connecting "all sorts and conditions of men," the trope of Jacob and Esau also underscored the perils of fraternity. Although Esau and Jacob were the offspring of Isaac and Rebecca, they were also progenitors of two warring nations, the Edomites and the Israelites. When Rev. Brooke Lambert asked readers of the *Contemporary Review* to heed the plaintive call of Esau and play the part of Jacob in bettering the lot of their slum brethren, he warned that Esau's cry "may soon become a howl—the howl of a crowd of injured brothers." The East London Esau, unlike his Biblical counterpart, would advance not with four hundred but with "400,000 men to meet us."[2] Samuel Barnett, the gentle rector of St. Jude's, Whitechapel, one of East London's poorest parishes, admonished the rich, "before they go to deal with their poor, disinherited brother" to wrestle, as Jacob had, "with the spirit which haunts their path."[3]

What did it mean to liken the affluent men of London to the patriarch Jacob? What "spirit" haunted the path of Jacob and his would-be imitators in the 1880s? For champions of popular rights and privileges, this "spirit" could only have been the legacy of Jacob's ill-gotten gains. Jacob, the man of learning and peace, was also a thief and usurper who used his intelligence to steal Esau's birthright and his paternal blessing. Since the late eighteenth century, radicals had frequently likened the despoliation of the prerogatives of laboring men to the starving Esau's bartering his birthright for "a mess of pottage." As Lambert insisted, the men who raise the cry of outcast London "have lost their birthright and have no blessing."

If brotherhood seemed to promise a way to escape the horrors of urban class warfare, it was also linked to the sex wars and gender anxieties of the fin-de-siècle. The language of fraternity was unabashedly male and framed the major problems and the solutions confronting modern Britain—poverty, class conflict, and debates about citizenship—in wholly masculine terms. The popularity of fraternal ideologies in the 1880s must be set against the backdrop of women's increasingly vociferous attempts to wrest control of their destinies from fathers, brothers, and husbands. Men had no choice but to reconsider what it meant to be a man in response to women's experiments with new public and private roles. As male reformers set about putting their visions of cross-class fraternity into concrete form through missions, settlement houses, clubs, and classes for the poor, they necessarily found themselves promoting particular visions of relations between men and men, men and women, rich and poor. Remaking men and redefining masculinity were explicit aims of many of their class-bridging projects in the slums and grew out of their need to understand their own gender and sexual identities.

The first all-male settlement houses established in the slums of East London in the 1880s, high Anglican Oxford House and pan-denominational Toynbee Hall, were late Victorian Britain's most celebrated experiments in cross-class brotherhood. Their intertwined histories are the subject of this chapter.[4] As residential colonies of young bachelor graduates of Oxford and Cambridge that were established in the heart of slum districts, Oxford House and Toynbee Hall were, I argue, sites for testing out both innovative solutions to urban poverty and distinctly heterodox conceptions of masculinity and male sexuality.[5] This chapter examines the impact of male settlers' religious beliefs and practices on their ideas about social reform, gender, and sexuality. It assesses the consequences of their attempt to extend the all-male Edens of their Oxford and Cambridge colleges into the turbulent spaces of the metropolitan slums. Situating the men's settlement movement within the broader context of growing public concerns in the mid-1890s about homosexuality and intimate friendships among men, I examine the sexed codes of self-expression prevailing at Toynbee Hall and Oxford House. Finally, I turn to the politics of brotherly love in two institutions attached to these two places: C. R. Ashbee's Guild and School of Handicraft and the Oxford House Club for Working Men. The micro-politics of these two institutions make it possible to evaluate the relationship between the optimistic rhetoric of fraternity and the contentious realities of social practice.

I structure my comparisons between the first settlements by focusing on two seemingly opposed ways in which the first generations of male settlers responded to the slums and came to understand their own masculinity and sexuality: asceticism and aestheticism. A few definitions and caveats are in order here, since I return repeatedly to these two terms. By asceticism, I mean the impulse to renounce material pleasures and luxury voluntarily as a way to purify the individual and society. Asceticism was not only a bodily regime by which some men chose to regulate their daily lives. It was also essential to how they saw themselves as men and to their sense of what was wrong with the industrial capitalist metropolis as a center for the profligate consumption of goods and services.

Defining aestheticism is a more difficult matter because my usage must necessarily compete with its frequent invocation by men and women in the nineteenth century and subsequently by art historians, literary critics, and historians. By aestheticism, I refer to the assertion of the centrality and power of art and beauty in modern life. The men I examine in this essay, as admiring readers of Thomas Carlyle, John Ruskin, and William Morris, all believed that true beauty was at once the handmaiden and expression of goodness and necessary to social well-being. At the same time, there were many other devotees of Victorian aestheticism such as Walter Pater and Oscar Wilde, for whom beauty did not *necessarily* serve any social or moral function. Aestheticism was never a single well-defined movement. Men and women could pay allegiance to aesthetic ideals through the decoration of their homes and the clothes they wore or by writing essays proclaiming the moral virtues of the arts and crafts and joining organizations devoted to bringing beauty into the lives of the poor.[6] Aestheticism generated many different signs and symbols that individual men and women freely appropriated in their self-fashioning. Male settlers mobilized aestheticism not only as a personal style and creed—as a way to define themselves—but to help them formulate approaches to urban poverty.[7] They were determined to eradicate the oppressive ugliness of the slums, which they believed trapped its denizens within a spiritual and cultural wasteland. As such, they participated in a much broader, pan-European tendency in the late nineteenth century to filter their vision of the city through aesthetic lenses.[8]

From the 1880s until the 1920s, male settlers at Oxford House and Toynbee Hall distinguished themselves as leading members of Parliament, civil servants within municipal and state bureaucracies, bishops and archbishops of the Church of England, and expert policy makers within the London County Council who expanded the role of government in the daily lives of Londoners.[9] Apart from the public schools and ancient universities themselves, London's male settlement houses arguably had more success than any other institution in late Victorian and Edwardian Britain in launching their residents and associates into positions that allowed them to define not only what was or was not a "social problem," but also to influence official church, governmental, and private voluntary responses to these problems. The experiences of these young men in the London slums and its formative impact on their perceptions of urban poverty and of themselves as men constitute an important chapter in the making of modern British social and sexual politics.

THE SOURCES OF "BROTHERHOOD" IN LATE VICTORIAN ENGLAND

Men in late Victorian Britain had an enormous range of sources to draw upon—some ideological, but many others personal and institutional—in articulating their ideas of fraternity. While we can find scattered remarks about brotherhood in the writings of English radicals such as Godwin and the Owenites, it was Frederick Denison Maurice (1805–1872) who rehabilitated "fraternity" in clothing that suited the tastes and temper of Victorian society. To a remarkable extent, the men who couched their demands for social reform in the rhetoric of brotherhood acknowledged Maurice as their inspiration.[10] A Unitarian turned Anglican clergyman, scholar, and polemicist, Maurice was arguably the most influential theologian in nineteenth-century Britain. He constructed his Christian socialist theology out of the fact of the fatherhood of God, which, he insisted, necessarily implied the brotherhood of mankind. Maurice's universal claims for brotherhood, his belief that it encompassed and bound together all of humanity, differed markedly from the formulations of brotherhood that were associated with the rites and mysteries of societies organized along fraternal lines, such as the Freemasons, and with nationalist movements in the nineteenth century, such as the Fenians. Fraternity, understood in these latter terms, emphasized not only the connections between those who claimed to belong to the nation or organization, but also the exclusion of those who did not. The challenge for Maurice and his followers in the slums of London was to resolve the tension between social cohesion and exclusivity, democracy and brotherhood.[11]

Maurice's ideas about brotherhood clashed with the theology and the aesthetics of masculinity of the Oxford movement whose adherents were attracted to John Henry Newman's charismatic personality and his claims on behalf of the apostolic origins of the Church of England. The leaders of the Oxford movement including Newman, Richard Hurrell Froude, and John Keble, struck alarmed observers (Maurice among them) in the 1840s as a band of brothers devoted to dangerously papist rituals and to an unnatural fascination with celibacy and ascetic denial.[12] Nor was Maurice any more sympathetic to the influence of Evangelicals, whose spirituality, politics, and social ministry among the poor grew out of an abiding sense of their own sinfulness and the doctrine of atonement.[13] Maurice's God was loving and compassionate, less focused on judging the ultimate fate of men's souls than bettering their earthly lot. The life on earth of the incarnate Jesus and His sympathy for the physical needs of the poor and the fallen animated Maurice's conviction that the mighty and the powerful had far-reaching obligations toward their less fortunate brethren. In Maurice's theology and social politics, fraternity was the basis of association both within and across social classes.[14]

If Maurice found the roots of his Christian Socialism in Scripture, they were also bound closely to the political, economic, and social imperatives of the 1830s and '40s. These were decades of economic dislocation and hunger, of the unprecedented emigration of Irish men, women, and children escaping famine, and of incendiary Chartist politics. Maurice's friend and contemporary, the renowned novelist and clergyman Charles Kingsley, contended that Christian Socialism arose phoenix-like out of the ashes of Chartism, the broad-based and heterogeneous working-class political movement that was intent on securing full political citizenship for laboring men. The disintegration of organized Chartism after the massive demonstration in Kennington Common in south London in April 1848 did not mark the "death day of liberty," Kingsley argued, but instead galvanized the birth of Christian Socialism.[15] Nor were the Christian Socialists alone in responding constructively to the apparent dangers and subsequent demise of Chartism. The mass meeting at Kennington Common so unnerved Queen Victoria and Prince Albert that they sought advice from the leading evangelical reformer, Lord Shaftesbury, about how best they should express their love for their poor subjects. Shaftesbury wisely enjoined Albert to link the interests of the monarchy to the needs of the people by heading up "all social movements in art and science . . . as they bear upon the poor" and thus set in motion the invention of the "welfare monarchy" in modern Britain.[16]

Maurice's conviction that Chartism had singularly failed to inculcate reason and order among its rank and file—habits of mind essential to the well being of individuals and societies—prompted him to found the Working Men's College in London in 1854. He aspired to making the College into a "Society of which teachers and learners are equally members, a Society in which men are not held together by the bond of buying and selling, a Society in which men meet not as belonging to a class or caste, but as having a common life which God has given them and which He will cultivate in them."[17]

Distrusting "general tumultuous assemblies" as incompatible with education, Maurice and his cofounders controlled the government of the institution, its pedagogical form and content.[18] While Maurice championed the gradual extension of the franchise to laboring men, he emphatically distinguished brotherhood from equality. Maurice's radicalism was muted by his misgivings about the untutored will of the people; he often found himself in the uncomfortable position of condemning the democratic impulses of the College's most active students and council members. Maurice's contention that the preservation of liberty was compatible with—and sometimes even depended upon—accepting the existence of social hierarchy was deeply engrained within British political and intellectual culture. Most male settlers, even those committed to progressive social and political change, brought these values with them well into the twentieth century.[19]

If well-to-do Victorians celebrated the plenitude of goods and services available to them, they also displayed a voracious appetite for the jeremiads condemning their materialism served up not only by Maurice, but by other "sages" as well.[20] Practical idealists, not rigorous intellectual theorists, male settlers eclectically combined elements of Maurice's teachings about brotherhood with ideas drawn from other thinkers as well in their own essays, reports, and appeals to the public. Samuel Barnett, for example, carried a volume of Matthew Arnold in his back pocket and brought Maurice's lectures on the Epistles to read out loud to his beautiful bride, Henrietta, on their honeymoon before returning to their modest slum vicarage in Whitechapel. He and Henrietta read Ruskin's *Sesame and Lilies* together as they talked over their hopes and dreams about married life.[21] A High Church heir to the Oxford movement inspired by Maurice's incarnational theology, Henry Scott Holland "perspired" just listening to the "gorgeous eloquence" of Ruskin's Slade Lectures on art at Oxford. He longed to throw himself into the squalor and frenetic pace of life in the London slums which, he conceded, made his daily existence at Oxford seem pale and effete.[22] C. R. Ashbee saw himself through the prism of Carlyle's fictional hero, Prof. Teufelsdrockh (literally, Professor Devil's Shit) from *Sartor Resartus*. His ideas about cross-class brotherhood were heavily tinged with the radical moral and economic aesthetics of Ruskin and Morris as well as with the sexually charged vision of male comradeship and democracy of the Sheffield socialist, Edward Carpenter. The varied ideological and spiritual debts we find among male social reformers, bound together by dense networks of affiliation and discipleship, suggest that the intellectual fabric of the late Victorian age was tightly woven out of twisted and distorted threads, not disconnected and discrete ideological strands.

Victorian conceptions of fraternity derived not only from the musings of theologians and social theorists but from models of brotherliness provided by social and political clubs, friendly societies, and trade unions. Clubland remained overwhelmingly male despite—and because of—the growth of societies for educated and well-to-do women in the late 1880s and '90s.[23] The club played a crucial role in the social and political identities of elite Englishmen throughout the nineteenth century who prided themselves on being "the most clubbable of animals."[24] Victorians believed that a gentleman's club, with its distinctive political, social, or artistic coloration, told a great deal about the character of the man himself.[25] Because so many elite men spent the better part of their lives moving from one exclusive all-male "club" to another—from public schools to Oxford and Cambridge colleges and, finally, to Parliament or the higher reaches of the civil service—the fraternal ethos of the club all too often insinuated itself into the way they believed the world ought to work.[26]

Gentlemen did not monopolize club life in the metropolis. Brotherly associations, albeit of a more humble kind, also figured prominently in the lives of working people. A network of working-men's and radical clubs spread throughout London from the 1860s onward as places of recreation, education, and political activism. The promoters of working-men's clubs touted them as desirable and rational alternatives to pubs and music halls, which they condemned as dens of commercial vice and intemperance.[27] For the poor, the term "club" also referred to locally based mutual aid societies providing lump-sum payments to members to cover funeral expenses. Building upon these deeply rooted traditions of mutual aid, trade unionists and socialists also insisted that their members stood in a brotherly relationship with one another.[28] However, most trade unionists understood brotherhood to consist of protecting the particular economic and social interests of their members, for example, wages, hours, and conditions of labor, property in skill, etc., from the encroachment of outsiders, including laboring women.[29] Members of newly emerging socialist organizations of the 1880s and '90s, such as the Social Democratic Federation, the Socialist League, and the Independent Labour Party, by contrast, sought to preserve a more inclusive and democratic conception of fraternity in their political rhetoric, though in practice they sometimes were intolerant of the cultural habits and attitudes of fellow laboring men and women.[30]

Among the most outspoken socialist proponents of "brotherhood" was Edward Carpenter, a Cambridge-educated poet and erstwhile curate for F. D. Maurice himself. While Carpenter's egalitarian ideas about women placed him in the vanguard of the movement, he was especially committed to an eroticized (albeit elevated) view of cross-class male comradeship. He lived the "simple life" with his working-class lover, George Merrill, on a farm outside of Sheffield, which became a mecca of sorts not only for homosexuals, vegetarians, and socialists, but for many other men seeking alternative ways to think about themselves and their society.[31] Carpenter admired the homoerotic poet of American democracy, Walt Whitman, and published his own epic poem, *Towards Democracy* (1883), which gained an increasingly wide audience by the end of the century and was frequently reprinted and quoted. Carpenter had close ties to leading social reformers in London (male and female), who sought out his advice in devising class-bridging philanthropic enterprises and who in turn served as models for Carpenter as he developed his theories about sexuality, gender, and altruism.[32]

The fraternal ties binding members of elite and plebian clubs, Carpenterian conceptions of cross-class male love, and the defensive rhetoric of male trade unionists bore faint resemblance to what Maurice had in mind when he enunciated his gospel of brotherhood in the 1840s. But all of these sources contributed to the protean meanings attached to brotherhood in late-nineteenth-century London. In a society that exalted the right to form voluntary societies of all kinds as a hallmark of English liberty, fraternal associations such as clubs not only left their imprint on individual men but also significantly shaped what the Victorians believed it meant to be English. Clubs and club ideals smacked pleasingly of an older, more human way of ordering social relationships. The proliferation of various "guilds" devoted to uplifting the poor and the weak—the Guild of Play, the Guild of Help, the Guild of the Brave Poor Things, the Women's Co-operative Guild—reflected the Victorians' infatuation with a medieval past of their own invention.[33] But these neo-corporatist institutions and idioms also addressed a widely felt need to soften the hard edges of urban modernity and anonymity by reviving faintly anachronistic forms of community. The "archaic ring" of appeals to fraternal solidarity helps to explain its appeal to men and women acutely aware of the accelerating pace of change in their daily lives.[34] The revival of fraternity as a means to address the urgent problems besetting the late industrial metropolis is yet another example of Britons' attraction to what Alison Light, writing about interwar Britain, has called "conservative modernity."[35]

Late Victorian thinking about fraternity—what, for want of a more felicitous phrase, we might call "fraternalism"—was a mongrel ideology forged out of disparate elements.[36] Brotherhood was conceptually unstable, riddled with tensions between inclusive universalism and its seemingly inescapable dependence upon various forms of exclusion. Not surprisingly, it also meant different things to different people. The rituals of comradeship among members of an Oxford literary society differed markedly from the "brotherly" practices of trade unionists. This did not, however, make it any the less attractive to reformers in the 1880s and '90s. They eagerly embraced fraternal rhetoric as an alternative to the language of class division in establishing a wide array of social, educational, cultural, and religious institutions for the London poor, none more important than Oxford House and Toynbee Hall, the first university settlements in East London

"Modern Monasteries," "Philanthropic Brotherhoods," and the Origins of the Settlement House Movement

The settlement movement gave tangible expression to male reformers' acute desire to translate their fraternal ideals into practice; but it also reflected their deeply felt awareness that their own lives of ease were proof that they had sinned against the poor. Between 1883 and 1887, revelations of horrific squalor in the slums, fiery free-speech demonstrations in Trafalgar Square, and surging crowds of embittered East Londoners marauding in the streets of West London left an indelible imprint of the volcanic potential of Outcast London on polite society.[37] Individual settlers' allegiances spanned the entire political spectrum, but they collectively believed it was their special duty to remind members of the Victorian ruling class that they rightfully possessed, and needed to exercise authority to care for the poor. Because settlers were so self-evidently part of the establishment they criticized, they could, without exciting the anxiety of their peers, champion progressive causes within the metropolis, the nation, and the empire. Settlers' jeremiads against unfair social and economic practices served simultaneously as social criticism and justification for their self-chosen roles.

The university settlement movement captured all too well the paradoxical blend of arrogant self-confidence and anxious self-doubting of the late Victorian ruling classes. Without apology, the leaders of the first settlements manipulated widespread public fears about tensions between labor and capital in the early 1880s to gain supporters and financial backers for their fledgling scheme. But they also confidently heralded the potency of the high culture of the universities—what Matthew Arnold had famously called the "best that had been thought and said"—to bring order to the anarchic spaces of metropolitan poverty. The first two settlements, Toynbee Hall and Oxford House, were founded in 1884 in the midst of East London's most notorious slum districts as residential "colonies" for male university graduates. Their leaders intentionally played on the popular trope that likened the savagery and mysteries of the East End to those of Britain's eastern empire and compared Darkest London to Darkest Africa as places ripe for conversion. Promoters of settlements encouraged their well-to-do supporters to imagine that their slum locations were simultaneously safely distant from the elegance of West London and yet conveniently close enough for a late-afternoon or evening visit. Settlements combined elements of an Oxford or Cambridge college with many of the characteristics of a local center for social work and investigation, education, and cultural elevation. The audacious scope of their weekly activities—the sheer magnitude and variety of the charitable work residents undertook in their local communities, the inquiries into social conditions they conducted, and the clubs, classes, concerts, and lectures they sponsored—reflected the determination of the movement's leaders to transform the mental and physical landscapes of slum dwellers.

Samuel Barnett launched the movement in mid-November 1883, when he outlined his plans for what he called a "university settlement" to an audience of enthusiastic Oxford undergraduates. For nearly a decade he and his wife, Henrietta, had toiled to make St. Jude's, Whitechapel, into a great slum parish, with a network of interlocking social and religious institutions. But despite their rising fame in social reform circles, the local poor had proved remarkably impervious to their spiritual blandishments.[38] The university settlement movement promised them a way to build on their experiences while liberating them from the constraints of parish work. It also offered a means to deflect the criticisms volleyed at them by traditional churchmen, who distrusted the Barnetts' use of oratorios and picture exhibitions in the place of sermons when reaching out to the poor in their parish.

The Barnetts were the most notable and controversial promoters of aesthetic philanthropy in the metropolis. They closely linked the contemplation of beauty in its myriad forms with godliness and ethics. The establishment of a university settlement close to but entirely independent of St. Jude's and the authority of the Church of England was an ideal vehicle for applying the Barnetts' spiritualized aesthetics to the problems of Whitechapel.[39]

The survival of a draft speech that Barnett began to write around June 1883 (but almost certainly never delivered in this form) makes it possible to glimpse the evolution of his thinking about the relationship between settlements and established church agencies, in particular missions. It also quite literally bears the traces of Barnett's own struggle to grapple with the tension between ascetic and aesthetic, religious and secular, approaches to metropolitan poverty. In this speech, which was drafted for an audience of Oxford men and entitled "A Modern Monastery: A Suggestion for a Mission," he contemplated establishing a "modern monastery" as a new instrument of social and spiritual regeneration in the slums. In the months after he first began to draft his speech, Barnett thought better of his initial formulation and discarded both "modern monastery" and "mission." By November, he had systematically substituted the phrase "university settlement" each time the words "modern monastery" or "mission" appeared in his text.[40] In the years ahead, he zealously insisted that settlements should never be confused for missions. Why? What initially had drawn Barnett to the idea of a "modern monastery?" What accounts for his emphatic rejection of it in favor of "settlement?"

Barnett's desire to establish a "modern monastery" may well have reflected his admiration for Thomas Carlyle's critique of the cash nexus in his depiction of the virtues of monastic life at the all-male Abbey of St. Edmundsbury in *Past and Present*.[41] More immediately, Barnett may also have had in mind the "delightful bachelor households" formed by groups of university men who, from the late 1870s until the founding of Toynbee Hall in 1884, worked with him and Henrietta during their long vacations and affectionately called their residence the Friary.[42] Barnett must have come to realize that monasticism had unfavorable connotations to most Englishmen in the 1880s, who associated it with Roman Catholicism, with outdated forms of association, and with the unnatural asceticism and sexuality of mendicant orders.[43] While the terms "mission" and "monastery" smacked of self-denying clerical proselytism and celibacy, "settlement" emphasized the residents' commitment to their newly chosen community. Missionaries were by definition outsiders; settlers, at least in theory, claimed to be insiders. They were literally affirming the traditional duties and privileges of legal "settlement" within a parish. Only one element of the monastic ideal conspicuously survived Barnett's editing. The settlement remained an exclusively male enclave devoted to the cultivation of close friendships between men.[44]

Barnett's corrections and amendments to the draft suggest that he increasingly came to believe that the ascetic sensibility of the mission priest was incompatible with the spiritual aestheticism at the heart of his vision of the needs of the modern city and the university settlement as an instrument to address them.[45] At the same time, his flirtation with the notion of founding a mission—albeit a "modern monastery"—suggests that the affinities, as much as the differences, between missions and settlements, between ascetic and aesthetic impulses, probably underpinned his later determination to distinguish between them.[46]

Samuel did not need to convince his Oxford audience that the poor of East London had powerful claims over them. Oxford's finest preachers, lay and clerical alike, had prepared the way for him.[47] For the past several years, Oxford men had struggled to give definite form to their inchoate longings to help in the arduous work of cleansing the spaces of metropolitan poverty and moralizing their inhabitants. One correspondent to the February 1883 issue of the *Oxford Magazine* felt that Oxonians men had already taken their ideas about brotherhood too far. He complained that the "dirty vigor of Walt Whitman," whom he dismissed as a "nauseous" sign of these democratic times, had encouraged Oxford men to enter into an "unnatural fraternity" with the "uncultivated." Just as critics of the Oxford movement of the 1840s had detected something effeminate in its adherents, so, too, this writer hinted that the new Oxford movement of the 1880s, characterized by the "vogue" for cross-class brotherhood, was neither pure nor manly.[48] The leaders of the settlement movement struggled with the tensions between their sense of noblesse oblige and democracy and between their desire to forge intimate bonds of friendship with laboring men and boys while avoiding any suggestion of "unnatural" homoerotic desires.[49]

But it was not the handful of English followers of Whitman at Oxford who most fully captured the mood of the early 1880s, although Whitmanic conceptions of comradeship and democracy did constitute a significant strand of the ethos and ideology of Toynbee Hall. Many more of the most talented undergraduates had fallen under the spell of two quietly charismatic Balliol men, Thomas Hill Green and Arnold Toynbee, each of whom had incorporated elements of Maurice's Christian Socialism in his approach to spiritual and social questions.[50] Both men had inspired their Oxford followers to seek forgiveness from and reconciliation with the laboring poor. Green's call for a more expansive role for the state in rectifying social inequalities (even as he continued to exalt the efficacy of voluntary associations and individual moral action and growth) powerfully influenced the first few generations of male settlers.[51] Toynbee had insisted that Oxford men, as students, constituted a peculiarly disinterested class whose moral, intellectual, and social standing impelled them to mediate between the conflicting claims of labor and capital. His youthful idealism and sincerity, his "good looks and sweet voice," and his attempt to marry his passion for "political economy" with the outward demeanor of "the aesthetic young man of *Punch*" added to his appeal as an apostle of a new Oxford movement, at least in the eyes of that pioneering social scientist, Clara Collet.[52] She associated Toynbee with a distinctly idealistic approach to social questions and with a distinctly new form of masculine self-presentation. Green's premature death in 1882, closely followed by Toynbee's a year later, only heightened Oxford's desire to take up the kind of practical work in the slums that Barnett laid out in his scheme.

Settlements, the Barnetts hoped, would serve as bulwarks against the mechanization of benevolence and the impersonal forces of the market, bureaucratization, and urbanization. They would make possible the multiplication of friendships whose ever widening spheres of influence promised to bring social peace to the warring classes and Arnoldian "sweetness and light" to the darkest corners of the metropolis. The Barnetts demanded that settlers give their best selves, not doles, to the poor.[53] In emphasizing personal ties of loving sympathy between rich and poor— what J. R. Green, the East End vicar and great historian of the English people, called the "femininities of clerical life"—the Barnetts espoused a style of philanthropy identified with women.[54] Doing so placed the Barnetts in a somewhat difficult position. While applauding women's consolidation of social authority through their benevolent labors in the slums, Samuel feared that men might abandon slum philanthropy entirely to women rather than blur the boundaries separating men's and women's work, paid and unpaid. Male reformers in the 1880s increasingly recognized the precariousness of their position within the feminized world of charity workers, which led some of them to exaggerate the fecklessness of "charitable ladies" who "distributed shillings broadcast" with no regard for the consequences of their actions.[55]

The Barnetts' decision to make their university settlement an exclusively male institution—albeit one devoted to a style of charity identified with "real sympathy and womanly feeling"—reflected discomfort with a hardened, disengaged bourgeois manliness and their commitment to offering men alternative models of social citizenship.[56] From the outset, the Barnetts sought not only to expand the horizons of the poor, but also to encourage the most talented male graduates of Oxford and Cambridge to think in new ways about their public and private selves. If settlements were explicitly experiments in reimagining class relations, they were also implicitly sites to invent a new kind of man who was manly but capable of deep empathy, public-spirited because he was attuned to the private grief of his neighbors.[57]

The Barnetts staked out their own idiosyncratic middle ground between liberal individualism and the collectivist politics espoused by socialists in the 1880s. During their first years in Whitechapel, the Barnetts adhered to the individualist policies of the Charity Organisation Society (COS), with its conception of the limited role of the state in regulating people's lives. But by the early 1880s, they had begun to break away from the orthodoxies of the central committee of the COS and embarked on their long path toward what they called "practicable socialism." Educating East Londoners to appreciate beauty in all its forms remained an important part of the Barnetts' practicable socialism. For example, the Barnetts' renowned Whitechapel Picture Exhibitions, which brought great British art to East Londoners, sought to enrich the aesthetic experiences of East Londoners and ensured that male aesthetes interested in social questions attached themselves to Toynbee. Other schemes, such as the Barnetts' plans to cleanse the city and provide model housing for the poor, combined aesthetics with social hygiene. Still others, such as farm colonies for the unemployed, sought literally to remove the poorest of the poor from the city itself. Samuel was an early and outspoken supporter of old age pensions. As early as 1889 he declared to his brother Frank that "Free School Free Doctors Free Books and Free Church are plan[k]s in my platform."[58] Even as the Barnetts supported an expansion in the state's obligations to its citizens, they continued to emphasize the instrumentality of culture, as well as relationships between men of culture and the poor, in shaping individual character and in civilizing the urban wilderness.[59]

Their ideas about philanthropy and culture were not always easy to reconcile with their thinking about fraternity. They admonished university men to avoid all traces of condescension in their dealings with their poorer brethren. At the same time, they seemed to concur with the elitist view that the "mere presence of a gentleman" in a slum district would raise the moral tone of those around him.[60] Samuel enjoined settlers "to make common what is best" by striving after "an ideal that stops not short till beauty, knowledge, and righteousness are nationalised, and every noble source of joy is opened to the people."[61] They would do this, not by affecting the poverty of their neighbors, but by making the settlement into an oasis of cultivated beauty.

While Oxford warmly received Barnett's speech introducing the settlement idea, two important details of his plan excited considerable commentary and disapproval: his criticism of slum missions and his determination that the settlement should have no official links with the Church of England and impose no religious test on residents. At a time when denominational rivalries were intensifying and Christians felt the pressure of secularism and atheism, the Barnetts' approach struck some as misplaced and dangerous. C.G.L. (probably Cosmo Gordon Lang) suggested that the settlement must have "at least an indirect connection with the clergy of the parish. . . . [I]t ought never to abandon the religious element." While avoiding the taint of party spirit and dogma, it must nevertheless remain true to Christianity.[62]

By January 1884, discontent with Barnett's proposal centered on a group of men at Keble College. Keble was a recent creation, established in 1870 in reaction to the reforms that opened up Oxford degrees to Nonconformists. Its founders were committed to the Anglo-Catholic ideals of the Oxford movement, whose theology, emphasis on rituals, and sacramental practices had been so badly discredited by numerous well-publicized conversions to Roman Catholicism. Born in a defensive spirit of reaction, Keble College was Oxford's prickly High Church conscience. By the early 1880s, Keble's leaders were ready to showcase not only their commitment to the theatricality of incense, priestly vestments, and processions in their services, but also their wholesale embrace of many of the social principles of Maurice's Christian Socialism. The High Church party at Oxford decided to establish their own rival scheme for a men's settlement along distinctly Anglican lines. Edward Talbot, the warden of Keble, urged his undergraduates to "lend us the help of your brains; you must think out the laws of science, of political economy, of ethics, which govern the conditions . . . of these masses; you must give them the help of your sympathies."[63] Talbot later admitted without apology that Keble men had played the part of the "cuckoo" for "they in a degree stole Canon Barnett's idea and put it to their own purposes."[64]

While the Barnetts' supporters debated among themselves, the Keble men rapidly moved forward with their plans. On January 27, 1884, over 800 supporters assembled at Keble to hear the Bishop of Bedford, Walsham How, and the famed housing reformer, Octavia Hill, inaugurate a new campaign against metropolitan poverty. Lavinia Talbot, wife of the warden of Keble, recalled the day in her diary. "I shall never forget the impression of O. Hill—a little brown skimp woman with splendid eyes." Dressed in black silk, alone on the platform with "the great mass of men before her," Hill's "whole being vibrat[ed] with passion."[65] Hill's decision to join ranks with the Keble men deeply pained the Barnetts because she had been one of their closest friends at the outset of their married life.[66] Samuel made no effort to conceal his chagrin that his plan to unite university men had already become the focus of party controversy. "The Keble people are very vigorous," Barnett allowed, "and it will strain one's charity to be in spirit their fellow-workers. I must begin by quenching the desire to say what I think. Words do a great deal to give form to thought."[67] Even before the leaders of the settlement movement had put their ideas about cross-class fraternity to the test of slum life, they struggled with their own unbrotherly feelings of competition with one another.

By the spring of 1884, plans for two distinct settlements had taken definite shape. The Barnetts' proposal gathered supporters not only at Oxford but in Cambridge and London as well; the organizing committee selected Samuel as its first warden and named the settlement after Arnold

Toynbee. In honoring Toynbee's memory, the founders of Toynbee Hall not only ensured its identification with its namesake's youthful idealism but also with perceptions of Toynbee as *Punch*'s iconic "aesthetic young man." The Keble supporters wasted no time working out the details of their settlement, which they called Oxford House because only Oxford men were eligible to live there. The Rev. G. W. Knight-Bruce, a muscular Christian and high Churchman, agreed to take charge of the parish of St. Andrew's in Bethnal Green and supervise the work of the nearby university settlers. The settlement would form an extraordinary part of the parish apparatus although its residents, unlike workers at conventional missions, were free to pursue their work beyond the borders of the parish itself. At the outset Oxford House differed very little from the home missions founded in the 1870s under the auspices of the bachelor cleric and ritualist clergyman, Edward King, Oxford's beloved professor of pastoral theology.

In defiance of the Barnetts' views, the leaders of Oxford House often used the terms "mission" and "settlement" interchangeably. By so doing, they encouraged the philanthropic and Christian public to associate their scheme with the growing fame of several charismatic ritualist Anglican priests who launched their own missions in East London in the 1880s. As with most other missionary enterprises, the dictates of Christian love came before the principles of scientific charity. One head of Oxford House made no attempt to conceal his habit of distributing small sums of his own money to the local poor as he walked the streets.[68] Almost from its founding, Oxford House sponsored a shelter for homeless wanderers and vagrants and thereby provoked the disapproval of the ever-vigilant Charity Organisation Society.[69] Such an enterprise, with its potential to demoralize the poor by undermining their capacity for self-help, would have been inconceivable at Toynbee Hall. Despite this ostensible lapse in judgment, "the philanthropic brotherhood" of Oxford House, as the COS's secretary C. S. Loch called them, eventually earned the bona fides of the COS.[70]

The leaders of Oxford House chose an abandoned national school adjacent to the parish church as the site for the settlement and immediately set a team of local workmen to transform the empty schoolrooms into a modest residence designed to accommodate three or four university men. The Talbots came to visit the site in May 1884. Lavinia found it "excellent in many ways," but she wryly observed that its was "p'raps too close to the Ch[urch] and Vic[arage] for quite the right independence and too close I think to Mr. Barnett and Whitechapel."[71] Only a fifteen-minute stroll separated Oxford House from Toynbee Hall.

By October 1884, with the plaster not yet dry, Oxford House opened its doors to Oxford graduates and the people of Bethnal Green. It was a small and unimpressive institution and attracted little notice in the press. The ground floor served as clubhouse, dining room, and common room. "A sort of garret in the upper part, roughly divided off into compartments was the first dormitory," recalled Warden Spooner of New College, Oxford. The residents were "attacked by rats, their luggage and belongings were carried off by thieves, the cooking left much to be desired."[72] James Granville Adderley, one of the first heads of Oxford House and the youngest son of Lord Norton, fondly recalled the "primitive times" at the settlement, but he did so in order to make light of his sacrifice and to amplify his fortitude. The spartan physical conditions of the house and its location in the "wilds" of Bethnal Green made it easier for Oxford House men to model themselves after the early Christians, who had brought forth the light of truth in a hostile world of heathen ignorance and unbelief. Adderley later came to mock settlers' assumption that their poor neighbors were in any meaningful sense "savages."[73] In a satirical reversal of roles, he claimed that Oxford House served as a shelter for the "rich unemployed," members of a wanton class he described as "submerged gentlemen"—a mocking allusion to the notorious "submerged tenth" beloved of social statisticians.[74]

In marked contrast to Oxford House, asceticism had no place in the Barnetts' plans for the settlement or for themselves.[75] The Barnetts welcomed the first settler into the new settlement on Christmas Day, 1884, three months after the opening of Oxford House. By January 1885, Toynbee overflowed with hundreds of "guests," a dozen residents, and journalists anxious to gather copy for their newspapers. Only three years later Baedeker's guide to London confirmed Toynbee Hall's status as a major landmark and tourist destination by including a paragraph about the building and the work of its residents. The hall, a derelict boys' industrial school rebuilt to look like a neo-Elizabethan manor house, was a rather grand affair, especially compared to the squalid tenements and cheap lodging houses surrounding it (figure 5.1).[76] When the art-loving Christian Socialist Percy Dearmer stopped by to visit Toynbee Hall in 1892, he found it a "most luxurious place."[77] A substantial courtyard buffered its main rooms from the noise of Commercial Street, one of East London's busiest and most cosmopolitan thoroughfares. The Barnetts ushered their visitors through an Arts and Crafts style arched doorway into elegantly appointed public rooms strewn with Persian rugs and tasteful paintings and sculptures (figures 5.2a–d). Everything about the interior decoration of Toynbee Hall declared its founders' and leaders' allegiances to that mingling of good taste and advanced politics rightly associated with the Arts and Crafts movement. An early resident, C. R. Ashbee and the rough lads from the neighborhood in his School of Handicraft spent over two thousand hours decorating the "aesthetic tint

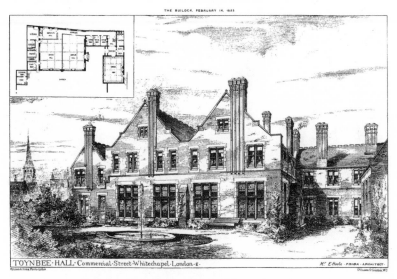

FIGURE 5.1.   Toynbee Hall. (From the *Builder*, February 14, 1885.)

[ed]" walls of the dining hall with a "frieze of escutcheons from the colleges at Cambridge and Oxford."[78] (These friezes are visible in figure 5.2b.) Each spring Oxford House men prepared for Easter through their own private Lenten self-renunciations; the Barnetts, Toynbee Hall, and their friends madly prepared for the apotheosis of their aesthetic calendar: the Easter Sunday opening of the annual Whitechapel Fine Art Picture Exhibition, which displayed pre-Raphaelite paintings (among many others) on walls decorated with goods donated by that avatar of high-minded aestheticism, Liberty and Morris.[79]

Compared to the ramshackle dormitory available to the first residents of Oxford House, Toynbee Hall offered its residents their own comfortable rooms to which no East Londoner had access, except perhaps the "admirable staff of servants" who knew their place and remained anonymous to the gentlemen they served (figure 5.2b).[80] Ironically, the division of labor and space within the settlement reproduced precisely those social and economic inequalities that made cross-class fraternity such an elusive goal in East London. The Barnetts hoped that Toynbee Hall would be the center of community life in Whitechapel, but in crossing its threshold, East Londoners entered into a world utterly alien from anything else they knew in their daily lives.

Oxford House never quite emerged from the shadow of Toynbee Hall and has been all but forgotten by historians. But it, and not Toynbee

a

b

FIGURE 5.2.   Henrietta Barnett included figures 5.2a and 5.2c in her biography of her husband, Samuel. While they depict the two main rooms within the residential part of Toynbee Hall, Henrietta chose images of them without people. Her intention, we can infer, was to memorialize the advanced good taste of the interiors, which were decorated in a style indebted to the Arts and Crafts movement. Robert Woods, the American social reformer and sometime resident of Toynbee Hall, included images of the same two rooms in his study, "The Social Awakening in London" (first published in *Scribner's Magazine* in 1892). But these images convey an altogether different message, one which exposes some of the internal contradictions of the institution's class-bridging aspirations. Rather than depicting young university men dining with their East End friends at a

c

d

communal meal, we see two domestic servants, in their white caps and apron, hard at work (figure 5.2b). The picture of the drawing room (figure 5.2d) is crowded with figures, but all of them are ladies and gentleman. The conspicuous absence of laboring men and women within these two public "domestic" spaces, except in the role of servants, provides an ironic critique of Toynbee's failure to establish relations of genuine equality with its Cockney neighbors. (5.2a and c from Henrietta Barnett, *Canon Barnett: His Life, Work, and Friends*, London, 1919; 5.2b and d from Robert Woods, *The Poor in Great Cities*, New York, 1895.)

Hall, was the first settlement to begin work in East London. While Toynbee Hall captured the public's imagination in a way that Oxford House never did, most settlements in Britain followed the lead of Oxford House by attaching themselves to various religious denominations. Sectarian rivalries, rather than a spirit of fraternal cooperation, fueled the proliferation of settlement houses in London for the next three decades as Wesleyan Methodists, Catholics, Quakers, and many other religious denominations established their own slum outposts. These settlements in turn reshaped the settlement idea to suit their needs. Some, such as Browning House in south London, even abandoned the notion of single-sex residential halls in favor of families integrated within neighborhoods.[81] Even before the first settlement had begun its work in London, there was no single ideal of what a settlement was or ought to be. That statement needs to be underscored because historians have wrongly generalized about the movement as a whole based solely on their understanding of Toynbee and have ignored the rich diversity of perspectives settlers brought to their work.

RELIGION AND CODES OF MASCULINITY

The Barnett's aestheticized spirituality and the ascetic vision of Christian missionary work held by the founders of Oxford House powerfully shaped the early histories of the two institutions and the ethos of the movement as a whole. The marked dissimilarity in the outward appearances of Oxford House and Toynbee Hall not only grew out of the institutions' divergent conceptions of religion and social reform, but also reflected the quite distinct visions of masculinity and femininity that each promoted. Religious beliefs and gender ideologies worked hand in hand at the two settlements, each reinforcing and helping to articulate the other. Analyzing settlers' ideas about family, women, and faith makes it possible to begin to decipher the subtle codes of masculinity prevailing at Oxford House and Toynbee Hall.

Rev. Scott Holland, an admirer of Samuel Barnett and a major force behind Oxford House, was an eloquent spokesman for the corporatist vision underlying the first two male settlements. "It was absolutely unnatural," he explained, "that human society should grow to such a scale that the ordinary relations of life which tie together men of different capacities and gifts should separate them."[82] Rather obtusely, Holland and many other pioneers of the settlement movement refused to see that it was equally "unnatural" for a band of wealthy graduates to live in single-sex male communities in the heart of a London slum. The oddness of the settlement enterprise, especially relations between settlers and their neighbors, disturbed the young American Robert Woods during his tour of Britain's institutions of benevolence and social welfare.[83] Woods, destined to play an important role building a transatlantic world of social reformers and interpreting English social movements to a broad American audience, confided to his friend Anna Dawes that the relation between settlements in London and their neighbors is an "artificial one."[84] If Toynbee Hall resembled an Oxford college transplanted into the heart of Whitechapel, its proponents also claimed it was a domestic space whose occupants were encouraged to see themselves as members of an extended family. As one enthusiastic resident recalled, nothing disturbed "the peace of the family" at Toynbee Hall during the year and a half he lived there.[85]

Several factors insured that settlements were at best unconventional families. While both Toynbee Hall and Oxford House restricted residence to men, relationships between men and women were quite different at each institution. From the outset, Toynbee Hall provided many opportunities for well-to-do and educated women to contribute to its work as associates.[86] As Bolton King, one of the settlement's earliest and best respected residents, explained, "comradeship" among students at Toynbee Hall "has known no difference of sex." "Women have found here respect and reverence, and have been treated as equals."[87] Several families attached themselves to the settlement and lived in lodgings nearby. Toynbee benefited from Henrietta Barnett's powerful intellect and assertive personality and from the able female workers whom she had gathered around her at St. Jude's in the 1870s and early 1880s.[88] Samuel and Henrietta's household, lodged in the rectory of St. Jude's, also provided male residents with a model of conjugal domesticity.[89]

Women were much scarcer at Oxford House, especially in the years before the founding of its sister settlements, St. Margaret's and St. Hilda's, a few blocks away.[90] Even after these women's settlements began their work, most Oxford House residents had few ties with their female counterparts. Oxford House had a much more distinctly all-male character than Toynbee Hall, a tendency only accentuated by the monastic longings of several of its early leaders. James Adderley and H. H. Henson, another early head of Oxford House, saw in the settlement an opportunity to realize their ambition to establish a celibate community of laymen devoted to serving the poor. They adopted suitably monastic nicknames for one another: Abbot Adderley and Prior Henson.[91]

Edward Cummings, an acerbic young American resident at Toynbee Hall in 1888 and father of the poet, saw nothing natural about life at Toynbee. He captured the distinctly anti-domestic tone of the settlement in its early days. He believed that settlements brought your unregenerate man in contact with the most artificial and ephemeral phase of civilized life . . . of leaving him with an ideal in which eternal youth, free from the ties of family life, entertains its friends with dinners, pipes, lectures, songs and magic lanterns, in ample halls adorned with mysterious things aesthetic, and in the end discusses the evils of society over black coffee and unlimited cigarettes.[92]

Cummings's assessment was ungenerous, perhaps even a bit unfair. But he astutely noticed that settlement life entailed not only a commitment by residents to probe social questions but also a willingness to adopt a particular and rather peculiar masculine persona.

Given the large number of Toynbee men for whom the aesthetic theories of the art critic John Ruskin were a sort of religious creed, it is hardly surprising that the settlement's walls were adorned with "mysterious things aesthetic." Many of Toynbee Hall's leaders, friends and residents, such as Alfred Milner, Claude Montefiore, C. R. Ashbee, and E. T. Cook, were ardent Ruskinians who shared his paternalistic radicalism and his conviction that ethics and aesthetics were indivisible.[93] But the Ruskinian "aesthetes" of Toynbee Hall should not be confused for their close cousins, the followers of the bachelor Oxford don, Walter Pater.[94] Pater, in his essays on the Renaissance, had famously and scandalously championed "art for art's sake" and enjoined his readers to experience the ecstasy of moments of extreme but necessarily fleeting, aesthetic gratification. Toynbee residents believed that art had too much important work to do in improving the world to be left in the hands of Paterian aesthetes. More damningly, many of Pater's contemporaries felt that his adulation of male beauty, like his sensual vision of aesthetic experience, crossed the line separating pure intellectual inquiry from impure thinking, homosocial fraternity from homoerotic passion. Toynbee Hall "aestheticism" tended more toward Ruskin's high moralism and manly love of adventure than to Pater's effeminizing worship of pagan beauty.[95]

Religion mattered a great deal at Toynbee Hall, but rarely in a way calculated to console traditional churchmen. As an early resident of Toynbee Hall observed in a poetic satire of its annual report, the Barnetts gathered around them "those elements contrary/ The man of Bxllixl and the Missionary." Agnostic, Anglican, Dissenter, Jew, Tory, Liberal, and Radical: all flocked to Toynbee Hall to imbibe Samuel's wisdom. During the settlement's first decade, approximately a quarter of the residents were clerics or clergymen "crawling in the caterpillar stage."[96] But it was the seekers and doubters, not the men of faith, who gave Toynbee its distinctive character. The journalist J. A. Spender typified many of the young men who ventured to Whitechapel in the 1880s. In the post-Darwinian world of Higher Criticism, he saw himself condemned to the "outer darkness" of unbelief. At a time when so many men and women experienced shattering crises in faith, Spender struggled "to get an idea of God which had any meaning or reality." In Samuel Barnett he found a guide to direct him through his perplexities. Barnett "gave you the whole of his wise, subtle and original mind," Spender recalled. "At Toynbee we called him the 'seer'; and no one that I have known better deserved the name."[97] Barnett's clerical successor at St. Jude's offered a much less sympathetic estimate of Toynbee Hall and its warden. During a private conversation with an interviewer sent by Charles Booth as part of his survey of religious life in the metropolis, Rev. Bayne blasted Toynbee as an "irreligious influence" and complained that "infidelity and non-church going stand out as the swagger thing."[98]

The residents of Oxford House were cut from very different cloth. The settlement attracted men with strong religious convictions, many of whom viewed residence in Bethnal Green as preparation for clerical careers. Oxford House drew strength from the solidarity and fellowship of men who shared similar views about God and religious practice. Committed to ministering to the needs of the poor, they favored a blend of ceremonial liturgical practices and incarnational theology that found its highest expression with the publication of *Lux Mundi* (1889) under the editorial direction of Charles Gore, the first principal of Pusey House.[99] If Toynbee residents gave full vent to exploring their spiritual doubts with one another in earnest and angst ridden conversations and often expressed their desire to do good through art and culture, Oxford House encouraged its residents to bolster their faith through doing God's work. The whirlwind of daily and weekly activities at Oxford House left little time for indulgent self-reflection. The settlement's most effective and charismatic head, Arthur Foley Winnington Ingram, asked a young man struggling to find his faith to "come and pray with us, and not talk about your doubts." With evident satisfaction, Winnington Ingram recalled the results of the prohibition he had imposed. The man came to Oxford House and "for five years he worked among the poor, and he never talked about his faith at all. What was the result? Why, in working for others his faith came back to him: he saw the Gospel in action."[100]

Cosmo Gordon Lang (a future archbishop of Canterbury), knew both settlements well in the 1880s; he found the atmosphere at Oxford House "less strained and self-conscious [than at Toynbee]. The residents and visitors seemed to have less sense that they were . . . studying problems or testing theories. . . . [T]hey were, rather, loyally accepting something old and tried and sure and bringing it as a gospel, a good gift, to the people. This seemed to give them a greater simplicity and cheerfulness."[101]

Lang was surely right that "simplicity" was the hallmark of Oxford House in its early years. But what did Oxford House residents and supporters mean by "simplicity?" On the most obvious level, simplicity referred to the physical conditions of the settlement. The bare-bones domestic arrangements at the settlement added a patina of romance to the manly adventure of life in the slums and sustained settlers' illusions that they were truly sharing in the "primitive" life of Bethnal Green itself. In the lexicon of Oxford House residents, "simplicity" meant much more than this. It figured prominently in their conception of their Christian mission to Bethnal Green and in the way they described their relationships with their neighbors. While theologians and historians fiercely debated the historicity of Scripture, Oxford House men congratulated themselves on conveying "simple" Christian truths to the poor in straightforward language. They called themselves Church of England and did not trouble over "theological quarrels."[102] According to an early circular intended to recruit graduates, the complex task of forging cross-class fraternal bonds was merely a matter of facilitating "simple personal intercourse" between the men of Oxford and Bethnal Green.[103] In sum, they claimed to bring simple truths to their simple friendships with the poor while living under conditions of simple austerity. By claiming simplicity in their theological views, Oxford House implicitly disavowed the morbid, unmanly, and supposedly arcanely convoluted religious and personal musings of the founding fathers of the Oxford movement. Their emphasis on action rather than contemplation as a way to transform spiritual doubt into spiritual strength contributed to their identity as "muscular Christians" and manly men.

For Oxford House residents, simplicity of life at the settlement was integral to their rejection of what they took to be the materialistic norms of bourgeois masculinity in the late nineteenth century. As one early resident confessed, he "long[ed] to throw all aside, and to be an ascetic as was [St.] Francis."[104] By residing at Oxford House, settlers could safely (and only for a short time) "throw all aside" without compromising their future prospects or their sense of themselves as "manly" men. How better to understand the lives of the poor, they asked themselves, than to minimize the material differences separating them from the beneficiaries of their altruism? The evangelical Wilfred Thomason Grenfell, the iconoclastic founder of the Labrador medical mission, had no sympathy with the high churchmanship of Oxford House; but he was captivated by the way its leaders were "proving that they were real men—men who had courage as well as faith."[105]

Oxford House residents' sense of themselves as men was closely tied to their investment in viewing East London as an aboriginal space free from the stultifying constraints of bourgeois respectability. We see this clearly in the way Henry Scott Holland, one of the Oxford House's most influential spokesmen, wrote and talked about the impact of his visits to "rough" London in the 1870s. He thrilled to the

> sight of the black and brutal street reeling with drunkards, and ringing with foul words, and filthy with degradation—and the little sudden blaze of light and colour and warmth in the crowded shed, with its music and its flowers and its intense, earnest faces, and its sense of sturdy, stirring work, quick and eager, and unceasing—God alive in it all. It is most wonderful to me—the contrast with our rich solemn days, our comfortable Common Rooms and steady ease.

He concluded with a paean to the therapeutic value of his sojourns into the slums: "[I]t certainly does one good to get touched up by a rough strong bit of reality, like that."[106]

Repulsion and attraction, moral and aesthetic sensibilities, oddly jockey with one another for primacy in Holland's imagination. In this passage, Holland attempts to force the profane to merge into the divine; or, perhaps more aptly, he insists that the sacred depends upon the dirt and squalor of the slum to make itself visible. The raw and uncultivated energies of East London become a sign of God's animating presence and function as an antidote to the "ease" of Oxford where Holland felt himself hidden away from the "fullness of the new life."[107] At the same time, Holland's rhetoric betrays anxiety about his own claims to make sacred the splendid squalor of the slums. The short interjection "God alive in it all" stands apart from, rather than concludes, his long and sensuous description of the excitations of the slums. It is too abrupt, perhaps even contrived, to be wholly convincing. The clause betrays Holland effort to contain, to justify, and to moralize the aesthetic sensations that threaten to make him into part of the spectacle he witnesses. He and his readers are left breathless and "reeling" along with "the drunkards."

The atavistic forces of the slum give Holland knowledge of God while stirring within him "primal sympathies" which put him in touch with the "spirit of the irregulated democracy."[108] Holland seems to believe that he can only tap into his own Christian manliness by inventing and encountering East London as a place of "heightened actuality" and brutal, eroticized excitations. As he explained to one of his closest friends, "you must see actual living, actual dying, actual sinning, real good hearty vice, naked sin: drunkenness, murder, revelling and such like."[109] Holland relishes the opportunity provided by his benevolent work in the slums to immerse himself in the uncouth but invigorating squalor of the East End. At the same time, his mission there is to tame the very forces he finds so appealing in the poor and that he awakens in himself. Implicit in all of Holland's remark is a critique of the illusory virtues of bourgeois codes of male conduct, which cut men off from their deepest selves and sympathies.[110]

It was not just overheated images of the primitive invoked by male slum philanthropists like Holland that connected their benevolent projects in the East End of London to Britain's imperial fortunes.[111] Many Victorian men devoted to missionary work at home and abroad believed that living manly and simple lives among the heathen denizens of the London slums was excellent preparation for evangelizing in the distant corners of empire. And some, like Robert Morant, reversed this trajectory and lived in Toynbee Hall after his long sojourn to Siam serving as a tutor in the royal household.[112] It was no accident that Balliol College, Oxford, under the leadership of Benjamin Jowett, sent many of its best and brightest students to Toynbee Hall and to the Indian civil service. Both were suitable destinations for men who saw themselves as servants of their nation and as champions of a progressive ideology that legitimized their self-assured ethos of imperial dominion.

If, as I have argued, the leaders of the first two settlements mobilized the opposition between the "aesthete" and the "ascetic" in defining and representing the religious and social reform agendas of their respective institutions, this opposition often proved impossible to sustain. Oxford House asceticism may have entailed forsaking the material and sexual prerogatives closely associated with men of wealth, but, as Scott Holland's words make clear, slums also provided ample sensory rewards. The very act of denying themselves certain kinds of pleasure could and did often produce intensely stimulating sensations as compensation. As Holland himself explained in a sermon entitled "Christian Asceticism," true Christian asceticism entailed not an act of repudiation but rather the joy of redemption.[113]

Despite their insistent representation of themselves as ascetic apostles of simplicity, Oxford House residents practiced an intensely and self-consciously aestheticized form of Anglo-Catholic worship.[114] Their strategy in appealing to poor parishioners relied upon making services a feast of beautiful sights, sounds, and smells. Elaborately choreographed processions, masses, and worship services rivaled, and perhaps also oddly paralleled the marketing strategies of their enemies, the owners of music halls and pubs, who poured tens of thousands of pounds into decorating their establishments. As one Anglo-Catholic missioner in the East End acknowledged, his mission was "a sort of chapel and music-hall combined."[115] When Winnington Ingram left Oxford House to become the Bishop of Stepney, he joyously processed through streets thronging with tens of thousands of East Londoners. These processions, with their colorful banners and striking robes, were intended to be aesthetic as well as religious experiences, at once celebrations of spiritual community and street carnival (figure 5.3).

FIGURE 5.3.   Winnington Ingram did not see himself as a ritualist per se, although he was closely associated with many leading ritualists and linked High Churchmanship with social reform in the 1880s and '90s. The neochivalric iconography used in his religious processions through slum neighborhoods lent color and pageantry to religious events and helped broaden the church's appeal to the poor. Neomedieval and chivalric imagery also figured prominently in the visual culture of advanced aestheticism. (From S. C. Carpenter, *Winnington-Ingram*, London, 1949.)

The aesthetically sensuous forms of worship favored by Oxford House presented several challenges as the settlement sought to carve out for itself a distinct niche within the overlapping worlds of philanthropic and religious London. In an age of widespread anti-Catholicism exacerbated by the development of vibrant religious communal institutions among London's Irish Catholic poor, Oxford House needed to unambiguously stand apart from Roman Catholicism and Roman Catholic practices. It also could ill afford to be too closely identified with London's famous—and notorious—ritualist Anglo-Catholic slum priests such as Father Stanton, Father Lowder, Father Dolling and Father Osborne Jay. Differentiating itself from these slum priests was no easy task for Oxford House because the two groups of men had so much in common. The founders and leaders of Oxford House admired these clergymen and appealed to the same constituencies for support in Oxford and London.[116] Like the men of Oxford House, Anglican slum priests adopted celibacy and simplicity in their daily lives as part of their religious vocation and program of social reform. They, too, were outspoken in their commitment to nurturing cross-class brotherly love to heal the injuries of class and poverty. To compound confusion between the settlement and the missionary enterprises of slum priests, Father Dolling's mission in East London in 1884 was called the "Oxford House Movement, Magdalen College Branch."

But Dolling and Jay and their ilk, unlike the men of Oxford House, courted controversy and regularly flouted the authority of the Anglican hierarchy.[117] They were out and out ritualists—that is, they were Anglicans whose services incorporated many of the symbolic gestures, religious artifacts, and ceremonies used by Roman Catholics that were not sanctioned forms of Anglican worship. Evangelical zealots and duly appointed ecclesiastical commissioners alike regularly scrutinized slum priests' religious services in the 1880s and '90s. Such observers were only too happy to interpret a bent knee at the altar as a covert priestly genuflection—yet another sign of dangerous Romanizing tendencies among men required to uphold the articles of faith of the Church of England.[118] Whereas Oxford House increasingly hoped to awaken Anglicans to their obligations to the poor by helping former residents achieve positions of influence *within* the church, Dolling and Jay and several other Anglo-Catholic slums priests, including the Christian Socialist Stewart Headlam, seemed to relish their status as gadflies and outsiders.

Not encumbered by the need or desire to please their clerical superiors, slum priests tended to be much bolder than their peers at Oxford House in practicing their ideas about brotherly love. The East London vicar under whom both Dolling and Jay served briefly in the mid-1880s wrote scathing and frantic letters to his bishop accusing his charismatic curates of fomenting "democratic and socialistic agitation" and countenancing gambling and swearing at the mission.[119] Headlam's vicar, Septimus Hansard, himself a noted radical in the 1850s, was even more intemperate in his condemnation of his wayward curate's defense of working men's right to enjoy music halls and his bohemian radicalism. In a series of vituperative letters to the bishop of London, he insinuated that Headlam was not only deviant in his priestcraft but a "pernicious" moral influence on the young as well.[120] While the vicarious delights of so much slum work depended upon juxtaposing but not merging the high and the low, men like Jay and Dolling dangerously obliterated the boundaries separating them. Dolling regularly told irreverent jokes with the "slummiest" of men whom he invited into his own home for a smoke and a chat. Jay's sleeping quarters were located within his mission complex in Shoreditch, and visitors noted with horror mingled with admiration that the "exhalations from the gas and the men's bodies" rose into Jay's small overhanging room from the gymnasium, boxing club, and homeless shelter below.[121]

Almost exaggeratedly masculine in their powerful physical presence, these slum priests nonetheless struck many observers as sexually ambiguous. Headlam was briefly married to a lesbian who entered and then quickly departed their conjugal home with her lifelong companion; he, along with James Adderley, conspicuously offered Oscar Wilde spiritual succor at a time when even the latter's friends shunned him. While one young soldier described Father Dolling as a "manly" man, a coworker commented that Dolling's "masculine strength" was balanced by "immense reserves of deep sentiment" characteristic of his nobly "feminine" character (figures 5.4a and 5.4b).[122] Jay's manner was likewise disconcerting. His "almost brutal exterior"—he was a "stout, plain, coarse looking fellow with all the appearance of a prize fighter out of training"—contrasted sharply with the sumptuous and refined beauty of the mission church he built, with its splendid glass and mosaic work.[123] It was difficult to reconcile the refinement of Jay's aesthetic sensibility in the design and decoration of his church with his self-denying way of life and his rough manner and appearance. Jay's persona puzzled contemporaries because it consisted of a transgressive mixing of aestheticism with asceticism. He possessed the refinement of a West London religious dandy and the plebeian crudeness of a Cockney boxer. Their ritualism, antiauthoritarianism, and disdain for social and gender conventions made Headlam, Jay, and Dolling into celebrities, the darlings of journalists in search of colorful copy, but it also ensured that Oxford House never openly cast its lot with them. To do so would have compromised its growing reputation as a training center for men eager to make their mark within the church.

Just as Oxford House men needed to find a balance between manly simplicity and the aesthetic attractions of their devotional practices, so, too, many of the aesthetic philanthropists of Toynbee Hall extolled the virtues of living the simple life in the slums, free from the artifices they associated with bourgeois respectability. Despite their refusal to live in apostolic poverty, Toynbee men imagined that they had embraced a purer form of existence. Like their Oxford House counterparts, they believed that by living in the slums they were criticizing and, at least for a time, abandoning, the sham rituals of respectable society. They, too, often saw the London poor through a self-serving gaze that transformed their "neighbors" into recipients of charity and their "brothers" into desirable objects of fraternal love and sociological inquiry.

In her searing 1888 novel, *Out of Work*, Margaret Harkness offered a bitterly ironic perspective on Oxford House and Toynbee Hall residents. Harkness's narrator described the physical appearance of her Christlike

OUR SAILORS.

a

SOME OF OUR WORKERS.

b

FIGURE 5.4. Slum priests and other High Church male slum workers, while typically committed to celibacy and living in all-male communities, were often remarkably successful in attracting female followers and financial supporters. Robert Dolling was particularly adept at moving between the homosocial worlds of the clubs he established for slum boys and young sailors (figure 5.4a) and the world of spinsterly charity he supervised with assistance from his unmarried sisters (figure 5.4b). (From Charles Osborne, *Life of Father Dolling*, London, 1903.)

proletarian protagonist, Joseph Coney, and imagined the effect his hair-style would have upon residents of the two settlements.

> As he took off his hat, and wiped his forehead with a red cotton pocket-hand-kerchief, one noticed that his brown hair stood upright, short and sharp on his head. It showed no parting. Men of his class often dispense with partings; they wear their hair on end, cropped close to the skin. One does not see this sort of hair-dressing in the fashionable parts of London, but it is not unbecoming.

The passage archly concluded that "no doubt some day one of the gentlemen at aesthetic Toynbee Hall or ascetic Oxford House, will adopt it, and set the fashion in the West End."[124]

Harkness's readers in the 1880s would have immediately understood that Jos's spiky hair was a sign of his poverty, worn by some poor men out of convenience or involuntarily imposed upon them by poor-law, military, and prison barbers. By suggesting that the well-to-do men of Oxford House and Toynbee Hall would mimic this plebeian style, Harkness slyly lampooned their pretensions to have become East Londoners merely by living for a few months in a slum settlement. The passage also suggests that just as slumming itself had become a craze in the 1880s, so, too, the masculine personae of male settlers were themselves fashion statements—elaborate performances of new ways of being a man. The narrator's quip that a shaved head would equally serve the purposes of the "aesthete" and the "ascetic" implies that the distinctions between these styles of masculinity could not withstand critical scrutiny. Harkness seems to be arguing here that the Toynbee Hall "aesthete" and the Oxford House "ascetic" were insincere masculine poses, different from one another but also interchangeable.

"TRUE HERMAPHRODITES REALISED AT LAST": SEXING THE MALE SETTLEMENT MOVEMENT

If, as I have argued, male settlers criticized and reworked conventional ideas about religion, social reform, and masculinity, many of them also discovered in the corporate life of settlements a congenial place to experiment with heterodox ideas about male sexuality. Some expressed their sexuality through its ostensible rejection: that is, celibacy. Others found in their benevolent labors a way to gain deeper intimacy with the poor, particularly men and boys, upon whom they lavished their love and affection. If settlements provided a bridge between the cloistered world of the university and the adult world of work and family, they also constituted a haven where young men, many of whom had moved from all-male public schools to all-male colleges, could sort out for themselves their own sexual and social identities. Most male settlers eventually married, whereas a much larger proportion of their female counterparts remained single. But settlement house homosociability, with its spirit of brotherly love, contained powerful, albeit subterranean, currents of homoeroticism, which seeped into male settlers' approach to religious and social questions. Analyzing closely how male settlers such as Winnington Ingram and C. R. Ashbee wrote about themselves and their work in the slums—listening for the subtle nuances of tone and inflection in their prose—provides one way to recover the sexed dimension and sexual politics of the men's settlement house movement.

For a man who we can safely assume never had sex, Winnington Ingram thought and worried a great deal about it. He was profoundly devoted to sexual purity both in his private life and in his public pronouncements. His determination to cleanse the slums of London of immorality was matched by his devotion to his own rituals of bodily purification.[125] His biographer informs us that throughout his adult life, Winnington Ingram shaved twice and bathed three times per day. He seems to have relished the boyish impression he made on his contemporaries, who repeatedly likened him to that notably sexless, perennial adolescent, Peter Pan. Nor should it come as a surprise to learn that real-life Peter Pans in the slums, adolescent boys and young men, were the particular object of Winnington Ingram's pastoral energies and affections. His only apparent romantic entanglement with the opposite sex ended as precipitously as it had begun when his fiancée mysteriously broke off their brief engagement.[126] As soon as he ascended to the See of London at the precocious age of forty-three, Winnington Ingram sought wise counsel about the church's views on clerical—and in particular, episcopal, celibacy. He must have been disappointed, although apparently not persuaded, when the dean of Westminster identified "eunuchs for the kingdom of Heavens's Sake" as practicing a form of asceticism associated with the subversive and rejected doctrines of Gnosticism.[127]

The character of the settlement changed significantly under Winnington Ingram's stabilizing influence and boundless enthusiasm. He transformed a modest outpost of High Church Oxford into a permanent institution in the local life of generations of men, women, and children in Bethnal Green and an important force within the Church of England during the first half of the twentieth century. Within a few years of his arrival, he raised the money and supervised the construction of an impressive though plainly designed building, which remains to this day the settlement's center for its work in the community. But several aspects of the inchoate vision of its first residents endured: a commitment to an uncritical High Churchmanship; a sense of bringing the gospel as a good gift to the poor; an underlying missionary impulse; and a sexually ambiguous but robust masculinity. Winnington Ingram left so profound an imprint on the settlement that it took two world wars to alter the pattern and tone of life he established there.

Henry Wood Nevinson, a journalist and close affiliate of Toynbee Hall, visited Oxford House in 1893. A brilliant observer of men and manners, he left a detailed account of his impressions of the settlement, its head—Winnington Ingram—and its residents. He found Oxford House "a more genuinely monastic establishment than Toynbee." He liked the solidity and plain design of the rooms, which, unlike Toynbee Hall, were "quite free of pictures and tinsell decorations." At lunch, he met a dozen residents, "fine ingenious Oxford youths," who struck him as "kindly and honest enough" but "just in danger of self-sacrificial priggery." As lunch began, Winnington Ingram, "who had been celebrating sexts or some such function," appeared. Winnington Ingram was, Nevinson noted, a "tallish thin man of 35 with smooth black hair and clothes, the gold cross on watch chain very conspicuous: it pervaded his presence. Face thin, pale and rather wasted without being as yet distinctly ascetic. Eyes blue or very light grey, and a little watery; hands white and sacerdotal." For Nevinson, Winnington Ingram's outward appearance was an apt mirror of the inner man.

> Figure pliant and like the face having a look of being always wrinkled into an inviting and encouraging smile, as much as to say, "Don't you suppose for a moment I am at all superior to you; I am but a human brother devoted to God's service and the Church can be as jolly in her holiness and purity as the most debased groveller of you all. Like all that sect he was of course as polite as a model and laughed copiously if not heartily at everyone and everything.

Nevinson, as a true Toynbee man, couldn't bear "that sect." They all seemed "exactly alike" with "no variety of thought or speech or manner." He concluded that Winnington Ingram and his type were "the true hermaphrodites realised at last."[128]

Nevinson's biting description captured the essence of Winnington Ingram's charisma and of the Oxford House man as a new masculine type in fin-de-siècle philanthropic London. Without denying Winnington Ingram's sincerity, Nevinson's tone is skeptical; he doesn't quite believe that Winnington Ingram and his residents are what they appear to be. Just as the residents are almost but not quite prigs and Winnington Ingram is almost but not quite ascetic, so, too, the group as a whole constitutes an intermediate sex, neither male nor female.[129] As "hermaphrodites," they are simultaneously supersexed—endowed with the sex organs of men and women—and oddly unsexed. They seem capable of cloning themselves without depending on the reproductive labors of women. But whereas the religious, sexual, and gender identities of renegade slum priests such as Jay and Dolling made them dangerous and exciting personalities, another Toynbee man, Ernest Aves, pinpointed the qualities that enabled Winnington Ingram to succeed at Oxford House and within the Church of England. Winnington Ingram was "attractive and safe" and made each person he met feel as if he were "the man [whom Winnington Ingram] has been waiting to see for the last six months."[130]

The absence of artifice at Oxford House, Nevinson hinted, was itself a carefully crafted pose self-consciously adopted by residents to serve several specific goals. It enabled them to differentiate their simple venture from that of Toynbee Hall, where both the walls of its drawing room and the personalities of many of its residents were more than a little tinged with aesthetic hues. The Oxford House man was ascetic in his personal habits, eschewing male pleasures of sex and drink, but he also wasn't afraid to enjoy himself in games and strenuous sports. He embraced the traditional symbols of Christianity while rejecting the trappings of bourgeois manhood. In short, he was thoroughly modern and reassuringly anachronistic, orthodox in his faith while attending to the changing needs of the people, zealous in his attention to liturgical ritual and heterodox in his masculinity and sexuality.

Only a year after Nevinson recorded his impressions, John Francis Bloxam, an undergraduate at Exeter College, Oxford, published a daring short fiction probing the libidinal drives fueling the mixture of asceticism and ritualism that was such a marked feature of the masculine personae of Oxford House men.[131] Bloxam's story, "The Priest and the Acolyte," appeared under an alias in the sole number of the Oxford-based journal he edited, the *Chameleon*.[132] It chronicles the attempt of a young, "ascetic" upper-class cleric to sublimate his same-sex desires in self-denying work as a priest in a small mission chapel in the countryside. But the priest's longing for the golden-curled, fourteen-year-old acolyte sent to serve him overmasters him and they become lovers. Bloxam's narrator and protagonist explicitly link the aesthetic attractions of religious life to homoerotic appreciation of youthful male beauty. Rejecting entirely the possibility of interpreting his story as the immoral exploitation of a youth by an older man, Bloxam's narrator confirms his protagonist's self-serving claim that he is a "martyr" in "the struggle against the idolatrous worship of convention"(358). "The Priest and the Acolyte" suggests that asceticism, aestheticism, the rejection of conventional norms, and male same-sex desire are intertwined components of a coherent and moral approach to manly life.

If Bloxam's imagined space of homosexual freedom (albeit only fleeting) within the framework of his fiction was the English countryside, he spent the final years of his own working life as the vicar of St. Saviour's,

Hoxton, the most notoriously ritualist slum parish in the East End of London in the early twentieth century.[133] Bloxam owed his appointment to none other than Winnington Ingram, then the bishop of London, who viewed Bloxam as a safe appointment in comparison to his predecessor at St. Saviour's. We can only assume that Winnington Ingram had no knowledge of Bloxam's youthful literary efforts and his close association with Wilde's circle at Oxford in the 1890s.[134] During the previous decade, Winnington Ingram had been forced to discipline severely the previous incumbent of St. Saviour's, Ernest Edward Kilburn, whose commitment to enticing the poor of Hoxton into his the church was exceeded only by his love of ritual.[135]

Toynbee Hall, like Oxford House, served as a magnet for men discontented with existing relations between rich and poor and with prevailing conceptions of gender and sexuality. "Comradeship" at Toynbee Hall flirted dangerously on the boundaries between homosociability, homoeroticism, and homosexuality. When English admirers of Walt Whitman rallied to provide financial support for the poet of democracy and comradely love in 1885, they found allies at Toynbee Hall. William Michael Rossetti was pleased that T. Hancock Nunn, a leading resident at Toynbee Hall, "the headquarters of those University Men who are endeavouring to tinge the grime of the East end of London with a little civilization" proposed to "do something, himself and others" to help Whitman.[136] Samuel Barnett also admired Whitman, though it seems he, along with so many of his contemporaries, either could not or would not acknowledge the homoerotic themes saturating Whitman's work. He dreamed that one day Toynbee Hall and its residents would succeed in transforming the soulless and impersonal metropolis into Whitman's "City of Friends." In this city, the poor would have "the personal care of a brother man better equipped than himself with gifts of time; and all men from the lowest to the greatest would delight to know one another."[137]

The elevating virtues of passionate male friendships among social equals and across class lines was one subject about which residents of the first male settlements all waxed rhapsodic. H. Clay Trumbull's 1892 tome, *Friendship the Master Passion or The Nature and History of Friendship, and its Place as a Force in the World*, is a notably uninhibited monument to the Anglo-American cult of "friendship-love," his translation of the biblical word "agape," which he defined as love that neither demanded nor desired control over the beloved.[138] Friendship-love was precisely what Toynbee Hall and Oxford House had in mind when they enjoined settlers to make friends with one another and the poor. One Toynbee resident put the matter quite simply: "It is love that begets love," which in turn binds together the disparate parts of the nation. "We have done almost everything for our working classes," he continued, "but love them."[139] Acting on this imperative for the man of West London to love his forgotten brother in the East End was the essential work of the settlement movement. Barnett had famously enjoined settlers to express their fraternal love for the poor through what he called the "personal touch." Despite its apparent endorsement of tactile intimacy, Barnett's idea of touch was emphatically not sexual. For him, the personal touch was merely a figure of speech to describe constructing bridges of mutual sympathy between East and West London through friendships between individual settlers and individual working-class men and boys. In language echoing Carlyle's *Sartor Resartus*, Barnett insisted that cross-class friendship entailed stripping away outward signs of social distinction "to get at the man hidden within the clothes."[140]

At least a few men who came to work or live at Toynbee Hall quite literally lusted after the man "hidden within the clothes." C. R. Ashbee conspicuously interpreted Barnett's ideas about friendship, touch, and the democratic possibilities of a "world out of clothes" to serve his own needs and ideas. During his association with Toynbee Hall (1886–89), Ashbee tested the Barnetts' determination to preserve the settlement movement from the taint of "unnatural fraternity." Ashbee arrived at Toynbee Hall in 1887 after three years in the intellectual and social hothouse of Kings College Cambridge. At Kings, Ashbee had found a group of young men who shared his passion for Carlyle and Ruskin, for the riddles of art, poetry, and philosophy, and, above all else, for one another's company. Ashbee and his friends Roger Fry and Goldsworthy Lowes Dickinson formed a circle of frustratingly chaste comrades who worshipped the beautiful while seeking "to serve humanity" amidst the dirtiness of the slums.[141] They revered not only Edward Carpenter's social and sexual philosophy, but the way he lived by his principles. After staying with Carpenter and his working-class lover, George Merrill, at Millthorpe in December 1885, Ashbee proclaimed that Carpenter "come[s] nearer to ones ideal of *the Man* than anyone I have ever met."[142] So when Ashbee arrived at Toynbee Hall, he hoped to find in Samuel Barnett another Carpenter, and in his relations with fellow residents and laboring men, the building blocks to create his idealized "comradeship in the life of men."[143] He was destined to be bitterly disappointed in both Barnett as a mentor and Toynbee Hall as a place to develop his daring but muddled ideas about art, sexuality, and cross-class brotherhood.

During the Michaelmas term of 1887, Ashbee launched a new venture in aesthetic philanthropy and brotherly love for the benefit of Whitechapel. Two weeks after dining with the pre-Raphaelite painter Edward Burne-Jones, with whom he discussed "dreams and schemes and promises" for East London, Ashbee confided in his journal the stirring of his plan: "*The inauguration of an Idea.*"[144] Ashbee's idea grew out of a project he had undertaken with members of his Ruskin reading class at Toynbee Hall to decorate the settlement's dining room with heraldic friezes of the Oxford and Cambridge colleges supporting the settlement.[145] In Ashbee's adoring eyes, his erstwhile Cockney students were "my boys and men," who gave him "upwards of 2000 hours of love time." Ashbee's thoughts were rapidly moving beyond the social constraints imposed by the classroom. They were *his* men and boys, and they gave him, not merely time, but "love time."

Ashbee's enthusiasm for Cockney youths was widely shared among philanthropic men in the slums, many of whom idealized the youths' "high spirits" as proof of their unrealized human potential. The aristocratic Hugh Legge, a resident at Oxford House in the early 1890s, described his affectionate relations with the rough lads who attended the boys' club that he managed in terms strikingly similar to Ashbee's. They were "my lads" and "my boys," whose earthy smells, physical strength, and pluck he admired.[146] Winnington Ingram's official biographer believed his subject's work among the roughest lads "most attracted" him. He was most fully himself among these "lads" and believed their power of reciprocal affection "far surpassed that of a woman."[147] So deeply did the working-class boy appeal to the imaginations of sexually dissident elite men that one scholar has recently argued that he was a sort of femme fatale, an iconic object of erotic and altruistic desires.[148]

In the months ahead, as Ashbee formulated his plans for the Guild and School of Handicraft, Ruskinian ideas about craft production fused with Carpenter's vision of male comradeship across class lines.[149] Ashbee proposed to establish his School of Handicraft devoted to training young men and boys from the slums in the arts and crafts and to instilling in them a love of beauty and design. The burden of instruction would fall on Ashbee and on the adult members of the professional Guild of Handicraft, which was run on democratic and cooperative principles. Ashbee's closest friends at Toynbee Hall—Arthur Laurie, Hubert Llewelyn Smith, Hugh Fairfax-Cholmeley, and A.G.L. Rogers—joined him as members of the governing committee. Barnett delighted in Ashbee's initiative while Carpenter praised Ashbee's "real love for the rougher types of youths among the 'people', which of course will help you much—without which indeed one could do but little."[150]

Within a few months of the founding of the guild and school in 1888, Ashbee had grown disillusioned with Toynbee Hall and Samuel Barnett. It seems likely that as Ashbee came to discover that Samuel Barnett's conception of fraternal love was entirely sexless, his initial adoration for the saintly Barnett quickly turned to virulent hatred. "A man very great but very evil," Ashbee decided. "He is primarily a eunuch—in spirit and heart—that is the reason for his coldblooded saintliness. He plays fast and loose with the moral enthusiasm of young men, and has not the strength either to lead or to be led by them."[151] Ashbee's assessment is largely self-revelatory and many years later, upon rereading these words, he asked "forgiveness of Barnett's shade."[152] His sexually charged image of Barnett as a moral eunuch must have contrasted disastrously, in Ashbee's mind, with Carpenter's robust manliness. As Ashbee grappled with his own ever more urgent same-sex desires, he sought to consolidate "the love of my friends . . . making the bulwarks of real human love so strong in the hearts of our men and boys [the East London guildsmen and students] that no castrated affection shall dare face it."[153]

By March 1889, Ashbee had shaken Barnett off his back and along with some of his fellow Toynbee residents had established his own splinter group in Beaumont Square, a short distance away from Toynbee Hall (figure 5.5).[154] If Barnett could not give Ashbee the affection he craved, the boys at the school more than satisfied his needs. They were "Treasures of the New Socialism," chosen by Ashbee's friend, Arthur Laurie, from his pupils at the People's Palace, one of late Victorian London's best-known attempts to bring education and entertainment to the poor. Ashbee felt that "eternal love" had been "sealed" between him and his "rough lads" as they frolicked together on a country holiday he organized to the Isle of Wight.[155]

What did these youthful "Treasures" think about the Toynbee men in their midst? The son of an out-of-work saddle maker, Frank Galton[156] went on several such excursions with Ashbee's fellow workers, A.G.L. Rogers and Hubert Lewellyn Smith, and left a vivid account of what such holidays meant to him. A gifted student who avoided both drink and the music hall, Galton toiled as an errand boy in an engraving shop while attending classes at the Working Men's College. This work eventually led him to Toynbee Hall and Ashbee's group of friends where he hoped to improve his skills as a draftsman. He found the atmosphere congenial and spent countless evenings "drawing from plaster models, working on bits of metal." While he gained valuable skills, the Toynbee men were the "main interest." Hubert Llewelyn Smith, A.G.L. Rogers and Vaughan Nash "opened a new world to me." "They were from the public schools and university," Galton remembered, "and were entirely new phenomenon to us, we had never met people of their kind before." The university men took Galton and his classmates on weekend excursions to Epping Forest, which were "red letter days" for Galton. They all slept in hammocks, and women from the neighboring cottages brought tea and did the housekeeping for the young university men and their band of East Enders. They romped through the forests, played "chase the stag," cricket, and rounders, and enjoyed "substantial plain dinners."[157]

This was the sort of utopian gambol that appealed deeply to philan-

FIGURE 5.5. Ashbee ultimately translated his disappointment with the Barnetts and the demise of his connection with Toynbee Hall into aesthetic form through a series of images. The upper two convey his aspiration of using craft training to build bridges of comradeship between university men and working-class East Londoners. The bottom image is a visual allegory of his departure—along with the Guild and School of Handicraft—from the familiar shores of Toynbee Hall. (From C. R. Ashbee, *A Few Chapters in Workshop Reconstruction and Citizenship, and an Endeavour Towards the Teaching of Ruskin and Morris*, 1894.)

thropic men in the slums, especially to the Toynbeeites who founded the School and Guild of Handicraft. Galton felt that these heady adventures changed the course of his life. "It is impossible to exaggerate the value of these short weekends to us two boys." The beauty of the forest, the bracing exercise, and "above all the society of three young men of high culture and great ability, all combined to produce an effect it is difficult to describe and impossible to over rate."[158] Galton may not have been the typical East London boy, but the gratitude he felt so unreservedly toward male settlers is echoed by the handful of working-class memoirists associated with clubs and classes at Toynbee Hall and Oxford House.[159]

If relations between the settlers and their band of working-class youths seemed idyllic, among the settlers themselves, tensions mounted. Undoubtedly, Ashbee's insistent and difficult egoism lay at the heart of the internecine conflicts at the school and guild. Ashbee was uncharacteristically reticent about this period in his life. He destroyed his journal for these months, perhaps because the memories were too painful. All we know definitely is that by Christmas 1890, Ashbee was entirely isolated. His colleagues had resigned from the committee of the school and were ensconced in a rival craft school close by Toynbee Hall. A letter from the publisher Kegan Paul to Arthur Rogers implies that Ashbee had attempted to push comradeship beyond what his peers would tolerate. "I agree," Paul wrote, "with those who oppose his [Ashbee's] action, and that I am sure your hitherto joint work cannot be carried on on his lines . . . that any raising of boys to a different level and to companionship with those who have had so different training must be on a basis of fact and manly life, not on sentiment and moonshine." While no hint of any sexual scandal ever appeared in print about Ashbee's relations with his Cockney boys, he seems to have pushed "companionship" with his boys beyond what even his friends and supporters could tolerate.[160]

Ashbee's endeavors at Toynbee Hall and his subsequent break with it—whether an expulsion or self-imposed exile—made visible an erotic dimension discernible, albeit only faintly, in so much male slum work in late Victorian Britain. Toynbee Hall proved to be a much less fertile ground for planting the seeds of an erotic but elevated form of male comradeship than Ashbee initially had supposed. Just as Oxford House could not allow its High Churchmanship to turn into outlawed ritualism, so, too, Toynbee Hall needed to preserve friendship-love from the dangers of same-sex passion. Far from idealizing celibacy, as did the founders of Oxford House, or expecting chastity of its unmarried residents, as did Toynbee Hall, Ashbee spent much of his subsequent adult life seeking to satisfy his sexual needs with working-class men and boys at home and abroad, and, occasionally, with his remarkable comrade wife, Janet, whom he married in 1898.[161]

Leaders of the men's settlement movement were acutely aware of the paramount importance of policing the uncertain boundaries separating male friendship-love from homosexuality, all the more so from the mid-1890s onward when the trials of Oscar Wilde cast suspicion on relations between all elite men, especially those identified as "aesthetes," and poor slum youths.[162] Wilde had ironically appropriated the rhetoric of aesthetic philanthropy and child rescue when asked to explain to the court why he had treated two young working-class men to an expensive dinner at Kettner's, a well-known bohemian haunt in Soho. A "passion to civilize the community" was his arch reply, a passion that compelled him to take beautiful "street arabs" into private rooms for confidential chats.[163] The crusading journalist W. T. Stead feared that public exposure of "a few more cases like Oscar Wilde" would seriously impair "the freedom of comradeship" that served the British "race" so well.[164]

Wilde's civilizing "passion" among working-class boys and youths echoed a scene from the 1881 pornographic urban fantasy, *Sins of the Cities of the Plain, Or Confessions of a Maryanne*, a book that Wilde apparently had read.[165] The anonymous author exploited the homoerotic underbelly of male slumming in his gruesome tale of a gentleman who, masquerading as a philanthropist, "went down Whitechapel way" and picked up a beautiful thirteen-year-old shoeblack living in a Ragged School Refuge.[166] Tender benevolence—the gentleman gives the boy a bath and buys him new clothes—suddenly turns into coerced sexual aggression. After raping the boy, the gentleman sells him into prostitution. While this fictional narrative should not be read as a statement of historical facts, it does, as Morris Kaplan argues, emphasize "the difficulty of separating the exaggerations and projections of fantasy from documentary representations of social reality."[167]

In the years following Oscar Wilde's trials and Ashbee's break with Toynbee, Barnett had continued to pursue his goal of mingling love and learning while remaining ever vigilant to the imperative to maintain sexual purity at the settlement. To achieve true "fellowship in pursuit of knowledge," Toynbee Hall established a students' union and club room and two residential hostels catering to university extension students: Wadham House, named after Barnett's alma mater, and Balliol House, in homage to the ties binding together the renowned college and settlement. Barnett hoped that these residence halls would form the nucleus of "a great democratic university, as popular and as far-reaching as the medieval universities were."[168] Like Toynbee Hall itself, Wadham House was designed to appeal to men longing to free themselves from the suffocating decor and norms of respectability.

Why, it seemed to its founders, should not men engaged in business—school masters, clerks, artizans—fly from the Inferno of London lodgings—from muslin curtains and antimacassars, and enlarged portraits of the dear deceased—from cheerless tea and toast and the pipe of solitude—to a social life which would brace their energies and feed their intellects and souls? . . . Each man has his private room—small but not afflicting to the artistic soul. The community share a common room. The place is to a large extent self-governing—much more so than an Oxford college, though it rejoices in the paraphernalia of warden, dean, and censor of studies.[169]

The writer's lighthearted tone implies that Wadham House was intended to provide refuge for men of modest means and bohemian cast of mind.

H. H. Asquith, the future Liberal prime minister, visited one of the residential hostels, which he hoped would become a "nursery of great ideals, the training school in which men should be disciplined to be strenuous and valiant servants."[170] However, daily life at the residential hostels was both more prosaic and less virtuous than either the Barnetts or Asquith had expected. In 1896, Samuel Barnett nearly incited a rebellion among the residents of Balliol House when he expelled a member for getting drunk.[171] More disappointingly, virtually no working men—neither skilled artisans nor mechanics—resided at the hostels, in large measure because the weekly charge for room and board of 18–19 shillings was beyond the means of even well-paid laboring men in East London.

Wadham House residents proved themselves to be at least as unconventional as their varsity counterparts at Toynbee Hall. The residents created and circulated privately among themselves the "Wadham House Journal," which mischievously chronicled the activities and interests of house members.[172] The journal is self-consciously and exuberantly a product of aestheticism, a work determined to parody all forms of high mindedness and its own literary-artistic pretensions. It is not a document that can or should be read too literally, although its entries appear to have corresponded loosely to events in the life of the house and in the broader community. Its creators mingled poems with journalistic satires of current events and mock extracts from house committee deliberations; photographic images vied with drawings of neochivalric emblems (figure 5.6).

In both its form and content, the "Wadham House Journal" of 1905 displays one of the distinctive features of Toynbee Hall in its first decades—the overlap of aestheticism, social reform, and dissident sexuality. Its dominant mode is double entendre; its dominant themes are invasion, contamination, and imminent moral corruption. Nothing means quite what it says; each entry seems calculated to confuse any reader who is not already privy to the secrets shared by house members. While claiming to sound a cautionary note, the contributors celebrate the decay of

FIGURE 5.6.   The "Wadham House Journal" and its predecessor, the "Interhouse Journal" (begun in 1893 for Wadham and Balliol Houses), were created both to contain information about the collective life of the two student halls and as aesthetic objects. The cover of the "Wadham House Journal" is decorated with a neoheraldic drawing of a helmet and sword in red and green. The table of contents page of the 1905 journal, shown here, is whimsical in its use of odd angles and a pastiche style that self-consciously strives for an "aesthetic" effect.

morals of various residents. Reworking the homoerotic tone and tropes of A. E. Housman's *Shropshire Lad* (1896), the author of a fictional piece entitled "Musings upon a Blighted Life" recounts the degeneration of John Burgis, a Wadham House resident and erstwhile "Berkshire lad," whose early life was "bright and gay," "his morals sound and hearty too. . . . [N]o sin was *he* a party to." After living with his fellow residents, the "seven devils" of Wadham House, the lad is now "lost in gloom," his life "blighted." Another poem, "Assossiette! Assossiette!," parodies two Housman poems, "When the lad for longing sighs" and "On your midnight pallet lying." It features a "pious youth" with "pale . . . cheek," "bristling . . . hair," "brow . . . sad with toil and care." The poem impressionistically conjures up a mood of intense and eroticized mystery as the youth overhears through a bedroom door the "groaning" and "moaning" of an "alien" Frenchman who cries out in his sleep "this fearful word for thing so nice; / 'Assossiette! Assossiette!'" Does "assossiette" refer to the way a Frenchman would say the English word "associate," which was the technical term used by Toynbee Hall to describe the status of Wadham House residents at the settlement? Or does "assossiette" refer to a woman associated with Wadham House? The calculated indeterminacy of the poem and of the meaning of the "fearful word" "Assossiette" contributes to the sexually ambiguous masculinity put on view in the journal.

A satiric prose entry offers another version of the events described in "Assossiette, Assossiette" and suggests that vice in general, and dissident male sexuality in particular, constitute the "open secret" (the phrase comes from the journal itself) of life at Wadham House. It records the invasion of Wadham House by "aliens," including a stout anarchist Finn and "a heathen Frenchman, the most disreputable of the lot, who has already succeeded in bringing down by several grades the moral tone of the House and would achieve its total corruption if such a thing were possible." During the Easter vacation, "most self-respecting residents fled away," leaving those "obliged to stay" to "whisper . . . their experiences." The writer disingenuously concluded with a bit of titillating provocation that played upon the sexualizing of secrets between men. In an extended footnote to a section of text recorded only as blank underlining, the editor explained that "we have thought it our duty to the homes in which this Journal is honourable known, to hush down into honest silence the whispers of our correspondent's friends."[173] The self-contradicting formulation "honest silence" captures the mock-serious tone of the journal as a whole, which made fun of several contemporary anxieties: the impact of the invasion of "aliens," that is, Jews in Whitechapel; and fears about links between aestheticism, male homoeroticism, and immorality. Whereas the authors of the journal explicitly ascribe the source of "contamination" at Wadham House to the foreignness of its residents, the texts themselves point to other, unnameable misdeeds and desires.

The notices about Wadham House published during 1905 in the *Toynbee Record*, the official organ of the settlement and its many branches, make no allusion to the presence of either Gallic invaders or the "moral corruption" of the house. We learn instead that several members of Wadham House fared well on civil service examinations and that William Beveridge—who along with his future brother-in-law, Richard Henry Tawney, served as university extension lecturers during the spring term— was subwarden of Toynbee and censor of studies at Wadham and Balliol Houses. One cannot help but be struck by the vast discrepancy between what the official, published records tell us about this philanthropic off-shoot of Toynbee Hall and the unauthorized history of its inner life re-vealed, albeit in fragmentary glimpses and self-mocking language, by the chance survival of the house journal.

If, as I have argued throughout this book, the slums of London were sexed spaces in the Victorian cultural imagination, settlements were them-selves places were young men could try on new masculine styles and ex-plore dissident sexual desires while basking in the limelight for their al-truistic sacrifices. Intent on explaining the men's settlement movement as a paradigmatic response to the crises between labor and capital of the 1880s, scholars have failed to notice that settlements were not only apt sites for reckoning with class alienation and segregation, but also for ex-perimenting with new conceptions of masculine subjectivity. The aesthetic young men of Toynbee Hall, the ascetic would-be slum clergymen of Ox-ford House, and London's celibate High Church slum priests never achieved the iconic notoriety of the insurrectionary New Woman. Nor should they have. The cultural burdens they bore were much less restric-tive than those confronting the New Women of the '80s and '90s, and their rebellion against these burdens correspondingly less far-reaching.[174] Their defiance of prevailing gender and sexual norms was accompanied— and perhaps to some extent, also concealed—by their socially sanctioned tasks of bringing social peace and religious instruction to the poor at a particularly anxious moment in the history of the metropolis. Their phil-anthropic labors made it possible for these men to moralize all sorts of de-sires—to bind the wounds of a class-divided society and to free them-selves, at least for a time, of the manacles of bourgeois respectability.

Can we go so far as to claim that these ascetics and aesthetes in the slums were "New Men?" Certainly, this is what James Adderley came to believe about himself. In 1896 Adderley embarked on nearly six weeks of tramping, preaching, and begging in London and southern England as part of his missionary work as superior of the fledgling Society of the Di-vine Compassion. Dressed in a dark cowl and sandals and sleeping in six-pence "doss" houses night after night, Adderley was subjected to considerable ridicule. In his slumming diary, he recorded that he was fre-quently taunted with the cry, *The New Woman! The New Woman!* Sometimes he was even called, *The New Man!* Far from objecting to the epithets, Adderley reflected that the phrase "New Man" aptly ex-pressed "just what I am trying to be!"[175] Two years earlier, the New Man had appeared in the humor magazine *Punch*. Playing on the theme of sexual and gender inversion, *Punch* decided that the "New Man" was, in a word, "Woman."[176] The sexual ambiguities that were such an important part of the public personae of men like Adderley, Dolling, Ashbee, and Winnington Ingram contributed to the public's confusion about who or what these New Men were.[177]

Even in Barnett's first tentative exploration of the settlement idea in his draft speech, "A Modern Monastery," we can detect a tension between monastic self-denial on the one hand, and a celebration of the power and beauty of art and culture on the other. The contrasting interior and exterior designs of Oxford House and Toynbee Hall and the masculine personae fostered by each settlement were symptomatic of deeper differences in the way each settlement expressed the relationship between religion, social reform, and masculinity. The early settlers' keen attention to the way they represented themselves—the distinct sense of style they conveyed—was one important though subtle means by which Oxford House and Toynbee Hall men expressed their differences from one another. While contrasting views about religion provided the initial justification for the creation of Oxford House, different conceptions of masculinity, which were embedded in ideological and aesthetic beliefs, came to be just as important in distinguishing the two from each other.

At the same time, it is important not to exaggerate these differences. The men of Oxford House and Toynbee Hall fed off and responded to the same set of social, economic, religious, and sexual anxieties. Many residents were neither aesthetes nor ascetics; still others were drawn toward and actively supported both institutions. The opposition between the "aesthete" and the "ascetic" belies the porous character of the boundaries separating these masculine personae. The aesthete and the ascetic in the slums were oscillating modes of masculinity, at once opposed to one another and yet part of a shifting continuum of masculine subjectivities and behaviors.

It is clear that the innovative masculine personae forged by male settlers and slum priests in the late nineteenth century were related to the contemporaneous emergence of the homosexual as a distinct medical, sexual, and social category of persons. But how? Let me answer this question by beginning with what we know with certainty and then moving to more speculative or suggestive approaches to it. Considerable evidence demonstrates that the most outspoken defenders of "Greek love" between men and of homosexual rights in Victorian Britain were drawn to slum benevolence in general and to Toynbee Hall in particular. Oscar Browning, who had been sacked from Eton amidst rumors of sexual scandal and was an ardent defender of platonic love between men, served on the original Cambridge Committee for the University Settlement that became Toynbee Hall.[178] Edward Carpenter supported the Barnetts' work and corresponded with C. R. Ashbee as he developed his ideas about comradeship and craftsmanship. The homosexual scholar of the Renaissance John Addington Symonds told members of the Elizabethan Literary Society at Toynbee Hall that he "sympathise[d] deeply with your work at Toynbee Hall. I congratulate you heartily on the success you have achieved."[179] Carpenter's and Symonds's enthusiasm for men's settlements is hardly surprising given the central role of cross-class love between men in their own sexual and social ethics.[180]

In the first decades of the twentieth century, novelists, psychologists, and sexologists alike increasingly viewed male settlement house and club work with boys in the East End of London as potential signs of homosexual desire. E. M. Forster, in his novel *Maurice* (written 1913–14), sent his homosexual protagonist Maurice fleeing to a college settlement in the south London slums after Clive, his erstwhile aristocratic lover, throws him over for a woman and marriage.[181] Recuperating from sexual loss through slum benevolence, Maurice represses and sublimates but also gives vent to, his same-sex desires by playing football and teaching arithmetic and boxing to the rough lads living near the settlement.[182] In 1927, T. A. Ross published "A Case of Homosexual Inversion," which concerned a gentleman of culture and business acumen who was tortured by the belated discovery of his sexual feelings for men. Horrified by the romantic attentions of women, the gentleman "thereafter . . . occupied much of his spare time in philanthropic society . . . chiefly among boys in the east of London." At first, "no trace of conscious sex feeling was aroused" by his contact with slum boys, but later "he began to realize that there were some constituents among his ideas concerning the male sex besides those of normal philanthropy."[183]

At the same time, the evidence presented in this chapter strongly suggests that there is no reason to believe that the endeavors of settlers and slum priests, such as James Adderley, to become New Men in the slums were culturally constrained fumblings toward homosexuality. The opposition between "homosexuality" and "heterosexuality," which gained currency in late-nineteenth-century Britain, is simply too crude, both descriptively and theoretically, to accommodate the kinds of masculine subjectivities that elite men like Scott Holland, Adderley, Winnington Ingram, and Dolling attempted to fashion for themselves through their cross-class fraternal philanthropy in the slums.[184] The erotic ambiguities of Toynbee Hall aestheticism and Oxford House asceticism *may* well have made these settlements attractive to a small number of male residents and associates who actively pursued sexual relationships with other men. Ashbee's self-revealing and self-serving archive of letters and journals provides the most compelling evidence in support of this supposition.[185] However, Ashbee's break with Toynbee demonstrates that while the leaders of male settlements encouraged the cultivation of loving friendships among men, they refused to tolerate any hint of sex between men. Most male settlers, unlike their female counterparts, ultimately chose to marry and seemed to have had little difficulty balancing their intense youthful attachments with other men with opposite-sex love and romance as mature adults. It would be misguided and unfair to identify men like Winnington Ingram, who so resolutely understood themselves through their devotion to celibacy, with the homosexual—a person whom sexologists defined by and through sexual desires and acts.[186] We are much better served placing the emergence of the "homosexual," like the philanthropic "aesthete" and "ascetic," as one of many fin-de-siècle masculine personae constructed at the interstices of new ideas about sexuality and gender, and religious and social-reform impulses.

A Door Unlocked: The Politics of Brotherly Love in the Slums

Just as the opposition between the aesthete and the ascetic was unstable, so, too, the distinctions between "agape" and "philia"—the sexual purity of the "true hermaphrodite" and the "unnatural depravity" of the homosexual comrade—were more subtle than most Victorians would have been willing to admit. We get a sense of the affinities drawing these seemingly opposed types of men together in C. R. Ashbee's enthusiastic appreciation for Winnington Ingram, who invited Ashbee to dine with him in July 1901 at Fulham Palace, his London residence. On the face of it, they make an unlikely pair of dinner companions, the celibate bishop with a passion for purity and the married homosexual aesthete and guild socialist. But apparently the evening was a great success as the two men discussed their mutual love of East London and its people. Ashbee was charmed to discover that Winnington Ingram had converted the palace library into a sanatorium for his "East end friends" where he had installed two little slum children recovering from scarlet fever. In Ashbee's admiring and perhaps envious eyes, Winnington Ingram was "the Bachelor Bishop with the heart of a boy" who had literally been taken out of his carriage by an East London crowd and been "shouldered by the mob for joy at his appointment" to the episcopal see of London. What Winnington Ingram lacked in intellectual cleverness he made up for with his candor and unaffected good fellowship. Winnington Ingram got what he wanted, Ashbee decided, not through sophisticated disquisition but merely by "put[ting] his arm around your neck," precisely the sort of comradely gesture Ashbee adored. At first, Ashbee was puzzled how "so papistical a parson" could inspire such love from the people; but, upon reflection, he decided that, regardless of what Winnington Ingram himself believed, the appeal of ritualism was wholly "aesthetic."[187]

Divided by an immense gulf in their views about God and sexuality, Ashbee and Winnington Ingram found ample common ground in their conviction of the necessity of forging ties of brotherly love across the class divide and in their cultivation of boyish hearts. More surprisingly, the bohemian socialist Ashbee and the cautiously conservative High Church Winnington Ingram also believed that they had the right and obligation to impose their will on the laboring men with whom they claimed fraternal equality.[188] Two examples, one drawn from Ashbee's management of the Guild and School of Handicraft and the other from Winnington Ingram's oversight of the Oxford House Club for working men, demonstrate just how willing each was to forsake the leveling possibilities of cross-class fraternal love in favor of asserting the hierarchical politics of class difference.

Ashbee readily abandoned all pretension of being either a democrat or a socialist when one member of his Guild of Handicraft, John Pearson, privately sold custom-crafted metalwork to a better-established rival in 1890 or, more disastrously, when an unskilled member, William Flowers, produced on the guild's premises metalwork that he insisted he had a right to sell for his exclusive profit. Ashbee obliged Pearson to restore his profit to the guild while he summarily demanded Flowers's resignation.[189] Ashbee's high-handed assertion of authority throughout 1891 provoked his own shop steward, C. V. Adams, to remind Ashbee of the cooperative and socialistic principles of their scheme: no man, Adams explained, should "assume the position of proprietor or master." Another demanded to know whether the guild "was a democratic or autocratic concern."[190] The minutes of the guild make clear that it was democratic in theory but autocratic in practice.

While Ashbee was locked in the struggle with his guildsmen, Winnington Ingram's faith in the probity of the working men of Bethnal Green was put to the test. During his tenure as head of Oxford House, its flagship clubs for working men, the University Club and the Oxford House Club, were singled out for high praise by the sociologist Charles Booth and widely applauded in the press.[191] Winnington Ingram believed that clubs were instruments well suited to kindling a spirit of brotherhood within Bethnal Green and reconciling East and West London.[192] While drinking cocoa or playing billiards, club men would gain the independence of mind and character to equip them for their new roles as citizens in a democratic state. However, unlike dozens of rival political and social clubs in East London which working men managed entirely by and for themselves, democracy did not mean self-rule at Oxford House Club.[193]

When one enterprising senior member of the club's rowing society, Mr. Welch, raised money from a local publican without first seeking approval from the club manager, Oxford House residents were appalled by his apparent violation of the temperance principles of the club. After weeks of heated debate and increasingly acrimonious negotiations, Winnington Ingram decided to quash the burgeoning rebellion. He insisted that accepting the tainted money "would imply the smash-up of the Club." "As landlords of the premises," Winnington Ingram declared, he and the Council of Oxford House "would probably consider it undesirable to allow their premises to be used by the Club."[194]

Winnington Ingram must not have anticipated just how well club members had honed their skills in debate and learned their lessons in citizenship. A longtime and well-respected member, Mr. Price, distilled the essence of the entire debate over publican subsidies in a few sentences. His words, strikingly reminiscent of Ashbee's guildsmen in 1891, reveal just how politically sophisticated at least some laboring men in late Victorian London were. Price "had always understood that this was a democratic Club," he began. "But if it was entirely under the control" of its Oxford benefactors, Price reasoned, "this was evidently not the case." He boldly asked the meeting whether they considered it "fair-dealing to threaten them with expulsion if they did not do exactly as the Council wished." Price appealed in vain to fellow club members, whom Winnington Ingram had bullied into silence.[195] In the years ahead, Winnington Ingram and Oxford House retained firm control over the club but not over the loyalty of club men, whose numbers declined sharply.

Did either Ashbee or Winnington Ingram ever reflect on their apparent failure to live up to their own fraternal principles? Or did they prefer to see themselves as upholders of principles too precious to compromise merely for the sake of democratic processes? Surviving sources provide no answers to these questions; however, the mere fact that they chose to preserve minute books filled with pages of detailed evidence of internal struggles between laboring men and their benefactors suggests that Ashbee and Winnington Ingram believed they had nothing to hide. These two intensely idealistic men apparently saw no contradiction between their commitment to promoting democratic habits among laboring men *and* their "autocratic" assertion of class-based power. Winnington Ingram's confrontation with clubmen neither diminished his belief that "human brotherhood . . . is the great truth of this age"[196] nor muted his voice in condemning business enterprises whose pursuit of profit harmed his beloved East Londoners.[197]

As these examples make all too clear, there was a world of difference between proclaiming the virtues of democracy and acting democratically; between saying you love your brother and being loved in return by him. Male slum philanthropists found it easy to lavish their affection on and exercise authority over working-class boys and youths, whose physical vigor, high spirits, and independence they unfailingly praised. But these same attributes were much more threatening in adult working men, and all the more so when these men refused to proffer what many elite male settlers demanded from them: "freely accorded social homage."[198] When working men dared to demand a real share in decision making, Ashbee and Winnington Ingram abandoned the rhetoric of brotherly love and crudely asserted their power. These may have been bitter lessons for all involved, but they also captured the limits of what fraternity and democracy were—and were not—in late Victorian London.[199]

The spatial relationship between Oxford House and its flagship club aptly reflected the aspirations and contradictions of male settlers' fraternal ideology. The Oxford House Club and the settlement house proper, with residents' private and public rooms, literally shared a common roof—tangible proof of the settlement's commitment to building bridges of friendship between rich and poor. A single door connected the two institutions. But that door remained tightly locked from the day the settlement opened until World War II and the arrival of that maverick head of house, Guy Clutton-Brock and his wife Molly. The Clutton-Brocks vividly recalled the moment they first opened the door when a club member exclaimed, "Ah, you've opened the door from the Club to the House and the House to the Club." They noted, "That was a very big thing, that door." Unlocking "that door" in the middle of World War II was an event at once trivial and momentous, a symbol of hopeful progress and shameful anachronism.[200]

Why were settlers so slow to share "frankness and fraternal trust" with the working men they sought to befriend?[201] Many residents of Toynbee Hall and Oxford House were deeply attracted to the slums of East London because they perceived them as simultaneously lying within and beyond the boundaries of civilization. For these elite men, slums presented urgent contemporary problems while slum residents remained stranded in an archaic past. Settlers' determination to see slum dwellers as primitives was tied not only to their ideas about class but to the way they understood their own robustly heterodox masculinity.[202] In the decades following the First World War, settlers continued to engage in what one contemporary scathingly described as a "central Africa style of philanthropy."[203] Their rhetorical and psychological investment in this style of philanthropy proved disastrously resilient. We see this clearly in the career of Walter Carey, a prominent clergyman in Britain and South Africa. Carey served as bishop of Bloemfontein in the 1920s and '30s, an appointment held several decades earlier by the first head of Oxford House, G. W. Knight Bruce.[204] Carey was drawn toward the religious and social ideals promoted by Oxford House. A rugged man, a superb athlete, and a devout High Churchman, he idealized Scott Holland and Winnington Ingram ("a real knight of Christ") and praised Oxford House for its success in putting Christian fraternal principles into action in the slums.[205] Like so many others of his generation, he dutifully disguised himself as a tramp to see how the poor lived. Charismatic and effective in bringing the Gospel to working men in Britain and to "natives" in South Africa, Carey also romanticized them as unspoiled primitives. He described the natives he met in South Africa as "simple, lovable, irritating by their backwardness, yet true and faithful." Not surprisingly, when he went to present the views of his fellow bishops on the "native question" to the father of the Republic of South Africa, the Afrikaner General Hertzog, Carey admitted to Hertzog that he did not think there were more than one thousand native men "fit for an equal vote with the European." Nor did he believe that native men were "yet capable of farming land well."[206] The discourse of the "primitive" made it easy for men like Carey to modulate brotherly love into a fatherly assertion of power in articulating their vision of the relationship between authority and democracy, church and state.

In 1984, Fred Gore recalled with annoyance and amazement the attitudes he encountered among well-intentioned Oxford men who came to enlighten him and his friends in the years between the wars. One of eight children of a French polisher in the furniture trade of Bethnal Green, Gore happily attended the well-appointed clubs for working boys and men at Oxford House. According to Gore, the kindly manager of the boys' club at Oxford House he joined, who later became an Anglican bishop, had completely misjudged the poor. "I learnt donkey's years later," Gore explained, that he came down to Bethnal Green under the impression that he was going down to meet some sort of Central American tribe." "You see, it's incredible," Gore continued, "that educated people should come down with such a wrong impression. These people down here, as poor as they were, when you looked out of our back window and you saw all the yards, they turned their little yard into a garden, and they kept rabbits and pigeons and things like that. They had their own culture, you see."[207]

Unfortunately there was nothing incredible about the persistence of such views among reform-minded university men in late-nineteenth- and early-twentieth-century Britain. For settlers, seeing the poor both as their brothers and as savages was tied to the way they understood themselves as manly men and as bearers of the elite culture of the universities. They repeatedly described the poor as downtrodden Esaus—leaving themselves, without trace of irony, to play the part of Jacob, the civilizer but also the thief who stole his brother's birthright.

Choosing to live outside what they took to be the geographical, psychological, and social boundaries of respectable society, slum priests and settlers refused to emulate the bourgeois paterfamilias's devotion either to traditional family life or to the single-minded pursuit of individual self-interest in the market place. By settling in the slums, these men carved out for themselves a social space where, with the approval of society, they could place fraternity before domesticity. Their experiences living on the social margins, far from removing them from the center of power, only augmented their authority to define, speak, and write about pressing social issues confronting Britons. Their fraternal ideologies were, at least in their own eyes, well suited to the complexities of their task: to harmonize the conflicting claims of rich and poor; East and West; altruism and self-interest; womanly sympathy and manly strength; secular imperatives and Christian duties. Male settlers' fraternal ideologies sustained not only their claims to educate, uplift, and govern their poor brethren but also to love and befriend them as well. The elite men examined in this chapter yearned to transcend and transform the suffocating systems of class and gender privilege, which they believed poisoned social relations and inhibited their own self-development. At the same time, the cultural logic of slumming powerfully informed their vision of poverty and the poor, constraining them from initiating a truly democratic reordering of class, gender, and sexual hierarchies even within their adopted slum neighborhoods. Theirs was less a failure of intention than of imagination.

Conclusion

─❧❧❧─

> The mission of Christians to the city in the 1880s is an
> invitation to us a hundred years later to answer the same
> challenge of increasing inequality and social disintegration
> which our predecessors so clearly saw and so vigorously
> met. They turned resolutely to what Henrietta Barnett
> called *Practicable Socialism*. Today we seek a new
> vocabulary to express renewed faith in the city.
> —*Faith in the City*

CONFRONTED BY the violence of social dislocation and the
desperate loss of hope accompanying endemic poverty in the
early 1980s, politicians, activists, religious leaders, and academics on the right and left in Great Britain have had a great deal at stake in laying claim to their own competing versions of the Victorian past. For some of them, Victorianism stands in for dynamic economic expansion at home, military preeminence abroad, and entrepreneurial bravado unfettered by self-serving trade unions and a wasteful welfare state. For others, the Victorian past offers a cautionary tale about the evils and excesses of free-market capitalism and the racist brutality of imperialism.

As Prime Minister Margaret Thatcher's Conservative government consolidated its power by dismantling a century of state-subsidized social entitlements, abolishing the Greater London Council, and defanging trade unionism, the archbishop of Canterbury, Robert Runcie, assembled a blue-chip commission in 1983 to investigate "Urban Priority Areas."[1] Dismissed as "Marxist rubbish" by outraged Conservatives,[2] the commission's report, published as *Faith in the City* in December 1985, offered a trenchant interpretation of Victorian approaches to urban poverty while blasting the Conservative government's "more or less crude exaltation of the alleged benign social consequences of individual self-interest and competition."[3]

Faith in the City remains "hugely influential" in British politics, and leaders of both major parties continue to hearken back to it in their public pronouncements.[4] An ambivalent testament to the enduring legacy of slumming and slum benevolence, it provides a way to reflect upon long-term continuities and changes in modern British social and sexual politics.

Like their Victorian predecessors, the archbishop's commissioners voyaged into the slums to "see . . . the human reality behind the official statistics"; they, too, drew their conclusions "above all by . . . direct experience" of witnessing urban poverty and listening to the voices of the poor.[5] They established their expert credentials through pastoral work in slums and leadership of social welfare institutions, including an East London docklands settlement house and Oxford's Barnett House (named in honor of Samuel Barnett), its academic unit devoted to social work and public policy. The modern incarnations of Victorian philanthropies, including Barnardos, the Salvation Army, and the Family Welfare Association (the contemporary name for what was once called the Charity Organisation Society), all submitted evidence to the commission.

In all these ways, *Faith in the City* descends directly from late-nineteenth-century journalistic and sociological surveys of urban poverty and dozens of others parliamentary commissions and proceedings of church congresses. At the same time, the authors of *Faith in the City* notably distanced themselves from the mental world of Victorian slumming. They refused to position the poor as erotic objects of elite spectatorship, in marked contrast to so many of the philanthropists, evangelical "rescuers," journalists, and social workers discussed in this book. They vehemently rejected the racist tropes of domestic imperialism that likened the poor to exoticized heathen *subjects* in favor of remaking the city and the church in the image of its multiracial, multi-confessional *citizens*. The report recognized the imperative to attend to the human dignity of those in need of assistance. The decaying physical infrastructure of Britain's urban core, much of it dating back to the late nineteenth century, functions both as a material fact and as a metaphor for the continuities binding "Urban Priority Areas" to Victorian slums as well as the immense historical gulf separating them.

Faith in the City invoked the Victorian past, not as an exercise in nostalgic moralizing about lost certainties, but rather to inaugurate spiritual renewal and a progressive vision of social and economic justice. Its authors clearly believed that the success of their policy recommendations depended, at least in part, upon the history within which they embedded them. In "self-lacerating" prose,[6] the report chastised the church for its long neglect of the cities and their poor and reconstructed a usable past of Victorian worthies whose labors on behalf of the urban poor merited both remembrance and selective emulation. The historical prologue to *Faith in the City* ultimately divides men and women into two clear-cut groups. On the one hand, it condemns the vast majority who tragically reproduced the church's "paternalistic," "male-dominated," and "mainly middle class" values in their dealings with the urban poor.[7] On the other, it uncritically celebrates the achievements of a handful of visionary mavericks, precisely those "evangelicals and Anglo-Catholics," Christian socialists, municipal reformers, and university settlers scrutinized in this study.

Conceptualizing the past in terms of heroes and villains, saints and sinners, may serve a powerful, even necessary, political message. It does not, however, make for very good history. I have done my best to avoid this trap. In its place, I have tried to produce a portrait, no less dramatic, in shades of gray. Just as slum explorers sought to illuminate the dark corners of the metropolis, this book has cast a critical light upon them, their ideas, their methods, their institutions, programs, and policies. Without diminishing their achievements, I have called attention to their problematic and consequential assumptions about freedom and democracy, equality and deference, fraternity and hierarchy, gender and sexuality. I have reassembled the complex web of sexual and social politics out of which emerged many of the most influential and enduring monuments of Victorian philanthropy and so much of the twentieth-century welfare state.

Eros and altruism, self-gratification and self-denial, the desire to love the poor and to discipline their disruptive power: these seemingly opposed impulses were tightly and disconcertingly bound to one another. Far from offering an apologia for slummers—reformers, missionaries, journalists, sociologists, and social workers—I have focused on moments of particularly acute ethical ambiguity in their careers. Readers have encountered James Greenwood in the act of lying about his identity in order to discover sexual abominations supposedly secreted in London's casual wards; Dr. Barnardo accused of abusing the children he rescued and circulating images many found indecent; Elizabeth Banks acknowledging that cash not kindness motivated her slumming; Winnington Ingram invoking his power as landlord and threatening to shut down the working-men's club founded on principles of cross-class brotherly love. In each of these cases, the poor responded to and negotiated with their social betters. Some, like the parents of several children Barnardo photographed, expressed outrage at Barnardo's "artistic fictions" and testified against him at his arbitration. Others, like Mrs. Stevens, manipulated lady slum visitors' preoccupation with dirt to increase the alms she received. Still others, like Mr. Price of the Oxford House Club, demanded that male settlers live up to their own principles. In these moments and in their resolution we see most clearly the often invisible costs of benevolence paid for by the poor themselves. We also glimpse class relations, not as an abstraction, but concretely produced, reproduced, and changed through encounters between rich and poor.

Rather than caricaturing philanthropists as hypocritical agents of class interest, I have shown how satisfying their own varied needs—religious, social, sexual, psychological, and class—informed how they served others and conceptualized poverty. The women and men I have discussed in this book were far too ill at ease with their inherited middle-class social, sexual, and gender norms—too deeply engaged in seeking out new ways of understanding themselves—to defend the status quo. Engagement with slum benevolence often stimulated a critical, rather than complacent, cast of mind about relations between the sexes and the classes.

Well-to-do men and women voyaged into the slums of Victorian London to bear direct personal witness to the hardships of the poor. In unprecedented numbers, they experienced for themselves the sounds, smells, sights of slum life that they took to be irrefutable facts about poverty. In this sense slumming as a technique of gathering and organizing social knowledge suited the entrenched empiricism that was such a distinctive characteristic of British sociology. However, slumming and slum benevolence also tapped into the unruly passions of the moral imagination and into attempts to reconfigure class and gender relations and sexuality. The slums of London, I have argued, proved to be a fruitful crucible for the cultivation of heterodox sexual and social subjectivities. At least for some men and women, slums were spaces free from the inhibitions and prohibitions of middle-class domesticity and conjugality.

The readiness of philanthropists and their public to imagine the sufferings and squalor and vice of the poor fueled a remarkable flowering of charitable creativity and institution building in Victorian and Edwardian London. But it also opened up a gap between facts and fantasies into which elite men and women could and did project their own needs, desires, and values. To put it another way, it led contemporaries to debate what was fact and what was fantasy. In the intertwined naked bodies of men and boys in the Lambeth Casual Ward, the journalist James Greenwood saw sodomy and sexual depravity whereas the homeless man called the Real Casual saw desperation to keep warm and survive a freezing winter night in a miserably inadequate open shed. The logic of Greenwood's depiction of his night in a workhouse pointed toward increasing surveillance of the poor and the regulation of male same-sex behaviors, which in turn contributed to the equation of homelessness and homosexual acts with the 1898 Amendment to the Vagrancy Act. The logic of the Real Casual would have required public officials to provide the homeless poor with shelters that respected and protected their dignity.

Greenwood and fellow slummers deftly transformed their sojourns in the slums into literary, social, political, and cultural capital. "A Night in a Workhouse" literally rescued the *Pall Mall Gazette* from bankruptcy. Dr. Barnardo widely circulated his erotically charged visual and written narratives about street waifs to raise the hundreds of thousands of pounds upon which his philanthropic empire rested. Elizabeth Banks quite happily admitted that she paid her bills by selling her tales of slumming to the highest bidder. Educated women used their knowledge of the poor to establish new professions within the public and private sector enabling them to live with one another and without men. Six months or a year's residence at Toynbee Hall and Oxford House proved to be a valuable credential for young men eager to advance within the Church of England or the emerging social welfare bureaucracies of central and local government.

Philanthropists' success in serving their own interests infuriated the working-class socialist and lifelong East Londoner, George Lansbury. In Lansbury's eyes, most slum philanthropy, even at well-intentioned Toynbee Hall, was merely selfishness passing for altruism. "The one solid achievement of Toynbee Hall," he bitterly observed in his 1928 autobiography, "has been the filling up of the bureaucracy of government and administration with men and women who went to East London full of enthusiasm and zeal for the welfare of the masses, and discovered the advancement of their own interests." These men and women had conveniently decided, Lansbury continued, that "the interests of the poor were best served by leaving East London to stew in its own juice while they became members of parliament, cabinet ministers, civil servants. . . . [They] discovered . . . that after all, all the poor in a lump were bad and reform and progress must be very gradual; that the rich were as necessary as the poor—and indeed, that nothing must ever be done to hurt the good-hearted rich who keep such places as Toynbee Hall going out of their ill-gotten gains."[8]

Leading scholars have so often quoted Lansbury's withering critique, which was published in his 1928 autobiography, that it behooves me to evaluate it carefully.[9] He had not always been so critical of Toynbee Hall and late-Victorian social reformers. In 1907, on an occasion Lansbury did not include in his autobiography, he offered a stunningly different version of the history and effects of late-nineteenth-century London's class-bridging movements. He shared the platform at New College Hall, Oxford, with a most unlikely companion: Lord Hugh Cecil. Scion of the great aristocratic house of Cecil, bachelor son of the Conservative prime minister Lord Salisbury, and a former resident of Oxford House, Lord Hugh is now best remembered as the irrational, "gauntly Elizabethan" diehard who refused to allow the Liberal prime minister, H. H. Asquith, to deliver his speech on the Parliament Bill on the floor of the House of Commons during the Revolt of the Lords in 1911. He was also the author of the classic manifesto of the Conservative Party, Conservatism (1912).[10] Drawing upon the lessons he had learned as a resident of Oxford House, Lord Hugh articulated an organic, deferential vision of social relations, stressing interdependence and hierarchy, that lay at the heart of the Conservative Party's approach to the urban poor from the 1890s until World War II.[11] The work of Oxford House, Lord Hugh explained in language anticipating his argument in Conservatism, "built together the separate atoms of society; it cemented together what had become divided and individual, so that they founded again a healthy social organisation." When the applause subsided, Lansbury rose to speak. Far from attacking the words of the noble lord, he extended the heartfelt thanks of laboring men for the good work of Oxford House and Toynbee Hall. He had come to admire and respect these men of wealth and education and hoped that more would come to share in their "good work." "Oxford was not sending her men" to the slums of London, he insisted, "with any ulterior object" beyond their desire to improve society.[12]

What had happened between 1907 and 1928, when Lansbury published his autobiography, to account for his drastic reevaluation of the settlement movement? Lansbury's remarks in 1907 and 1928 need to be read for what they are: interpretations of Victorian slum benevolence that reflected the concerns of a specific historical moment. In 1907, trade unionists and socialists, including Lansbury, had just begun to form themselves into the Labour Party and were still seeking allies across the political spectrum among those committed to improving the lives of laboring people. By 1928, the Labour Party was eager to reclaim its fragile claim to office and determined to erase all traces of its former ties with the pre–World War I world of liberals, progressives, and social reformers.

How can the evidence presented in this book help to take stock of Lansbury's antithetical claims? Is it possible to make sense of two such apparently irreconcilable judgments? In one key respect, Lansbury's criticisms in 1928 hit the mark directly. The educated men and women who lived and worked in the slums did become leading members of Parliament, cabinet ministers, civil servants, and social welfare workers. They staked out their authority to define and propose solutions to ills besetting society based on their experiences living in the slums.

His scornful claim that they left East London to "stew in its own juices" while advancing their individual and collective class interests is both simplistic and inaccurate. No doubt from his perspective, the salaries of civil servants, politicians, and social workers seemed munificent compared to the wages East Londoners earned as jam workers and laundresses, French polishers and gas fitters. Such a comparison, however, obscures the reality that these men gave up lucrative careers in business and the professions—readily available to them by virtue of their class, familial connections, intelligence, and education—to pursue much more modestly remunerated and less glamorous work as public servants.

While few stayed on in their adopted districts as permanent residents, most could never quite get away from the scenes of their youthful slum labors. For example Clement Attlee, Lansbury's own deputy in the 1930s and the Labour prime minister after World War II, returned over and over to his days at Toynbee Hall and the club for boys "mostly barefoot and ragged" in Limehouse that he managed.[13] He concluded his major speech in the House of Commons in support of the National Insurance Bill (based largely on the policy recommendations of another Toynbee Hall man, William Beveridge) by recalling the indelible impression of the poverty he had witnessed "forty years ago in Limehouse."[14] Far from confirming Attlee's sense of class superiority and his satisfaction with the status quo, his fourteen years in East London made him a thoroughgoing democrat who was highly sensitive to the relationship between poverty and cultural values.[15]

Living in the slums did not necessarily lead women and men to a single party affiliation or ideological destination. Slum philanthropists spanned the political spectrum, from ardent Christian Socialists such as the historian R. H. Tawney to reactionary paternalists such as Lord Hugh Cecil to maternalist Conservatives such as Lady Astor. What so many of them shared in common was a determination to look closely at the human face of poverty and find ways to redress the injuries of class. We can find their signatures on most landmark social welfare legislation of the first half of the twentieth century, from the collaboration of Margaret McMillan and Robert Morant in securing the passage of the Medical Inspection of School Children Act of 1907 to the implementation of the Beveridge Report in the aftermath of World War II.

With that smug but anxious arrogance of youth, William Beveridge wrote to his fretful parents in 1903 assuring them that *his* interest in Toynbee Hall and East London and the poor had nothing to do with either "slumming" or "social problems." He utterly distrusted "the saving power of culture and missions and isolated good feelings as a surgeon distrusts 'Christian Science.'"[16] There is no reason to doubt for a moment that Beveridge meant what he said. But his disavowal of slumming and social problems belies the much deeper streams of thought, feeling, and belief that flowed between sympathy and science, private philanthropy and public welfare, eros and altruism. For better and for worse, British social policy after World War II was as much the consummation of a century of slumming as it was an emphatic rejection of it.

MANUSCRIPT SOURCES

Addams, Jane. Papers. Peace Collection. Swarthmore College, Swarthmore, PA

Ashbee, C. R. Papers. Kings College Archive Centre, Cambridge

Banks, Elizabeth. Papers. Special Collections.University of Tulsa Library, Tulsa, OK

Barnett, Samuel. Papers. Lambeth Palace Library, London (Ms 1463–1466)

Barnett, Samuel. Papers. London Metropolitan Archives (formerly the Greater London Record Office, GLRO)

Benson, Edward. Diaries. Trinity College, Cambridge

Benson, Edward. Papers. Lambeth Palace Library, London

Beveridge, William. Papers. British Library of Political and Economic Science (BLPES), London School of Economics

Booth, Charles. Papers. British Library of Political and Economic Science (BLPES), London School of Economics

Cairns, Hugh McCalmont, First Earl. Papers. PRO 30/51, Public Record Office, Kew

Charity Organisation Society (COS). Files and Papers. Family Welfare Association (FWA), London Metropolitan Archives (formerly the Greater London Record Office, GLRO) (While I have used the papers of the COS extensively throughout this book, they contain the key collection of letters, papers, and reports on the Barnardo arbitration.)

Cockerell, Sydney. Papers. Bodleian Library, Oxford

Collet, Clara. Papers. Modern Record Office, University of Warwick

Davidson, Randall. Papers. Papers of the Archbishops of Canterbury. Lambeth Palace Library, London

Elmy, Elizabeth. Papers. British Library

Ensor, R.C.K. Papers. Bodleian Library, Oxford

Fry, Roger. Correspondence with Goldsworthy Lowes Dickinson. Kings College, Cambridge

Fulham Papers (Papers of the Bishops of London), Lambeth Palace Library. (Within the Fulham Papers, I used extensively correspondence and papers for Bishops Jackson, Creighton, Temple, and Winnington Ingram on parochial affairs in London.)

Galton, Frank. Papers. Coll. Misc. 315. British Library of Political and Economic Science (BLPES), London School of Economics

Hill, Octavia. Papers (correspondence with Henrietta and Samuel Barnett). British Library of Political and Economic Science (BLPES), London School of Economics

Holland, Henry Scott. Correspondence with Lavinia (Mrs. Edward) Talbot. Keble College, Oxford (Note: this correspondence is now deposited at York University: Borthwick Institute of Historical Research)

Holland, Henry Scott. Papers. Lectures and Sermons. Christ Church, Oxford (Note: these papers are now deposited at York University: Borthwick Institute of Historical Research)

Image, Selwyn. Papers. Bodleian Library, Oxford

Interhouse Journal of Balliol and Wadham Houses, Barnett Research Centre, Toynbee Hall

Lady Margaret Hall Settlement. Papers. Lady Margaret Hall Settlement, Lambeth (Note: this collection has been divided and deposited in the Lambeth Archive Department and the London Metropolitan Archives)
Account Books
Annual General Meeting Minute Books
Household Account Books
Katherine Thicknesse, typescript and manuscript Recollections
M. Child, Recollections of the Duke of Clarence Boys Club
Misc. Correspondence
Olive Butler, Some Personal Recollections
Typescript, Settlement Conference on Training, 1939
Winifred Locket, Recollections

Lambeth Board of Guardians. Minute Book, 1865–1866. London Metropolitan Archives (formerly the Greater London Record Office, GLRO)

Lee, Vernon (Violet Paget). Papers. Special Collections. Colby College Library, Colby College, Waterville, ME

Lester, Muriel. Papers. Peace Collection. Swarthmore College, Swarthmore, PA

Loch, Charles Stewart. Diary. Goldsmith's Library, University of London

London County Council. Reports of Inspectors of Licenses. London Metropolitan Archives (formerly the Greater London Record Office, GLRO)

Mansbridge, Albert. Papers. British Library

Ministry of Health, Public Record Office, London

Poor Law Commission and Successors:. Correspondence with Asylum Districts and Boards (MH17)

Local Government Board, Misc. Correspondence and Papers (MH25)

Minutes and Records of the Guild and School of Handicraft, Victoria and Albert Museum Library, London

Nevinson, Henry. Papers. Bodleian Library, Oxford

Nightingale, Florence. Papers. British Library, London

Oxford House University Settlement. Papers. Oxford House University Settlement, Bethnal Green, London (Note: most of the archives of Oxford House are now deposited in the Local History Library, Tower Hamlets)
Minute Books, Council of Oxford House
Minute Books, Oxford House Club
Tapes and transcripts, Oral History Project

Passfield, Baron (Sydney Webb) and Beatrice Webb. Papers. British Library of Political and Economic Science (BLPES), London School of Economics

Pettingell Collection of Plays (microfilm). University of Kent, Canterbury

Rogers, Thorold. Papers. Bodleian Library, Oxford

Royden, Maude. Papers. The Women's Library (formerly the Fawcett Library), London Metropolitan University

Spooner, William Archibald. Papers. New College, Oxford

Talbot, Lavinia (Mrs. Edward). Diaries. Hagley Hall, Stourbridge, West Midlands, UK

Tillyard, Frank. Papers. Shaftesbury, Dorset (in private hands)

Tower Hamlets Library. Local History (cuttings, photographs, and newspaper clippings)

Toynbee Hall. Papers and Misc. Correspondence. Barnett Research Centre, Toynbee Hall

Toynbee Hall. Papers. London Metropolitan Archives (formerly the Greater London Record Office, GLRO)

Toynbee Travellers Journal. Barnett Research Centre, Toynbee Hall

Wadham House Journal. Barnett Research Centre, Toynbee Hall

Women's University Settlement. Papers. Women's University Settlement, Blackfriars, Southwark, London (Note: most of these papers are now deposited at the Women's Library, formerly the Fawcett Library, London Metropolitan University)

Executive Committee Minute Books

Helen Barlow Recollections

M. E. King, Reminiscences and Notes on Acland Club

Octavia Hill, Correspondence on housing

Woods, Robert. Papers. Harvard University, Houghton Library

NOTES

INTRODUCTION
SLUMMING: EROS AND ALTRUISM IN VICTORIAN LONDON

1. See Frank Owen, *Tempestuous Journey, Lloyd George, His Life and Times* (New York: McGraw-Hill Book Company, 1955), 63–64.

2. Karl Baedeker, *London and Its Environs* (Leipzig: Karl Baedeker, 1887).

3. In 1892, Frederick Engels described the phenomenon of elite's interest in East London as a "momentary fashion among bourgeois circles of affecting a mild dilatation of Socialism." See Engels's "Preface to the English Edition," in Frederick Engels, *The Condition of the Working Class in England* (1892 ed. of 1887 trans., reprinted with an introduction by Eric Hobsbawm, London: Granada, 1969; repr. Chicago: Academy Chicago Publishers, 1969), 34. Citation is to Academy edition.

4. James Adderley, *In Slums and Society: Reminiscences of Old Friends* (London: Fisher Unwin, 1916), 26.

5. T. P. Stevens, *Father Adderley* (London: T. Werner Laurie, 1943). The poem and dedication are in the unnumbered front pages of the book.

6. Ibid., 5.

7. The close attention I pay to individual men, women, and children—their actions, thoughts, feelings, and representations—differs markedly from the approach pioneered by Michel Foucault in *The History of Sexuality: An Introduction*, vol. 1 (New York: Harmondsworth Penguin, 1978), which is a history largely without historical actors or human agents. At the same time, my approach also draws upon Foucault's work on "discourse," "technologies of power and knowledge," and their relationship to sexual and social institutions, ideologies, and identities.

8. See José Harris, *Private Lives, Public Spirit: Britain, 1870–1914* (Oxford: Oxford University Press, 1993); Susan Pedersen and Peter Mandler, *After the Victorians: Private Conscience and Public Duty in Modern Britain* (London: Routledge, 1994).

9. In conceptualizing the relation between sexual and social politics, I have benefited particularly from Judith Walkowitz, *City of Dreadful Delight: Narratives of Sexual Danger in Late-Victorian London* (Chicago: University of Chicago Press, 1992).

10. Henry W. Nevinson, *Changes and Chances* (New York: Harcourt, Brace and Company, 1924), 121.

11. On the interplay of the "imagined" and "real" slum in newspaper representations of slum life, see Alan Mayne, *The Imagined Slum: Newspaper Representation in Three Cities, 1870–1914* (Leicester, England: Leicester University Press, 1993). On the role of the late Victorian press in covering social problems and in producing Jack the Ripper as a Victorian sensation, see L. Perry Curtis, *Jack the Ripper and the London Press* (New Haven: Yale University Press, 2001). See also Curtis's important work on representations of the Irish in print and po-

litical caricatures, *Apes and Angels: The Irishman in Victorian Caricature* (Washington, DC: Smithsonian Institution Press, 1971).

12. For a provocative treatment of these issues in Chicago and New York, see Kevin J. Mumford, *Interzones: Black/White Sex Districts in Chicago and New York in the Early Twentieth Century* (New York: Columbia University Press, 1997).

13. Ann Douglas has brilliantly evoked the ways in which Harlem in New York City between the wars functioned as a similar site of benevolence, license, experimentation, and sexual and racial transgression in *Terrible Honesty, Mongrel Manhattan in the 1920s* (New York: Farrar, Strauss and Giroux, 1995). Likewise, Christine Stansell captures the mingling of transgressive bohemianism and reformism in *American Moderns: Bohemian New York and the Creation of a New Century* (New York: Metropolitan Books, 2000).

14. Royal Commission on Historical Manuscripts, Sixth Report, 1877 [c. 1745] 367–368. My thanks to Robert Bucholz for sending me this reference.

15. See Stefan Collini, *Public Moralists: Political Thought and Intellectual Life in Britain, 1850–1930* (Oxford: Clarendon Press, 1991).

16. On the phenomenon of the attractions of those who are designated low or unclean to those occupying "high" or central locations in society, see Peter Stallybrass and Allon White, *The Politics and Poetics of Transgression* (Ithaca, NY: Cornell University Press, 1986)

17. Henry James, *Princess Casamassima* (New York, 1886; Middlesex, England: Penguin, 1977, rprt., 1985), 184–185 (Citations are to the reprint edition). On James's debt to and rewriting of investigative slum journalism and surveillance of the poor, see Mark Seltzer, "The Princess Casamassima: Realism and the Fantasy of Surveillance," *Nineteenth-Century Fiction* (March 1981): 506–534.

18. For a sensitive and panoramic reconstruction of the cultural and social logic underpinning the lives of the poor in Victorian London and their responses to the well-to-do, see Ellen Ross, *Love and Toil: Motherhood in Outcast London, 1870–1918* (Oxford: Oxford University Press, 1993).

19. Nor were Adderley's criticisms misplaced. When Archbishop Benson presided at the opening of the University Club at Oxford House, he seemed disappointed in the "extreme punctiliousness and propriety" of the men, whom, he assumed were "the better sort of small shopkeepers." He was surprised to learn they were bona fide laborers. Benson, diary, February 18, 1888, p. 49, Benson Diaries. See also A. C. Benson, *The Life of Edward White Benson*, vol. 2 (London: Macmillan, 1899), 202.

20. Adderley's use of the word "slumming" retained some of its early- and mid-nineteenth-century connotations of fraudulence given by writers such as Pierce Egan and Henry Mayhew—of blackening newly counterfeited coins to pass them off as legitimate or forging false begging letters. See "slum" as noun and verb, and "slumming" in Eric Partridge, *The Dictionary of the Underworld* (London: Routlege and Kegan Paul, 1950; repr., Wordsworth: Hertfordshore, UK, 1995), 642–643. Citations are to Wordsworth edition.

21. Arthur Pillans Laurie, a resident at Toynbee Hall in the 1880s, could not bear the publicity and fanfare surrounding the settlement, although he did not

hold the leaders of the settlement responsible. "We were supposed to be noble young men engaged in trying to do good to the poor. We did not feel noble and were quite incapable of doing good. . . . [Toynbee Hall] was very much in the limelight then, and irritating flocks of gaily arrayed young men and young women used to descend upon us from the West End." With some friends, Pillans set up his own small colony in nearby Stepney Green. A. P. Laurie, *Pictures and Politics: A Book of Reminscences* (London, 1934), 74.

22. See Louisa Hubbard, "Statistics of Women's Work," in Angela Burdett-Coutts, ed., *Woman's Mission: A Series of Congress Papers on the Philanthropic Work of Women by Eminent Authors* (London: S. Low, Marston and Co., 1893), 364. See also Anne Summers, "A Home from Home: Women's Philanthropic Work in the Nineteenth Century," in Sandra Burman, ed., *Fit Work for Women* (New York: St. Martin's Press, 1979), 33–63. On women and philanthropy in nineteenth-century Britain, see Frank Prochaska, *Women and Philanthropy in Nineteenth-Century England* (Oxford: Clarendon Press, 1980). See also Jane Lewis, *Women and Social Action in Victorian and Edwardian England* (Stanford, CA: Stanford University Press, 1991); Ronald Walton, *Women in Social Work* (Boston: Routledge and Kegan Paul, 1975); Kathleen Woodroofe, *From Charity to Social Work in England and the United States* (London: Routledge and Kegan Paul, 1962). On women's work in the Salvation Army, see Pamela Walker, *Pulling the Devil's Kingdom Down: The Salvation Army in Victorian Britain* (Berkeley, CA: University of California Press, 2001), esp. chs.1 and 5. On Ranyard Bible women, see Frank Prochaska, "Body and Soul: Bible Nurses and the Poor in Victorian London," *Historical Research* 60 (1987): 337–348; see also Mary Poovey, *Making a Social Body: British Cultural Formation, 1830–1864* (Chicago: University of Chicago Press, 1995) ch. 2.

23. His work *The New Floreat* explicitly addressed the public-school-educated boy as the audience for his message about social obligation. James Adderley, *The New Floreat: A Letter to an Eton Boy on the Social Question* (London: Wells Gardner Darton and Co., 1894). Likewise, a pioneering woman social investigator, Helen Dendy Bosanquet, blasted members of her own sex for their selfish pursuit of sensation through slumming. " 'Do show me some cases of unmitigated misery,' is a request said to have been made by a young lady in search of sensation,' " Bosanquet recalled. See Helen Dendy Bosanquet, *Rich and Poor* (London: Macmillan, 1896), 5.

24. The rector of the slum parish St. George's in the East, the "rich and racy" Rev. Harry Jones, asserted that his "knowledge of the East of London" was "direct and connected." "I have not dipped into it on philanthropical errands from the West," he protested. Without trace of acknowledgement that he regularly transformed his observations of life among the poor into colorful anecdotes for his spirited dinner parties and the very article he had written, Jones insisted that he had not "hunted within its [East London's] border for curious literary materials." Harry Jones, "Life and Work among the East-London Poor," *Good Words* 25 (1884), 50. On Jones and his wife's life in East London and their style of housekeeping, see Henrietta Barnett, *Canon Barnett: His Life, Work, and Friends*, vol. 1 (Boston: Houghton Mifflin Company, 1919), 224. Likewise the novelist and writer on social problems, Cyril Gull, simultaneously lamented the

tendency of novelists to "exploit" the East End for their own ends even while admitting that he sought out a slum philanthropist "hidden away . . . in the East End of London" because he seemed to present a "strange personality, and one offering considerable interest to a novelist." See Cyril Gull, *The Great Acceptance: The Life Story of F. N. Charrington* (London: Hodder & Stoughton, 1912), 2–3. Gull published his novels under the pseudonym Guy Thorne.

25. "The Slums," *Link* (October 20, 1888), 1. For another example of this pattern of discrediting slumming see "An East-End Worker: After Ten Years in Outcast London," *St. James's Gazette* (January 12, 1894), 4.

26. Besant used a graphic description of slumming in Edinburgh to explain her transition from espousing radical individualism, free thought, neo-Malthusian birth control, and atheism to her more systematic critique of capitalism as a Fabian socialist. See Annie Besant, *An Autobiography* (1893; 2d ed., London: T. Fisher Unwin, 1920), 308–311.

27. William Beveridge to Annette Beveridge, January 10, 1900, IIa 41, Beveridge Papers.

28. Henry Mayers Hyndman, *The Record of an Adventurous Life* (New York: Macmillan, 1911), 46–47.

29. H. J. Dyos argued that the study of the slums "requires a sociology of language, for it was being applied with varying force over the period and with different emphasis at any one time by different social classes; it was being used in effect for a whole range of social and political purposes. . . . It is not possible now to invent a satisfactory definition of a slum, even a London one, in the nineteenth century." H. J. Dyos, "The Slums of Victorian London," in David Cannadine and David Reeder, eds., *Exploring the Urban Past: Essays in Urban History by H. J. Dyos* (Cambridge: Cambridge University Press, 1982), 132. Dyos's densely suggestive essay remains an excellent starting point for analyzing the concept and representation of the slum in Victorian culture.

30. The *OED* (2004 on-line edition) did not bother to specify the social background of those who went slumming; that is, it assumes readers will know that only the well-to-do engage in this sort of activity. The verb forms "to slum" or "to go slumming" came into widespread usage only in the 1880s, although contemporaries felt free to use the term to characterize earlier philanthropic work. For example, an admiring biographical resumé of Lord Shaftesbury's life in *Good Words* from 1887 noted that "he had taken tea hundreds of times in workmen's houses; he had 'slummed' so far back as 1846, and the result was the Model Lodging House Act." Presumably the word "slummed" was in quotations to indicate its newness and its status as slang. See John Rae, "Lord Shaftesbury as a Social Reformer," *Good Words* 28 (1887), 238.

31. Rev. Prebendary Rogers, rector of St. Botolph, Bishopgate, sermon preached in Balliol College Chapel, Sunday, February 4, 1883, as reported in *Oxford Magazine* (February 14, 1883), 75.

32. The novelist Arthur Morrison constructed a complex web of authorial poses in his tales of slum life to complicate his relationship to his own working-class origins. He claimed insider knowledge of East London, not by virtue of being an East Londoner, but through the knowledge he gained as sympathetic outsider who had studied East End life. Morrison had researched carefully the

slum district he immortalized in *A Child of the Jago* by working closely with Rev. Osborne Jay (discussed at length in chapter 5). In the preface to the third edition of *A Child of the Jago*, he wrote that he had "for certain years lived in the East End of London, and have been, not an occasional visitor but a familiar and equal friend in the house of the East Ender in all his degrees." See Arthur Morrison, *Child of the Jago*, ed. Peter Miles (London: J. M. Dent, 1896; London: Everyman, 1996), 7. Citation is to Everyman edition.

33. See Eric Hobsbawm on the "labour aristocracy" and divisions within the working class, in Eric Hobsbawm, "The Labour Aristocracy in Nineteenth-Century England," *Labouring Men, Studies in the History of Labour* (Garden City, NY: Doubleday, 1964). Historians have wrestled with the problem of finding an appropriate language by which to describe and characterize social groups. For important contributions to this discussion, see Geoffrey Crossick, "From Gentlemen to the Residuum: Languages of Social Description in Victorian Britain," in Penelope Corfield, ed., *Language, History, and Class* (Oxford: Basil Blackwell, 1991), 150–178. José Harris offers a subtle and persuasive critique of "two class models" of late Victorian Britain. Harris takes into account "micro-divisions and conflicts within class groups, as well as macro-divisions and conflicts between the two giant formations of capital and labour. Snobbery, class rivalry, and social differentiation cropped up at least as often between groups that were close to each other in status as between those that were far apart." See Harris, *Private Lives, Public Spirit*, 8.

34. As Ellen Ross explains, social "explorers used old and vague terms like *rich* and *poor*, *gentleman* and *working man* (or plurals or female forms of the latter pair). And these continue to make better sense in describing London's mixed industrial, craft, and court society than do *employers* and *employed*, *masters* and *hands*, or *proletarians* and *bourgeoisie*. The poor themselves seem to have accepted this nomenclature, though more significant in their daily lives were gradations among the poor." Ellen Ross, *Love and Toil: Motherhood in Outcast London, 1870–1918* (New York: Oxford University Press, 1993), 12.

35. David Edwards, Report of Inspection of the Rose and Crown [on December 29, 1890] and Subsequent Administrative Proceedings, LCC/Min/10/855, GLRO.

36. Ibid.

37. See Jonathan Rose, *The Intellectual Life of the British Working Class* (New Haven: Yale University Press, 2002) on the impressive extent and depth of working-class reading.

38. Beatrice Potter, "A Lady's View of the Unemployed at the East," *Pall Mall Gazette* (February 18, 1886).

39. Ella Pycroft to Beatrice Potter, February 26,1886, II, (1), ii, 7 ff 467, Passfield Papers.

40. Potter and Pycroft chronicled these ongoing struggles in "Record of the Inhabitants of Katherine Buildings," Coll. Misc. 43, BLPES, as well as in Pycroft's letters to Potter, II, (1), ii, 7, Passfield Papers. See Rosemary O'Day, "How Families Lived Then: Katherine Buildings, East Smithfield, 1885–1890," in *Studying Family and Community History*, vol. 1, ed. Ruth Finnegan and Michael Drake (Cambridge: Cambridge University Press, 1994), 129–167. Ruth Livesy

offers a nuanced reading of these materials in "Domesticating the Slums: Lady Rent-Collectors and their Tenants, 1870–1914." Unpublished essay in author's possession. Aarons did write one surviving letter to Potter on March 2, 1886. II (1) ii, 8 ff 566–567, Passfield Papers.

41. Herbert Spencer to Beatrice Potter, November 12, 1887, II, (1), ii, 1, Passfield Papers. Interestingly, we find these views echoed, albeit from a very different perspective in the memoir of George Acorn, a laboring man who frequented Toynbee Hall. The patent falseness of slummers' pretensions to have become slum dwellers infuriated him. He acerbically commented that the philanthropist's "heart and mind might be deeply concerned with the dreadful mystery, the inconceivable entanglement of it all; but he [unlike a real slum dweller] would not have the whole horizon of his life hopelessly encumbered with difficulties and obstacles and appearing at once narrow and insurmountable." See George Acorn, *One of the Multitude* (London: Heinemann, 1911), xi.

42. Potter had a great deal more at stake than sociological research in her masquerade as a sweated Jewish trouser fitter. She believed that she had Jewish ancestry, a putative lineage that fascinated and bothered her. Thus disguising herself as a Jewess was also a way for Potter to come to know better a hidden part of herself and her family's past about which she had deep ambivalence. See Deborah Nord, *The Apprenticeship of Beatrice Webb* (Ithaca, NY: Cornell University Press, 1985), 165–170.

43. Amy Levy, the Jewish poet of platonic love between women and of urban despair, captured well the demotic pleasures of seeing the city from the top of an omnibus in her "Ballade of an Omnibus." See Amy Levy, *The Complete Novels and Selected Writings of Amy Levy, 1861–1889*, ed. Melvyn New (Gainesville, FL: University Press of Florida, 1993), 386.

44. Sigmund Freud was intrigued by these questions as well and provided his own set of psychosexual answers. He described a group of people who "protect themselves against the loss of the object by directing their love, not to single objects but to all men alike; and they avoid the uncertainties and disappointments of genital love by turning away from its sexual aims and transforming the instinct into an impulse with an inhibited aim. . . . Perhaps St. Francis of Assisi went furthest in thus exploiting love for the benefit of an inner feeling of happiness." See Sigmund Freud, *Civilization and Its Discontents*, trans. James Strachey (New York: W. W. Norton and Co., 1961), 49.

45. His widow, Margaret, and her sister, Caroline Haddon, edited several substantial volumes of his heretofore unpublished writings throughout the 1880s. As Margaret Hinton reminded readers in the 1884 preface to her husband's *The Law Breaker and the Coming of the Law*, "the throbbings of his heart are repeated in ours who read his words, and his hope for the world—a hope whose credentials are the more perfect love of the whole human brotherhood—is ever finding a wider response." Margaret Hinton, preface to *The Law Breaker and the Coming of the Law*, by James Hinton (London: Kegan, Paul, Trench, 1884), v. In March 1884, *Oxford Magazine* characterized the new Oxford movement at the ancient university, with its emphasis on cross-class brotherly love in the slums, as an outgrowth of Hinton's plea for the well-to-do to serve their poor brethren in East London.

46. A founding member of the Metaphysical Society in 1868, Hinton debated his ideas with the most influential male thinkers and writers of his day, including Alfred Tennyson, William Gladstone, Thomas Huxley, James Stephen, John Ruskin, F. D. Maurice, Henry Sidgwick, and Walter Bagehot. See R. H. Hutton, "The Metaphysical Society, A Reminiscence," *Nineteenth Century* (August 1885): 177–196.

47. Hinton, journal entry, 1870, as quoted in Ellice Hopkins, *Life and Letters of James Hinton* (London: C. Kegan Paul and Co., 1878), 290.

48. On "nature" in Hinton's philosophy, see James Hinton, *Man and His Dwelling Place: An Essay towards the Interpretation of Nature* (London: Smith, Elder, 1872) and *Life in Nature* (New York: D. Appleton and Company, 1872).

49. Hinton's arguments about women's freedom bear close resemblance to Ruskin's in *Sesame and Lilies*, where Ruskin exalts women's moral power and queenly authority based on their capacity for sacrificing for the social good. See Caroline Levine, "Self-Forgetfulness: The Radical Women of Sesame and Lilies" paper presented at the Mid-Atlantic Conference on British Studies, April 2001, New York, NY. Ruskin admired Hinton, "who could have taught us much," and lamented his untimely death. See John Ruskin, vol. 29 of *The Works of John Ruskin*, ed. E. T. Cook and Alexander Wedderburn (George Allen: London, 1907), 67.

50. James Hinton, vol. 3 of *Unpublished Manuscripts* (London, privately printed), 487–491.

51. Hinton looked to his own life to validate his claims: "I have," he wrote in February 1872, "ever since I lived in Whitechapel—for it was that that did it— desired service, and acted for it—desired with a desire that has no second, no second even in the sum of all other desires I have ever had. . . . Now what has it meant? That I have acted according to my pleasure." James Hinton to Caroline Haddon, February 1872, as quoted in Ellice Hopkins, ed., *Life and Letters of James Hinton* (London: C. Kegan Paul and Co., 1878), 307.

52. Mrs. Havelock Ellis [Edith Lees Ellis], *Three Modern Seers: James Hinton, Nietzsche, Edward Carpenter* (New York: Mitchell Kennerley, 1910), 24.

53. The first biographical essay on Hinton appeared soon after his death as an extended obituary in *Mind*. See J. F. Payne, "James Hinton," *Mind* (April 1876): 247–252. Ellice Hopkins, who had access to Hinton's now lost diaries, manuscripts, and correspondence published the next major study of his life two years later. See Hopkins, *Life and Letters*.

54. Spiritually adrift and seeking a vocation, Havelock Ellis had journeyed to the remote Australian outback at the age of nineteen where he first read Hinton's *Life in Nature*. "In an instant," he recalled more than a half century later, "the universe changed for me. I trod on air; I moved in light." A few weeks later, he eagerly consumed Ellice Hopkins's *Life and Letters*, which convinced him that he should emulate Hinton and become a doctor, an idea that he claimed "had never before so much as entered my head." Havelock Ellis, *My Life* (Boston: Houghton Mifflin Co., 1939), 164, 169. Throughout the 1880s, Havelock Ellis tried hard to ensure that Hinton's ideas would be accessible to a rising generation of men and women seeking solutions to sexual and social problems. See H[enry]. Havelock Ellis, "Hinton's Later Thought," *Mind* (July 1884): 384–405.

55. On the fellowship and its links to Hinton, see Willard Wolfe, *From Radi-*

calism to Socialism: Men and Ideas in the Formation of Fabian Socialist Doctrines, 1881–1889 (New Haven: Yale University Press, 1975), 152, 305–306. Ellis and the founder of the fellowship, Thomas Davidson, exchanged a series of lengthy letters about Hinton's teachings. See William Knight, ed., *Memorials of Thomas Davidson, The Wandering Scholar* (London: Ginn and Company, 1907), 37–43.

56. On Hopkins and Hinton, see Rosa Barrett, *Ellice Hopkins: A Memoir*, with an introduction by H. Scott Holland (London: Wells Gardner, Darton and Co., 1907), 86–101. For Hopkins's theology and her views about sex and gender reform, see Susan Mumm, "'I Love My Sex': Two Late Victorian Pulpit Women," in Joan Bellamy, Anne Laurence, and Gill Perry, eds., *Women, Scholarship and Criticism: Gender and Knowledge c. 1790–1900* (Manchester: Manchester University Press, 2000), and Susan Mumm, "Ellice Hopkins and the Defaced Image of Christ," in Julie Melnyk, ed., *Women's Theology in Nineteenth-Century Britain: Transfiguring the Faith of the Fathers* (New York: Garland Publishing, 1998).

57. On Noel and Hinton, see Desmond Heath, *Roden Noel, 1834–1894: A Wide Angle* (London: D. B. Books, 1998), 159–160. On Noel's slum benevolence among children, see the Hon. Roden Noel, *Selected Poems from the Works of the Hon. Roden Noel with a Biographical and Critical Essay by Percy Addleshaw* (London: Elkin Mathews, 1897), xx–xxi, xxix.

58. See Chushichi Tsuzuki, *Edward Carpenter: Prophet of Human Fellowship* (Cambridge: Cambridge University Press, 1980), 68.

59. The disappearance of his vast collection of unpublished manuscripts, manuscript autobiography, and letters (last owned by Edith Lees Ellis) has no doubt also curtailed scholarly interest in him.

60. These rumors can be traced most fully in the correspondence of Havelock Ellis and Olive Schreiner, with Ellis more often than not attempting to defend Hinton against the many charges levelled against him. Discussing Hinton did allow Ellis and Schreiner to enter into quite intimate exchanges about sexual ethics and desire at a time when they were still sorting out their own romantic feelings for one another. See Yaffa Claire Draznin, ed., *"My Other Self": The Letters of Olive Schreiner and Havelock Ellis, 1884–1920* (New York: Peter Lang, 1992).

61. Such charges must have been a terrible blow to his disciple Ellice Hopkins, who repeatedly emphasized in her adulatory *Life and Letters of James Hinton* her subject's complete devotion to purifying relations between the sexes and righting the "wrongs and degradation of women" that weighed so heavily upon him. See Hopkins, *Life and Letters*, 14.

62. Members of the Men and Women's Club, who have received a great deal of scholarly attention, had good reason to feel anxious about their reputations. Club members were caught up in overlapping romances and complex love triangles even as they engaged in supposedly disinterested and scientific debates about sex questions. See Walkowitz, *City of Dreadful Delight*, ch. 5. Henrietta Barnett, for example, never mentions the influence of Hinton on her development as a social reformer, though she did acknowledge her debts to the Haddon sisters. I have found only one reference to Hinton in Samuel's writings and correspondence,

both published and unpublished. See Samuel Barnett to Frank Barnett, September 1906, as quoted in Barnett, *Canon Barnett*, vol. 2 (1919), 197.

63. For a brilliant and influential analysis of the link between collar wearing as sign of respectability and the contextual nature of social roles and identities, see Peter Bailey, "Will the Real Bill Banks Please Stand Up? Towards a Role Analysis of Mid-Victorian Working-Class Respectability," *Journal of Social History* 12 (1979): 336–353. Gail Ching-Liang Low analyzes the "visual and imaginative pleasure of stepping into another's clothes" within the imperial and metropolitan contexts as "one of the central legacies of orientalism." She offers nuanced insights into the relation between "cross-class dressing" and "cross-cultural dressing." See Low, "White Skins/Black Masks: The Pleasures and Politics of Imperialism," *New Formations* (Winter 1989): 83–103.

64. H. M. Hyndman caustically observed that "Englishmen of apparently decent character," when far removed from the censorious gaze of rigidly respectable Mrs. Grundys, "stripped off" "conventional manners and morality as easily and almost as quickly" as they divested themselves of their tall hats and black coats. See H. M. Hyndman, *The Record of an Adventurous Life* (New York: The Macmillan Company, 1911), 130. The well-to-do Katherine Roberts could not bear to take off her nurse's uniform even after she had stopped working at a maternity hospital for poor women because it allowed her to "wander about in the evenings, or drop into the Pavilion for a bit, and have supper at a cheap restaurant, and feel Bohemian . . . for a little longer." She believed that "one's personality would change" the moment she put back on her usual costume of jewels and a smart frock. Katherine Roberts, *Five Months in a London Hospital* (Letchworth: Garden City Press, 1911), 144.

65. William James to Henry Rutgers Marshall, February 8, 1899, in Henry James, ed., *The Letters of William James*, vol. 2 (Boston: Atlantic Monthly Press, 1920), 88.

CHAPTER ONE
WORKHOUSE NIGHTS: HOMELESSNESS, HOMOSEXUALITY, AND
CROSS-CLASS MASQUERADES

1. The *Lancet* articles appeared in weekly installments in 1865 and 1866. Hart later became editor of the *British Medical Journal*. Through his marriage to Alice Rowland, Hart became closely tied to two of the leading social reformers of the day, his sister-in-law, Henrietta Rowland Barnett, and her husband, Rev. Samuel Barnett, the founders of the first university settlement in Whitechapel, Toynbee Hall. Hart published two articles summarizing the findings of the commission and put forward remedies. See Ernest Hart, "The Condition of Our State Hospitals," *Fortnightly Review* 3 (December 1865): 218–221; and "Metropolitan Infirmaries for the Pauper Sick," *Fortnightly Review* 4 (April 1866): 460–462. In February 1866, in the midst of the furor surrounding "A Night," Hart slightly modified and published in pamphlet form his first *Fortnightly Review* essay. The *Lancet* reports were also republished in single volume form as *Report of the Lancet Sanitary Commission for Investigating the State of the Infirmaries of Workhouses, 1866*. On Ernest Hart, see George Behlmer, "Ernest Hart and the

Social Thrust of Victorian Medicine," *British Medical Journal* (October 3, 1990): 711–713. *Punch* viewed Hart as a hero in the affair (as a man who had a "hart") and sang his praises with its usual comic flair. See *Punch* (April 14, 1866), 160.

2. See leader article in the *Times* (February 9, 1867), 7.

3. Nightingale's interest in workhouse infirmaries predated the Lancet series and had been prompted by the Liverpool philanthropist William Rathbone. See Cecil Woodham-Smith, *Florence Nightingale, 1820–1920* (New York: McGraw Hill, 1951), 296–303. She detailed her scheme for placing trained female nurses in workhouse infirmaries to the great sanitarian, Edwin Chadwick. See Nightingale to Edwin Chadwick, July 9, 1866, in Martha Vicinus and Bea Nergaard, eds., *Ever Yours, Florence Nightingale, Selected Letters* (Cambridge, MA: Harvard University Press, 1990), 270–274. For an excellent contemporary account of the Lancet's campaign and workhouse infirmary reform, see Thorold Rogers, ed., *Joseph Rogers, M.D., Reminiscences of a Workhouse Medical Officer* (London: T. Fisher Unwin, 1889).

4. On this campaign and the reform of workhouse infirmaries, see Gwendoline Ayers, *England's First State Hospitals and the Metropolitan Asylums Board, 1867–1930* (Berkeley: University of California Press, 1971), chs. 1 and 2.

5. On the early history of the *Pall Mall Gazette*, see J. W. Robertson Scott, *The Story of the Pall Mall Gazette, of Its First Editor, Frederick Greenwood, and of Its Founder, George Murray Smith* (London: Oxford University Press, 1950).

6. Frederick Greenwood acknowledged the key role of the *Lancet* and lamented the fact that the government only responded to social ills once they had been made into a "sensation." He argued that the neglect of the health needs of "disabled poor" were probably more shocking and injurious than the "curious and picturesque" workhouse revelations of "A Night." See Frederick Greenwood, "Curiosities of the Public Service," *Pall Mall Gazette* (October 24, 1867), 1.

7. In this respect, I follow Keating, who reprinted "A Night in a Workhouse" as the first text in his primary source anthology *Into Unknown England, 1866–1913: Selections from the Social Explorers* (Manchester: Manchester University Press, 1976) and offers a cursory analysis of it in *The Working Classes in Victorian Fiction* (London: Routledge and K. Paul, 1971). As Lynda Nead succinctly and rightly argues, "social investigation should be understood as one of the centres in the nineteenth century which produced definitions of sexuality." See Nead, *Myths of Sexuality: Representations of Women in Victorian Britain* (Oxford: Basil Blackwell, 1988), 150.

8. "The London Workhouses," *London Review* (January 27, 1866), 112.

9. *The Gladstone Diaries*, ed. H.C.G. Matthew vol. 6, 1861–1868, entry for February 5, 1866 (Oxford: Clarendon Press, 1978), 416.

10. *South London Journal* (January 27, 1866), 4.

11. Many articles discussed the various reprints of "A Night" and its circulation across social groups. See *South London Journal* (January 27, 1866), 4.

12. *Pall Mall Gazette*, March 7, 1866, hereafter cited as *PMG*. The French press reveled in the embarrassment "A Night" caused English officialdom. A complete version of "A Night" was translated and published in the *Revue Britannique* and reprinted in many other journals and papers. See for example, *L'Écho de la France* (April 20, 1866; and May 4, 1866). The provincial press in

Britain also reprinted "A Night." See for example, *Liverpool Daily Post*, supplement (January 15, 1866), 2; (January 16, 1866), 2; and (January 17, 1866), 2; the *Birmingham Journal* (January 20, 1866), 3. All the local papers serving individual neighborhoods in London, such as the *Clerkenwell Journal* and the *Shoreditch Advertiser*, reprinted "A Night" as well.

13. On Mearns, see Anthony Wohl, ed. and introduction, *The Bitter Cry of Outcast London* (Leicester: Leicester University Press; New York: Humanities Press, 1970) and Gareth Stedman Jones, *Outcast London: A Study in the Relationship between Classes in Victorian Society* (Oxford: Clarendon Press, 1971), esp. chs. 11 and 16. On Stead, see Deborah Gorham, "The Maiden Tribute of Modern Babylon Re-Visited," *Victorian Studies* (Spring 1976); and Judith Walkowitz, *City of Dreadful Delight: Narratives of Sexual Danger in Late-Victorian London* (Chicago, 1992), chs. 3 and 4.

14. "A Night" was first anthologized by Peter Keating, ed. in *Into Unknown England 1866–1913: Selections from the Social Explorers* (Manchester: Manchester University Press, 1976) and then by Sharon Winn and Lynn Mae Alexander, ed., *The Slaughter-House of Mammon: An Anthology of Victorian Social Protest Literature* (West Cornwall, CT: Locust Hill Press, 1992). Historians of workhouses and homelessness invariably discuss "A Night" without mentioning its sexual dimensions. See for example, Rachel Vorspan, "Vagrancy and the New Poor Law in Late-Victorian and Edwardian England," *English Historical Review* (January 1977): 66; Lionel Rose, *"Rogues and Vagabonds": Vagrant Underworld in Britain, 1815–1985* (London: Routledge, 1988), 114; Peter Wood, *Poverty and the Workhouse* (Wolfeboro Falls, NH: Alan Sutton, 1991), 154–155. Mark Freeman has recently examined the genre of writings about incognito slum exploration in the Victorian and Edwardian period. While he devotes considerable attention to Greenwood and "A Night in a Workhouse" and notes the emphasis on themes of "incest, squalor, violence, and ignorance" in the literature, he misses entirely the homoerotic dimension that made "A Night" into a sensation. Freeman's primary focus is on the methodologies used by these sociologists–slum explorers. See Mark Freeman, "'Journeys into Poverty Kingdom': Complete Participation and the British Vagrant, 1866–1914," *History Workshop Journal* 52 (Autumn 2001): 99–121.

15. "Queer" most frequently meant "odd" or out of the ordinary in the 1860s, though increasingly from the 1880s onward it was often used in specific contexts that also implied oddness or deviance in sexual arrangements. Here, I capture the ambiguity of its contemporary usage to convey both oddness and the possibility of sexual irregularity. On London as a "queer metropolis," see Matt Houlbrook, "'A Sun Among Cities': Space, Identities, and Queer Male Practices, London, 1918–1957" (Ph.D. diss., University of Essex, 2002). On East London as a queer space, see Gavin Brown, "Listening to Queer Maps of the City: Gay Men's Narratives of Pleasure and Danger in London's East End," *Oral History* (Spring 2001): 48–61.

16. On the relationship between the organization of space and sexual desire, see David Bell and Gill Valentine, eds., *Mapping Desire: Geographies of Sexuality* (London: Routledge, 1994); on post–World War II London in particular, see Frank Mort, "Mapping Sexual London: The Wolfenden Committee on Homo-

sexual Offences and Prostitution: 1954–7," *New Formations*, 37 (1999): 92–113; see also, Matt Houlbrook, "Towards a Historical Geography of Sexuality," *Journal of Urban History* 27, no. 4 (2001): 497–504.

17. W. T. Stead claimed that "A Night" led to the beginning of the reform of the Poor Laws. W. T. Stead, "Character Sketch: February. The Pall Mall Gazette," in *The Review of Reviews* 7 (February 1893): 145.

18. By beginning my study with Greenwood and the 1860s, I am following the periodization of E. P. Hennock, who argues for the "close relation of the social thought of the 1860s and that of the 1880s." "Poverty and Social Theory in England: The Experience of the 1880s," *Social History* (January 1976): 89.

19. Neil Bartlett, in his provocative and insightful biography of Oscar Wilde and the "forging" of gay selfhood, claimed that despite intense competition among journalists, including Mayhew and Greenwood, "to expose the worst evils," sex between men was conspicuously and completely absent from their writings. See Neil Bartlett, *Who Was That Man? A Present for Mr. Oscar Wilde* (London: Serpent's Tail, 1988), 143–145.

20. His books were usually collections of previously published articles.

21. On the pose of the "gent" in relation to the "swell," see Peter Bailey, "Ally Sloper's Half Holiday: Comic Art in the 1880s," *History Workshop Journal* 16 (Autumn 1983): 13.

22. For an extended history of Greenwood's family, see Scott, *The Story of the Pall Mall Gazette*, esp. ch. 12.

23. Edmund Yates, *Fifty Years of London Life, Memoirs of a Man of the World* (New York: Harper and Bros., 1885), 197. On Yates's editorial career, see Joel Weiner, "Edmund Yates: The Gossip as Editor," in Joel Weiner, ed., *Innovators and Preachers: The Role of the Editor in Victorian England* (Westport, CT: Greenwood Press, 1985): 259–274. On the cultural and social milieu of London's bohemian journalists, see P. D. Edwards, *Dickens's 'Young Men,' George Augustus Sala, Edmund Yates, and the World of Victorian Journalism* (Aldershot, UK: Ashgate, 1997); Christopher Kent, "The Idea of Bohemia in Mid-Victorian England," *Queens Quarterly* 80 (1973): 360–369. Jerrold Siegel places journalists at the heart of Bohemian Paris at mid-century. See Jerrold Seigel, *Bohemian Paris: Culture, Politics, and the Boundaries of Bourgeois Life, 1830–1930* (New York: Penguin Books, 1987).

24. The year after "A Night," Greenwood scored another major journalistic coup about sex with his exposé of the "Wrens of Curragh," a community of female prostitutes attached to the barracks in Curragh. He initially published his findings in the *Pall Mall Gazette*, October 15–19, 1867, and later in a pamphlet. Greenwood noted that the community of wrens admitted unattached, homeless women who were not always engaged in prostitution. See Maria Luddy, "An Outcast Community: The 'Wrens' of the Curragh," *Women's History Review* 1, no. 3 (1992), 341–355. My thanks to James Adams, whose unpublished graduate seminar paper, "The Wrens of the Curragh" (May 2003) vastly expanded my knowledge of this controversy.

25. See James Greenwood, "The Wren of the Curragh. No. 1," *Pall Mall Gazette* (October 15, 1867), 9. Greenwood also explicitly linked this exposé to

"A Night" by criticizing the horrors of the local workhouse and explaining the women's aversion to it.

26. For Greenwood's age and date of death, see B. I. Diamond and J. O. Baylen, "James Greenwood's London: A Precursor of Charles Booth," *Victorian Periodicals Review* (Spring/Summer 1984): 42.

27. For a vivid recreation of low haunts and depressed state of Lambeth at this time, see Simon Winchester, *The Professor and the Madman: A Tale of Murder, Insanity, and the Making of the Oxford English Dictionary* (New York: Harper Perennial, 1999).

28. "Private Correspondence Column," *Birmingham Journal*, supplement (January 27, 1866), 4.

29. Stead, "Character Sketch," 144.

30. Frederick Greenwood as quoted in B. I. Diamond, "A Precursor of the New Journalism: Frederick Greenwood of the *Pall Mall Gazette*" in Joel Wiener, ed., *Papers for the Millions: The New Journalism in Britain, 1850s to 1914* (Westport, CT: Greenwood Press, 1988), 27.

31. On the cotton famine's impact on the theory and practice of poor relief, see Lynn Lees, *The Solidarities of Strangers: The English Poor Laws and the People, 1700–1948* (Cambridge: Cambridge University Press, 1998), ch. 7.

32. Passed on a provisional one year basis in 1864, it was made into permanent law in 1865.

33. See Metropolitan Houseless Poor Act, 27 & 28 Vict. c. 116 (1864); 28 & 29 Vict. c. 34 (1865).

34. Sidney and Beatrice Webb, *English Poor Law Policy* (London, 1910), 97.

35. In 1866, the government of London remained extremely chaotic and highly localized. Each workhouse had its own board of guardians who served as trustees of the institution and involved themselves with the supervision of paid staff and regular inspection of the premises. London's vestrymen were responsible not only for poor relief, but also for most other local government functions such as education and roads.

36. On tensions between local guardians and the emergence of more centralized government in London see David Owen, *The Government of Victorian London, 1855–1889: The Metropolitan Board of Works, the Vestries, and the City Corporation* (Cambridge, MA: Belknap Press, 1982); On the politicization of London vestries, see John Davis, *Reforming London: The London Government Problem, 1855–1900* (London: Oxford University Press, 1988), 23–24.

37. As the history of "A Night" makes clear, Thomas MacKay was wrong to claim that the effect of the Metropolitan Houseless Poor Act was "instantaneous: all the metropolitan boards, with one exception, provided, for the most part adequately, the accommodation required by the Act." Thomas MacKay, *History of the English Poor Law*, vol. 3 (New York, 1900), 379.

38. See Louisa Twining, *Recollections of Workhouse Visiting and Management during Twenty-Five Years* (London: C. K. Paul, 1880). Twining alludes to, but never mentions by name, "A Night." She goes out of her way to establish that women had entered the field of workhouse reform before men. For Millicent N., see *Victoria Magazine for Women* (September 1866), 463.

39. Nightingale wrote to Gathorne Hardy, president of the Poor Law Board, that she was "as stern a political economist as any man and I would make the able bodied pauper either really work or starve." See Nightingale to Gathorne Hardy, February/March 1867, AdMss. 45787, ff 131, Nightingale Papers, British Library.

40. Frederick Greenwood, "Birth and Infancy of the Pall Mall Gazette," *Pall Mall Gazette* (April 14, 1897), 2.

41. The seeming disinterest of the press in discovering his actual name suggests that journalists were not particularly concerned about his fate as an individual, but rather saw his death as an opportunity to draw attention to a social problem and sell papers.

42. My thanks to Louise Yelin for suggesting this source for "A Night." For example, see "A Walk in a Workhouse," *Household Words* (May 25, 1850). Dickens's depiction of the workhouse in *Oliver Twist* and Fagin's relations with his "street arabs" constitute yet another set of his influence on the sorts of themes treated by Greenwood.

43. See Eve Sedgwick, "Homophobia, Misogyny, and Capital: The Example of *Our Mutual Friend*," in Eve Sedgwick, *Between Men: English Literature and Male Homosocial Desire* (New York: Columbia University Press, 1985), ch. 9. On Dickens's use of disguise, and more generally, the history of disguise in Victorian literature, see John Reed's suggestive analysis in *Victorian Conventions* (Athens, OH: Ohio University Press, 1975), ch. 13.

44. In a sermon preached for the benefit of the bishop of London's Fund, the Bishop of St. David's elaborated on the unique status and claims of London on the nation. "It is the seat of government, of legislation, of the supreme and permanent administration of justice; the main storehouse of the national wealth, material and intellectual; the depository of the most precious treasures of art and knowledge; the chief laboratory of all the inventions which contribute to cheer, adorn, and ennoble human life; the mart of all productions which minister to every kind of desire; the centre in which every ambition finds its highest aim." Lord bishop of St. David's, Connop Thirlwall, *The Wants of the Great City: A Sermon Preached at Whitehall Chapel, May 13, 1866* (London, 1866), 2, 3.

45. See Keith McClelland, "England's Greatness, the Working Man," in Catherine Hall, Keith McClelland, and Jane Rendall, *Defining the Victorian Nation, Class, Race, Gender, and the Reform Act of 1867* (Cambridge: Cambridge University Press, 2000), esp. 96–102.

46. See José Harris, "Between Civic Virtue and Social Darwinism: The Concept of the Residuum," in David Englander and Rosemary O'Day, eds., *Retrieved Riches: Social Investigation in England, 1840–1914* (Aldershot: Scolar Press, 1995).

47. According to W. T. Stead, James was "greatly assisted by the independent observations of [Bittlestone] his companion. Four eyes were better than two, and one memory assisted the other." Stead, "Character Sketch," 144.

48. Ibid.

49. At this point in Greenwood's story, he used the pronoun "he" to describe the gentleman slummer. Once he reveals the fact that he is the slum investigator, he used the first person singular pronoun.

50. These terms figure prominently in the first annual report of the COS. See *Meeting of the Society for Organising Charitable Relief and Repressing Mendicity, Held at Willis's Rooms, on March 30th, 1870* (London, 1870), esp. 6–8.

51. As Nina Auerbach has argued, amateur theatricals were immensely popular among the well-to-do, precisely those people whom the *PMG* hoped to capture as readers. See Nina Auerbach, *Private Theatricals* (Cambridge, MA: Harvard University Press, 1990).

52. See Gail Ching-Liang Low, "White Skins/Black Masks: The Pleasures and Politics of Imperialism," *New Formations* (Winter 1989), 93.

53. See Harry Cocks, "The Trials of Sodom: Sodomy Trials and the Regulation of Male Homosexuality, 1830–1885," unpublished paper presented to the North American Conference on British Studies, Chicago, 1996. Cocks discusses the use of disguises and entrapment within the broader problem of policing sodomy and using evidence provided by the police in various prosecutions for homosexual offences in *Nameless Offences: Homosexual Desire in the Nineteenth Century* (London: I. B. Tauris, 2003), ch. 2. He examines the use of disguises—and forms of cross-dressing—by men seeking sex with other men in ch. 3.

54. See C. W. Craven, *A Night in the Workhouse* (London, 1887), 5. Craven's narrative sticks very closely to Greenwood's and ends with his claim to have been an "amateur casual" for an evening.

55. Striptease did not emerge as widespread form of erotic dance until the early twentieth century. My thanks to Judy Walkowitz for pointing this out to me.

56. See Louis Chevalier's analysis of Sue in *Laboring Classes, Dangerous Classes* (Princeton, NJ: Princeton University Press, 1973). See also Edward R. Tannenbaum, "The Beginnings of Bleeding-Heart Liberalism: Eugene Sue's *Les Mystères de Paris*," *Comparative Studies in Society and History* 23, no. 3 (July 1981), pp. 491–507.

57. According to Stead, in its early days the *Pall Mall Gazette* was believed to be a paper "for gentlemen by gentlemen." Stead, "Character Sketch," 141.

58. "Legalized Abominations—The Christian Hells of England," *Reynold's Newspaper* (January 21, 1866), 3.

59. The Poor Law Board had met during the first week of January 1866 to establish uniform standards of food and work requirements for workhouses. See Lambeth Board of Guardians, minute book, 1865–1866, Greater London Record Office.

60. See David Armstrong, *The Political Anatomy of the Body* (Cambridge: Cambridge University Press, 1983) for a general framework about the relationship between disease, social hygiene, and shifting attempts to regulate bodies.

61. George Woolcott, *Public Baths and Wash-Houses: Suggestions for Building and Fitting Up Parochial or Borough Establishments* (London, 1850); E. T. Bellhouse, *On Baths and Wash-Houses* (Manchester, 1854), 4, 13. The pamphlet was reprinted from the *Transactions of the Manchester Statistical Society* for June 1854.

62. For a vivid account of the cholera epidemic of 1865–1866 and its links to anxieties about fouled water and East London squalor, see Norman Longmate, *King Cholera: The Biography of a Disease* (London: Hamish Hamilton, 1966), ch. 20.

63. The appropriation of institutions of public hygiene as sites of male same-sex contact and desire in twentieth century London has been analyzed by Matt Houlbrook. See "The Private World of Public Urinals: London, 1918–1957," *London Journal* 25, no. 1 (2000): 52–70. Houlbrook's article turned my attention to the first queer guidebook to London. Its author, "Paul Pry," the pseudonym of Thomas Burke, likewise playfully and ironically used the language of hygiene as a way to talk about queer sex in 1937. The guidebook opens with one of its two main characters, Mr. Mumble, searching the *Sanitary World and Drainage Observer* for information—ostensibly about public urinals but in fact about sites for illicit sexual contact between men. He literally uses London County Council drainage and sewer maps and his own map of London's public conveniences to construct a map of public refuges for sex between men. See Paul Pry, *For Your Convenience: A Learned Dialogue Instructive to All Londoners and London Visitors, Overheard in The Theleme Club and Taken Down Verbatim* (London: George Routledge, 1937).

64. Frederick Greenwood quoted by Stead in "Character Sketch," 144.

65. See Ellen Ross on the "oatmeal wars," in *Love and Toil: Motherhood in Outcast London, 1870–1918* (New York: Oxford University Press, 1993), 36–37.

66. George Bernard Shaw, *Complete Plays with Prefaces*, vol. 1 (New York: Dodd Mead and Co., 1962), 215.

67. John Timbs's vast compendium of club life (*Clubs and Club Life in London* [London: Richard Bentley, 1866]) was published that same week and widely reviewed.

68. On the 1842 Mines Act and the committee report that preceded it, see Angela John, *By the Sweat of Their Brow* (London: Routledge & Kegan Paul, 1984).

69. See Anthony Wohl, *The Eternal Slum: Housing and Social Policy in Victorian London* (Montreal, 1977); and "Sex and the Single Room: Incest among the Victorian Working Classes," in Anthony Wohl, ed., *The Victorian Family: Structure and Stresses* (New York: St. Martin's Press, 1978).

70. See Edwin Hodder, *The Life and Work of the Seventh Earl of Shaftesbury* (London, 1887), 470. Shaftesbury was closely involved with all these campaigns. See also Frank Mort, *Dangerous Sexualities: Medico-Moral Politics in England since 1830* (London: Routledge & Kegan Paul, 1987), Part 1.

71. The *Weekly Dispatch* of March 21, 1836, complained that the New Bastilles drove "men from the marriage bed to sleep with boys." See Anna Clark, *The Struggle for the Breeches: Gender and the Making of the British Working Class* (Berkeley: University of California Press, 1995), 190.

72. See Ronald Hyam, *Empire and Sexuality: The British Experience* (Manchester: Manchester University Press, 1990), 102.

73. Thirty years later, Frederick Greenwood reiterated the unspeakable and unnamable character of the casual ward abominations as well as the teasing rhetorical strategy used to encourage readers' dark imaginings. "All that might have been written after this visit to a casual ward was not written: could not be described in public print at that insufficiently advanced period of the century. But what was suppressed could be otherwise made known." Greenwood, "Birth and Infancy of the 'Pall Mall Gazette,'" 2.

74. While Greenwood's slum explorations are saturated by sexual themes and images, homoeroticism is *not* an overarching characteristic of his total body of writings. There are, however, several other examples of Greenwood's prurient-philanthropic fascination for handsome youths. In *Seven Curses*, he reproduced an advertisement published in a newspaper addressed to the "Aged and Unprotected" by "a young man, aged twenty-two, well-built, good-looking, and of a frank and affectionate disposition" desirous "of acting the part of a son towards any aged person or persons who would regard his companionship and constant devotion as an equivalent for his maintenance and clothes and support generally." Was the advertiser a male prostitute seeking economic support in exchange for his frank affection and companionship? Greenwood's commentary indicates that he was particularly intrigued by the advertisement and advertiser: "Although it is difficult without a struggle to feel an interest in this young gentleman's welfare, we cannot help feeling curious to know what success his advertisement brought him. Is he still a forlorn orphan, wasting his many virtues and manly attributes on a world that to him is a wilderness?" Given the thousands of destitute men and women in London, it is not clear why Greenwood was so drawn to this case or why he cared to imagine what had become of the youth's "manly attributes." *Seven Curses of London* (1869; repr. Oxford: Oxford University Press, 1981), 170.

75. Farnall's entry to the Lambeth visitor's book was reproduced in "The Houseless Poor and the Workhouse," *Daily News* (January 15, 1866), 2.

76. For example, the journal for Barnardo's work was named *Night and Day* to signify his vigilance at all hours, his commitment to rescuing children from the terrors of sleeping on the streets at night, and to indicate the ways in which philanthropy transformed the darkness of night into the healthy brightness of day for children.

77. On the construction and regulation of space based on the rhetoric of dirt and disease, see David Sibley, *Geographies of Exclusion: Society and Difference in the West* (London: Routledge, 1995).

78. The Harding Collection, Bodleian Library, Oxford, contains two broadside retellings of Greenwood's "A Night": Harding B, 13 (154) "A Night in a London Workhouse," and Harding B, 13 (155) entitled "A Night's Repose in Lambeth Workhouse."

79. Frederick Greenwood, "Casual Wards," *Pall Mall Gazette* (January 16, 1866), 1. Frederick's editorial response to the Wrens exposé included a substantial analysis of "A Night." He argued that both series of articles had revealed official incompetence and refusal to act to serve the public's best interests. See Frederick Greenwood, "Curiosities of the Public Service," *Pall Mall Gazette* (October 24, 1867), 1.

80. "A Night in a London Workhouse," n.d. (Digby, St. Giles, London) Bodleian Library.

81. John Smeaton, "Workhouse Governors," *Pall Mall Gazette* (January 19, 1866), 3.

82. James Greenwood, *Seven Curses of London*, 173.

83. *Pall Mall Gazette* (January 15, 1866), 5.

84. "A Ministerial Midnight Visit," *Tower Hamlets Express* (January 19, 1866).

85. J. H. Stallard, *The Female Casual and Her Lodging: With a Complete Scheme for the Regulation of Workhouse Infirmaries* (London: Saunders, Otley and Co., 1866), 12. Ellen Stanley's reports of her visit were first published in serial form and widely reprinted in London. See for example "The Female Casual at Whitechapel, Pt. 1," *East London Observer* (September 1, 1866), 2. These articles did not come close to matching the sensation accompanying Greenwood's initial revelations.

86. Northumbrian [pseud.], "Legalized Abominations—The Christian Hells of England," *Reynolds's Newspaper* (January 21, 1866), 3.

87. *Times* (January 29, 1866), 2–3.

88. The *Observer's* first critical notice of "A Night" appeared in an article on January 14 and focused on Farnall's, not Greenwood's, findings.

89. "Midnight Visits to the Casual Wards of London, No. 3," *Observer* (February 11, 1866), 5.

90. For the most part, *Observer* articles detailed facts in straightforward prose about casuals wards (their dimensions; the numbers of inmates; the character of the bedding and clothing provided; the condition of the bathwater) and highlighted local variation in their management. However, the *Observer* was forced to acknowledge conditions in the workhouse of St. James, Clerkenwell, were even more horrible than what the Amateur Casual had discovered in Lambeth. But, unlike the *PMG*, it refused to specify what its reporters had seen. "Midnight Visits . . . No. 4," *Observer* (February 18, 1866), 5.

91. "Midnight Visits . . . No. 1," *Observer* (January 28, 1866), 5.

92. This was the argument developed in "Home, Sweet Home," *All the Year Round* (April 7, 1866), 303.

93. I explore the relationships between news as commodity, slum investigation, and gender in detail in chapter 3, "The American Girl in London." For a superb study of the relationship between gender, sex, and scandal in the emergence of the press in New York city, see Amy Srebnick, *The Mysterious Death of Mary Rogers: Sex and Culture in Nineteenth-Century New York* (New York: Oxford University Press, 1995).

94. The best introduction to debates about the history of New Journalism is Joel H. Wiener, ed., *Papers for the Millions: The New Journalism in Britain, 1850s to 1914* (New York: Greenwood Press, 1988). See especially B. I. Diamond's contribution, "A Precursor of the New Journalism: Frederick Greenwood of the *Pall Mall Gazette.*"

95. See the *Observer* (February 11, 1866), 5.

96. See Jim Davis, "A Night in the Workhouse, or The Poor Laws as Sensation Drama," *Essays in Theatre* 7, no. 2 (May 1989): 111–126.

97. Ibid., 118. The prompt copy contains one page of "speeches to be omitted," which include phrases such as the "guardians of the poor are but their oppressors."

98. Note written on ms. prompt copy of *The Casual Ward* original in the Frank Pettingell Collection of Plays, University of Kent, Canterbury; microfilm from "The Popular Stage: Drama in Nineteenth Century England," series one, part 1, reel 11, in the same collection.

99. *South London Journal* (February 3, 1866), 4.

100. "An 'Amateur Casual' in Trouble," *Lloyd's Weekly* (January 28, 1866), 7.

101. *South London Journal* (February 3, 1866), 4

102. Stallard, *The Female Casual* 2, 37, 47. For a more extensive treatment of this investigation, see ch. 4, "The Politics and Erotics of Dirt."

103. Farnall's official inspection on January 13 immediately halted the use of the crank shed as a sleeping place and set in motion the installation of hot and cold running water for the baths to replace the old system of carrying pails of water by hand. He also demanded that Lambeth Workhouse officials send casuals who could not be accommodated in the regular wards to a nearby licensed lodging house at the expense of the newly established metropolitan-wide common fund. However, beyond noting Farnall's recommendations and Sir Richard Mayne's offer that the police should act as relieving officers, the minute book of the Lambeth guardians for January and February 1866 betrays neither traces of the scandal surrounding the guardians nor evidence of any discord among the guardians. See *Minute Book*, January 16 and January 23, 1866, LaBG 133/30, Lambeth Board of Guardians.

104. Northumbrian [pseud.], "Legalized Abominations," 3.

105. See report of Lambeth vestry meeting of January 18, 1866, in *South London Journal* (January 20, 1866), 4, 5.

106. *Daily News* (January 20, 1866), 4.

107. The outpouring of articles condemning vestrymen and poor law guardians was immense.

108. *Daily News* (January 26, 1866), 4.

109. Farnall's surviving correspondence files for this period surprisingly contain almost no information about metropolitan casual wards. See PRO/MH12/12474. Farnall's own shifting stance on workhouse reform was closely scrutinized, often unfavorably. The *Journal of Social Science*, a newly established organ for sanitary reform, commented sarcastically that "it must be a matter of surprise to every one to find that he has so suddenly [after the Lancet Commission and "A Night"] become the advocate for workhouse reform. For years he has been . . . the apologist for the very evils he now condemns." *Journal of Social Science* 1, no. 10 (1865–1866): 553.

110. See C. P. Villiers, "Destitute and Houseless Poor in the Metropolis," minute of the Poor Law Board, December 23, 1863, in the Select Committee of the House of Lords on Poor Law Relief, 1888, appendix 8, p. 140. See also "Report of Andrew Doyle, esq., Poor Law Inspector, to the President of the Poor Law Board," *Sessional Papers, 1866*, vol. 35, Paper no. 3698.

111. Edwin Chadwick, "Administration of Medical Relief to the Destitute Sick of the Metropolis," *Fraser's Magazine* (September, 1866), 355.

112. John Wilson to secretary of Poor Law Board, January 22, 1866. PRO/MH25/17.

113. See Jeremy Bentham, "Offences Against One's Self," (1785), ed. Louis Crompton, first published in the 1978 summer and fall issues of *Journal of Homosexuality*.

114. For a critique of such night refuges in the aftermath of the publication of "A Night," see J. C. Parkinson, "A Real Casual on Refuges," *Temple Bar* (April 1869): 32–44.

115. Rev. John Llewelyn Davies, "The Poor Law and Charity," *Macmillan's Magazine* (December 1866), 131.

116. See chapter 2 for a lengthy discussion of the history of the COS and its monitoring of metropolitan philanthropy.

117. Thomas Murray Browne, honorary secretary of the Discharged Prisoners' Relief Committee, had paid similar homage to Greenwood in his speech "Night Refuges," given at the Conference of Managers of Reformatory and Industrial Institutions the year before in April 1869. Reprinted in *Conference on Night Refuges Held at 15 Buckingham Street, Strand*. June 8th, 1870 (London: Society for Organising Charitable Relief, 1870), 21.

118. C. J. Ribton-Turner, *A History of Vagrants and Vagrancy and Beggars and Begging* (London, 1887; repr., Montclair, New Jersey: Patterson Smith, 1972).

119. *Pall Mall Gazette* (January 29, 1866), 9.

120. Greenwood, *Pall Mall Gazette* (January 15, 1866), 9. On the concept of "anachronistic space"—the rhetorical invention of people and societies supposedly occupying a space in a time before civilization—and its racial, gender, and class dimensions, see Anne McClintock, *Imperial Leather: Race, Gender, and Sexuality in the Colonial Contest* (New York: Routledge, 1995), 40–42.

121. For a sampling of Greenwood's writing about exotic savagery, see *Curiosities of Savage Life* (London: S. O. Beeton, 1864) and *Low-Life Deeps: An Account of the Strange Fish to Be Found There* (London: Chatto and Windus, 1876), esp. 134, 173, 180, 267.

122. The immense popularity of *Arabian Nights* ensured that readers would immediately recognize Haroun Al Raschid and presumably also link his name and the term "street arab" to the complex erotic valences of that text's representation of medieval Islam.

123. See G. R. Sims, *My Life: Sixty Years' Recollections of Bohemian London* (London: Eveleigh Nash, 1917) esp. chapter 29.

124. On vagrants as members of a "fraternity," see "Report of Andrew Doyle," 62–63.

125. For a reading of this short story against Mayhew's journalism, see Audrey Jaffe, "Detecting the Beggar: Arthur Conan Doyle, Henry Mayhew, and "the Man with the Twisted Lip," *Representations* (Summer 1990).

126. On representations of the poor in relation to anthropology, see M. C. Cowling, *The Artist as Anthropologist: The Representation of Type and Character in Victorian Art* (Cambridge: Cambridge University Press, 1989).

127. James Greenwood, *The Wilds of London* (London: Chatto and Windus, 1874), 357–358.

128. On the links between parliamentary reform, race, and gender politics in Jamaica at this time, see Catherine Hall, Keith McClelland, and Jane Rendall, *Defining the Victorian Nation: Class, Race, Gender and the Reform Act of 1867* (Cambridge: Cambridge University Press, 2000). See Bernard Semmel's analysis of the impact of Morant Bay on British political debate in *The Governor Eyre Controversy* (London: MacGibbon & Kee, 1962).

129. The *PMG*'s assessment was reprinted in the *Daily News* (January 26, 1866), 2.

130. "The Great Crime Again," *Orb* (January 25, 1866), 56.

131. *Hansard Parliamentary Debates*, 3d series, vol. 185 (1867), 1862–1866.

132. G. R. Sims as quoted by P. J. Keating, introduction to *Into Unknown England* (Manchester: Manchester University Press, 1976), 16.

133. "'Daddy and the Photographer,'" *Daily Telegraph*, as reprinted in *Lloyd's Weekly London Newspaper* (February 11, 1866), 7.

134. "Lays of Lambeth," *Punch* (February 17, 1866), 66.

135. See *Era* (Feb. 18, 1866), as cited in Davis, "A Night," 115.

136. See G. S. Jones treatment of the "culture of consolation" and music-hall songs in "Working-Class Culture and Working-Class Politics in London, 1870–1900: Notes on the Remaking of a Working Class" in Gareth Stedman Jones, *Languages of Class: Studies in English Working-Class History, 1832–1982* (Cambridge: Cambridge University Press, 1983). In several path-breaking articles, Peter Bailey has probed deeply the social, cultural, and psychic resources of music halls as key constituents of popular culture. See Peter Bailey, "Ally Sloper's Half Holiday: Comic Art in the 1880s," *History Workshop Journal* 16 (Autumn, 1983): 4–31 and "Champagne Charlie: Performance and Ideology in the Music-Hall Swell Song," in J. S. Bratton, ed., *Music Hall: Performance and Style* (Milton Keynes, England: Open University Press, 1986). On the meaning and uses of popular art in general, and music-halls and melodrama in particular, see Patrick Joyce, *Visions of the People: Industrial England and the Question of Class, 1848–1914* (Cambridge: Cambridge University Press, 1991), part 4.

137. See John Law [Margaret Harkness], *In Darkest London: A New and Popular Edition of "Captain Lobe, A Story of the Salvation Army"* (London: William Reeves, 1891), 143–144.

138. "A 'Casual' Supper," *PMG* (February 15, 1866), 9. For Shaftesbury's account of this supper, see Hodder, *The Life and Work of the Seventh Earl of Shaftesbury*, 613–614.

139. William Williams, letter to the editor, *PMG* (February 21, 1866), 3–4.

140. J. C. Parkinson, "On Duty with the Inspector," *Temple Bar* (June 1865), 349. *Temple Bar* was edited by his close friend, Edmund Yates. Yates mentions Parkinson frequently in his autobiography, *Fifty Years of London Life: Memoirs of a Man of the World* (New York: Harper & Brothers, 1885).

141. The following is the text of Parkinson's advertisement: A NIGHT IN A WORKHOUSE.—One Sovereign will be paid to any CASUAL PAUPER who slept in the labour-shed of LAMBETH WORKHOUSE on the night of Monday, 8th January, and who will communicate with T. Thompson, Post-office, Bradley-terrace, Wandsworth-road, S. See J. C. Parkinson, "A Real Casual on Casual Wards," *Temple Bar* (March 1866), 497, hereafter cited as Parkinson, "A Real Casual."

142. This theme is well developed in another story written by one of the "respectable men who slept in the Lambeth labour-shed on the same night as the 'Amateur Casual.'" See "Told by a Tramp," *All The Year Round* (April 28, 1866), 371–374.

143. Parkinson, "A Real Casual," 509.

144. Ibid., 515.

145. Ibid., 517.

146. Ibid., 509.

147. *South London Journal* (January 27, 1866), 4.

148. Ibid. (February 3, 1866), 4.

149. "Police Intelligence," *Daily News* (January 20, 1866), 3.

150. Symonds disliked the term "homosexual" and never used it to describe himself or others committed to what he instead called "Arcadian" or "Greek love."

151. Given Symonds's preoccupation with his own "double life," he may well have been particularly intrigued by Greenwood's use of an incognito to reveal the unintended but sexually dissident life of male casuals. Drawing heavily on Symonds's autobiographical writings, Ed Cohen argues that "the representation of a constituent doubleness 'within' male subjects opened the possibility for signifying non-normative or even transgressive forms of male sexuality." Incognitos made literal the performance of "a constituent doubleness." See Ed Cohen, "The Double Lives of Man: Narration and Identification in Late-Nineteenth-Century Representations of Ec-Centric Masculinities," in Sally Ledger and Scott McCracken, eds., *Cultural Politics at the Fin de Siècle* (Cambridge: Cambridge University Press, 1995), 111.

152. *The Memoirs of John Addington Symonds*, ed. Phyllis Grosskurth (New York: Random House, 1984), 187–188.

153. Ibid., 188.

154. Symonds frequently changed pronouns in his published poems to conceal that a man was the object of his romantic longings.

155. Symonds wrote two letters to Dakyns that day. This is the second and briefer of the two. John Addington Symonds to Henry Graham Dakyns, January 17, 1866, in vol. 1, 1844–1968 of *The Letters of John Addington Symonds*, ed. Herbert Schueller and Robert Peters (Detroit, 1967), 610.

156. See Morris Kaplan, "Who's Afraid of John Saul? Urban Culture and the Politics of Desire in Late Victorian London," *GLQ: Journal of Lesbian and Gay Studies* 5, no. 3 (1999): 267–314. As Paul Robinson argues, the "central problem of Symonds' life was to negotiate an accommodation between his moral convictions and his erotic needs. It found expression, above all, in his effort to rationalize homosexuality in terms of two powerful—and related—nineteenth century ideas, Hellenism and democracy." Paul Robinson, *Homosexual Autobiography from John Addington Symonds to Paul Monette* (Chicago: University of Chicago Press, 1999), 8. On the role of cross-class erotics in the making of homosexual identity, see Stephen Donaldson, "Eroticization of the Working Class," in the *Encyclopedia of Homosexuality*, ed. Wayne R. Dynes, 1990, 1405–1406.

157. See Phyllis Grosskurth, *John Addington Symonds: A Biography* (London: Longmans, 1964), 266.

158. Grosskurth, *Memoirs*, 116. Tramps and soldiers appear throughout Symonds's poetry as figures of men who love other men. He longed for "the open road, field, ocean, camp, / Where'er in brotherhood men lay their heads. / Soldier with soldier, tramp with casual tramp." This poem is quoted in Timothy D'Arch Smith, *Love in Earnest* (London: Routledge, 1970), 13.

159. John Addington Symonds to Henry Graham Dakyns, January 17, 1866, in *Letters of John Addington Symonds*, vol. 1, 610.

160. See Charles Upchurch, "Forgetting the Unthinkable: Cross-Dressers and

British Society in the Case of the Queen vs. Boulton and Others" *Gender and History* 12, no. 1 (2000): 127–157, on the ways in which the eruption of public knowledge about male same-sex practices during the Boulton and Park trial led officials to stifle discussion of them which contributed to the acquittals of the defendants. Upchurch elsewhere argues that the mainstream press from the 1820s onwards, including the *Times*, powerfully shaped perceptions of same-sex desire and activity in its regular coverage of unnatural assault cases. He shows that newspapers did much more than provide information about sex acts and offenses but instead offered readers normative judgments about appropriate and inappropriate male social identities and same-sex behaviors. See Charles Upchurch, "'. . . and every Solicitation, Persuasion, Promise, or Threat': The Regulation of Male Same-Sex Desire in London, 1820 to 1870' (Ph.D. diss., Rutgers University, 2003), esp. ch. 5.

161. On tensions within their collaboration, in particular Symonds's critique of arguments based on heredity and neuropathy, see Joseph Bristow, "Symonds's History, Ellis's Heredity: Sexual Inversion" in Lucy Bland and Laura Doan, eds., *Sexology in Culture, Labelling Bodies and Desires* (Chicago: University of Chicago Press, 1998), 79–99.

162. Fear of legal problems led Ellis to publish the work first in German. The first English edition of *Sexual Inversion* appeared under both Ellis's and Symonds's name. See Havelock Ellis and John Addington Symonds, *Sexual Inversion* (London: Wilson and Macmillan, 1897; repr., New York: Arno Press, 1975). When it was published in English, the British government prosecuted it as an obscene publication, which led Ellis to republish it and his other major studies of sexuality in Philadelphia. My citations will refer to the more widely available American edition that was published as the second volume of Havelock Ellis's *Studies in the Psychology of Sex*.

163. See *Sexual Inversion*, 85–90.

164. Ibid., 169, 170.

165. Ibid., 18.

166. On working-class and middle-class links between work, independence, and masculinity see Sonya Rose, *Limited Livelihoods: Gender and Class in Nineteenth Century England* (Berkeley, CA: University of California Press, 1992), chapter 6.

167. See Ellis, *Sexual Inversion*, appendix A, "Homosexuality among Tramps," by Josiah Flynt, 219–224. Jeffrey Weeks notes that homosexual slang overlapped with and was closely related to the language of tramps. *Coming Out, Homosexual Politics in Britain from the Nineteenth Century to the Present* (London: Quartet Books, 1990), 42.

168. Josiah Flynt, *Tramping with Tramps: Studies and Sketches of Vagabond Life* (New York, 1907), 3. The first edition was 1893. Flynt's chapters had appeared as essays in various periodicals during the preceding fifteen years.

169. Ellis, *Sexual Inversion*, 13.

170. On the status hierarchies, gender, and sexual systems structuring erotic relations between working-class "punks" (young men) and other men "exceptionally disengaged from the family and neighborhood," such as "hoboes" (called "wolves") in New York City, see George Chauncey, *Gay New York: Gen-*

der, *Urban Culture, and the Making of the Gay Male World, 1890–1940* (New York: Basic Books, 1994), esp. 86–97. Chauncey underscores the ways in which gender structured sexual relations between men, many of whom conceived of themselves as deeply manly men in contrast to the effeminacy of the "fairy." See also Lesley Hall's analysis of the class basis of sexual categories in Hall, *Hidden Anxieties: Male Sexuality 1900–1950* (Cambridge: Polity Press, 1991), 3–4.

171. See *Times* (March 15, 1898), 6.

172. Angus McLaren discusses the link between vagrancy and male sexual deviance in *The Trials of Masculinity: Policing Sexual Boundaries, 1870–1930* (Chicago: University of Chicago Press, 1997), 16–18. Louise Jackson notes the application of the act to police sex between men in *Child Sexual Abuse in Victorian England* (London: Routledge, 2000), 105.

173. See Jeffrey Weeks, *Sex, Politics and Society: The Regulation of Sexuality since 1800* (London: Longmans, 1981). Matt Cook argues that "what the 1898 provision [of the Vagrancy Act] did was to heighten the significance of behaviour that was not explicitly sexual [such as make-up and the way a man walked] . . . and of places that had a reputation. . . . The police did not arrest because sexual acts had actually been committed but on the basis of a judgment they had made about the propensity of an individual to commit them." See Matt Cook, *London and the Culture of Homosexuality, 1885–1914* (Cambridge: Cambridge University Press, 2003), 44.

174. On Ellis's objections to the "gross indecency" clauses of the Criminal Law Amendment Act, see *Sexual Inversion*, 209–211.

175. Michel Foucault focused on the period between 1870 and 1900 as crucial to the emergence of sexual categories and identities. For one influential analysis of "essentialist" versus "constructionist" accounts of homosexuality, see David Halperin, *One Hundred Years of Homosexuality and Other Essays on Greek Love* (New York: Routledge, 1990), esp. 43–45. Rictor Norton, by contrast, does not view the late nineteenth century as particularly foundational for the making of homosexuality and homosexual identities. Rictor Norton has elaborated his stance in a variety of published works including *Mother Clap's Molly House: The Gay Subculture in England, 1700–1830* (London: Gay Men's Press, 1992) and *The Myth of the Modern Homosexual: Queer History and the Search for Cultural Unity* (London: Cassell, 1997).

176. See Deborah Nord, *Walking the Streets: Women, Representation, and the City* (Ithaca, NY: Cornell University Press, 1995). Nord's account begins with London in the 1820s and Pierce Egan's famous "Tom" and "Jerry."

177. See Frederic Harrison, *Fortnightly*, November 1867, as reprinted in ed. Carl Dawson and John Pfordesher, eds., *Matthew Arnold, Prose Writings: The Critical Heritage* (London: Routledge and Kegan Paul, 1973), 226; see James MacDonell, *Daily Telegraph*, September 1866, as reprinted in *Critical Heritage*, 165–166.

178. The *South London Journal* described Greenwood as the "The Exquisite" (February 3, 1866), 4.

179. Arnold thought of these two works as forming a whole, and from the 1883 American edition onward, they were usually published in a single volume.

180. See "My Countrymen," in *Complete Prose Work's of Matthew Arnold*,

vol. 5, *Culture and Anarchy with Friendship's Garland and Some Literary Essays*, ed. R. H. Super (Ann Arbor, Michigan: University of Michigan Press, 1965).

181. See "Dedicatory Letter," in *Complete Prose Works*, vol. 5, *Culture and Anarchy with Friendship's Garland and Some Literary Essays*, 351. See also his letter to the editor of the *Pall Mall Gazette*, January 17, 1866, which compared the appalling state of workhouse infirmaries to conditions in schools. See Matthew Arnold, "Mansion House Meeting," in *The Complete Prose Works of Matthew Arnold*, vol. 4, *Schools and Universities on the Continent*, ed. R. H. Super (Ann Arbor: University of Michigan Press, 1964), 11.

182. "Dedicatory Letter" in Arnold, *Culture and Anarchy*.

183. See Stefan Collini, *Arnold* (Oxford: Oxford University Press, 1988), ch. 5.

184. They began work on *London* in 1869, but its completion and publication was delayed until 1872, after the Franco-Prussian War.

185. Blanchard Jerrold, *Life of Gustave Doré* (London, 1891), 185.

186. *Lloyds* commented extensively on "A Night" in January and February of 1866. See especially January 21 and 28, and February 4, 1866.

187. Jerrold and Doré, *London: A Pilgrimage* (London: Grant, 1872; rprt., New York: Dover Publications, 1970), 142.

188. On Arnold's love of masquerade, see Park Honan, *Matthew Arnold: A Life* (New York: McGraw Hill, 1981), 353.

189. Blanche Roosevelt, *Life and Reminiscences of Gustave Doré* (New York: Cassell, 1885), 350.

190. Jerrold noted with pride that he had accompanied Prince Charles Bonaparte and the Marquis de Bassano on a night tour of the East End on February 5, 1872. See Jerrold and Doré, *London*, 148.

191. Ibid., x, 5.

192. Ibid., 143.

193. Griselda Pollock provides a probing examination of *London: A Pilgrimage* as a representation of the city "as a matrix articulating an array of ideologies in contest, expressed through anxieties about the country-versus-city conflict, the threat of criminal classes and the residuum, the dread of pauperism, the scourge of alcoholism, inventions of schemes of social control and surveillance, investigation, and classification." She observes that in London, "proximity and sexuality, those recurrent concerns of bourgeois writers criss-cross and deposit an array of unspecified meanings fixating upon bodily corruption, degeneration, and reproduction." Pollock notes that Doré and Jerrold's expedition was "an adventure" in slumming "in the manner of James Greenwood, rather than Henry Mayhew," but she fails to note the sexual themes of "A Night." See Pollock, "'Vicarious Excitements': *London: A Pilgrimage* by Gustave Doré and Blanchard Jerrold, 1872," *New Formations* (Spring, 1988): 26, 35, 36.

194. Jerrold, *Life of Gustave Doré*, 153–154.

195. See also Doré's "Mixing the Malt," which celebrates the physical prowess of half-naked malt men working in a huge vat. Jerrold and Doré, *London*, 130. Alan Woods describes Doré's visual rhetoric as "Gothic romanticism." See Alan Woods, "Doré's 'London'—Art as Evidence," *Art History* 1, no. 3 (1978): 356.

196. Several scholars have noted a literary tradition linking Greenwood to London and Orwell, but none have commented on the role of sexuality in their narratives. See P. J. Keating, *The Working Classes in Victorian Fiction* (London: Routledge and Kegan Paul, 1971), 38; and Nord, *Walking the Streets*, 239.

197. George Orwell, *The Road to Wigan Pier* (London: Victor Gollancz, 1937; rprt. New York: Harcourt, Brace, 1958), 121, 124. (Citations are to the Harcourt edition.)

198. Raymond Williams, *Culture and Society, 1780–1950* (New York: Harper and Row, 1958; rprt., with a new introduction by the author, New York: Columbia University Press, 1983), 289–290. Citation is to the Columbia edition.

199. See Andrew Sinclair, "A View of the Abyss," in Jacqueline Tavernier-Courbin, ed., *Critical Essays on Jack London* (Boston, MA: G. K. Hall, 1983). See also, Robert Barltrop, *Jack London: The Man, the Writer, the Rebel* (London: Pluto Press, 1976), ch. 6. See also Joseph McLaughlin, "Writing London, East End Ethnography in Jack London's *The People of the Abyss*," in McLaughlin, *Writing the Urban Jungle: Reading Empire in London from Doyle to Eliot* (Charlotteville, VA: University Press of Virginia, 2000).

200. Jack London to Anna Strunsky, August 21, 1902, in vol. 1, 1896–1905, of *The Letters of Jack London*, ed. Earle Labor, Robert Leitz, and I. Milo Shepard (Stanford: Stanford University Press, 1988), 306.

201. On the influence of *People* on Orwell, see Orwell, *The Road to Wigan Pier*, 140.

202. See Clarice Stasz, *Jack London's Women* (Amherst, MA: University of Massachusetts Press, 2001), chapter 4.

203. Jack London, *The People of the Abyss* (New York: Grosset and Dunlap, 1903), 15.

204. Ibid., 39. London's narrative closely parallels Greenwood's in many respects including its playful account of his donning his disguise as a tramp, his mandatory bath in water made filthy by previous tramps, and his therapeutic ritual of bodily purification in baths for the well-to-do which end each episode.

205. George Orwell, *Down and Out in Paris and London* (London: Victor Gollancz, 1933; repr., San Diego: Harcourt Brace, 1961, 1933), 129. Citation is to the Harcourt edition.

206. Ibid., 145.

207. Old Daddy figures prominently in the article version published as "The Spike" in *The Adelphi* (April 1931), reprinted in Peter Davison, ed., *The Complete Works of George Orwell, vol. 10, A Kind of Compulsion, 1903–1906* (London: Secker & Warburg, 1997–1998), 200. He is not mentioned in *Down and Out*.

208. There are six roller towels in the version of this scene he originally published as "The Spike," in *The Adelphi*, Davison, *Complete Works*, vol. 10, 198.

209. Orwell, *Down and Out*, 147.

210. The closest Orwell comes to spending time with a Kay-like young man is the borstal boy named Ginger, "a strong athletic youth of twenty six" with whom he went hop picking in August and September 1931. Davison, *Complete Works*, Vol Ten, 216. He later explains that Ginger is aggressively homophobic and had helped to beat and rob a "Nancy Boy" in Trafalgar Square (218).

211. Copy of *Down and Out* given to Brenda Salkeld and annotated by Eric Blair (George Orwell). Annotations of fictitious changes published in Davison, *Complete Works, vol. 10*, 300.

212. Orwell, *Down and Out*, 159.

213. Driberg's biographer Francis Wheen offers some comparisons between Driberg and Orwell. See Francis Wheen, *Tom Driberg: His Life and Indiscretions* (London: Chatto and Windus, 1990), 86.

214. Tom Driberg, *Ruling Passions* (London: Jonathan Cape, 1977), 75–76, 133–136.

215. John Worby, *The Other Half: The Autobiography of a Tramp* (New York: Lee Furman, 1937), 28–29, 184–189, 246–252, 266–303. Worby explained how he came to publish his tramp memoirs in *Spiv's Progress* (London, 1939), chapter 24 and 25. While the second memoir contains lots of discussion of sex with women, it notably mentions no homosexual encounters. Matt Houlbrook suggests that neither homosexuality nor homophobia can help explain the sexual dynamics between working-class men and their better-off male sexual partners as their relationships sometimes moved between "intimate friendship and brutal assault." "Intimacy, sex, blackmail, theft, and assault constituted a continuum within the same cultural terrain, all underpinned by dominant understandings of masculinity." See Matt Houlbrook, "Soldier Heroes and Rent Boys: Homosex, Masculinities, and Britishness in the Brigade of Guards, circa 1900–1960," *Journal of British Studies* 42, no. 3 (July 2003): 362.

CHAPTER TWO
DR. BARNARDO'S ARTISTIC FICTIONS:
PHOTOGRAPHY, SEXUALITY, AND THE RAGGED CHILD

1. *Times* (29 January 1866).

2. Blake Morrison, "Lost and Found: The Forgotten Legacy of Dr. Barnardo," *The Independent on Sunday* (June 11, 1995), 6–11. The BBC documentaries shown in July 1995 highlighted issues about race and the pathos of separating children from the parents and siblings. In this way they extended the work of Gillian Wagner and Joy Parr on Barnardo's philanthropic abduction of children from the hands of their impoverished—and sometimes Roman Catholic—parents. See Joy Parr, *Labouring Children: British Immigrant Apprentices to Canada, 1869–1924* (London: Croom Helm, 1980), esp. 67–69; and Gillian Wagner, *Children of the Empire* (London: Weidenfeld and Nicolson, 1982).

3. See Raphael Samuel, "Mrs. Thatcher's Return to Victorian Values," in T. C. Smout, ed., *Victorian Values* (Oxford: Oxford University Press, 1992).

4. See Gertrude Himmelfarb *Poverty and Compassion: The Moral Imagination of the Late Victorians* (New York: A. A. Knopf, 1991); see also *The De-Moralization of Society: From Victorian Virtues to Modern Values* (New York: A. A. Knopf, 1995).

5. Gertrude Himmelfarb, "The Victorians Get a Bad Rap," *New York Times* (January 9, 1995), A11; and "Remoralizing America," *Wall Street Journal* (February 7, 1995), A26. Himmelfarb discusses some of the controversies that dogged Barnardo's work and concludes that "the Barnardo Homes are a testimo-

nial to a philanthropic impulse that survives in defiance of all predictions, and to social needs that are not adequately satisfied by the state." See *Poverty and Compassion*, 230–234.

6. Some of the major biographies of Barnardo include A. E. Williams, *Barnardo of Stepney: The Father of Nobody's Children* (London: G. Allen and Unwin, 1946); J. Wesley Bready, *Doctor Barnardo: Physician, Pioneer, Prophet* (London: G. Allen and Unwin, 1930).

7. James Greenwood, *Seven Curses of London* (London: S. Rivers, 1869), 3, 11.

8. T. J. Barnardo, *Night and Day* (June 16, 1877), 83. Barnardo used his magazine *Night and Day* to publicize his work and raise money.

9. The Barnardo arbitration needs to be understood within the context of growing public outrage about the exploitation of children. For an excellent treatment of the movement to protect children, see George Behlmer, *Child Abuse and Moral Reform in England, 1870–1908* (Stanford: Stanford University Press, 1982).

10. George Reynolds, *Dr. Barnardo's Homes Containing Startling Revelations* (London: Printed for George Reynolds, 1877) hereafter cited as *Startling Revelations*. Very little is known about George Reynolds besides what one can learn about him in connection to the Barnardo arbitration. His sprawling, ill-tempered attack on Barnardo, *Startling Revelations*, is the sole example of his writing to survive, an ironic testimony to how well-founded his jealousy of Barnardo was. He was minister of a small independent Baptist church in Stepney called the Cave of Adullum. Reynolds may well have resented the fact that some East Londoners attended religious meetings under Barnardo's auspices instead of joining a regular church such as his own. He apparently lacked charisma as a preacher. Church membership remained so small that years after the arbitration, Charrington had to rescue it by including it under the umbrella of his own extremely successful operations.

11. On Charrington, see *The History of the Tower Hamlets Mission* double number of the *The Witness: A Monthly Record* (March 1880). The cover of the first biography of Charrington, *An Oasis in the Desert*, was subtitled, *Fredk. N. Charrington, the Ex-Brewer and His Work in the East of London*. His biographer, Guy Thorne, claimed that Charrington was Walter Besant's model for his famous novel *All Sorts and Conditions of Men*. Guy Thorne, *The Great Acceptance: The Life Story of F. N. Charrington* (London: Hodder and Stoughton, 1912), 6. Several years after the Barnardo arbitration, the Duke of Westminster gently encouraged him to be more receptive to the People's Palace under construction only a few hundred yards up Mile End Road from Charrington's headquarters: "I believe Mr. Charrington had some little fear, I won't say jealousy, but some little fear of competition to his own great scheme, but I believe from what I hear and from what he has told us, that there is ample room in this Mile End Road for two, or even more Institutions such as it is proposed to erect." The Duke's conciliatory words fell on deaf ears, and Charrington vigorously denounced the trustees of the People's Palace for permitting drink on its premises and substituting the "varnish of modern culture" for the gospel of the Saviour." Speech of Duke of Westminster, *The Quarterly Record of the Tower Hamlet's*

Mission (July 4, 1885), 7. To make matters worse, his cousin Mr. Spencer Charrington lavishly supplied the People's Palace with free Charrington's beer for its jubilee supper in 1887. Ironically, although Charrington was closely allied with the COS during its investigation of Barnardo, the COS questioned the principles by which Charrington ran his own organization in East London, the Tower Hamlets Mission. The COS vouched for Charrington's personal integrity but for the next five decades secretly informed correspondents that it could not "recommend that support be given to the [Charrington's] Mission on the ground of its material work." COS report on Frederick Charrington's Tower Hamlet's Mission, November 13, 1877, A/FWA/C/D57/1, COS Files and Papers. Unaware of the COS's long standing criticisms of his work, Charrington left the COS £5000 at his death. The Family Welfare Association (FWA) archives are the case files and records of the Charity Organisation Society.

12. We get a sense of Charrington's desire to protect his philanthropic turf from Barnardo's encroachment in an account of one of the shortlived attempts to reconcile Barnardo and Charrington. See copy of letter from Thomas Stone to W. E. Shipton, October 25, 1875, A/FWA/C/D10/2, COS Files and Papers.

13. Barnardo had initially played an active part in promoting Charrington's work by introducing him to wealthy and influential Evangelicals. On this aspect of their relationship, see *East London Observer* (September 8, 1877). Charrington's love of publicity was lifelong. At age 65 he quietly entered the House of Commons, strode to the speaker's chair, grasped the mace, and denounced the existence of a drinking bar for MP's use in the nearby lobby as an example of the government's complicity with the drink trade. See *Illustrated Record of the Tower Hamlets Mission* (Summer 1915), 5.

14. Notes taken by A. L. Baxter of interview with Edwin Kerwin, January 19, 1898, Charles Booth Papers, B183, ff. 103, 107. Baxter was one of Charles Booth's assistants for his survey of religious life in London. Kerwin was Charrington's longtime lieutenant and assistant.

15. The major histories of the COS include Charles Loch Mowat, *The Charity Organisation Society, 1869–1913: Its Ideas and Work* (London: Methuen, 1961); Helen Bosanquet, *Social Work in London, 1869 to 1912, A History of the Charity Organisation Society* (London: J. Murray, 1914); Madeline Rooff, *A Hundred Years of Family Welfare: A Study of the Family Welfare Association (formerly COS), 1869–1969* (London: Joseph, 1972); Jane Lewis, *The Voluntary Sector, the State, and Social Work in Britain: The Charity Organisation Society/Family Welfare Association since 1869* (Aldershot: E. Elgar, 1995); and Robert Humphreys, *Sin, Organized Charity, and the Poor Law in Victorian England* (New York: St. Martin's, 1995).

16. Kathleen Heasman claims that "as many as three-quarters of the total number of voluntary charitable organisations in the second half of the nineteenth century can be regarded as Evangelical in character and control." These included lavish coffee palaces and temperance tabernacles; shoeblack and woodchopping brigades; mothers' meetings; seaside convalescent homes; bible and pure literature depots, etc. See Kathleen Heasman, *Evangelicals in Action: An Appraisal of their Social Work in the Victorian Era* (London: Geoffrey Bles, 1962), 14. See also Donald Lewis, *Lighten Their Darkness: The Evangelical Mission to Work-*

ing-Class London (New York: Greenwood Press, 1986) and J. Wesley Bready, *England: Before and After Wesley, The Evangelical Revival, and Social Reform* (London: Hodder and Stoughton, 1938).

17. Almost from its inception, the COS tried to curtail charities that offered food and shelter to all in need, regardless of the economic and moral status of the recipient.

18. The distinction between the Central Office of the COS, dominated by a few full-time employed officers, and its various branches scattered throughout the metropolis is quite important. The COS files indicate that some local branches of the COS were much more tolerant of Barnardo than others. Because most histories of the COS focus on official pronouncement emanating from its Central Office, historians have tended to assume that the practices and ideologies of the COS were much more uniform than they were. Robert Humphrey's study, *Sin, Organized Charity, and the Poor Law* (New York: St. Martin's Press, 1995) notably departs from this historiographical tradition by examining the work of provincial committees.

19. See Gillian Wagner, *Barnardo* (London: Weidenfeld and Nicolson, 1979); see also her "Dr. Barnardo and the Charity Organisation Society: A Re-Assessment of the Reynolds-Barnardo Arbitration Case of 1877" (Ph.D. diss., London School of Economics, 1977). These two works provide superb accounts of the arbitration, the COS, and evangelical charity in London.

20. See Alan Trachtenberg's review of the 1974 exhibition held at the National Portrait Gallery: "The Camera and Dr. Barnardo," *Aperture*, 19, no. 4 (1975): 72.

21. Charles Booth, *London North of the Thames: The Inner Ring*, vol. 2 of *Life and Labour of the People in London*, Third Series: Religious Influences (London, 1902), 46–47.

22. *East London Observer* (August 4, 1877), 7.

23. See Boyd Hilton, *The Age of Atonement, The Influence of Evangelicalism on Social and Economic Thought, 1785–1865* (Oxford: Oxford University Press, 1988), chapter 9.

24. It was the term Hicks, the former governor of the London Debtor's Prison, used to describe Barnardo's performance at the opening of a coffee palace in West London. G. M. Hicks to Ribton Turner, January 12, 1877, A/FWA/C/D31/1, COS Files and Papers.

25. "Cant," *Temple Bar* (October 1866), 410.

26. T. J. Barnardo, *Rescue the Perishing* (London: Morgan and Scott, 1875), viii.

27. Barnardo's views on the relationship of fact and fiction, real life and art were not always consistent. See *Night and Day* (May 16, 1877), 60; and *Night and Day* (November 1, 1877), 121.

28. Anna Shipton, *Following Fully* (London: Morgan and Scott, 1865; 2d. ed. 1872). For her ideas about facts and fictions, see especially iii.

29. R. M. Ballantyne, *Dusty Diamonds Cut and Polished: A Tale of City Arab Life and Adventure* (London: J. Nisbet, 1884), preface. On Ballantyne's life and work, in particular his North American adventure fiction in relation to Victorian masculinities, see Richard Phillips, *Mapping Men and Empire: A Geography of Adventure* (London: Routledge, 1997), esp. ch. 2.

30. G. Holden Pike, *Pity for the Perishing: The Power of the Bible in London* (London: J. Clarke, 1884), 85.

31. Pike made only minor modifications to Barnardo's original, such as substituting "he" for "I" to produce a third person instead of first person narrative.

32. See Mary Poovey, *Making a Social Body: British Cultural Formation, 1830–1864* (Chicago: University of Chicago Press, 1995).

33. COS case records also constitute a narrative genre. For some recent work on humanitarian narratives in the early nineteenth century, see Thomas Laqueur, "Bodies, Details and the Humanitarian Narrative," in Lynn Hunt, ed., *The New Cultural History* (Berkeley: University of California Press, 1989); and Sonya Michel, "Dorothea Dix; or the Voice of the Maniac," *Discourse* 17, no. 2 (Winter 1994–95).

34. Evangelicals had played central roles in interpreting and popularizing the political economy of Malthus, Smith, and Ricardo and in applying these ideas to social policies from the 1820s to 1860s. The leader of the reform-minded Evangelicals, Lord Shaftesbury, also served as an early vice president of the COS. See Mowat, *The Charity Organisation Society*, (London, 1960) 16. Barnardo himself presented a paper at the 1876 meeting of the Social Science Congress.

35. T. J. Barnardo, *Something Attempted, Something Done* (London: E. and J. F. Shaw, 1890), 37.

36. Barnardo published the paper he presented to the Social Science Congress in October 1876 in *Night and Day* (January 15, 1877), 3.

37. See diary of Charles Stewart Loch, typescript, entry for September 14, 1876. Goldsmith's Library, Senate House, University of London.

38. *Daily Chronicle* (October 20, 1877).

39. Perhaps the most famous critics from within of the COS who ultimately broke with it were two of its earliest members, Samuel and Henrietta Barnett. See chapter 5 on the Barnetts.

40. W. Y. Fullerton, *J.W.C. Fegan, A Tribute* (London, n.d. [c. 1925]), 9–13.

41. J.W.C. Fegan to Mr. Scott, February 3, 1883, A/FWA/C/D68/1, COS Files and Papers.

42. Fegan detailed the beginning of his career rescuing children in a small pamphlet which is remarkably similar to those produced by Barnardo. See J.W.C. Fegan, *How I Found My First Arab* (London, n.d.), 11.

43. The honorable secretary for the Deptford COS described Fegan as "a gentleman of undoubted probity and having independent means." Mr. Kemp to Ribton Turner, June 6, 1876, A/FWA/C/D68/1, COS Files and Papers. After the dissolution of the Deptford COS's ties to Fegan, the Central Office investigated him more aggressively. See "Report of Charles Carthew's Interview with Mr. Fegan to COS Central Committee on the Boys' Home, Deptford" April 12, 1880, A/FWA/C/D68/1, ibid.

44. See H. G. Henderson to Central Office, June 30, 1876, A/FWA/C/D10/1, ibid.

45. Ralph Ellis to Ribton Turner, June 19, 1877, A/FWA/C/D10/1, ibid.

46. See circular by C. T. Ackland, vice chairman, Kensington Committee, A/FWA/C/D10/2.

47. Reynolds, *Startling Revelations*, 49–51.

48. E. P. Thompson described Methodism as "psychic masturbation" in *The Making of the English Working Class* (London: Victor Gollancz, 1963), 368.

49. Syrie Barnardo and James Marchant, *Memoirs of the Late Dr. Barnardo* (London: Hodder and Stoughton, 1907), 33–34. On his lack of interest in women, see J. Wesley Bready, *Doctor Barnardo* (London, 1930), 166.

50. James Eli Adams, *Dandies and Desert Saints, Styles of Victorian Masculinity* (Ithaca, NY: Cornell University Press, 1995), 22.

51. Letter to the editor from Thomas Barnardo, *Tower Hamlets Independent* (August 25, 1877).

52. Barnardo wrote an indignant letter to the *East London Observer* on August 25, 1877, explaining the situation. "I understand that a very imperfect proof of a miserable photograph of myself, condemned when first taken, and never since circulated, has been recently exposed for sale in certain East End shops. The professed likeness is a wretched caricature. . . . I am compelled to authorize the publication of a carte-de-visite which shall faithfully depict my physiognomy for the satisfaction of those who are kind enough to care for the same either from motives of curiosity or feelings of regard" (6).

53. On Lord Cairns involvement with Thesiger and Barnardo during the trial, see Cairns Papers, PRO/30/51/21 ff. 73–79 and PRO/30/51/9 ff. 36–38. See also Wagner, *Barnardo*, 171–172.

54. "Thesiger's Summing Up," *East London Observer* (September 8, 1877).

55. On Fitzgerald's employment by the COS, see Alsager Hay Hill to Organising Department, COS, November 4, 1876, A/FWA/C/D10/1, COS Files and Papers. Wagner notes that Fitzgerald was employed by Charrington and was an important though not very effective witness against Barnardo. See Wagner, *Barnardo*, 141. On the social and cultural world of policemen as members of the "uniformed working class," see Carolyn Steedman, *The Radical Soldier's Tale: John Pearman, 1819–1908* (London: Routledge, 1988), 58.

56. Mrs. Andrews to Dr. Barnardo, September 13, 1876. Copy of letter in COS Files and Papers, A/FWA/C/D10/3.

57. *Tower Hamlets Independent* (August 25, 1877).

58. Edward Fitzgerald to George Reynolds, November 26, 1877, copy COS Files and Papers. A/FWA/C/D10/2.

59. Manuscript fragment, no attribution or date. A/FWA/C/D10/3, ibid.

60. See chapter 1 for a detailed account of Greenwood's casual ward experiences.

61. Thomas Barnardo, "A Very Restless Night," *Night and Day* (April 16, 1877), 40. Mrs. Barnardo reprinted parts of this story in *Memoirs*, 67–73.

62. Barnardo, "A Very Restless Night," 40.

63. Ibid., 42.

64. On the relationship between mimesis and nemesis, see Homi Bhabha, "Of Mimicry and Man: The Ambivalence of Colonial Discourse," *October* 28 (1984): 125–133. Incognito slumming reverses Bhabha's trajectory: it is the powerful who "imitate" the powerless, albeit in order to gain knowledge about the powerless.

65. *Times* (October 19, 1877), 6.

66. Ibid.

67. Henry Labouchère's assault on Barnardo and his photographs anticipated his later campaigns, conducted in the pages of his magazine, *Truth*, against deceptive advertisements, what we would now call truth in advertising. On Barnardo's photographs, see *Truth* (July 19, 1877), 92.

68. Barnardo reprinted this leaflet in *Night and Day* (November 1, 1877), 143.

69. The use of posed before-and-after photographs to demonstrate the effects of missionary work was not limited to Barnardo. In the United States, American Indians were subjected to similar photographic poses. See David Wallace Adams, *Education for Extinction: American Indians and the Boarding School Experience, 1875–1928* (Lawrence, KS: University Press of Kansas 1995), ch. 4. My thanks to Paula Fass for pointing this out to me.

70. On the general issue of children and sexuality, see James Kincaid, *Child Loving: The Erotic Child and Victorian Culture* (New York: Routledge, 1992); Graham Ovenden and Robert Melville, *Victorian Children* (New York: St. Martin's, 1972); see also Carol Mavor, *Pleasures Taken: Performances of Sexuality and Loss in Victorian Photographs* (Durham, NC: Duke University Press, 1995), ch. 1. For a powerful critique of Kincaid, see Carolyn Steedman, *Strange Dislocations: Childhood and the Idea of Human Interiority* (Cambridge, MA: Harvard University Press, 1995), esp. 166–168. Harry Hendrick argues that poor children in Victorian culture were viewed as both victims of and threats to society. Thus reformers emphasized that children were simultaneously dangerous sources of criminality and disorder, on the one hand, and sentimental objects of pity and sympathy, on the other. See Harry Hendrick, *Child Welfare: England, 1872–1989* (London: Routledge, 1994), esp. pp. 7–12.

71. T. J. Barnardo, *A City Waif: How I Fished for and Caught Her* (London: E. and J. F. Shaw, 1883), 6. The dates of publication of Barnardo's chapbooks bore no relationship to the date during which the events recounted in them transpired. For this reason, it is impossible to determine whether Barnardo encountered Bridget before or after the arbitration.

72. Ibid., 20–21.

73. See John Lupton to C. J. Ribton-Turner, January 10, 1877; T. J. Barnardo to John Lupton, January 15, 1877; John Lupton to C. J. Ribton-Turner, January 20, 1877; and T. J. Barnardo to C. J. Ribton-Turner, January 24, 1877, A/FWA/C/D10/1, COS Files and Papers.

74. This story appeared in W. Y. Fullerton, *J. W. C. Fegan, A Tribute* (London, n.d.), 53. A longer version appeared in a pamphlet published around 1883, *Mr. Fegan's Work Among Our Waifs and Strays by a Lady* (London, n.d.), A/FWA/C/D68/13/10, COS Files and Papers, 12–13.

75. See Valerie Lloyd's perceptive and informative, *The Camera and Doctor Barnardo* (Hertford, 1974), 10–13. A woodcut of Rejlander's "Poor Jo" later served as the symbol of the Ragged School Union (and its successor, the Shaftesbury Society) until World War II. On Rejlander's pseudo-documentary photographs of ragged children, see Jadviga M. Da Costa Nunes, "O. G. Rejlander's Photographs of Ragged Children: Reflections on the Idea of Urban Poverty in Mid-Victorian Society," *Nineteenth Century Studies* 4 (1990): 105–136.

76. See Stephanie Spencer, "Art and Photography: Two Studies by O. G. Rej-

lander," *History of Photography* 9, no. 1 (January–March 1985); and Malcolm Daniel, "Darkroom vs. Greenroom: Victorian Art Photography and Popular Theatrical Entertainment," *Image* 33 (1990): 1–2.

77. O. G. Rejlander, *Journal of the Photographic Society of London* (April 21, 1858).

78. *Photographic Notes*, as quoted in Edgar Yoxall Jones, *Father of Art Photography: O. G. Rejlander, 1813–1875* (Greenwich, CT: Newton Abbot, David & Charles, 1973), 23.

79. There is an enormous bibliography on this question. For a contemporary summary of the debate, see *The Photographic Times* (May 1877), 103. Some examples that are particularly germane to Barnardo's photographs include the treatment of the issue in Edgar Yoxall Jones, *Father of Art Photography: O. G. Rejlander, 1813–1875* (Greenwich, CT, 1973); Aaron Scharf, *Art and Photography* (London: Allen Lane, 1968), esp. chapter 5; Jeff Rosen, "Posed as Rogues, The Crisis of Photographic Realism in John Thomson's *Street Life in London*," *Image* 36, no. 3/4 (1993): 9–39; John Tagg, *Burden of Representation: Essays on Photographies and Histories* (Amherst, MA: University of Massachusetts Press, 1988); Griselda Pollock, "'With my own eyes': Fetishism, the Labouring Body, and the Colour of Its Sex," *Art History* 17, no. 3 (September 1994): 342–382.

80. *Night and Day* (November 1, 1877), 143.

81. See the essays by Julian Treuherz and Susan Casteras in Julian Treuherz, *Hard Times: Social Realism in Victorian Art* (London: Lund Humphries, 1987); see also Ira Nadel and F. S. Schwarzbach, eds., *Victorian Artists and the City: A Collection of Critical Essays* (New York: Pergamon Press, 1980), esp. Sheila Smith's essay, "'Savages and Martyrs': Images of the Ragged Poor in Victorian Art."

82. On Marks, see Rev. T. Mardy Rees, *Welsh Painters, Engravers, Sculptors, 1527–1911* (Carnarvon: J. E. Southhalls, 1912), 104.

83. *Art Journal* (June 1873): 467.

84. On Frith's means of finding various street roughs to sit for him as models for his paintings of the poor, see W. P. Frith, *My Autobiography and Reminiscences* (New York: Harper, 1888) esp. chapters 28, 30, and 39. On the model for the "Crossing Sweeper," see pp. 208, 411–413.

85. My discussion of Darwin's photographs is drawn from Phillip Prodger, "Illustration as Strategy in Charles Darwin's 'The Expression of the Emotions in Man and Animals'" in Timothy Lenoir, ed., *Inscribing Science: Scientific Texts and the Materiality of Communication* (Stanford: Stanford University Press, 1998), 140–181.

86. See Janice Hart, "Photography, Pornography, and the Law: The First Fifty Years," *The Photographic Collector* 4 (Winter 1983): 287–299. See also, Lynn Hunt, ed., *The Invention of Pornography: Obscenity and the Origins of Modernity, 1500–1800* (Cambridge, MA: Zone Books, 1993). On the sexual geography of Victorian London and its relationship to obscene images and texts, see Lynda Nead, *Victorian Babylon: People, Streets and Images in Nineteenth-Century London* (New Haven: Yale University Press, 2000), part 3. As Nead argues, "obscenity created a spatial economy in the city, which drew together into a dangerous proximity the centres of official power and their transgressive other" (150).

87. In 1858, Dodgson posed and photographed in rags the daughter of the dean of Christ Church, Alice Liddell (the girl on whom he modeled the celebrated protagonist of *Alice in Wonderland* and *Alice through the Looking Glass*), thereby making her look the part of a street waif. Far from rescuing Alice, Dodgson's image of her bared limbs and ragged clothes manipulated Victorian visual iconography to appear to place Alice in sexual danger. Carol Mavor argues that the photograph of Alice Liddell as a beggar child "allowed Carroll to play in a space of difference, a simulated difference of class," which she sees as quite different from the effects of Barnardo's photographs of real beggar girls. Carol Mavor, *Pleasures Taken: Performances of Sexuality and Loss in Victorian Photographs* (Durham, NC: Duke University Press, 1995), esp. 39–42. See also Morton Cohen, *Lewis Carroll, Photographer of Children: Four Nude Studies* (Philadelphia: Philip H. and A.S.W. Rosenbach Foundation, 1978); Lindsay Smith, 'Take Back Your Mink': Lewis Carroll, Child Masquerade, and the Age of Consent," *Art History* (September 1993): 369–385; Susan Edwards, "Pretty Babies: Art, Erotica, or Kiddie Porn?" *History of Photography* 18, no. 1 (Spring 1994): 38–46.

88. Mario Perniola, "Between Clothing and Nudity" in Michel Feher, ed., *Fragments for a History of the Human Body* (Cambridge, MA: MIT Press, 1989), 237.

89. Raggedness could also be deployed to produce highly sentimental images of childhood innocence and insouciance. Mrs. H. M. Stanley called her first model "a dear little child in tatters" and called street children "little ragamuffins." Mrs. Stanley was the wife of the famed African explorer. See Mrs. H. M. Stanley (Dorothy Tennant), *London Street Arabs* (London: Cassell and Company, 1890), 5.

90. *The Charity Organisation Society and the Reynolds-Barnardo Arbitration* (London, 1878), 35.

91. *Night and Day* (November 1, 1877), 130. This was originally published by Reynolds in *Startling Revelations* (1876), 7. The version of Reed's testimony in the handwritten transcript of his testimony given at the arbitration in the files of the COS does not contain the phrase "After he had disfigured me."

92. The word "unnatural" was used by St. John Wontner. Given this sequence of events, it is difficult to understand why, in the version of Reed's story that Reynolds published, Reed claimed that "in consequence of Dr. Barnardo having torn my clothes in pieces I was ashamed to walk through the streets to the Home." Reynolds, *Startling Revelations*, 7. This raises the question of whether Reed was then forced to get out of the new uniform and put back on the ripped clothes.

93. Ibid., 12.

94. See Ian Gibson, *The English Vice: Beating, Sex, and Shame in Victorian England and After* (London: Duckworth, 1978), esp. chs. 5 and 6. Apart from Swinburne's writing, most flagellant literature, Gibson explains, depicted male and females, not males with other males (282).

95. Reynolds, *Startling Revelations*, 8.

96. Karen Halttunen, "Humanitarianism and the Pornography of Pain in Anglo-American Culture," *American Historical Review* (April 1995): 325, 334.

97. Reynolds, *Startling Revelations*, 7–8.

98. The arbitrators accepted Barnardo's version of the events surrounding the flogging of Reed for insubordination. See *Night and Day* (November 1, 1877), 128.

99. Ibid., 130.

100. First published separately as Leaflet No. 6 (Second Series), the story was reprinted in *Rescue the Perishing* (1875), lxxiii–lxxvi.

101. [Henry Gladwyn Jebb], *Out of the Depths* (London, 1860). On the publication of the novel, see Derek Hudson, *Munby, Man of Two Worlds* (Boston: Gambit, 1972), 22.

102. T. Barnardo, *Rescue the Perishing*, lxxv. Caroline Bressey has used Barnardo's admission and case records for the Williams children to reconstruct their history with some precision. The information about the children and their mother contained in these records differs considerably from the story Barnardo first published about them, along with their photograph, in *Rescue the Perishing* (1875) and later retold as "Three Woolly Black Heads" in his magazine, *Night and Day* (February 1898). The admission record describes the children's father, Peter Williams, as an "Englishman" and ship's cook whereas Barnardo's published account makes him into a "mulatto" and "coloured" sailor. Presumably, Barnardo believed that the English public would be less sympathetic to the plight of Mrs. Williams if they knew that she had been married to a white Englishman. Bressey argues that Barnardo intentionally sought to produce the impression that Peter and Elizabeth Williams had once been slaves. See Caroline Bressey, "Forgotten Histories: Three Stories of Black Girls from Barnardo's Victorian Archive," *Women's History Review* 11, no. 3 (2002): 351–374.

103. Barnardo notably tells us nothing about the fate of the youngest child, a boy, whom, we must assume, enters the less familial setting of the barracks in the boys' home.

104. The image simultaneously draws upon deeply racist rhetorics while demonstrating that Barnardo, unlike so many of his contemporaries, accepted people of all races into his homes as a matter of policy. For a perceptive reading of issues of race and empire in Barnardo's photographs, see Lindsay Smith, "The Shoe-Black to the Crossing Sweeper: Victorian Street Arabs and Photography," *Textual Practice* no. 10, 1 (1996): 29–55. On the photographs of the Williams children, see 41–45.

105. Examination of George Collins, July 9, 1877, A/FWA/C/D10/3, COS Files and Papers.

106. For a careful reconstruction of Merrick's life, see Michael Howell and Peter Ford, *The True History of the Elephant Man* (New York: Penguin, 1980). Howell and Ford note that Merrick's disabilities made him an ideal object of charity since he clearly could not support himself except as a freak. I develop this idea more fully in this section.

107. The most sophisticated cultural analysis of Merrick is Peter Graham and Fritz Oehlschlaeger, *Articulating the Elephant Man, Joseph Merrick and his Interpreters* (Baltimore: Johns Hopkins University Press, 1992). Graham and Oehlschlaeger approach Merrick's story both through an analysis of transhistorical archetypes and through its relationship to other cultural developments in Victorian Britain.

108. Wilfred Thomason Grenfell, *A Labrador Doctor: The Autobiography of Wilfred Thomason Grenfell* (Boston: Houghton Mifflin Company, 1919), esp. ch. 4 on his time at the London Hospital. There are several good biographies of Grenfell which examine his work with poor youths in the London slums. See Ronald Rompkey, *Grenfell of Labrador: A Biography* (Toronto: University of Toronto Press, 1991) ch. 2; and J. Lennox Kerr, *Wilfred Grenfell: His Life and Work* (London: George G. Harrap, 1959), ch. 2.

109. For Halsted's perspective, see D. G. Halsted, *Doctor in the Nineties* (London: Christopher Johnson, 1959), ch. 2.

110. Sir John Bland-Sutton, *The Story of a Surgeon* (London: Methuen, 1930), 139.

111. Sir Frederick Treves, *The Elephant Man and Other Reminiscences* (London: Cassell and Company, 1923), 2–5.

112. Ibid., 22.

113. These photographs are reproduced in Howell and Ford's *True History of the Elephant Man.*

114. Treves, *The Elephant Man*, 36.

115. As Edward Said concluded about Kipling's depiction of the division between white and nonwhite: "A Sahib is a Sahib, and no amount of friendship or camaraderie can change the rudiments of racial difference." See Edward Said, *Culture and Imperialism* (New York: Alfred Knopf, 1993), 135. Likewise, Twain's *Prince and the Pauper* (1881), while praising the wider vision the prince and the pauper acquire from their masquerades in one another's clothes and lives, insists on the rightness of restoring each to his original station.

116. Nadja Durbach demonstrates that Merrick's body appeared in the "Register of Bodies Used for Anatomical Examination" but suggests that his corpse was not, per se, dissected. See Nadja Durbach, "Monstrosity, Masculinity, and Medicine: Re-Examining the Elephant Man," unpublished paper in another's possession. My thanks to Prof. Durbach for sharing her findings with me.

117. In addition to scathing attacks in the press, the COS received many angry letters as well. Lt. Col. Richard Oldfield, for example, wrote to Ribton Turner on September 18, 1877, that he would influence his friends to "try and direct any monies they may be inclined to give to yr. society to Dr. Barnardo." For this and other critical letters, see A/FWA/C/D10/2, COS Files and Papers.

118. *Lloyd's Weekly Newspaper* (October 28, 1877).

119. On this aspiration, see G. M. Hicks to Ribton-Turner, August 14, 1877. A/FWA/C/D10/1, COS Files and Papers.

120. COS Council Minute Book, entries for July 2–November 19, 1877, A/FWA/C/A1/5.

121. This did not stop others from borrowing his techniques. For an account of the way an evangelical spinster, Miss Crimp, used photographs to promote her work, see "Visit to King Edward Industrial Schools," *Ragged School Union Magazine* (April 1882), 67.

122. John Tagg, *The Burden of Representation* (Basingstoke, UK: Macmillan Education 1988), ch. 3.

123. For a comprehensive analysis of this legacy, see Hugh Cunningham, *The Children of the Poor: Representations of Childhood since the Seventeenth Century*

(Oxford: Blackwell, 1991), chs. 5 and 6. On street arabs, see Anna Davin, *Growing Up Poor: Home, School, and Street in London, 1870–1914* (London: Rivers Oram Press, 1996), 160–164. See also Anna Davin, "Waif Stories in Late Nineteenth-Century England," *History Workshop Journal*, 52 (Autumn 2001): 67–98.

124. On Stead's campaign and subsequent trial, see Judith Walkowitz, *City of Dreadful Delight: Narratives of Sexual Danger in Late-Victorian London* (Chicago: University of Chicago Press, 1992), chs. 3 and 4; on Stead within the context of campaigns against child abuse, see George Behlmer, *Child Abuse and Moral Reform* (Stanford, CA: Stanford University Press, 1982), 73–77.

125. The Barnardos were so certain that the girls they saved would otherwise have become prostitutes that Mrs. Barnardo described girl streets waifs as "not yet fallen." *Sowing and Reaping*, 11th Annual Report of East End Juvenile Mission (1877), xxxi.

126. In the 1880s, debate over age-of-consent legislation in Britain and India was quite fierce. On the Indian context and its impact on British understandings of masculinity, see Mrinilina Sinha, *Colonial Masculinity: The 'Manly Englishman' and the 'Effeminate Bengali' in the Late Nineteenth Century* (Manchester: Manchester University Press, 1995).

127. For an example of the way one elite gay man in interwar Britain appropriated and reworked Barnardo's visual lexicon to serve his own explicitly homoerotic (and not philanthropic) ends, see James Gardiner, *A Class Apart: The Private Pictures of Montague Glover* (London: Serpent's Tail, 1992). From 1916 to the mid-50s, Glover assembled a vast archive of sexually revealing photographs of working-class boys and men, many of whom he photographed costumed in soldiers uniforms and in ragged clothes (their own or provided by him). The clothes of the ragged child and the soldier/sailor were interchangeable signifiers of fetishized male same-sex desire in Glover's photographic rhetoric.

128. See Viviana Zelizer, *Pricing the Priceless Child: The Changing Social Value of Children* (New York: Basic Books, 1985). On Barnardo's use of photographs as advertising tools, see Alec McHoul, "Taking the Children: Some Reflections at a Distance on the Camera and Dr. Barnardo," *Continuum: The Australian Journal of Media and Culture 5*, no. 1 (1991). George Reynolds used the phrase "making capital" in reference to Barnardo's sale of photographs in *Startling Revelations*, 12.

129. In her analysis of several different late-twentieth-century attempts to photograph destitute children in the United States, Julia Ballerini argues that despite the radical intentions of the photographers, their work individualizes poverty and reinforces rather than challenges the status quo. "Documentary photography, especially among the disadvantaged, has always been an ideological minefield. . . . It is easy for work to signify in ways contrary to those intended by its producers." Julia Bellerini, "Photography as a Charitable Weapon: Poor Kids and Self-Representation," *Radical History Review* (Fall, 1997): 169, 180.

130. Carole Howlett, foreword, to Tink Palmer and Lisa Stacey, *Stolen Childhood: Barnardo's Work with Children Abused through Prostitution* (London: Barnardo, 2002).

131. Rachel Knott, "Questions and Answers, Abuse through Prostitution Advertising Campaign," at *www.barnardos.org.uk/AboutBarnardos/CampAdv/QA.html* (Nov. 3, 2002). Controversy continues to surround Barnardo's photo-

graphic practices even as this book moves into proofs. Its most recent campaign in late 2003 against childhood poverty featured a computer-generated advertisement depicting a baby with a cockroach crawling out of his mouth accompanied by the caption, "Baby Greg is one minute old. He should have a bright future. Poverty is waiting to rob Greg of hope and spirit and is likely to lead him to a future of squalor." The advertisement was banned by the Advertising Standards Authority (ASA) after it received 466 complaints—the highest number received for an advertisement campaign in 2003. See John Carvel, "Child poverty adverts banned," *Guardian* (December 10, 2003), http://society.guardian.co.uk/campaigning/story/0,8150,1103491,00.html. Undaunted by the ban, *Campaign Magazine* voted the advertisement one of the ten best of 2003.

132. The campaign has been so successful that it has been invoked in parliamentary debates in Scotland to support the creation of the office of Commissioner for Children and Young People. See *Proceedings of the Scottish Parliament*, Wednesday, September 25, 2002, afternoon, Speech by Cathy Jamieson, the Minister for Education and Young People, column 14045.

133. Edward Fuller, *The Right of the Child: A Chapter in Social History* (London: Victor Gollancz, 1951), 91–93.

134. Save the Children, *Focus on Images* (London: Save the Children UK, 1994). The document was first published, but without photographic illustrations, in 1988. It has been revised several times, and according to staff at Save the Children, is once again under discussion and revision. According to Alan Thomas, photo librarian for Save the Children, the guidelines and pamphlet stimulated "many discussions" and "most aid agencies now have their own version of the guidelines." Personal communication to author, July 19, 2001.

135. Mrs. Barnardo and James Marchant, *Memoirs of the Late Dr. Barnardo* (London, Hodder and Stoughton, 1907), 59.

CHAPTER THREE
THE AMERICAN GIRL IN LONDON: GENDER, JOURNALISM, AND SOCIAL INVESTIGATION IN THE LATE VICTORIAN METROPOLIS

1. "The Wares of Autolycus," *Pall Mall Gazette* (November 22, 1893), 5. See G. R. Sims, "Mustard and Cress," *The Referee* (November 19, 1893), 7.

2. Ibid., (November 29, 1893), 5.

3. Mary Billington, "Leading Lady Journalists," *Pearson's Magazine* (July 1896), 111.

4. Mary Billington, "The Adventures of a Lady Journalist," *Young Woman* (January 1899), 135.

5. Elizabeth Banks, *The Autobiography of a "Newspaper Girl"* (New York: Dodd, Mead and Company, 1902), 308, hereafter cited as *Autobiography*.

6. A decade later, Banks's fellow countryman, Jack London, also hired a photographer to illustrate his incognito escapades in the London slums for *The People of the Abyss* (New York: Macmillan, 1903). But London's photographs included interiors of shelters, street scenes, and poses of him with "real" tramps. London's images make much greater documentary claims than Banks's, though obviously they could not have been taken at the time he was masquerading to be a tramp without revealing that he was not who he claimed to be.

7. Banks discussed her photographs frequently with her literary agent, W. Morris Colles of the Authors' Syndicate. Her interest in them was confined to their part in promoting publicity and sales of her books. See Elizabeth Banks to W. Morris Colles, December 6, 1893, box 1, folder 1; December 6, 1901, box 1, folder 2; March 13, 1902 and April 23, 1902, box 1, folder 3, Banks Papers.

8. She claimed to have been born in 1870 and hence graduated from college at the exceptionally precocious age of 17, but census records strongly point to 1865 as her actual date of birth. See Jane Gabin, "Elizabeth Banks: An American on Fleet Street," in her Introduction to a reprint of Elizabeth Banks, *The Remaking of an American* (Gainesville, FL: University Press of Florida, 2000), xvi–xvii, and esp. note 1, xlvii. While Gabin's useful essay notes several of Banks's autobiographical inaccuracies, she nonetheless accepts most of what Banks wrote about herself as factual, rather than as literary performances intended to construct a persona. Gabin's essay is the first published scholarly assessment of Banks, but it is marred by a variety of historical errors, such as dating the Paris Commune of 1870 in 1898 and placing Oscar Wilde's trial in between the Spanish American and Boer Wars (it preceded both!)

9. For example, just as James Greenwood insisted in "A Night" that he had braved the Lambeth Casual Ward by himself but had, in fact, been accompanied by his friend Bittlestone, so, too, Banks liked to emphasize her arrival in London as a friendless single girl. However, in an interview conducted in the autumn of 1894, we learn that she shared her "snug maisonette flat" with her sister, who had come to London sometime before Banks. See Marion Leslie, " 'An American Girl in London,' An Interview with Miss Elizabeth Banks," *Young Woman* (November 1894), 59.

10. In the twilight of her career as a journalist in 1926 as Banks prepared to write a book on "democracy pure and undefiled," she acknowledged her penchant for writing only partial truths. She told a fellow reporter without trace of apology that she was "going to print the whole truth for the first time in her life." See "Women Who Figure in News of the Day," the *New York Sun*, (November 15, 1926), clipping in *Sun* morgue file for Elizabeth Banks, held in the New York Public Library.

11. Will of Elizabeth Banks, Somerset House, London.

12. The largest collection consists of forty-six letters that Banks wrote to her literary agent detailing her negotiations for book contracts and deals, etc. See Elizabeth L. Banks Papers, University of Tulsa. See also Banks's short note to Theodore Dreiser, whom she had met in New York, praising the "truths" of his *Sister Carrie*. Elizabeth Banks to Theodore Dreiser, February 25, 1908, Dreiser Papers, folder 381, Special Collections, University of Pennsylvania.

13. Polly Pollock [Elizabeth Banks], "In an English Compartment Car," *Anglo-American Times* (March 11, 1893), 200.

14. Banks, *Autobiography*, 25–26, 212. See also Elizabeth L. Banks, "American 'Yellow' Journalism," *Nineteenth Century* (August 1898), 333–334.

15. Elizabeth Banks to W. Morris Colles, December 10, 1901, box 1, folder 2, Banks Papers.

16. "She Is an American," *New York Daily Tribune* (October 15, 1896), 5;

American Woman's Home Journal, Special Commencement Number (June 6, 1897), 9.

17. Ishbel Ross, *Ladies of the Press* (New York: Harper, 1936), 18.

18. Marion Leslie, "An American Girl," *Young Woman* (November 1894), 58.

19. See Polly Pollock [Elizabeth Banks], *Anglo-American Times* (January 7, 1893), 61–62; and "Female Suicides," *Anglo-American Times* (January 28, 1893), 109.

20. She cut short her time working in a laundry because "Saturday brought me such weariness of the flesh that I decided I had better resign" before being fired. See Elizabeth Banks, *Campaigns of Curiosity: Journalistic Adventures of an American Girl in London* (Chicago: F. T. Neely, 1894), 196, hereafter cited as *Campaigns.* Bank's rediscovery by scholars in the past few years has led to the reprinting of her *Campaigns* with an introduction by Mary Suzanne Schriber and Abbey Zink. See Elizabeth Banks, *Campaigns of Curiosity, Journalistic Adventures of an American Girl in Late Victorian London* (Madison, WI: University of Wisconsin Press, 2003).

21. Banks, *Autobiography,* 220–221.

22. Ibid., 222.

23. William Allen White used the term "harpies" in his famous "What's the Matter with Kansas" editorial of August 1896 in reference to the flamboyant platform speaking of the Populists' star woman performer, the Kansan Mary Elizabeth Lease. See Michael Goldberg, *Army of Women: Gender and Politics in Gilded Age Kansas* (Baltimore, MD: Johns Hopkins University Press, 1997); and Marily Dell Brady, "Populism and Feminism in a Newspaper by and for Women of the Kansas Farmer's Alliance, 1891–1894" and June Underwood, "Civilizing Kansas: Women's Organizations, 1880–1920" in *Kansas History* 7 (1984–85): 280–290, and 291–306.

24. Elizabeth Banks, "Electioneering Women, An American Appreciation," *Nineteenth Century* (November 1900), 791–794.

25. "Women for Sound Money," *New York Sun* (October 4, 1896), 4; see also "M'Kinley Women Rejoice," *New York Sun* (November 8, 1896), 3.

26. Polly Pollock [Elizabeth Banks], "My 'At Home' Day," *Anglo-American Times* (April 8, 1893), 270.

27. This is one of the central arguments in David Rubinstein, *Before the Suffragettes: Women's Emancipation in the 1890s* (Brighton: Harvester Press, 1986).

28. There is a vast literature on the New Woman in Britain, much of it by literary scholars. See Sally Ledger, *The New Woman: Fiction and Feminism at the Fin de Siècle* (Manchester, UK: Manchester University Press, 1997); Gail Cunningham, *The New Woman and the Victorian Novel* (New York: Barnes & Noble Books, 1978); Angelique Richardson and Chris Willis, eds., *The New Woman in Fiction and in Fact: Fin-de-Siècle Feminisms* (New York: Palgrave, 2001); Ann Ardis, *New Women, New Novels: Feminism and Early Modernism* (New Brunswick: Rutgers University Press, 1990).

29. Banks, *Campaigns,* 153–154.

30. See Marion Marzolf on women in the United States in *Up from the Foot-*

note: A History of Women Journalists (New York: Hastings House Publishers, 1977), ch. 1; Laurel Brake, Subjugated Knowledges: Journalism, Gender, and Literature in the Nineteenth Century (Washington Square, NY: New York University Press, 1994); Cynthia White, Women's Magazines, 1693–1968 (London: Joseph, 1970); Margaret Beetham, A Magazine of Her Own?: Domesticity and Desire in the Woman's Magazine, 1800–1914 (London: Routledge, 1996), parts 1 and 2; Mark Hampton, "The Fourth Estate: Theories, Images, and Ideals of the Press in Britain, 1880–1914," (Ph.D. diss., Vanderbilt University, 1998), esp. ch. 5.

31. These journals were closely associated with the Langham Circle, whose members espoused radical sex equality based on liberal principles of political economy. See Sheila Herstein, "The English Woman's Journal and the Langham Place Circle: A Feminist Forum and its Woman Editors," in Joel Wiener, ed., Innovators and Preachers: The Role of the Editor in Victorian England (Westport, CT: Greenwood Press, 1985); Pauline Nestor, "A New Departure in Women's Publishing: The English Woman's Journal and the Victoria Magazine," Victorian Periodical Review 15 (3) (1982: 93–106; Jane Rendall, "'A Moral Engine'? Feminism, Liberalism, and the English Woman's Journal," in Jane Rendall, ed., Equal or Different? Women's Politics, 1800–1914 (Oxford: Basil Blackwell, 1987), 112–138. Similarly, American women journalists made no effort to emulate Victoria Woodhull's notorious career as a journalist in the United States in the early 1870s. She subsequently moved to England where she edited a progressive review devoted to social issues called the Humanitarian.

32. See Beetham, A Magazine of Her Own? 68–69.

33. Census data in Britain and the United States dramatically testifies to women's emergence into the profession of journalism. The 1841 census in Britain listed fifteen women professionally engaged as authors, editors, and journalists; by 1891 this number had soared to 660. Between 1890 and 1900 the U.S. census reported an increase in the number of female reporters and editors (a much narrower and more useful definition than the one available in the British census) from approximately 1,000 to almost 2,200.

34. As editors increasingly courted women readers through women's columns in the mainstream press or through newspapers and periodicals specifically geared toward female readers (such as the Woman's Herald, Queen, and the Lady's Pictorial), demand for women journalists increased. According to the Woman at Home in 1898, "hundreds of thousands of pounds of capital are employed in the ladies' newspapers of today; hundreds of bright, talented women, and men too, are busied incessantly in providing by pen and pencil every conceivable sort of information and illustration which can help to tell all the world what the feminine half is doing." Based on women's journalistic prominence, the article concluded that "the Victorian Era has been above all else the women's era." See "Two Great Ladies' Paper," The Woman at Home (April 1898), 561.

35. "His Vile Face and Vicious Eye. Mr. T. P. O'Connor on Descriptive Personal Journalism," St. James's Gazette (January 5, 1894), 5.

36. Many women journalists, including Banks, shared the belief that women possessed a distinctly female voice as journalists that suited them to do interviews and write in a light and charming manner. Mary Billington went even further and insisted that most women lacked "the more abstract ability to judge tendencies

and the feelings of masses" that was so essential for the serious work of reporting about questions of domestic politics and empire. More compellingly, the widespread perception that men and women reporters wrote differently reflected the widely varying character of the stories editors gave to them. There was very little competition between male and female journalists because their assignments reflected gendered notions of male and female spheres. There were a few notable exceptions, however, foremost among them Flora Shaw, the *Times's* colonial correspondent and analyst, and Emily Crawford, the special correspondent in Paris of the *Daily News*. On Shaw's involvement with politics, journalism, and imperialism, see Jonathan Schneer, *London 1900: The Imperial Metropolis* (New Haven, CT: Yale University Press, 1999), 134–146. On women's skills as interviewers, see Hulda Friederichs, "Difficulties and Delights of Interviewing," *English Illustrated Magazine* (1892), 338.

37. See the annual reports, The Society of Women Journalists, 1894 onward, British Library, 011899.e. The formerly all-male Journalists Institute granted women full and equal membership. As Mr. Clayden, president of the Journalists Institute (founded in 1889), proudly told the assembled audience at the First International Conference of the Press in Antwerp in July 1894, "There is no more democratic body in the world than the Institute of Journalists of the United Kingdom. It rests on universal suffrage as its basis, it knows no distinction between man journalists and woman journalists." Speech of Mr. Clayden as quoted by Catherine Drew, "Women as Journalists," *Englishwoman's Review* (October 15, 1894), 245. Some women established the Society of Women Journalists, which numbered more than two hundred women within a short time of its founding in 1895. The data on membership is compiled from several different articles. In addition to serving as a lobby to advance the professional interests of women journalists, the Society of Women Journalists offered free legal assistance and medical treatment for the one guinea subscription required of its members. For attacks on the single-sex basis of the society by a woman journalist, see "Woman's World," *St. James's Gazette* (February 21, 1894), 12. On professional associations of journalists, see Mark Hampson, "Journalists and the 'Professional' Ideal in Britain: The Institute of Journalists, 1884–1907," *Historical Research* 72, no. 178 (June 1999): 183–201.

38. Sheila Braine, "London's Clubs for Women," in G. R. Sims, ed., *Living London*, vol. 1 (London: Cassell, 1903), 116. See also, Amy Levy, "Women and Club Life," *Woman's World* 1 (1888), 364–367, reprinted in Melvyn New, ed., *The Complete Novels and Selected Writings of Amy Levy, 1861–1889* (Gainesville, FL: University Press of Florida, 1993). On women's clubs and the ways in which activist women "remapped" space in London in forging political, social, and professional networks, see Lynne Walker, "Home and Away: The Feminist Remapping of Public and Private Space in Victorian London," in Rosa Ainley, ed., *New Frontiers of Space, Bodies and Gender* (London: Routledge, 1998): 65–75.

39. A useful summary of women's entrance into the professions in international perspective is provided by *Women in Professions: Being the Professional Section of the International Congress of Women, London, July 1899* (London: T. Fisher Unwin, 1900).

40. Anonymous, "Ladies at Work," *The Spectator* (November 4, 1893), 635.

41. The flavor of this world is effectively conveyed by G. R. Sims, *My Life: Sixty Years Recollections of Bohemian London* (London: Eveleigh Nash Company, 1917); and Henry Vizetelly, *Glances Backwards through Seventy Years,* vol. 2 (London: K. Paul, Trench, Trubner, & Co., 1893), 35, 116.

42. See William Beveridge Papers, letters to his mother and R. H. Tawney, IIa/49–51, BLPES. On Beveridge's career as a journalist after leaving Toynbee Hall, see José Harris, *William Beveridge: A Biography* (Oxford: Clarendon Press, 1977), ch. 5.

43. The young Irishwoman Charlotte O'Conor Eccles felt keenly that all male institutions and prevailing norms of male and female behavior effectively barred most women from seeking and getting positions on metropolitan newspapers. "A man meets other men at his club," she opined in an anonymous article published in *Blackwood's Magazine* in 1893. "He can be out and about at all hours; he can insist without being thought bold and forward; he is not presumed to be capable of undertaking only a limited class of subjects but is set to anything." Even the physical layout of Fleet Street, the center of the London newspaper world, frightened her and prompted her to fantasize that its "mysterious little alleys and side streets" were "cut-throat sort of places" where a provincial young lady might be "robbed and murdered." See [Charlotte O'Conor Eccles], "The Experiences of a Woman Journalist," *Blackwood's Magazine* (June 1893), 831.

44. See Bram Dijkstra, *Idols of Perversity: Fantasies of Feminine Evil in Fin-de-Siècle Culture* (New York: Oxford University Press, 1986); and Elaine Showalter, *Sexual Anarchy: Gender and Culture at the Fin de Siècle* (New York: Viking, 1990).

45. G. Holden Pike, "Young Women as Journalists," *Girl's Own Paper* (March 1891), 396.

46. XYZ [pseud.], "Women in Journalism," *Author* (July 1892), 62.

47. Grant Allen's controversial and best-selling novel, *The Woman Who Did* (London: J. Lane, 1895), only confirmed XYZ's suspicions that the female journalist was a source of "morbid" danger to the social fabric. As critic John Stokes perceptively notes, it was no accident that Allen's heroine was a female journalist who advocated free love and was subjected to vicious attacks by press reviewers. See John Stokes's excellent analysis of gender, sexuality, and the New Journalism in *In the Nineties* (Chicago: University of Chicago Press, 1989), esp. ch. 1, "'Is It a Revolution?': The Economics of the New Journalism and the Aesthetics of the Body Politic." Stokes sets the New Journalism against aestheticism and decadence in this essay.

48. See the writings of the *Star's* leading female journalist, Miss Strutt-Cavell (who wrote under the nom de plume "Stella"), which perfectly capture the anxiety to be an advanced woman in journalistic methods while staunchly defending women's essentially domestic nature. See Stella, "Woman Up To Date," *Star* (December 9, 1893), 4. On Stella's work as a woman journalist, see Leily Bingin, "Some Interesting Experiences of Lady Journalists," *Cassell's Magazine* (September 1898), 356.

49. See Billington, "Leading Lady Journalists," 104; see also Bingen, "Some Interesting Experiences of Lady Journalists," 353–357.

50. Billington, "Leading Lady Journalists," 102.

51. See Seth Koven, "How the Victorians Read *Sesame and Lilies*," in Deborah Nord, ed., *John Ruskin's "Sesame and Lilies": Rereading the Western Tradition* (Yale University Press: New Haven, 2002).

52. Denise Riley offers an important analysis of the relation between the categories the "social" and "woman" in *Am I That Name?: Feminism and the Category of "Women" in History* (Minneapolis: University of Minnesota Press, 1988).

53. Elizabeth L. Banks, "London Invites Plague," *Chicago Evening Post* (August 6, 1901), 5; and "Pink in London Gloom," *Chicago Evening Post* (August 24, 1901), 3.

54. Mrs. Crawford, the Paris correspondent for the *London Daily News* and the *New York Tribune*, whose first-hand reports of the street battles of the Paris Commune in 1870 had laid the foundation for her illustrious career, reminded her readers that she was a wife and mother and that journalism was compatible with "home duties." At the same time, she acknowledged that the perils she confronted as a journalist had "deconventionalised" her. Emily Crawford, "Journalism as a Profession for Women," *Contemporary Review* (September 1893), 369–71.

55. W. T. Stead, "Young Women in Journalism," *Review of Reviews*, American ed. (November 1892), 452. This article is a reprint of a published interview in the magazine *The Young Woman*.

56. Apparently, Stead was impressed with Banks's "Cap and Apron" articles in the *Weekly Sun*. On Stead's views of Banks, see Frederick Whyte, *The Life of W. T. Stead*, vol. 2 (London: J. Cape, 1925), 70–71.

57. Banks, *Autobiography*, 185.

58. Ibid., 95–97.

59. Howard Good examined the interplay of autobiography and journalism in the work of several leading American women journalists of the late nineteenth and early twentieth centuries. See Howard Good, *The Journalist as Autobiographer* (Metuchen, NJ: Scarecrow Press, 1993), esp. 73–102.

60. Marion Leslie, "An American Girl in London," An interview with Miss Elizabeth Banks, *Young Woman* (November 1894), 60, hereafter cited as "Interview."

61. Nisbet and Co. published a pamphlet under the title "Only a Factory Girl," which recounted the experiences of two evangelical young ladies who had disguised themselves as factory girls "in order that they might visit their haunts, become acquainted with their habits and associations, and learn how best to meet their needs." The ladies ventured from the factory to the theatre, the music hall, and the gin-palace. See a short review of "Only a Factory Girl" in *The British Weekly* (July 1, 1887), 136. I have been unable to locate any record of this pamphlet's existence beside this short notice. See Judith Walkowitz's analysis of the social and cultural meaning of women's new access to the streets of London in the 1880s, *City of Dreadful Delight: Narratives of Sexual Danger in Late-Victorian London* (Chicago: University of Chicago Press, 1992), ch. 2.

62. Billington, "Leading Lady Journalists," 110.

63. Sarah Tooley, "The Growth of a Socialist: An Interview with Mrs. Sidney Webb," *The Young Woman* (February 1895), 148.

64. Deborah Nord, *The Apprenticeship of Beatrice Webb* (Ithaca: Cornell University Press, 1985), 154.

65. Banks was in Lima at the time Potter published her articles.

66. See Brooke Kroeger, *Nellie Bly: Daredevil, Reporter, Feminist* (New York: Times Books, 1994), 86–105. See also Jean Lutes, "Into the Madhouse with Nellie Bly: Girl Stunt Reporting in Late Nineteenth-Century America," *American Quarterly* 54, no. 2 (June 2002): 217–253.

67. Elizabeth L. Banks, "American Women as Journalists," *Author* (December 1893), 252–253.

68. See "The Newest Journalism," *Ladies Pictorial* (September 8, 1894), 322. One married woman journalist was appalled that Banks had disdained the generous food allowance her mistress had given her and demanded to know whether Banks, "our amateur casual—very 'amateur' and very 'casual'—knows that many respectable working men bring up large families" on the sum Banks had found inadequate to pay for her own luxurious meals. See "A Kensington Martha," letter to "Voice of the People" column, *Weekly Sun* (December 10, 1893).

69. Banks edited out her comments on female prostitution when she published her campaigns in book form.

70. Banks, *Campaigns*, xvi.

71. Marion Leslie, "Interview," 61.

72. Banks, *Autobiography*, 95–97.

73. Miss Heather Bagon, letter to "Voice of the People" column, *Weekly Sun* (November 3, 1893), 3. On the ways in which women readers constructed a sense of themselves and their worlds through women's magazines, especially the correspondence columns, see Lynne Warren, "'Women in Conference': Reading the Correspondence Columns in *Woman*, 1890–1910," in Laurel Brake, Bill Bell, and David Finkelstein, eds., *Nineteenth-Century Media and the Construction of Identities* (London: Palgrave, 2000): 122–134.

74. Elizabeth Banks, reply in "Voice of the People" column, *Weekly Sun* (November 12, 1893), 3.

75. E.L.S., letter to "Voice of the People" column, *Weekly Sun* (November 26, 1893), 3.

76. Arthur Chitty, letter to "Voice of the People" column, *Weekly Sun* (December 10, 1893), 3.

77. Lynne Warren has examined the ways in which women readers used correspondence columns and, more generally, shaped their identities "as progressive 'woman' or conservative 'lady'" through reading print media that targeted their sex. See Lynne Warren, "'Women in Conference': Reading the Correspondence Columns in *Woman* 1890–1910," in Laurel Brake, Bill Bell, and David Finkelstein, eds., *Nineteenth-Century Media and the Construction of Identities* (London: Palgrave: 2000): 123.

78. See "Another Woman Journalist," letter to "Voice of the People" column, *Weekly Sun* (November 19, 1893), 3.

79. Through the Social Science Association, women had played significant parts in these controversies from mid-century. See two fine studies about these contributions, Eileen Janes Yeo, *The Contest for Social Science: Relations and Representations of Gender and Class* (London: Rivers Orum Press, 1996), part

2; and Lawrence Goldman, *Science, Reform, and Politics in Victorian Britain: The Social Science Association* (Cambridge: Cambridge University Press, 2002), ch. 4. On the role of journalists in debates about women's work, see Carolyn Malone, "Sensational Stories, Endangered Bodies: Women's Work and the New Journalism in England in the 1890s," *Albion* 31 (Spring 1999): 49–71. On the rise of women's columns in the socialist press, see Chris Waters, "'Masculine Socialism' and the Development of Women's Columns in the British Socialist Press, 1884–1914." Paper presented to the work-in-progress seminar, Department of History, University of Sussex, May 1983.

80. See Liselotte Glage, *Clementina Black: A Study in Social History and Literature* (Heidelberg: Carl Winter, 1981), part 1.

81. On Black's intimate relations with Karl Marx's family, see Yvonne Kapp, *Eleanor Marx*, vol. 1, *Family Life* (New York: International Publishers, 1972), 219.

82. For an assessment of the editor of *The Nineteenth Century*, James Knowles, and his contributions to journalism, see Neil Berry, *Articles of Faith: The Story of British Intellectual Journalism* (London: Waywiser Press, 2002).

83. Clementina Black, "The Dislike to Domestic Service," *Nineteenth Century* (March 1893), 454–455.

84. F[rank]. M. Butlin, "International Congress of Women," *Economic Journal* 9, no. 35 (September 1899): 452.

85. For example, see Clementina Black, "London Tailoresses," *Economic Journal* 14, no. 56 (December 1904): 555–567.

86. Elizabeth L. Banks, "How the Other Half Lives, The Crossing Sweeper," *English Illustrated Magazine* (May 1894), 849.

87. Clementina Black, "Match-Box Making At Home," *English Illustrated Magazine* (May 1892), 625–629. Black modestly did not inform readers about the significant role she had played in the summer of 1888 in helping her friend Annie Besant organize a strike by matchgirls employed at starvation wages by the firm of Bryant and May. In February 1888, Besant and William T. Stead had founded a weekly paper, the *Link*, "simply and solely as the helper of the helpless, the friend of the oppressed, and the advocate and champion of the cause of the 'Disinherited our Race.'" Besant used her journalism not only to report abuses but as a way to organize supporters. On the editorial aims of the *Link*, see Annie Besant and William T. Stead, "To Our Fellow Servants," *Link* (February 4, 1888), 1. On the role of the *Link* in the subsequent strike, see Besant's articles for June and July 1888.

88. See Arwun Mohun, *Steam Laundries: Gender, Technology, and Work in the United States and Great Britain, 1880–1940* (Baltimore: Johns Hopkins University Press, 1999), esp. 119–125. See Patricia Malcolmson's pioneering study of the industry, with its emphasis on married women's work, "Laundresses and the Laundry Trade in Victorian England," *Victorian Studies* 24 (Autumn 1981): 439–462. Activist women and workers were deeply divided among themselves over the virtues and vices of such forms of state legislation that "protected" workers and limited their hours without compensation for lost earnings. See Rosemary Feurer, "The Meaning of 'Sisterhood': The British Women's Movement and Protective Labor Legislation, 1870–1900," *Victorian Studies* 31 (Win-

ter 1988): 233–260. See also Philippa Levine's treatment of these debates among activist women in *Victorian Feminism, 1850–1900* (Tallahassee, FL: Florida State University Press, 1987).

89. Skilled workers, Banks noted, who were paid weekly favored a state-mandated reduction in the working day from 12 to 10 hours. Workers paid by the piece defended their right to work longer hours to preserve their total wages.

90. Banks, *Campaigns*, 179.

91. These articles were quickly reprinted as two volumes, *Tempted London: Young Men* (London: Hodder and Stoughton, 1888); and John Law [Margaret Harkness], ed., *Toilers in London, or Inquiries Concerning Female Labour in the Metropolis* (London: Hodder and Stoughton, 1889). No individual is credited with editing the first volume, whereas the editor of the second volume is identified as the author of *Out of Work*. On the *British Weekly* and its editor, the Scottish minister William Robertson Nicholl, see Josef L. Altholz, *The Religious Press in Britain, 1760–1900* (New York: Greenwood Press, 1989), 63–64.

92. *British Weekly: A Journal of Social and Christian Progress* (February 24, 1888), 314; *British Weekly* (September 23, 1887).

93. Harkness to Webb, December 25, 1887, Passfield Papers.

94. Harkness's friend Annie Besant had brilliantly organized and publicized the strike through her paper the *Link*.

95. See *British Weekly* (May 18, 1888, and July 20, 1888). See also the *British Weekly* discussion of female emigration to Australia on September 21, 1888, and Harkness's recyling of the same material in *Captain Lobe*, on December 7, 1888, and December 14, 1888.

96. Thanks to the labors of a handful of literary scholars, Harkness has been rescued from her longtime status as the recipient of the letter in which Engels defined socialist aesthetics by criticizing Harkness's depiction of the passivity of the poor. Led by Beate Kaspar, scholars have fleshed out a fuller picture of her life and suggested a variety of frameworks by which to understand her achievements. John Goode stresses her contribution to the socialist novel and her engagement as a novelist with the class-based political struggles of her day. Eileen Sypher argues that the force of Harkness's political arguments was blunted by her commitment to conventional and conservative readers and heroines. Ingrid Von Rosenberg locates Harkness within the movement to adapt Zola's French naturalism to the needs of the English socialist novel. Deborah Nord places her within a tradition of urban social exploration and within the emerging community of "glorified" spinsters seeking to define new social roles for themselves. See Beate Kaspar, *Margaret Harkness: A City Girl* (Tubingen: M. Niemeyer, 1984) and Kaspar's and Joyce Bellamy's detailed reconstruction of her life in the *Dictionary of Labour Biography*, vol. 8, (London: Macmillan, 1972), 103–113; Ingrid Von Rosenberg, "French Naturalism and the English Socialist Novel: Margaret Harkness and William Edwards Tirebuck," in H. Gustav Klaus, ed., *The Rise of Socialist Fiction, 1880–1914* (Brighton: Harvester, 1987); John Goode, "Margaret Harkness and the Socialist Novel," and Kiernan Ryan, "Citizens of Centuries to Come: The Ruling-Class Rebel in Socialist Fiction," in H. Gustav Klaus, ed., *The Socialist Novel in Britain: Towards the Recovery of a Tradition* (New York: St. Martin's, 1982); Eileen Sypher, *Wisps of Violence: Producing Public and Private*

Politics in the Turn-of-the-Century British Novel (London: Verso, 1993), esp. ch. 6, "Margaret Harkness: Representing Politics in the Slums"; Bernadette Kirwan, introduction to Merlin Radical Fiction reprint of *Out of Work*; Peter Keating, *The Working Classes in Victorian Fiction* (London: Routledge and K. Paul, 1971), ch. 9; Deborah Nord, *The Apprenticeship of Beatrice Webb* and "Neither Pairs Nor Odd": Female Community in Late-Nineteenth-Century London, *Signs* 15, no. 4: 733–754 and the incorporation of this article into her larger study, *Walking the Victorian Streets* (Ithaca, NY: Cornell University Press, 1995).

97. These were the words Beatrice Potter used to describe her cousin in her diary entry for March 24, 1883. See *The Diary of Beatrice Webb, Glitter Around and Darkness Within, 1873–1892*, ed. Norman and Jeanne MacKenzie, vol 1 (Cambridge, MA: The Belknap Press of Harvard University Press, 1982), 79.

98. Margaret Harkness to Beatrice Potter, December 10, 1875; September 1876; Passfield Papers, BLPES. Deborah Nord has noted Harkness's ambivalent identification with feminist perspectives in "Neither Pairs Nor Odd" in *Walking the Victorian Streets*, 196–197.

99. One of Harkness's biographers believes she may have had a romantic attachment to a married man. See Kaspar and Bellamy, *Dictionary of Labour Biography*, 110.

100. Consumed by grief at the death of his unnamed beloved, the doctor finds consolation and freedom in the slums where he spends "whole nights prowling about the street." Because the book version of *Captain Lobe* is more readily available than its serialized form in the *British Weekly*, I will refer to the 1891 edition, which included an appreciative introduction by the founder of the Salvation Army, William Booth. See John Law [Margaret Harkness], *In Darkest London, Captain Lobe* (London: Bellamy Library, William Reeves, 1891), 82–83, 194.

101. "Our business," the *British Weekly* declared, "will be, in the most delicate and reticent manner, to lay the facts before the Church" and to call upon churchmen and women to take action. See "Tempted London: Young Women," *British Weekly* (April 13, 1888), 441.

102. See Judith Walkowitz, *Prostitution and Victorian Society: Women, Class, and the State* (Cambridge: Cambridge University Press, 1980).

103. Frederick Engels offered his oft-quoted definition of literary realism in response to Harkness's *City Girl*: "Realism, to my mind, implies, besides truth of detail, the truthful reproduction of typical characters under typical circumstances." Engels to Harkness, April 1888, in Lee Baxandall and Stefan Morawski, eds., *Marx and Engels on Literature and Art: A Selection of Writings* (St. Louis: Telos Press, 1973), 114–115. It was in this letter that Engels also expressed his disappointment at the way the London poor "passively submit [sic] to fate." My thanks to Louise Yelin for this reference.

104. Carolyn Steedman, *Strange Dislocations: Childhood and the Idea of Human Interiority, 1780–1930* (Cambridge, MA: Harvard University Press, 1995), 121.

105. "Tempted London: Young Women. No. 1. Flower Girls," *British Weekly* (May 4, 1888), 11.

106. Rudyard Kipling, *Times* (November 29, 1892), 8.

107. Elizabeth Banks, "On One Side Only. An American Girl's Reply to Mr. Kipling," *Times* (December 6, 1892), 5.

108. See *St. James's Gazette* (January 17, 1894).

109. See H. B. Marriott-Watson, "The American Woman," *Nineteenth Century* (September 1904): 433–442.

110. Gertrude Atherton, "English and American Girls," *Woman at Home* (October 1897), 42.

111. Matthew Arnold, "On Translating Homer," in R. H. Super, ed., *On the Classical Tradition* (Ann Arbor: University of Michigan Press, 1960), 140.

112. See Antoinette Burton, *At the Heart of the Empire: Indians and the Colonial Encounter in Late-Victorian Britain* (Berkeley: University of California Press, 1998); and Angela Woollacott, *To Try Her Fortune in London: Australian Women, Colonialism, and Modernity* (Oxford: Oxford University Press, 2001).

113. Elizabeth Banks, "American London," in G. R. Sims, ed., *Living London*, vol. 2 (London: Cassell and Co., 1903), 112.

114. Mrs. H. R. Haweis, "The American Girl," *Young Woman* (January 1894), 153–154.

115. C[ecil]. de Thierry, "American Women, From a Colonial Point of View," *Contemporary Review* (October 1896): 522.

116. "War on American Women," *New York Sun* (October 11, 1896), 7.

117. On Banks's description of her interview with Li Hung Chang, see Elizabeth Banks, "The Women of England and America," *New York Herald* (October 1896), sec. 6, p. 5. See also "She Is an American. The Wee Mite of a Woman Who Interviewed Li Hung Chang," *New York Daily Tribune* (October 15, 1896), 5.

118. Elizabeth L. Banks, "The Women of England and America," *New York Herald* (October 18, 1896), 5.

119. Elizabeth L. Banks, "The English Man Compared with the American Man. The Good Points of Both and Wherein Each Might Gain from Study of the Other," *New York Herald* (October 25, 1896), 5.

120. Elizabeth Banks, "Self-Help Among American College Girls," *Nineteenth Century* (March 1896), 502–513.

121. Marion Leslie, "Interview", 62.

122. Banks, "American 'Yellow' Journalism."

123. Hugh E. M. Stutfield, "The Psychology of Feminism," *Blackwood's Edinburgh Magazine* 161 (January 1897): 114–115.

124. Elizabeth Banks, "The American Negro and His Place," *Nineteenth Century* (September 1899), 459–474.

125. Celia [Elizabeth Banks], "People One Meets, Walking Lima's Streets," *Oshkosh Weekly Northwestern* (May 5, 1890), 8.

126. Banks, "The American Negro and His Place," 467–468. On an Indian woman's experiences in late Victorian women's colleges, see Antoinette Burton, *At the Heart of the Empire: Indians and the Colonial Encounter in Late-Victorian Britain* (Berkeley: University of California Press, 1998), ch. 3.

127. Banks, "The American Negro and His Place," 459–460, 474.

128. It was presumably through this association that she became close friends with Edith Lees Ellis, a former member of the Fellowship of the New Life and lesbian wife of Havelock Ellis. She calls Ellis, "Mrs. Havie." See Banks, *Remaking of an American*, 8.

129. I am borrowing the phrase from Antoinette Burton, "Making a Spectacle of Empire: Indian Travelers in Fin-de-Siècle London," *History Workshop Journal* 42 (1996): 96–117.

130. Unsigned review of *Autobiography of a 'Newspaper Girl,'* *Nation* (December 25, 1902).

131. Unsigned review, "Campaigns of Curiosity," *Pall Mall Gazette* (September 25, 1894), 4.

132. See Lisa Tickner, *The Spectacle of Women, Imagery of the Suffrage Campaign, 1907–14* (Chicago: University of Chicago Press, 1988).

133. See Olive Christian Malvery, *The Soul Market with Which Is Included 'The Heart of Things'* (London: Hutchinson, 1907). See Judith Walkowitz's analysis of Malvery's manipulation of race and gender categories in her journalism and photographs, "The Indian Woman, the Flower Girl, and the Jew: Photojournalism in Edwardian London," *Victorian Studies* 42 (Fall 1998). Walkowitz examines Malvery's manipulation of commercial venues for her work and contrasts the different ways in which she represented working girls, Jews, and other "aliens" in her writing and photographs as part of a broader crisis in liberalism.

CHAPTER FOUR
THE POLITICS AND EROTICS OF DIRT: CROSS-CLASS SISTERHOOD
IN THE SLUMS

1. George Orwell, *Down and Out in Paris and London* (London: Harpers and Brothers, 1933; 2d. ed., New York: Harcourt Brace Janovich, 1961), 9.

2. Many scholars in recent years have examined women's engagement with slum reform and investigation. See Judith Walkowitz, *City of Dreadful Delight: Narratives of Sexual Danger in Late-Victorian London* (Chicago: University of Chicago Press, 1992); Deborah Nord, *Walking the Streets, Women, Representation, and the City* (Ithaca, NY: Cornell University Press, 1995) and *The Apprenticeship of Beatrice Webb* (Ithaca, NY: Cornell University Press, 1985), esp. chs. 5 and 6; Ross McKibbin, *The Ideologies of Class: Social Relations in Britain, 1880–1950* (Oxford: Clarendon Press, Oxford University Press, 1990), ch. 6; Martha Vicinus, *Independent Women: Work and Community for Single Women, 1850–1920* (London: Virago, 1985); Jane Lewis, *Women and Social Action in Victorian and Edwardian England* (Stanford, CA: Stanford University Press, 1991); Eileen Yeo, *The Contest for Social Science: Relations and Representations of Gender and Class* (London: Rivers Oram Press, 1996); and Ellen Ross, *Love and Toil: Motherhood in Outcast London, 1870–1918* (New York: Oxford University Press, 1993).

3. Norman and Jeanne MacKenzie, eds., *The Diary of Beatrice Webb*, vol. 1 *Glitter Around and Darkness Within*, 1873–1892, (Cambridge, MA: Harvard University Press, 1982), 132; Margot Asquith, *An Autobiography*, vol. 1 (New York: George H. Doran Company, 1920), 108–116. See Walkowitz, *City of Dreadful Delight*, ch. 2 on shopping and slumming as expressions of women's new freedoms to move through urban space in the 1880s; see also Erica Diane Rappaport, *Shopping for Pleasure: Women in the Making of London's West End*

(Princeton: Princeton University Press, 2000), esp. introduction, "To Walk Alone in London."

4. The word "queer" appears constantly in both novels. It often means nothing more than "odd" or "unusual." But on other occasions it is freighted with subtle sexual connotations. In the text of this essay, I have cited several examples from *Miss Brown*. In *A Princess of the Gutter*, Joan's cousin Anne, a passionate musician, is uncomfortable with talk of marriage and feminine banter. Joan invites Anne to join her in her new slum residence in Shoreditch, but Anne is not yet ready to leave her conventional bourgeois home. Anne "wrenched her hands out of mine, and left me. She had already got back into her shell, and it was impossible for me to touch her or influence her in any way. Nevertheless, during the night which followed, my last night in the old house, I thought of Anne and her triumphant march [a piano piece] with a queer sense of excitement and pleasure" (114). By the novel's end, Anne and Joan are ensconced together as "sisters" in the slums. "Queer" linked with "pleasure" in this passage seems to convey some element of attraction that goes beyond its standard meaning of "unusual." This suggests that "queer" had begun to acquire its homoerotic connotations well before 1900. On the meaning of the word "queer" in Robert Louis Stevenson's *The Strange Case of Dr. Jekyll and Mr. Hyde* (New York: Vintage Books, 1886), see Elaine Showalter, *Sexual Anarchy* (New York: Viking Penguin, 1990), 112.

5. Mary Douglas, *Purity and Danger: An Analysis of Concepts of Pollution and Taboo* (London: Routledge and K. Paul, 1966), 159. See also Patricia Yaeger's brilliant analysis of dirt, race, gender, and sexuality in Southern women's fiction in *Dirt and Desire, Reconstructing Southern Women's Writing, 1930–1990* (Chicago: University of Chicago Press, 2000), esp. ch. 6.

6. After providing a graphic description of urban vice and physical squalor, Kay literally halts his narrative because he is "unwilling to weary the patience of the reader by extending such disgusting details." See J. P. Kay, *The Moral and Physical Condition of the Working Classes Employed in the Cotton Manufacture in Manchester, Second Edition Enlarged and Containing an Introductory Letter to the Rev. Thomas Chalmers* (London: James Ridgway, 1832), 37.

7. Mary Higgs, *Glimpses into the Abyss* (London: P. S. King and Son, 1906), 20.

8. See Derek Hudson, *Munby, Man of Two Worlds: The Life and Diaries of Arthur J. Munby, 1828–1910* (London: J. Murray, 1972), 89–90; Liz Stanley, ed., *The Diaries of Hannah Cullwick, Victorian Maidservant* (London: Virago, 1984); L. Davidoff, "Class and Gender in Victorian Britain," in J. K. Newton, ed., *Sex and Class in Women's History* (London: Routledge and Kegan Paul, 1983); G. Pollock, "'With My Own Eyes': Fetishism, the Labouring Body, and the Colour of its Sex," *Art History* 17 (September 1994): 342–382; Ann McClintock, *Imperial Leather: Race, Gender, and Sexuality in the Colonial Contest* (New York: Routledge, 1995). See also, Diane Atkinson, *Love and Dirt: The Marriage of Arthur Munby and Hannah Cullwick* (London: Macmillan, 2003).

9. Mary Poovey, *Making a Social Body: British Cultural Formation, 1830–1864* (Chicago: University of Chicago Press, 1995), esp. chs. 3–6.

10. John Ruskin, *Sesame and Lilies*, paragraph 86. For an extended analysis of the gender and sexual politics of *Lilies* in relationship to women's social work

in the slums, see Seth Koven, "How the Victorians Read *Sesame and Lilies,*" in Deborah Nord, ed., *John's Ruskin's Sesame and Lilies* (New Haven: Yale University Press, 2002). Unlike Leonore Davidoff and Catherine Hall, who suggest that by the 1840s and '50s, separate spheres ideology produced fixed lines of gender division in the middle class, I stress the ways in which the ideology and practice of separate spheres both permitted and required women to bring their "private" values into "public" life. See Leonore Davidoff and Catherine Hall, introduction to part 3, of *Family Fortunes: Men and Women of the English Middle Class, 1780–1850* (Chicago: University of Chicago Press, 1987), 319. While Davidoff and Hall argue that "only gradually did private functions retreat to a hidden core" (319), they also recognize the public character of middle-class women's philanthropic endeavors (416–436).

11. J. H. Stallard, *The Female Casual and Her Lodging with a Complete Scheme for the Regulation of Workhouse Infirmaries* (London: Saunders, Otley, and Co., 1866) 1, 2, 6, (hereafter cited as Stallard, *Female Casual*). This remarkable book consists of Dr. Stallard's introductory materials and conclusions along with a narrative of her incognito visits to the casual ward by Ellen Stanley, one of many pseudonyms assumed by the pauper widow. The narrative was heavily edited to make its language and images acceptable for a respectable reading public.

12. Stallard, *Female Casual*, 48, 49. On male sexual threats, see pp. 7, 52–53.

13. See chapter 3 for an extended analysis of women's incognito investigations in the 1880s and '90s.

14. On higher education, see Rita McWilliams Tullberg, *Women at Cambridge: A Men's University, though of a Mixed Type* (London: Gollancz, 1975); on women and local government, see Patricia Hollis, *Ladies Elect: Women in Local English Government, 1865–1914* (New York, Oxford: Oxford University Press, 1987).

15. In the September 1888 issue of the *Nineteenth Century* Beatrice Potter created a sensation with the publication of her "Pages of a Workgirl's Diary," a vivid record of her experiences masquerading as a trouser fitter and Jewess in a sweated workshop in East London, which she later dismissed as a "lark" and "romantic adventure." See Sarah Tooley, "The Growth of a Socialist, an Interview with Mrs. Sidney Webb," *The Young Woman* (February 1895), 148.

16. Katharine [Symonds] Furse, *Hearts and Pomegranates: The Story of Forty-Five Years, 1875–1920* (London: Peter Davies, 1940), 156.

17. "Overdoing It," *Punch* (December 22, 1883), 294.

18. Mary Higgs, *Glimpses into the Abyss* (London: P. S. King, 1906), x, 83.

19. Ibid., 94, 108–109, 113, 120.

20. See Mrs. Higgs's testimony of November 29, 1904, *Report of the Department Committee on Vagrancy, Minutes of Evidence*, vol. 2, Cd. 2891 (1906), 53.

21. Muriel Lester, letter no. 14, October 7–14, 1926, in Box 1, "Correspondence and form letters written from India," Lester Papers.

22. Kingsley Royden, "A Friend in My Retreat: Family Life in Bromley St. Leonard between the Wars," *East London Record*, no. 1 (1978).

23. Hulda Friederichs, "I Was In Prison—The Story of Miss Honnor Morten's Wonderful Work," *The Young Woman* (May 1900), 304.

24. Muriel Lester, *It Occurred to Me* (London: Harper and Brothers, 1937), 4–7, 20–23, 89.

25. For a balanced assessment of these activities, see George Behlmer, *Friends of the Family: The English Home and its Guardians, 1850–1940* (Stanford, CA: Stanford University Press, 1998), ch. 1. Behlmer's interpretation, while acknowledging the role of cross-class friendship, stresses the regulatory and disciplinary aspect of relationships between female sanitarians and the poor.

26. *Eighteen Years in the Central City Swarm*, n.d. (c. 1912), 34.

27. E. A. Pope, untitled article, *Monthly Record of the Bermondsey Settlement and St. George's Social Club* (May 1902), 76. At the time the stories she recounts actually occurred, Pope was still Miss E. A. Barrs.

28. Muriel Wragge, *The London I Loved: Reminiscences of Fifty Years Social Work in the District of Hoxton* (London: J. Clarke, 1960), 83.

29. Alice Hodson, *Letters from a Settlement* (London: E. Arnold, 1909), 12–15. A graduate of Lady Margaret Hall, Hodson worked at the college's settlement in South London with a boys' club at Waterloo Crypt. She noted that her father believed that a woman's sphere should be the home but also believed his daughter should be well informed and educated. Katherine Roberts shared Hodson's repulsion from and attraction to the dirtiness of her work among the poor. Roberts served as a nurse in a London Maternity Hospital for poor women. She wondered "why in Heaven's name can't they [the management of the hospital] get charwomen to do all the work? No wonder ladies don't often go in for this branch of [nursing] profession." Roberts regularly fled in a hansom cab to the comforts of tea and cakes, strawberries and cream with her friend "E" when she felt overwhelmed by her nursing duties. Like Hodson, Roberts also relished the signs of her violation of convention norms of gentile femininity and her rebellion against social convention. See Katherine Roberts, *Five Months in a London Hospital* (Letchworth: Garden City Press, 1911), 9, 18.

30. Ellen Ranyard's London Bible and Domestic Female Mission challenged this hierarchy by recruiting her Bible women and Bible Nurses from the churchgoing poor. Ranyard Bible Nurses themselves performed dirty labor for other working class women—scrubbing their homes and bodies in times of illness. See Frank Prochaska, "Body and Soul: Bible Nurses and the Poor in Victorian London," *Historical Research* 60 (1987): 336–348.

31. Anne McClintock, *Imperial Leather: Race, Gender, and Sexuality in the Colonial Contest* (London: Routledge, 1995), 154.

32. The founder of London's most renowned crèche, the evangelical Quaker Marie Hilton complained "that I sometimes read articles about the sin and vice of the East End, written by people who do not look below the surface, and cannot see the fine gold amid the dross. In spite of the pollution incident to the condition of the neighbourhood, many strive, and strive not in vain, to keep themselves unspotted from the world." See John Deane, *Marie Hilton: Her Life and Work, 1821–1896* (London: Isbister and Company Limited, 1897), 90.

33. On the body and image of the prostitute as a site of dirt and disease, see Lynda Nead, *Myths of Sexuality: Representations of Women in Victorian Britain* (Oxford: Basil Blackwell, 1988), 118–134.

34. E. S., "Women Who Ought to Work," *Eastward-Ho* (May 1885), 50–51.

35. Recent scholarly work on Loane suggests that the author "M. Loane" was not a single person, but was Loane, a well-published Queen's nurse, and her half-sister, Alice Ezra Loane. See introduction by Susan Cohen and Clive Fleay in M. Loane, *The Queen's Poor: Life as They Find It in Town and Country* (London: E. Arnold, 1905; facs. repr. London: Middlesex University Press, 1998). For a critical assessment of Loane's biases, see George Behlmer, *Friends of the Family: The English Home and its Guardians, 1850–1940* (Stanford, CA: Stanford University Press, 1998), 52–56.

36. M. Loane, *The Next Street But One* (London: E. Arnold, 1907), 99–100.

37. Another graduate of Lady Margaret Hall, Oxford, Winifred Locket, noted angrily that the indiscriminant charity of West End ladies had encouraged the poor in her neighborhood to cultivate "an appearance of poverty even if it was not there." Unpublished autobiographical manuscript, Winifred Locket, "Reminiscences," Lady Margaret Hall Settlement.

38. Joseph Williamson, *Father Joe: The Autobiography of Joseph Williamson* (New York: Abingdon Press, 1963), 41.

39. For an analysis of the way class divided women's attitudes toward mothering, see Jane Lewis, *The Politics of Motherhood: Child and Maternal Welfare in England, 1900–1939* (London: Croom Helm, 1980).

40. Maude Royden, *Bid Me Discourse*, unpublished autobiography, ff. 18/19. Fawcett Library, London. On Royden, see Sheila Fletcher, *Maude Royden: A Life* (New York, NY: Basil Blackwell, 1989). Jane Addams also noted the ways in which the hands of the poor served as unforgettable markers of their plight in *Twenty Years at Hull-House* (Boston: Bedford/St. Martin's, 1999), 70.

41. On Langridge's work, see Sister Gertrude, *Mother Edith, O.M.S.E.: a Memoir* (Beaconsfield, UK: Darwen Finlayson, 1964). See also Janet Courtney, *The Women of My Time* (London: Hogarth, 1934), 104–106.

42. Muriel Lester, *Kill or Cure* (Nashville: Cokesbury Press, 1937), 11.

43. In the aftermath of her husband's death, the wealthy and radical Charlotte Despard decided to live among the poor in the Nine Elms section of south London in 1891. Her years there, and in particular her poor-law visiting and work in Lambeth propelled her toward socialism and feminism. See Andro Linklater, *An Unhusbanded Life, Charlotte Despard: Suffragette, Socialist, and Sinn Feiner* (London: Hutchinson, 1980), esp. chs. 4 and 5.

44. Katharine Bruce Glasier put the matter well: "To be willing to live 'clean' oneself in airy, spacious dwellings, and to do nothing to help cleanse the world for others is simply to be 'unclean' in soul." See Glasier, "The Labour Woman's Battle with Dirt" in Marion Phillips, ed., *Women and the Labour Party* (New York: B. W. Huebsch, 1918).

45. Martin's feminist politics were quite idiosyncratic, neither identifiably socialist nor Labourite.

46. Martin was tied to Cambridge intellectual circles through her eminent brother-in-law, Professor James Ward, the philosopher and psychologist.

47. Anna Martin, "The Married Working Woman," *Nineteenth Century* (December 1910), 1107.

48. Susan Pedersen contexualizes Martin's proposals within a broad range of

social policy alternatives. See Pedersen, *Family, Dependence, and the Origins of the Welfare State: Britain and France, 1914–1945* (Cambridge: Cambridge University Press, 1993), 44–45. Martin figures prominently in Ellen Ross's sensitive analysis of elite women's slum philanthropy. See Ross, *Love and Toil*, esp. ch. 7.

49. See Seth Koven, "Borderlands: Women, Voluntary Action, and Child Welfare in Britain, 1840–1914," in Seth Koven and Sonya Michel, *Mothers of a New World: Maternalist Politics and the Origins of Welfare States* (New York: Routledge, 1993).

50. On women social explorers and reformers, see Jane Lewis's perceptive comparison of Helen Dendy Bosanquet and Beatrice Potter Webb, "The Place of Social Investigation, Social Theory and Social Work in the Approach to Late Victorian and Edwardian Social Problems: The Case of Beatrice Webb and Helen Bosanquet," in Martin Bulmer, Kevin Bales, and K. K. Sklar, eds., *The Social Survey in Historical Perspective, 1880–1940* (Cambridge: Cambridge University Press, 1991); A. M. McBriar, *An Edwardian Mixed Doubles: The Bosanquets versus the Webbs: A Study in British Social Policy, 1890–1929* (Oxford: Clarendon Press, 1987).

51. Carolyn Steedman, *Landscape for a Good Woman: A Story of Two Lives* (London: Virago, 1986), 2.

52. All historians of dirt are deeply indebted to the perceptive and much-cited work of Mary Douglas, *Purity and Danger* (New York: Praeger, 1966). My work also reflects the influence of Carroll Smith-Rosenberg's pioneering articles collected in *Disorderly Conduct: Visions of Gender in Victorian America* (New York: A. A. Knopf, 1985).

53. Miss Edith M. Sing, *What Do We Mean by a Women's Settlement* (Liverpool, 1897), 6, pamphlet, Widener Library, Harvard University.

54. Maude Stanley, *Work about Five Dials* (London: Macmillan, 1878), 6–7.

55. Margaret Nevinson, *Life's Fitful Fever: A Volume of Memories* (London: A. and C. Black, 1926), 80.

56. Olive Schreiner to Edward Carpenter, in Richard Rive, ed., *Olive Schreiner Letters,* vol. 1, 1871–1899 (Oxford: Oxford University Press, 1988).

57. See Ruth Brandon, *The New Women and the Old Men* (New York: W. W. Norton, 1990), ch. 2, esp. 74, and Walkowitz, *City of Dreadful Delight*, ch. 5, on this "romance."

58. Norman and Jeanne Mackenzie, *Diary of Beatrice Webb*, vol. 1, entry for April 1884, 115. See Deborah Nord's compelling interpretation of Potter's relationship with Chamberlain and its relationship to her philanthropic and literary work in *The Apprenticeship of Beatrice Webb*. On Schreiner's and Potter's attempts to stifle their own sexual needs in favor of social altruism, see Janet Oppenheim, *"Shattered Nerves": Doctors, Patients, and Depression in Victorian England* (New York: Oxford University Press, 1991), 216–221.

59. Norman and Jeanne MacKenzie, *The Diary of Beatrice Webb,* vol. 1, 132.

60. Barbara Pym, *Excellent Women* (New York: Dutton, 1978), 231.

61. Pycroft to Potter, July 6, 1886, Passfield Papers. On the role of gossip in working-class life, see Melanie Tebbutt, *Women's Talk? A Social History of 'Gossip' in Working-Class Neighbourhoods, 1880–1960* (Aldershot, UK: Scolar Press, 1995).

62. Pycroft to Potter, October 8, 1886, Passfield Papers.

63. Mary Talbot recalled that the working-class girls with whom she worked could not believe that she did not have a "young man" and rejected her reply that she intended to be "an old maid." Mary Talbot, "Women's Settlements," *Economic Review* (October 1895): 498. Likewise, the local poor hoped that the spinster rent collector Ellen Chase would "soon have a handsome husband, and a happy married life." Ellen Chase, *Tenant Friends in Old Deptford*, with a preface by Octavia Hill (London: Williams and Norgate, 1929), 69.

64. *The Monthly Record of Bermondsey Settlement and the St. George's Social Club,* (October 1903), 101.

65. Ibid. (May 1896), 53.

66. Ibid. (October 1898), 103.

67. H. M. Hyndman, *Record of an Adventurous Life* (New York: The Macmillan Company, 1911), 51.

68. *The Monthly Record of the Bermondsey Settlement and the St. George's Social Club* (February 1907), 18.

69. For an example of this anxiety, see Mrs. Maitland, speech at annual meeting, *Fourth Annual Report* (1891), 8, Women's University Settlement.

70. Emmeline Pethick-Lawrence, *My Part in a Changing World* (London: V. Gollancz, 1938), 67, 72.

71. Rev. Free, "Settlements or Unsettlements," *Nineteenth Century* (March 1908), 377–378. Nina Auerbach insightfully provides a framework for interpreting Free's strident remarks. She argues that the "Victorian old maid claims her place among the angels, not in their self-negation, but in their militant and dangerous potential to reverse life's comfortably familiar order." See Nina Auerbach, *Woman and the Demon: The Life of a Victorian Myth* (Cambridge, MA: Harvard University Press, 1982), 117.

72. Winifred Locket, "Recollections of L.[ady] M.[argaret] H.[all] S[ettlement]," c. 1956, Lady Margaret Hall Settlement Papers.

73. Vicinus, *Independent Women*, 290.

74. Anna R. Tillyard, *Second Annual Report*, Canning Town Women's Settlement, 17.

75. There are no writings by women—published or unpublished—comparable to the sexually frank diaries and letters of J. A. Symonds, C. R. Ashbee, or Lytton Strachey; and no transcripts of "sexual" trials of women comparable to the cases of Bolton and Park, Cleveland Street, and Oscar Wilde, which have proved such rich sources in reconstructing the history of male same-sex desire.

76. This is historian Susan Pedersen's explanation for the nature of the surviving Rathbone papers and archives. Pedersen is completing a new biography of Rathbone. Private communication with author.

77. For this reason, Martha Vicinus, author of many pioneering essays on same-sex erotics, largely ignores sexuality in her fine treatment of women's settlement houses in London. See Vicinus, *Independent Women*, ch. 6.

78. On the relationship of purity and feminism, see Lucy Bland, *Banishing the Beast: Sexuality and the Early Feminists* (London: Penguin, 1995). Bland emphasizes the normality and acceptability of passionate same-sex friendships. See p. 120.

79. See Sheila Jeffreys's use of novels in *The Spinster and Her Enemies: Feminism and Sexuality, 1880–1930* (London: Pandora Press, 1985), ch. 6.

80. Emmeline Pethick-Lawrence acknowledged the powerful impact of novels about social problems on the emergence of her engagement with social issues. She recalled that Walter Besant's *The Children of Gibeon* "made a profound impression and lived in my mind continuously." See Emmeline Pethick-Lawrence, *My Part in a Changing World* (London: V. Gollancz, 1938), 67. Mary Higgs condemned modern novels, with their "coloured picture of life" and exaggerated emphasis on sex for contributing to female immorality and destitution (*Glimpses*, 318) and instead believed that the solution to female vagrancy "belongs to womanhood to befriend womanhood" (323).

81. Muriel Lester, *Kill or Cure* (Nashville: Cokesbury Press, 1937), 13.

82. Vernon Lee, *Miss Brown, A Novel* (Edinburgh and London: William Blackwood and Sons, 1884); L. T. Meade, *A Princess of the Gutter* (New York and London: G. P. Putnam, 1896). There is a growing body of work on Lee. The work most closely related to my own is by Diana Maltz, who first set me thinking about Lee at the outset of my book project. See Diana Maltz, "Engaging Delicate Brains: From Working-Class Enculturation to Upper-Class Lesbian Liberation in Vernon Lee's and Kit Anstruther-Thomson's Psychological Aesthetics," in Talia Schaffer and Kathy Alexis Psomiades, eds., *Women and British Aestheticism* (Charlottesville: University of Virginia Press, 1999), 211–229. The two major biographies of Lee are Peter Gunn, *Vernon Lee: Violet Paget, 1856–1935* (London: Oxford Univesity Press, 1964); and Burdett Gardner, *The Lesbian Imagination (Victorian Style), A Psychological and Critical Study of "Vernon Lee"* (New York: Garland, 1987), which is a facsimile print of the author's 1954 doctoral dissertation. Scholarly articles on Lee are proliferating and include Adeline Tintner, "Vernon Lee's Oke of Okehurst," in *Studies in Short Fiction* 28, no. 3 (1991): 355–362; Ruth Robbins, "Vernon Lee: Decadent Woman?" in John Stokes, ed., *Fin de Siècle/Fin du Globe* (Basingstoke: Macmillan, 1992); Phyllis Mannocchi, "Vernon Lee and Kit Anstruther-Thomson: A Study of Love and Collaboration between Two Romantic Friends," *Women's Studies* 12, no. 2 (1986): 129–148.

83. It is not entirely clear that Lee's origins were as exotic as she claimed. Peter Gunn suggests that her father fabricated his Russian origins. See Gunn, *Vernon Lee.*

84. James penned many short portraits of Lee in his letters. See Rayburn Moore, ed., *Selected Letters of Henry James to Edmund Gosse* (Baton Rouge: Louisiana State University Press, 1988), 46.

85. Vernon Lee to her mother, June 20, 1881, in Irene Cooper Willis, ed., *Vernon Lee's Letters* (privately printed, 1937), 65.

86. Vernon Lee, *Countess of Albany* (London: Allen and Co., 1884), 291.

87. Lee immediately became persona non grata with the Morris's and Rossetti's, who quite rightly recognized themselves in Lee's characterization of their art, poetry, and romances with lower-class girls.

88. Lee, *Countess of Albany*, 282.

89. Vernon Lee, *Euphorion* (London: T. F. Unwin, 1884), 8, 13.

90. Lee, *Countess of Albany*, 303.

91. Ellis and Symonds, *Sexual Inversion* (1897; repr. New York: Arno Press, 1975), 200, 221.

92. Vernon Lee, diary fragment, 1884, Vernon Lee Papers. On the use of the word morbid, see John Stokes, *In the Nineties* (Chicago: University of Chicago Press, 1989).

93. Vernon Lee to her mother, July 23, 1885, in Willis, *Vernon Lee's Letters* (1937), 181.

94. Vernon Lee, diary fragment, 1883, Vernon Lee Papers.

95. Terry Castle, "Sylvia Townsend Warner and the Counterplot of Lesbian Fiction," in Joseph Bristow, ed., *Sexual Sameness: Textual Differences in Lesbian and Gay Writing* (London: Routledge, 1992), 134.

96. Lee, who knew John Addington Symonds well through her companion Mary Robinson, must have been familiar with Symonds's work on Michaelangelo's sexual passion for men. She also was familiar with Michaelangelo's masculinized female nudes of the Medici tomb.

97. On Sacha's perverse sexuality, see Ronald Pearsall, *Worm in the Bud: The World of Victorian Sexuality* (London: Weidenfeld and Nicolson, 1969) 484–485; on vampirism and dissident female sexuality, see Bram Dijkstra, *Idols of Perversity: Fantasies of Feminine Evil in Fin-de-Siècle Culture* (Oxford: Oxford University Press, 1986), ch. 10; and Nina Auerbach, *Our Vampires, Ourselves* (Chicago: University of Chicago Press, 1995).

98. Hamlin's divided self anticipates Robert Louis Stevenson's Dr. Jekyll and Mr. Hyde.

99. Kathy Psomiades, "'Still Burning from this Strangling Embrace': Vernon Lee on Desire and Aesthetics" in Richard Dellamora, ed., *Victorian Sexual Dissidence* (Chicago: University of Chicago Press, 1999), 26.

100. Here, I am modifying Linda Dowling's subtle analysis of the relationship of male homosexuality and hellenism. Dowling contends that the coded language used to express same-sex desire "does not operate as a simple inversion of the dominant discourse," but instead assumes a "discontinuous and constantly shifting relationship to the discourse of the dominant group" whose discourse is itself unstable. Linda Dowling, "Ruskin's Pied Beauty and the Constitution of a 'Homosexual Code,'" *Victorian Newsletter* 75 (1989): 1–8; see also her extended study, *Hellenism and Homosexuality in Victorian Oxford* (Ithaca: Cornell University Press, 1994).

101. Toynbee Hall, with its own tradition of tolerating sexual dissidence, was among her favorite slum destinations. See Willis, *Vernon Lee's Letters*, 341–342.

102. Vernon Lee to her mother, August 26, 1893, ibid., 362–363.

103. The dedication reads, "To Henry James I Dedicate, for Good Luck, My First Attempt at a Novel." The description of James's kindness comes from a letter Vernon Lee wrote to her mother in July 1884. See Willis, *Vernon Lee's Letters*, 155. James's relationship to Lee and Miss Brown was the subject of a series of articles and notes in the *PMLA* in 1953/54. See Carl Weber, "Henry James and His Tiger Cat," and Burdett Gardner, "An Apology for Henry James's 'Tiger Cat,'" in *PMLA* 68 (Sept. 1953): 672–687; and Leon Edel, "Henry James and Vernon Lee," *PMLA* 69 (June 1954).

104. Henry James to T. S. Perry, December 12, 1884, in Leon Edel, ed., *Henry James Letters*, vol. 3 (Cambridge: Belknap Press, 1980), 61. Lee was not the only author to dedicate a novel to James that explored morbid sexual themes. Howard Overing Sturgis dedicated his 1891 novel, *Tim*, about the love of two

Eton boys for one another, to James. James condemned the book and refused to communicate with its author. See Timothy D'Arch Smith, *Love in Earnest* (London: Routledge, 1970), 8.

105. Henry James to Vernon Lee, May 10, 1885, in Edel, *Henry James Letters*, vol. 3, 84–87.

106. See Henry James, *The Princess Casamassima* (New York: Penguin, 1985), 171, 427. A substantial body of literary criticism analyzes the theme of "homosexual panic" in James's writings, much of it inspired by Eve Sedgwick's *Epistemology of the Closet* (Berkeley: University of California Press, 1990). See also, "The Beast in the Closet: James and the Writing of Homosexual Panic," in Ruth Yeazell, ed., *Sex, Politics and Science in the Nineteenth Century Novel* (Baltimore: Johns Hopkins University Press, 1986).

107. The fullest analysis of "marginal masculinity" in James's *Princess* is Kelly Cannon, *Henry James and Masculinity* (New York: St. Martin's Press, 1994), esp. 45–47 and 94–95. Cannon underscores Hyacinth's refusal of both masculine aggression and the consummation of heterosexuality through marriage.

108. "Mrs. L. T. Meade at Home," *Sunday Magazine* 23 (1894), 616.

109. "How I Write My Books. An Interview with Mrs. L. T. Meade," *The Young Woman* 1 (1892–93), 122.

110. Sally Mitchell argues that by the mid-1870s Meade "had many of the characteristics that would make her a New Woman when the term became popular in the 1890s." See *The New Girl: Girls' Culture in England, 1880–1915* (New York: Columbia University Press, 1995), 10. Mitchell interprets Meade's various names somewhat differently than I do.

111. Helen Black, *Pen, Pencil, Baton and Mask, Biographical Sketches* (London: Spottiswoode, 1896), 226–227.

112. L. T. Meade, "A Peep at the Pioneer Club," *Young Woman* 4 (1895–96), 304, as quoted in Sally Mitchell, *The New Girl*, 10. On the Pioneer Club and, more generally, the institutions supporting activist women in the 1890s, see David Rubinstein's judicious study *Before the Suffragettes: Women's Emancipation in the 1890s* (London: Harvester, 1986), 222–25.

113. On the complexities of women's names and their social identities, see Kali Israel, *Names and Stories: Emilia Dilke and Victorian Culture* (New York: Oxford University Press, 1999).

114. Soon after its creation, Meade reported the aims of the SPCC in an article to the periodical devoted to philanthropy in East London, *Eastward Ho!* See L. T. Meade, "London Society for the Prevention of Cruelty to Children," *Eastward Ho!* (May 1885).

115. *Scamp and I* (London: John F. Shaw, 1892) chronicles the adventures of two street urchins, Flo and Dick, and their dog, Scamp, who is stolen and fated to be used in a vicious dog fight. It features several women philanthropists associated with Miss Octavia Hill's Courts (91).

116. L. T. Meade, "Story Writing for Girls," *The Academy and Literature Fiction Supplement* (November 7, 1903), 499.

117. "Mrs. L. T. Meade at Home," 620.

118. As Sally Mitchell has shown, the "girl culture" Meade helped to create through her novels and journalism celebrated the passionately affectionate ho-

mosocial worlds of girls' schools and women's colleges and settlement houses. Although Mitchell acknowledges the suggestion of homoeroticism in Meade's novels, she ultimately argues that such psychosexual interpretations would impose a modern sensibility on how Victorian girls read and understood Meade. Mitchell, *New Girl*, ch. 6, esp. 164–168.

119. There are dozens of these sort of comic references to the need of spinsters to find a man. See Ellen Chase, *Tenant Friends in Old Deptford* (London: Williams & Norgate, 1929), 68–69.

120. The term "rough gel" never achieved the popularity or homoerotic valences of its masculine counterpart, "rough lad." On the meaning of the later, see Seth Koven, "Rough Lads and Hooligans," in Andrew Parker et al., eds., *Nationalisms and Sexualities* (New York: Routledge, 1992).

121. By the 1930s, some female reformers were able to look back on the relationships they had witnessed in their youth at women's colleges and settlements and see them in sexual terms.

122. I analyze this scene and Harkness's social scientific, journalistic, and novelistic writings about poverty in "Converting East London: Sexuality, Salvationism, and Jewishness in Victorian East London." Paper presented at the Mid-Atlantic Conference of British Studies, March 2000, New York, NY.

123. Wragge, *The London I Loved*, 13.

124. Martha Vicinus, "Distance and Desire: English Boarding School Friendships, 1870–1920," *Signs* 9 (1984): 600–622.

125. There are many subtle homoerotic scenes, such as the moment when Joan lets down her gorgeous chestnut hair for Martha's benefit (131) or Martha's passionate declaration of love for Joan from her sickbed. As Joan nurses Martha during her illness, Martha proclaims, "I love you Jo-an; I think o' you day and night. There ain't nothing I wouldn't do for you—nothing—nothing" (185).

126. Edward Carpenter, *The Intermediate Sex* (London: G. Allen, 1912), 13, 72.

127. As Carroll Smith-Rosenberg observed, Havelock Ellis also noted the connection between emancipated women and lesbianism in *Sexual Inversion*. See "Discourses of Sexuality and Subjectivity: The New Woman, 1870–1936" in *Disorderly Conduct* (New York: A. A. Knopf, 1985).

128. My thanks to Martha Vicinus for suggesting the way Meade worked within this particular genre of writing about girls.

129. *Athenaeum* (October 17, 1896), 522.

130. Mitchell, *New Girl*, 21.

131. *Saturday Review* (November 30, 1895), 714.

132. See Gay Wachman, *Lesbian Empire: Radical Crosswriting in the Twenties* (New Brunswick, NJ: Rutgers University Press, 2001).

133. Virginia Woolf, *A Room of One's Own* (New York: Harcourt, Brace and Co., 1929), ch. 5, para. 1.

134. Roy Devereux [Mrs. Roy Pember-Devereux], *The Ascent of Woman* (London: John Lane, 1896), 58–59, 64.

135. The struggle over the representation of women in suffrage debates is brilliantly analyzed in Lisa Tickner, *The Spectacle of Women: Imagery of the Suffrage Campaign 1907–1914* (Chicago: University of Chicago Press, 1988), part 4, "Representation."

136. On the connections between dirt, domesticity, and domestic sciences in the United States, see Lynne Vallone's excellent essay, "'The True Meaning of Dirt': Putting Good and Bad Girls in Their Place(s)," in Claudia Nelson and Lynne Vallone, eds., *The Girl's Own: Cultural Histories of the Anglo-American Girl, 1830–1915* (Athens, GA: University of Georgia Press, 1994). On the emergence of women's scientific social work in Germany as a profession for middle-class women, especially Jewish women, see Marion Kaplan, *The Making of the Jewish Middle Class: Women, Family, and Identity in Imperial Germany* (New York: Oxford University Press, 1991), ch. 7.

137. For a sample of the syllabi of courses taught in sociology and in home economics, see *Calendar of King's College* [London], 1897–98, section on Department for Ladies, Kensington Square, 292–345. The department was later renamed King's College for Women. My thanks to Molly Sutphen for sending me copies of these calendars for several years.

138. Anna Martin, "The Married Working Woman," *Nineteenth Century* (December 1910), 1107.

139. Some few women, such as Beatrice Potter Webb, claimed for themselves the masculine privileges of the sociologist, but Webb consistently saw herself as an exceptional woman whose intellectual prowess entitled her to play a leading role in a variety of otherwise all-male political and intellectual settings.

140. Elmy to Harriet McIlquham, May 18, 1898, ff. 212, ms. 47451, Elmy Papers.

141. Not all female social workers supported such measures. An important minority associated with the Charity Organisation Society remained quite hostile to such infringements on family life. Catherine Davies, a member of a London County Council Care Committee in south London, was appointed to visit the homes of families receiving free meals under the act. She was quite critical of the act and its promotion of an unnatural dependence on the state in a report published in the *Charity Organisation Review*. See Catherine Davies, "Problems of Charity. Care Committee Home Visiting," *Charity Organisation Review* (April 1908), 218–219. For another interpretation of state welfare as a misguided and dangerous solution to "dirt" in poor women's lives, see Helen Dendy Bosanquet's many books, including *Rich and Poor* (London: Macmillan, 1896).

142. Miss A. T. Thompson, "National and Municipal Demands for Local Voluntary Work," *Charity Organisation Review* (July 1914), 48; see also Clara Grant's description of the transformation of her unofficial and voluntary work into an official function of the London County Council in *Farthing Bundles* (London: A. & E. Walter, 1931), 80–81. See Ellen Ross, "'Human Communion' or a Free Lunch: School Dinners in Victorian and Edwardian London," in J. B. Schneewind, ed., *Giving: Western Ideas of Philanthropy* (Bloomington, IN: University of Indian Press, 1996), 179–198 on the transformation of female-dominated care committees from private philanthropic to municipal bodies with the creation of the London County Council Care Committees.

143. Aldous Huxley, foreword (1946) to *Brave New World* (New York: Harper and Row, 1939; Bantam Modern Classic Edition, 1968), vii.

144. Wragge, *The London I Loved*, 53.

CHAPTER FIVE
THE "NEW MAN" IN THE SLUMS: RELIGION, MASCULINITY, AND THE MEN'S
SETTLEMENT HOUSE MOVEMENT

1. Rev. Montagu Butler, "Love the Brotherhood,"*Oxford Magazine* (October 31, 1883), 344.

2. Rev. Brooke Lambert, "The Outcast Poor. 1. Esau's Cry," *Contemporary Review* (December 1883), 916.

3. Samuel Barnett, "The Failure of Philanthropy," *Macmillan's Magazine* (March 1896), 396.

4. Historians have examined the contributions of male settlement house residents (most often called settlers) to social policy, philanthropy, and the church's mission to the poor. See Gareth Stedman Jones, *Outcast London: A Study in the Relationship between Classes in Victorian Society* (Oxford: Clarendon Press, 1971); Standish Meacham, *Toynbee Hall and the Search for Community* (New Haven, CT: Yale University Press, 1987); Asa Briggs and Anne Macartney; *Toynbee Hall: The First Hundred Years* (London: Routledge and K. Paul, 1984); Hugh McLeod, *Class and Religion in the Late Victorian City* (Hamden, CT: Archon Books, 1974); Kenneth Inglis, *Churches and the Working Classes in Victorian England* (London: Routledge and K. Paul, 1963); on Toynbee Hall and art, see Frances Borzello, *Civilising Caliban: The Misuse of Art, 1875–1980* (London: Routledge and K. Paul, 1987); and Peter D'Alroy Jones, *The Christian Socialist Revival: Religion, Class, and Social Conscience in Late Victorian England* (Princeton: Princeton University Press, 1968). The best analysis of Toynbee Hall remains Emily Klein Abel, "Canon Barnett and the First Thirty Years of Toynbee Hall" (Ph.D. diss., University of London, 1969). The work of David McIlhiney pays close attention to the religious differences between Toynbee Hall and Oxford House but is riddled with factual inaccuracies and unsubstantiated judgments about the two settlements. See "A Gentleman in Every Slum: Church of England Missions in East London, 1837–1914," Ph.D. diss., Princeton University, 1976. Geoff Ginn offers a meticulously researched comparison between Toynbee Hall and the People's Palace with an emphasis on the role of cultural philanthropy in the slums: "Gifts of Culture, Centres of Light: Cultural Philanthropy in the late Victorian East End" (Ph.D. diss., University of Queensland, 2001). Sara Burke has traced the transplantation of the English settlement ideal to Canada in *Seeking the Highest Good: Social Science and Gender at the University of Toronto, 1888–1937* (Toronto: University of Toronto Press, 1996). See also Kevin Murphy's treatment of sexual dissidence in male settlements in New York in "Socrates in the Slums: Homoerotics, Gender, and Settlement House Reform" in Laura McCall and Donald Yacovone, eds., *A Shared Experience: Men, Women, and Gender in U.S. History* (New York: New York University Press, 1998). Michael Rose has pioneered comparative work in Britain and the United States and has moved outside London in examining the British movement; see his "Settlement of University Men in Great Towns: University Settlements in Manchester and Liverpool," *Transactions of the Historic Society of Lancashire and Cheshire* (1989): 137–160; and "The Settlement House and Social Welfare:

Britain and the United States," *Working Papers in Economic and Social History,* University of Manchester, no. 6 (January 1991).

5. In his book *Making Men*, Waldo Eagar stresses the role of settlers in attempting to make men out of working-class boys but entirely ignores settlers' own attempts to remake themselves into new kinds of men. See *Making Men: The History of Boys' Clubs and Related Movements in Great Britain* (London: University of London Press, 1953), esp. ch. 6. Eagar was a resident at Oxford House in 1907. See *The Oxford House Chronicle* 21, no. 7 (July 1907): 1.

6. On the definition of aestheticism and the complex social and cultural affiliations it encouraged, see Diana Maltz, "Aestheticism in the Slums: University Settlements and the Case of the Toynbee Travellers," unpublished essay in author's possession. See also Ian Fletcher, "Some Aspects of Aestheticism," in O. M. Brack, Jr., ed., *Twilight of Dawn: Studies of English Literature in Transition* (Tucson, AZ: University of Arizona Press, 1987). See also Ruth Z. Temple, "Truth in Labelling: Pre-Raphaelitism, Aestheticism, Decadence, Fin-de-Siècle," *English Literature in Transition* 17 (1974).

7. On the links between aestheticism and dissident sexuality, see Richard Dellamore, *Masculine Desire: The Sexual Politics of Victorian Aestheticism* (Chapel Hill, NC: University of North Carolina Press, 1990).

8. See Daniel Rodgers's account of the impact of what he calls "aesthetic tourists" in shaping social politics in *Atlantic Crossings: Social Politics in a Progressive Age* (Cambridge, MA: Harvard University Press, 1998), 41–44; on aesthetics and urban social reform in Britain, see Helen Meller, ed., and introduction to Samuel Barnett, *The Ideal City* (1894: repr. Leicester: Leicester University Press, 1979).

9. Susan Pennybacker, *A Vision for London, 1889–1914: Labour, Everyday Life, and the LCC Experiment* (London: Routledge, 1995); see also Paul Thompson, *Socialists, Liberals, and Labour: The Struggle for London, 1885–1914* (London: Routledge & K. Paul, 1967).

10. On Maurice's inspiration, see Thomas Hughes to Samuel Barnett, December 31, 1878, Barnett Papers, Lambeth Palace Library.

11. On the tension between universalist and exclusionary uses of fraternity in France, see Felicity Baker, "Rousseau's Oath and Revolutionary Fraternity: 1789 and Today," *Romance Quarterly* 38 (August 1991): 273–287.

12. The publication of Hurrell Froude's *Remains*, with its revelation of his macabre fascination with bodily self-mortification, coupled with Newman's conversion to Roman Catholicism, merely confirmed the fears of the movement's most virulent critics that the movement was "unEnglish and unmanly." See David Hilliard, "UnEnglish and Unmanly: Anglo-Catholicism and Homosexuality," *Victorian Studies* 25 (Winter 1982): 181–210. For the links between Anglo-Catholicism and homosexuality in the mid-twentieth century, see Tom Driberg's autobiography *Ruling Passions* (London: Jonathan Cape, 1977), 16, 48. Driberg explicitly linked his pursuit of sex with working-class men and youths with his political radicalism and love of high Anglican ritualism. He saw nothing hypocritical about his various sets of sexual and political desires.

13. See Boyd Hilton, *The Age of Atonement: The Influence of Evangelicalism*

on Social and Economic Thought, 1785–1865 (Oxford: Oxford University Press, 1988).

14. Maurice insisted that "working men should understand that they are brothers, and can work together as brothers." Maurice wrote these words in support of the Society for Promoting Working Men's Associations in the *Christian Socialist* (December 5, 1848), as quoted in John Ludlow, *The Autobiography of a Christian Socialist*, ed. and introduction, A. D. Murray (London: F. Cass, 1981), 228.

15. Charles Kingsley, "Priests and People," vol. 2 of *Alton Locke* (New York: J. F. Taylor, 1899), 329.

16. Shaftesbury to Albert, as quoted in Frank Prochaska, *Royal Bounty: The Making of the Welfare Monarchy* (New Haven: Yale University Press, 1995), 84.

17. *First Circular of the Working Men's College*, as quoted in J.F.C. Harrison, *A History of the Working Men's College, 1854–1954* (London: Routledge and Paul, 1954), 21.

18. Frederick Denison Maurice, *Scheme* as quoted in Harrison, *Working Men's College*, 91.

19. The mingling of radical and reactionary ideas is one of the central themes of Raymond Williams, *Culture and Society, 1780–1950* (New York: Columbia University Press, 1958; reprint with new introduction by the author, 1983).

20. The concept of the Victorian sage was itself gendered as Carol Christ shows in "The Hero as Man of Letters: Masculinity and Victorian Nonfiction Prose," in Thaïs Morgan, ed., *Victorian Sages and Cultural Discourse: Renegotiating Gender and Power* (New Brunswick, NJ: Rutgers University Press, 1990).

21. Henrietta Barnett, *Canon Barnett, His Life, Work, and Friends*, vol. 1 (Boston: Houghton Mifflin, 1919), 59, 72.

22. Henry Scott Holland to Legard, March 1870, as quoted in Stephen Paget, ed., *Henry Scott Holland: Memoir and Letters* (London: J. Murray, 1921), 46.

23. Elaine Showalter notes that "fin-de-siècle Clubland existed on the fragile borderline that separated male bonding from homosexuality and that distinguished manly misogyny from disgusting homoeroticism." See Elaine Showalter, *Sexual Anarchy: Gender and Culture at the Fin de Siècle* (New York: Viking Penguin, 1990), 13. There were some notable exceptions to the all-male clubs, including the mixed-sex Whittington Club, which had been founded in 1846 along self-managed principles with an intended lower-middle-class clientele. See Christopher Kent, "The Whittington Club: A Bohemian Experiment in Middle Class Social Reform," *Victorian Studies* 18 (September 1974): 31–55.

24. Anonymous, "Anecdote and Gossip about Clubs," *London Society Magazine* (February 1867), 102–103.

25. That great chronicler of clubs and club life in London John Timbs conceded that clubs may not have existed in the time of Adam and Eve, but he felt sure they played an important role in the life of ancient Athens and Sparta. "Clubbism" was an engrained part of human nature, an offshoot of "man's habitually gregarious and social inclination" and the full flowering of clubs in London merely confirmed England's standing at the apex of civilization. See John Timbs, *Clubs and Club Life in London* (London: Chatto and Windus, 1872), 1–2.

26. Peter Gay associates these all male institutions with anxieties about women's activism and emerging feminism. See *The Bourgeois Experience: Victoria to Freud*, vol. 1 (New York: Oxford University Press, 1984), 288.

27. On rational recreation, see Peter Bailey, *Leisure and Class in Victorian England: Rational Recreation and the Contest for Control, 1830–1885* (London: Routledge and Kegan Paul, 1978); and Hugh Cunningham, *Leisure in the Industrial Revolution* (London: Croom Helm, 1980).

28. In 1871, it was still possible for C. E. Maurice to view trade unions as institutions capable of promoting a form of fraternity that would redefine the concept of liberty in England. See C. E. Maurice, "Fraternity," *Contemporary Review* (October 1871), 407–415.

29. See Sonya Rose's analysis of male trade unionists' desire to preserve male wages and work prerogatives from encroachment by women workers in *Limited Livelihoods: Gender and Class in Nineteenth Century England* (Berkeley, CA: University of California Press, 1992) esp. ch. 6.

30. See Stephen Yeo, "A New Life: The Religion of Socialism in Britain, 1883–1896," *History Workshop Journal* 4 (Autumn 1977): 5–56. Many leading male socialists puritanically frowned upon the "irrational" and "profligate" habits and leisure activities of their popular constituencies. See Chris Waters, *British Socialists and the Politics of Popular Culture, 1884–1914* (Stanford, CA: Stanford University Press, 1990). In addition, many male socialists' theoretical commitment to gender equality did not deter them from demanding that their female comrades subordinate sex-specific demands to the movement's distinctly male-centered political and social agenda. See Karen Hunt, *Equivocal Feminists: The Social Democratic Federation and the Woman Question, 1884–1911* (Cambridge: Cambridge University Press, 1996).

31. On Carpenter, see Sheila Rowbotham and Jeffrey Weeks, *Socialism and the New Life: The Personal and Sexual Politics of Edward Carpenter and Havelock Ellis* (London: Pluto Press, 1977).

32. Edward Carpenter, *The Intermediate Sex: A Study of Some Transitional Types of Men and Women* (London: G. Allen and Unwin, 1908). Julie Taddeo explores the fraternal and homoerotic sexual ideologies and practices of the Cambridge Apostles at the turn of the twentieth century in *Lytton Strachey and the Search for Modern Sexual Identity: The Last Eminent Victorian* (New York: Harrington Park Press, 2002), ch. 1.

33. For a study of one of these institutions, see Keith Laybourn, "The Guild of Help and the Changing Face of Edwardian Philanthropy," *Urban History* 20 (1993): 43–60.

34. The phrase is Anne Phillips' from her essay, "Fraternity," in Ben Pimlott, ed., *Fabian Essays in Social Thought* (London: Heinemann, 1984), 232.

35. See Alison Light, *Forever England: Femininity, Literature, and Conservatism between the Wars* (London: Routledge, 1991), 10.

36. On fraternity in the United States and its association with middle-class men belonging to fraternal orders such as the Odd Fellows, see Mark Carnes, "Middle-Class Men and the Solace of Fraternal Ritual," in Mark Carnes and Clyde Griffen, *Meanings for Manhood: Constructions of Masculinity in Victorian America* (Chicago: University of Chicago Press, 1990).

37. See G. S. Jones's superb account of this in *Outcast London* (London: Clarendon Press, 1971).

38. Barnett's growing frustration with the constraints of his work as a sort of mission-priest manqué is most evident in his annual parochial reports for St. Jude's, Whitechapel, and in his parish magazine. See Samuel Barnett's *Pastoral Addresses and Report of the Parish Work, St. Jude's, Whitechapel*, published annually, in British Library. See L. E. Nettleship, "William Fremantle, Samuel Barnett, and the Broad Church Origins of Toynbee Hall," *Journal of Ecclesiastical History* 33 (October 1982): 564–579.

39. See Seth Koven, "The Whitechapel Picture Exhibitions and the Politics of Seeing," in Daniel Sherman and Irit Rogoff, eds., *Museum Culture: Histories, Discourses, Spectacles* (Minneapolis: University of Minnesota Press, 1994).

40. Samuel Barnett, "A Modern Monastery: A Suggestion for a Mission," draft of speech, c. 1883, ms. 1466, ff 34, Barnett Papers. Lambeth Palace Library.

41. On Carlyle's vision of masculinity and homosocial dynamics, see Herbert Sussman, *Victorian Masculinities* (Cambridge: Cambridge University Press, 1994).

42. See H. Barnett, *Canon Barnett*, vol 1, 308.

43. The bitter controversies within the Church of England, surrounding monastic paradigms of religious organization, which were widely denounced as un-English and unmanly, bore no relation to the small numbers of men and women who actually entered sisterhoods and brotherhoods from mid-century onward. There is a growing and excellent body of work on single-sex religious communities in the nineteenth century. On sisterhoods, see Martha Vicinus, *Independent Women* (London: Virago, 1985), ch. 2; Susan Mumm, *Stolen Daughters, Virgin Mothers: Anglican Sisterhood in Victorian Britain* (London: Leicester University Press, 1999). On male and female religious communities within the Church of England, see Arthur Allchin, *The Silent Rebellion: Anglican Religious Communities, 1845–1900* (London: SCM Press, 1958); P. Bull, *The Revival of Religious Life for Men* (London: Richard Jackson, 1904); Rene Kollar, "Anglican Brotherhoods and Urban Social Work," *Churchman* 101, no. 2 (1987): 140–145; see also his *Abbot Aelred Carlyle, Caldey Island, and the Anglo-Catholic Revival in England* (New York: Peter Lang, 1995).

44. Despite Barnett's best efforts, several contemporary observers detected a distinctly monastic odor at Toynbee Hall. Henry Wood Nevinson called Barnett the Abbot of Toynbee Hall, "a monastic establishment where there were no vows." See Henry Wood Nevinson, *Changes and Chances* (New York: Harcourt, Brace and Company, 1924), 91. That quintessential aesthete, Selwyn Image, affectionately wrote to the renowned Arts and Crafts designer Mackmurdo in March of 1885, that he had just been to "St. Barnett's of Whitechapel" after a visit to Toynbee Hall. See Selwyn Image to Mackmurdo, March 26, 1885, Image Papers. Ironically, in recent years the Church of England has all but transformed Samuel and Henrietta into saints. Their anniversary is now celebrated in the Anglican calendar.

45. Barnett wrote to his brother Francis that "the Settlement will not add to the hardness of life, in every way it is likely to bring ease. We shall live in space, comfort, and quiet." Samuel Barnett to F. G. Barnett, March 1, 1884, F/Bar/2, Barnett Papers, London Metropolitan Archives.

46. See Samuel Barnett, "The Ways of 'Settlements' and of 'Missions,'" *Nineteenth Century* (December 1897), 977. In a letter to Jane Addams, Barnett insisted that the distinction "is one to be remembered if we wld. [would] preserve settlements from becoming what Mat Arnold called 'machinery.'" See Samuel Barnett to Jane Addams, September 20, 1897, Addams Papers.

47. Dr. Perceval used the occasion of his university sermon in January 1883 to explain that a man could only love God by loving his brother. See Dr. Perceval, University Sermon, *Oxford Magazine* (January 24, 1883), 14.

48. "Democracy and Culture, A Rejoinder" *Oxford Magazine* (February 14, 1883), 67. A decade later, the slum journalist G. R. Sims observed that "The Christian philanthropist of to-day is peculiar in his tastes. He loves his brother as himself, but always seems to select for special affection the brother who is a murderer or a miscreant, and a black murderer or miscreant for choice." G. R. Sims, "Mustard and Cress," *Referee* (October 15, 1893), 7. See David Hilliard "UnEnglish and UnManly"; and James Adams, *Dandies and Desert Saints: Styles of Victorian Manhood* (Ithaca, NY: Cornell University Press, 1995), 98–99 for his sensible correction of Hilliard's emphases and his more nuanced chronology of the conditions leading to the identification of Oxford movement effeminacy with sexual deviance. See also G. C. Faber, *Oxford Apostles: A Character Study of the Oxford Movement* (London: Faber and Faber, 1933).

49. For a treatment of a similar configuration of religious, reformist, and sexual desires in the American context during a somewhat later period, see George Chauncey, Jr., "Christian Brotherhood or Sexual Perversion? Homosexual Identities and the Construction of Sexual Boundaries in the World War I Era," *Journal of Social History* 19 (1985): 189–212.

50. In explaining the rise of the settlement movement, Barnett singled out Green's influence: "Men at the Universities, especially those who directly or indirectly felt the influence of T. H. Green, were asking for some other way than that of institutions by which to reach their neighbours." "University Settlements," in Will Reason, ed., *University and Social Settlements* (London: Methuen and Co., 1898), 12.

51. On Green, see Melvin Richter, *Politics of Conscience: T. H. Green and His Age* (Cambridge, MA: Harvard University Press, 1964); see also Andrew Vincent and Raymond Plant, *Philosophy, Politics, and Citizenship: The Life and Thought of the British Idealists* (Oxford: B. Blackwell, 1984); and Andrew Vincent, "T. H. Green and the Religion of Citizenship," in Andrew Vincent, ed., *The Philosophy of T. H. Green* (Aldershot, UK: Gower, 1986).

52. The archly admiring description was that of Clara Collet, who would soon work with Charles Booth on his monumental survey of London. See "Diary of an Assistant School Mistress," manuscript diary of Clara Collet, March 30, 1882, ms. 29/8/2, Collet Papers. On Toynbee, see Alon Kadish's excellent, *Apostle Arnold: The Life and Death of Arnold Toynbee* (Durham, NC: Duke University Press, 1986).

53. The Barnetts' ideas about personal service drew upon the writings and experiences of Edward Denison, son of the Bishop of Salisbury and an Oxford graduate, who had lived and worked among the poor in the 1860s. On Denison,

see Sir Baldwyn Leighton, ed., *Letters and Other Writings of the late Edward Denison, M. P. for Newark* (London: Richard Bentley and Son, 1872).

54. J. R. Green to W. Boyd Dawkins, April 1864, St. Peter's Parsonage, Stepney, as quoted in Leslie Stephen, ed., *Letters of John Richard Green* (London: Macmillan and Co., 1902), 143. In response to women's growing presence in the slums as charity workers, Green affectionately satirized their efforts in his "stray study" entitled "The District Visitor." In Green's eyes, the district visitor combined and surpassed the powers of her masculine counterparts, the parson and the almoner. Free from "manly" inhibitions, she "retails tittle tattle for the highest ends." He concluded that her influence over the poor "is a strange mixture of good and evil, of real benevolence with an interference that saps all sense of self respect, of real sympathy and womanly feeling with a good deal of womanly meddling, curiosity, and babble." See J. R. Green, "The District Visitor" in *Stray Studies from England and Italy* (New York: Harper and Brothers, 1876), 277.

55. See William Grey, "Recollections of Work Amongst the London Poor," (1889), 18, which was a published version of a talk he gave at Johns Hopkins to social science students on January 12, 1889. This pamphlet also includes extensive citations from "Leaves from the Summer Diary of an East End Almoner," originally published in the *Charity Organization Review* (January 1886).

56. Alan Sinfield notes that "the more the economy depended on brutal entrepreneurs, the more it seemed that the middle classes should evince the sensitivity and responsibility that they imagined had characterized the ancient gentleman." Alan Sinfield, *The Wilde Century: Effeminacy, Oscar Wilde, and the Queer Moment* (New York: Columbia University Press, 1994), 58.

57. T. H. Escott described the typical settlement house resident in the East End as "a gentleman in the prime of early and athletic manhood." See Escott, *Social Transformations of the Victorian Age* (London: Seeley and Co., 1897), 116–117. On openness to new modes of thoughts and action, see Henry Nevinson's description of the early 1880s as "a time of adventure and life renewed . . . of infinitely varied experiment." See *Changes and Chances* (London: Nisbet and Co., 1923), 110. Helen Lynd identified the "chief significance of the eighties" as the "beginning of a new phase in the recurrent struggle for individual freedom." See her still valuable classic study, *England in the Eighteen-Eighties: Toward a Social Basis for Freedom* (London: Oxford University Press, 1945), 9. For her assessment of settlements in relation to the church's outreach to the poor, see 321–324.

58. Samuel Barnett to Francis Gilmore Barnett, July 1888, F/Bar/78, Barnett Papers, London Metropolitan Archives.

59. See Helen Meller's assessment of Barnett views about culture and the city in Meller, *The Ideal City*.

60. The phrase comes from a letter written by Edward Denison on August 7, 1867 about the evils within communities that lacked "resident gentry" and the corrective power of gentlemen willing to work and live among the poor. See Sir Baldwyn Leighton, ed., *Letters and Other Writings of the late Edward Denison, M.P. for Newark* (London: Richard Bentley and Son, 1872), 37.

61. Samuel Barnett, "University Settlements in Great Towns," *Oxford Magazine* (November 21, 1883), 387.

62. C.G.L., "Letter to the Editor on University Settlements," *Oxford Magazine* (November 21, 1883), 397.

63. The Rev. Warden of Keble, Edward Talbot, sermon delivered at St. Mary's, January 27, 1884, *Oxford Magazine* (January 30, 1884), 28.

64. E. S. Talbot, Bishop of Rochester, Annual Meeting of Oxford House, held at Keble College, as quoted in *Oxford House Chronicle* (June 1896), 3.

65. Lavinia Talbot diary, March 7, 1884, Talbot Papers.

66. On Samuel's admiration for and disappointment in Hill, see Samuel Barnett to Francis Gilmore Barnett, March 1, 1884, F/Bar/2, Barnett Papers, London Metropolitan Archives.

67. Samuel Barnett to Francis Gilmore Barnett as quoted in Henrietta Barnett, *Life*, vol. 2, 29.

68. See S. C. Carpenter, *Winnington-Ingram: The Biography of Arthur Foley Winnington-Ingram, Bishop of London, 1901–1939* (London: Hodder and Stoughton, 1949).

69. On this shelter, see Charles Bethune and Harold Boulton, "Houseless at Night," *Fortnightly Review* (February 1887), 318–320; and Harold Boulton, "A London House of Shelter," *Fortnightly Review* (February 1894), 215–224. The annual reports of Oxford House always included a summary of the shelter's work during the year.

70. For the COS's cautious assessment of Oxford House and its House of Shelter "of a somewhat antediluvian character" see COS file on Oxford House, especially C. S. Loch to Edward Bond, June 5, 1890, A/FWA/C/D164/1, COS Files and Papers.

71. Diary of Lavinia Talbot, May 4, 1884, Talbot Papers.

72. Warden Spooner, autobiographical fragments, no. p., n.d., Spooner Papers.

73. See James Adderley, *Stephen Remarx: The Story of a Venture in Ethics* (New York: Dutton, 1894), 50. This short quasi-autobiographical novel was a surprise best-seller after being rejected by twenty publishers. Adderley's fame in his lifetime was always linked to his authorship of *Stephen Remarx*.

74. James Adderley as quoted in T. P. Stevens, *Father Adderley* (London: T. W. Laurie, 1943), 14.

75. In 1905, Samuel Barnett wrote that settlers "must live their own life. There must be no affectation of asceticism." See H. Barnett, *Canon Barnett*, vol. 1, 312.

76. For a detailed analysis of the paternalistic ideology of settlement houses by an architectural historian, see Deborah E. B. Weiner, *Architecture and Social Reform in Late-Victorian London* (Manchester: Manchester University Press, 1994), ch. 6.

77. Percy Dearmer to Stuart Johnson, Easter 1892, as quoted in Nan Dearmer, *Life of Percy Dearmer* (London: J. Cape, 1940), 54.

78. Ashbee Journals, August 28, 1887, Ashbee Papers; Edward Cummings, "University Settlements," *Quarterly Journal of Economics* (April 1892): 263.

79. The chairman of the Board of Oxford House, Sir William Anson criticized

Toynbee's programs in aesthetic education. See Sir William Anson, "The Oxford House in Bethnal Green," *Economic Review* (January 1893): 15.

80. This description comes from a note drafted in 1906 entitled "What Toynbee Hall Does for East London," A/TOY/22/3/6, Toynbee Papers, as cited in Geoff Ginn, *Gifts of Culture, Centres of Light: Cultural Philanthropy in the Late Victorian East End*, Ph.D. diss., University of Queensland, 2001, 188.

81. See Seth Koven, "Culture and Poverty: The London Settlement House Movement, 1870–1914," Ph.D. diss., Harvard University, 1987.

82. Henry Scott Holland, speech given at the Mansion House, January 21, 1891, appendix, Oxford House, Annual Report, 1891, 11.

83. For a superb analysis of the impact of such European "tourism" on shaping social welfare in the United States, see Rogers, *Atlantic Crossings*, esp. ch. 2–3.

84. Robert Woods to Anna Dawes, December 20, 1893, Woods Papers.

85. Second Annual Report, Toynbee Hall, 1886, 40. American historians have offered first-rate analyses of the role of settlements as domestic spaces. See Kathryn Kish Sklar, "Hull House as a Community of Women Reformers in the 1890's," in *Signs: Journal of Women in Culture and Society* 10, no. 4 (Summer 1985): 657–677 and Shannon Jackson, *Lines of Activity: Performance, Historiography, Hull-House Domesticity* (Ann Arbor: University of Michigan Press, 2000). Both of these works focus on a settlement headed by women, but male settlements also produced "domestic" spaces and ideologies within their institutions.

86. Clara Grant, a school visitor who ultimately established her own small settlement house, found Toynbee very open to her and other women engaged in social questions. She described herself as "a keen student at Toynbee Hall, where I found an intellectual home and came under the direct inspiring influence of its founder, Canon Barnett." She also served as a watcher-docent at the Barnetts' famous Whitechapel Picture Exhibitions. See Clara Grant, *Farthing Bundles* (London: A. & E. Walter, 1931) 79, 122–123.

87. Bolton King, speech given at first annual meeting of Toynbee Old Students' Association, *Toynbee Record* (July–August 1894), 134.

88. Henrietta acknowledged the artificiality of settlements and eventually made her most lasting contribution as founder of the Hampstead Garden Suburb, where rich and poor lived in family units in their own homes. A few Toynbee men decided to live near the settlement with their wives and children and played active roles in the settlement as associates. See Margaret Nevinson's vivid account of her ties to Toynbee Hall and her life nearby with her husband and children in *Life's Fitful Fever: A Volume of Memories* (London: A. & C. Black, 1926), 77–103.

89. The couple had no biological children of their own and many perceived Henrietta to be the more masculine of the two. On the Barnetts' marriage and relationship to Toynbee Hall, see Seth Koven, "Henrietta Barnett: (Auto)biography of a Late-Victorian Marriage" in Susan Pedersen and Peter Mandler, ed., *After the Victorians: Private Conscience and Public Duty in Modern Britain* (London: Routledge, 1994).

90. Only one Oxford House resident, Patrick Buchanan, was married. He and

his wife lived adjacent to the settlement's working men's club, the University Club. Perhaps because women had so few opportunities to contribute to the work of Oxford House in comparison to Toynbee Hall, where some taught classes and many others helped Henrietta, two small women's settlements (St. Margaret's and St. Hilda's) linked themselves loosely to Oxford House as sister settlements.

91. On Henson, see Owen Chadwick, *Hensley Henson: A Study in the Friction between Church and State* (Oxford: Oxford University Press, 1983), esp. 39–50. For Henson's own account of his time at Oxford House, see Herbert Hensley Henson, *Retrospect of an Unimportant Life*, vol. 1 (London: Oxford University Press, 1942), esp. ch. 2.

92. Edward Cummings, "University Settlements," *Quarterly Journal of Economics* (April 1892), 273.

93. A co-editor of the monumental *Works of John Ruskin* (London: G. Allen, 1911), Edward Tyas Cook was an early resident of Toynbee Hall, where he edited the settlement's periodical, the *Toynbee Journal*. The imperial administrator and future chairman of Toynbee Hall, Alfred Milner, had joined a group of idealistic undergraduates later closely associated with the Barnetts including Arnold Toynbee and the resolutely bohemian scion of one Anglo-Jewry's most distinguished families, Leonard Montefiore. On Montefiore's blending of high moral virtue and bohemianism, see H. Barnett, *Canon Barnett*, vol. 1, 304.

94. Like nearly every other intellectual and political celebrity of the day, Pater made his way to Toynbee Hall in 1890, where he delivered a lecture on Wordsworth with his eyes shut to a subdued and puzzled audience. A long-time Toynbee associate, Henry Wood Nevinson, wrote a witty sketch of the event in *Changes and Chances*, 84.

95. Alan Sinfield correctly observes that "aestheticism became a component in the image of the queer as it emerged, but it is a mistake simply to read this attitude back before the Wilde trials" (84). However, I am working with broader definitions of aestheticism and the aesthete than Sinfield. In this chapter, I show that aestheticism encompassed ideas and men not identified with effeminacy. See Sinfield, *The Wilde Century*, ch. 4. See also Linda Dowling's teasing out of codes of masculinity and sexual desire in *Hellenism and Homosexuality in Victorian Oxford* (Ithaca, NY: Cornell University Press, 1994).

96. J. E. Kelsell, "Suggested Report of Toynbee Hall," copy in Ashbee Journal, November 1886, ff. 399, Ashbee Papers.

97. J. A. Spender, *Life, Journalism, and Politics*, vol. 1 (New York: F. A. Stokes, 1927), 46. For similar and quite moving descriptions of Barnett's gentle spiritual magnetism, see the memoirs of a former Whitechapel vellum binder, Frederick Rogers, *Labour, Life, and Literature: Some Memories of Sixty Years* (London: Smith, Elder, 1913), 322. See also Beatrice Webb, *My Apprenticeship* (London: Longmans, Green and Co., 1926), 202.

98. Baxter interview with Rev. Bayne, notes for *Life and Labour of the People in London. Third Series. Religious Influences*, vol. 2, *London North of the Thames: The Inner Ring*, A 39, parish notes, District 7 and 8, Booth Papers. In the final published version, Booth entirely discounted Bayne's criticisms.

99. Deeply attached to the ancient traditions of the church and the veracity of

scripture as a record of historical events, such men insisted that "old truths" could best be preserved only by responding to "new needs, new points of view, new questions." Charles Gore, preface, *Lux Mundi: A Series of Studies in the Religion of the Incarnation* (London: J. Murray, 1890), vii–ix.

100. Winnington Ingram, as quoted in Carpenter, *Winnington-Ingram*, 39.

101. Cosmo Gordon Lang, as quoted in J. G. Lockhart, *Cosmo Gordon Lang* (London: Hodder and Stoughton, 1949), 50.

102. James Adderley, *In Slums and Society: Reminiscences of Old Friends* (London: T. Fisher Unwin, 1916), 47. Winnington Ingram's first official biographer, Percy Colson, contended that Winnington Ingram's character "has that great virtue which, of all qualities, is the most difficult to convey—perfect simplicity. There is nothing so subtle as simplicity." Percy Colson, *The Life of the Bishop of London: An Authorised Biography* (London: Jarrolds, 1935), 8.

103. James Adderley, "The Oxford House in Bethnal Green," April 1887, pamphlet, reprinted from the Notes for Working Members of the Associated Workers' League, 7. For this and other early circulars advertising Oxford House, see GALond 4° 132, Bodleian, Oxford.

104. But Henson also recognized that he, unlike his wealthy and aristocratic friend Adderley, could not afford to embrace a life of voluntary poverty permanently. See Henson, *Retrospect*, 14; and Chadwick, *Hensley Henson*.

105. Wilfred Thomason Grenfell, *A Labrador Doctor: Autobiography of Wilfred Thomason Grenfell* (New York: Houghton Mifflin, 1919), 60, 58, 84.

106. Henry Scott Holland, letter of October 1876, reprinted in Paget, *Memoir and Letters*, 88.

107. Ibid., 61.

108. Holland, letter of September 8, 1871, in ibid.

109. Holland, letter of September 1, 1871, in ibid.

110. Holland's sense that the disavowal of luxury could itself be a source of pleasure echoed observations of British imperial adventurers. Mansfield Parkyns, who traveled in Egypt and Abyssinia, suggested that leaving "luxury . . . [for] a few months' experience of hardship" would at first cause suffering but in the end lead to "real enjoyment." Parkyns reveled in what he called the "sweets of savage life." See Duncan Cumming, *The Gentleman Savage: The Life of Mansfield Parkyns, 1823–1894* (London: Century, 1987), 66, 70.

111. On the "primitive" in Victorian intellectual and social thought, see Henrika Kuklick, *The Savage Within: The Social History of British Anthropology, 1885–1945* (Cambridge: Cambridge University Press, 1993); and Adam Kuper, *The Invention of Primitive Society: Transformations of an Illusion* (London: Routledge, 1988). On the ways in which the discourse of the primitive functioned within a "sexualized field" of an imagined modern "us" and primitive "them," see Marianna Torgovnick, *Gone Primitive: Savage Intellects, Modern Lives* (Chicago: University of Chicago Press, 1990), ch. 1.

112. The mingling of ascetic self-denial, social reform, and imperial missionary impulses is strikingly evident in Robert Morant's longing to live and work among boys in England and Siam in the 1880s and '90s. As an undergraduate at New College, Oxford, in the early 1880s, Morant was ablaze with compassion for the poor and founded a "brotherhood" devoted to theological study and

work among the rough lads in a village on the outskirts of Oxford. He was ready to cast his lot with Oxford House at the time of its founding when a spiritual crisis made him question his Anglo-Catholic beliefs and led him toward Toynbee Hall. Uncertain which scheme spoke most directly to his heart and mind, Morant left England for Siam, where he zealously guarded his sexual purity while tutoring young princes and helping to shape that nation's system of education. Morant was happiest among poor boys in England and the "dear little" chaps in Siam with their "pearly white teeth and brown skin," upon whom he lavished his affections and from whom he received the love he craved. Morant was one of the most influential welfare bureaucrats of his generation, and his intimate relationships with the poor while he was a resident of Toynbee Hall in the 1890s only confirmed his deeply held conviction that the health of the democratic state depended upon the voluntary submission of the "impulses of the many ignorant to the guidance and control of the few wise." The "ignorant" many were to be loved, but not entrusted, with the nation's future. See Bernard Allen, *Robert Morant* (London: MacMillan, 1934), 20, 52, 126.

113. On this, see Henry Scott Holland, "Christian Asceticism," manuscript of undated sermon, Holland Papers. Holland insisted that true Christian asceticism entailed not an act of repudiation, but rather one of joyous redemption.

114. James Eli Adams provides a sophisticated analysis of the theatricality of asceticism. He argues that "every program of ascetic discipline requires holding a pose." See Adams, *Dandies and Desert Saints: Styles of Victorian Manhood* (Ithaca, NY: Cornell University Press, 1995), 42. I follow Adams's lead in proposing the instability of the oppositions between aestheticism and asceticism, muscular manliness and effeminacy.

115. This is how Robert Dolling described St. Martin's Mission in a tract dated December 31, 1884, which was reprinted in Charles Osborne, *Life of Father Dolling* (London: E. Arnold, 1903), 49.

116. Neither Jay nor Dolling had much respect for the work of men's settlements. Jay mocked Oxford House and Toynbee Hall as "little changing groups of stray residents" and once characterized Winnington Ingram's ideas as "amiable absurdities."

117. G. B. Shaw's Rev. Mavor Morrell in *Candida* is perhaps the best known literary representations of the unconventional slum priest-aesthete. G. B. Shaw, *Candida* (New York: Brentano's, 1905).

118. On the various controversies surrounding Anglo-Catholic ceremonial practices see James Bentley, *Ritualism and Politics in Victorian Britain: The Attempt to Legislate Belief* (Oxford: Oxford University Press, 1978). For an overview of ritualism in relationship to the history of High Churchmanship, see Kenneth Hylson-Smith, *High Churchmanship in the Church of England: From the Sixteenth Century to the Late Twentieth Century* (Edinburgh: T &T Clark, 1993), esp. part 4.

119. James Greaves to Bishop of London, October 11, 1886, ff 3, vol. 191, Fulham Papers.

120. Septimus Hansard to Bishop Jackson, January 22, 1878, vol. 8, letter "H," Fulham Papers. See also letters of Hansard to Jackson from December 5, 1877, and December 14, 1877. These files contain letters from a variety of people involved in Headlam's music-hall controversy, both his supporters and de-

tractors alike. As this evidence makes clear, McIlhiney's claim that Headlam's curacy under Hansard was the "only happy time period" in his official ministry is at best only partially true for the first years of their association. See McIlhiney, "A Gentleman in Every Slum," 88. On Headlam's music hall controversies, see John Orens, "The Mass, the Masses and the Music Hall: Stewart Headlam's Radical Anglicanism," *Jubilee Paper* (London: Jubilee Group, 1979).

121. Jay's celebrity was enhanced by the publication of Arthur Morrison's novel *A Child of the Jago* (1896), which was based on Morrison's observations of Jay and his slum neighbors. Morrison painted an affectionate portrait of Jay as the slum priest Father Sturt in the novel. Morrison also endorsed Jay's dismissal of the value of settlements by making fun of a thinly fictionalized version of Toynbee Hall called the East End Elevation Mission and Pansophical Institute. See Morrison, *A Child of the Jago* (London: J. M. Dent, 1996), ch. 2 and the excellent introduction by Peter Miles in the Everyman edition.

122. Osborne, *Life of Father Dolling*, 140, 178. Kenneth Leech examines the legacy of Dolling in post–World War II London in "The End of the Dolling Era? Fr. Joe Williamson in Stepney," in *The Anglo-Catholic Social Conscience: Two Critical Essays* (Croydon: Jubliee Group, 1991).

123. Interview with Father Jay, February 10, 1898, B228, district 9, ff. 37, 59, Booth Papers.

124. John Law (Margaret Harkness), *Out of Work* (London: Sonnenschein, 1888: rep., London: Merlin Press, 1990), 38–39. Citations are to Merlin edition.

125. For discussion of Winnington Ingram's involvement in campaigns against sexual immorality, in particular the use of movie theatres as places for homosexual encounters, see Dean Rapp, "Sex in the Cinema: War, Moral Panic, and the British Film Industry, 1906–1918," *Albion* (Fall 2002), 436, n. 53.

126. According to Winnington Ingram's biographer, he was briefly engaged to a woman he did not know well and who precipitously broke off the arrangement. He apparently never pursued any other romantic attachment. See Carpenter, *Winnington-Ingram*, 95, 116, 77.

127. Dean of Westminster to Bishop Winnington Ingram, September 28, 1900, in reply to a series of questions posed by Winnington Ingram. Fulham Papers.

128. H. W. Nevinson Diaries, February 11, 1893, ms. Eng.misc.e610/12, Nevinson Papers.

129. Here, I am alluding to Edward Carpenter's use of the term "intermediate sex" to describe men and women who were sexually attracted in different degrees to members of their own sex. Carpenter's sexology was based on a continuum of sexualities in which some were "purely" drawn to the opposite sex, and some to the same sex, others were in-between these pure forms, and hence "intermediates."

130. Interview with A. F. Winnington Ingram, December 28, 1898, by Ernest Aves, B228, ff. 34–35, Religious Census, Booth Papers.

131. No evidence suggests that Bloxam had in mind the men of Oxford House as he developed his protagonist, Ronald Heatherington. However, we can be fairly certain that he (along with most High Church students at Oxford) would have been familiar with the settlement and its work. For a perceptive

analysis of the connections between homoeroticism and Anglican theology and practice, see Frederick S. Roden, *Same Sex Desire in Victorian Religious Culture* (London: Palgrave, 2002).

132. The *Chameleon* reunited many of the same future clergymen and homosexual literati, including Oscar Wilde and Lord Alfred Douglas, who had contributed to the *Spirit Lamp* the preceding two years. Its publication excited considerable commentary, most of it very critical of the "unnatural" tone of its literary contributions. The work is reprinted in its entirety in Brian Reade, *Sexual Heretics: Male Homosexuality in English Literature from 1850 to 1900* (New York: Coward-McCann, 1971), 349–360. Page numbers in my text refer to this reprinted version of the story.

133. See *Crockford's Clerical Directory*, 1925 (London: Oxford University Press), 143.

134. No evidence discussing Bloxam's appointment or work survives in Winnington Ingram's episcopal files at Lambeth Palace.

135. See Carpenter, *Winnington-Ingram,* 170–175. According to the historian of St. Saviour's, Kilburn introduced vestments, reservation of the Sacrament, incense, and devotions to Our Lady and eventually banished all official Anglican service books in favor of the Latin Mass. Kilburn even organized massive processions of the Blessed Sacrament through Hoxton on the Feast of Corpus Christi. While Bloxam never provoked the level of public controversy that had surrounded Kilburn, he tenaciously preserved the style of services Kilburn had introduced. See John Harwood, "Vanished Church, Vanished Streets: The Parish of St. Saviour's, Hoxton," *East London Record* no. 9 (1986): 14–17.

136. Willliam Michael Rossetti to Mrs. Gilchrist, June 26, 1885, in Clarence Gohdes and Paul Baum, eds., *Letters of William Michael Rossetti concerning Whitman, Blake, and Shelly to Anne Gilchrist and Her Son Herbert Gilchrist* (Durham: Duke University Press, 1934; repr. New York: AMS Press, 1968), 149. Citations are to the AMS edition.

137. Samuel Barnett, "The Failure of Philanthropy," *Macmillan* (March 1896) as reprinted in *Living Age* (April 25, 1896), 231.

138. H. Clay Trumbull, *Friendship the Master Passion* (Philadelphia: J. D. Wattles, 1892), 386. The closest English equivalent, although one much more self-evidently seeking the historical origins of sexual love between men, is Edward Carpenter, *Iolaus: An Anthology of Friendship* (London: G. Allen, 1906). By using terms such as "comrade attachment" and "romantic comrades," Carpenter claimed that such relationships existed universally among both "primitive" and "civilized" peoples. Scott Holland was no stranger to "friendship love" and its "passionate strain." In such friendships, Holland recalled, the two male friends "in vain . . . reach out embracing arms to each other, in vain they cling to each other: the unity cannot attain its fullness, its satisfaction: they stand apart, confused, delicious sympathies may cross, and re-cross, from another touching, entwining, binding but not dissolving the barriers, not making the twain one." See Paget, *Memoir and Letters*, 94–95.

139. Thomas Hancock Nunn, "The Universities' Settlement in Whitechapel," *Economic Review* (October 1892): 479.

140. Samuel Barnett, manuscript of speech delivered at Toynbee Hall, July 2,

1889, ms. 1463, ff 60, Barnett Papers, Lambeth Palace. Barnett told Sarah Tooley, the interviewer sent by the *Humanitarian,* that "in the East you see Humanity as it is, in the West you see it clothed." In other words, he identified East London with both a metaphorical nakedness and truths about humanity. See Sarah Tooley, "The Social Problem In East London: An Interview with the Rev. Canon Samuel Barnett," *Humanitarian* (April 1899), 235.

141. Major biographies of Ashbee include Alan Crawford, *C. R. Ashbee, Architect, Designer and Romantic Socialist* (New Haven: Yale University Press, 1985); and Fiona MacCarthy, *The Simple Life, C. R. Ashbee in the Cotswolds* (Berkeley, CA: University of California Press, 1981). On Fry and his intimate but not sexual relation with Goldsworthy Lowes Dickinson, see Frances Spalding, *Roger Fry, Art and Life* (Berkeley, CA: University of California Press, 1980), ch. 2, esp. p. 27. On Dickinson and his desire "to serve humanity," see E. M. Forster, *Goldsworthy Lowes Dickinson* (London: E. Arnold and Co., 1934), 28.

142. C. R. Ashbee, journal, December 11, 1885, Ashbee Papers.

143. Ibid., July 25, 1886.

144. Ibid., August 20, 1887; September 8, 1887.

145. This episode in Ashbee's career at Toynbee echoed William Morris's equally self-conscious adventure in painting frescoes on the walls of the Oxford Union several decades earlier. Both gestures were public declarations of inchoate visions of society and confirmations of new directions in their private lives. On Morris, see E. P. Thompson, *William Morris, Romantic Revolutionary* (London: Lawrence & Wishart, 1955).

146. Ashbee Journals, August 28, 1887. See Hugh Legge, "The Repton Club," in John Matthew Knapp, ed., *The Universities and the Social Problem* (London: Rivington, Percival and Co., 1895), 133–47. I discuss many other effusive descriptions of rough lads by male philanthropists in "From Rough Lads to Hooligans" in Andrew Parker, et al. eds., *Nationalisms and Sexualities* (New York: Routledge, 1992).

147. Percy Colson, *Life of the Bishop of London* (London: Jarrolds, 1935), 32–33.

148. See Martha Vicinus, "The Adolescent Boy: Fin de Siècle Femme Fatale?" *Journal of the History of Sexuality* 5 (Summer 1994): 90–114.

149. See Ashbee's history of the School and Guild of Handicraft, *Endeavour Towards the Teaching of John Ruskin and William Morris* (London: E. Arnold, 1901).

150. Edward Carpenter to C. R. Ashbee, October 9, 1887, Ashbee Papers. The poet and socialist William Morris discouraged Ashbee. See Ashbee to Fry, December 14, 1887, and journal entry of approximately same date, Ashbee Papers.

151. Ashbee, journal, "Summing up of two years," end of 1888, Ashbee Papers.

152. See C. R. Ashbee, Memoirs, vol 1, *The Guild Idea,* introduction, written in 1938, p. 54, CRA/3, Ashbee Papers.

153. Ibid.

154. Ashbee, journal, March 21, 1889, Ashbee Papers.

155. Ibid.

156. Galton was the son of a highly skilled and well-paid saddle maker who

suffered a precipitous decline in earnings and social status in the 1870s as the saddle industry was deskilled and moved to mass production. By the age of three or four, Galton was living in a King's Cross tenement with one wash closet for twenty-five people; six years later his father became permanently unemployed. He later became a trade unionist, writer, and private secretary and researcher for Sidney and Beatrice Webb.

157. See manuscript "Autobiography of Frank Wallis Galton," Galton Papers.

158. Galton was perhaps the only working-class boy of his generation who later became a resident at a settlement house. He joined Mrs. Humphry Ward's settlement house in Bloomsbury.

159. For encomiums by working-class memoirists about Toynbee Hall and the Barnetts, see Frederick Rogers, *Labour, Life and Literature: Some Memories of Sixty Years* (London: Smith, Elder and Co., 1913), 81–82; and Thomas Okey, *A Basketful of Memories* (London: J. M. Dent, 1930), 50.

160. See Kegan Paul to Arthur Rogers, n.d., box 2, ff. 416, Thorold Rogers Papers. Kegan Paul was a sort of patron saint for Ashbee and his circle.

161. For Janet's contributions and perspective on their marriage, see Felicity Ashbee, *Janet Ashbee: Love, Marriage, and the Arts and Crafts Movement* (Syracuse, NY: Syracuse University Press, 2002). See especially ch. 3 on the concept of the "comrade wife."

162. On the identification of the "aesthete" and the "homosexual" as masculine types during the Wilde trial, see Ed Cohen, *Talk on the Wilde Side* (New York: Routledge, 1993), 135–136. See Eve Kosofsky Sedgwick's immensely influential analysis of tensions between acceptable homosocial relations and banned homosexual relations in *Between Men: English Literature and Male Homosocial Desire* (New York: Columbia University Press, 1985) and *Epistemology of the Closet* (Berkeley, CA: University of California Press, 1990). Sedgwick argues that "because the paths of male entitlement, especially in the nineteenth century, required certain intense male bonds that were not readily distinguishable from the most reprobate bonds, an endemic and ineradicable state of what I am calling male homosexual panic became the normal condition of male heterosexual entitlement." *Epistemology*, 185. On sex scandals between adult men and working-class male youths in Toronto, see Steven Maynard, "'Horrible Temptations': Sex, Men, and Working-Class Male Youth in Urban Ontario, 1890–1935," *Canadian Historical Review* 78, no. 2 (June 1997): 191–235.

163. H. Montgomery Hyde, ed., *Famous Trials 7: Oscar Wilde* (London: Penguin Books, 1962), 127–130. This quote comes from the first trial of the Marquess of Queensberry on the charge of criminally libeling Oscar Wilde. Wilde's writing frequently alluded to the mingling of aestheticism and philanthropy that was such a marked feature of Toynbee Hall and many other charitable schemes. The London slums figured prominently in his writings, both literary and journalistic, as a site for the expression of heterodox desires. Wilde was critical of and skeptical about the charitable practices of high-society philanthropists, and more generally, of contemporary altruists who, he believed, aggravated rather than solved the problem of poverty. However, he did reserve sincere praise for that group of men who, we must assume, were residents at Toynbee Hall and perhaps other men's settlement houses. In his essay "The Soul of Man Under Socialism,"

Wilde rejoiced that "at last we have had the spectacle of men who have really studied the problem and know the life—educated men who live in the East End—coming forward and imploring the community to restrain its altruistic impulses of charity, benevolence, and the like. They do so on the ground that such charity degrades and demoralises. They are perfectly right. Charity creates a multitude of sins." See Oscar Wilde, *The Soul of Man Under Socialism* (St. Louis, MO: Herman Schwartz, 1906), 3. The essay was first published in the *Fortnightly Review* (February 1, 1891).

164. W. T. Stead as quoted in Jeffrey Weeks, *Coming Out: Homosexual Politics in Britain from the Nineteenth Century to the Present* (London: Quartet, 1977), 21.

165. Jeffrey Weeks describes the prevalence of cross-age and cross-class sexual relations between well-to-do men and working class youths as a form of "sexual colonialism." Ibid., 40.

166. The chapter can also be read as a pornographic unmasking of the homoerotic tensions in Horatio Alger's story about the redemption of a New York shoeblack through the interventions of a middle-class gentleman. See Horatio Alger, *Ragged Dick* (Boston: Loring, 1868); on its homoerotic content, see Michael Moon, " 'The Gentle Boy from the Dangerous Classes': Pederasty, Domesticity, and Capitalism in Horatio Alger," *Representations* 19 (Summer 1987): 87–110. Alger himself had fled New England after acknowledging inappropriate sexual contact with a boy and was an ardent supporter of philanthropic schemes for shoeblacks.

167. See [John Saul], *Sins of the Cities of the Plain, Or Confessions of a Maryanne* (New York: Masquerade, 1992), ch. 12. I first analyzed this scene in "From Rough Lads to Hooligans," 370. Morris Kaplan has subsequently provided a much fuller reading of this text in its original published form in "Who's Afraid of John Saul? Urban Culture and the Politics of Desire in Late Victorian London," *GLQ* 5, no. 3, esp. 283–290.

168. *Toynbee Record* (December 1889), 26.

169. *Toynbee Record* (October 1889), 9.

170. H. H. Asquith, speech at Balliol House, reported in *Toynbee Record* (April 1891), 77.

171. Samuel Barnett to Francis Barnett, March 7, 1896, F/Bar/139, Barnett Papers, London Metropolitan Archives.

172. The "Wadham House Journal" existed only as a single manuscript copy. I have seen only one surviving issue, no. 8, for 1905. It contains eight parts but no pagination. The parts are 1. Editorial, 2. The Stones of London, part II, 3. The Anatomy of a Smile, 4. Notes and Jottings, 5. Wadham Notes, 6. Ancient Wales. Part II, 7. Spring Poetry: Assossiette and A Blighted Life, 8. Photographic Illustrations, Various. My deep thanks to Lorraine Blair for discovering the journal at Toynbee Hall itself, Barnett Research Center. All further references in my text are to this document.

173. Ibid. James Adams argues that "the reception of early Victorian brotherhoods . . . put in wide circulation a social semiotic that was to transform male secrecy into the sign of 'the closet,'" but he also warns against conflating all secrets with homosexual desire. See Adams, *Dandies and Desert Saints*, 13, 17.

174. On middle- and upper-class men's rejection of many elements of domesticity, see John Tosh, "The Making of Masculinities: The Middle Class in Late Nineteenth Century Britain," in Angela John and Claire Eustace, eds., *The Men's Share? Masculinities, Male Support, and Women's Suffrage in Britain, 1890–1920* (London: Routledge, 1997), esp. 41–47.

175. James Adderley, diary of "Tramping Without Tears in 1896," as quoted in Stevens, *Father Adderley*, 29.

176. *Punch* (November 24, 1894) as quoted in Linda Dowling, "The Decadent and the New Woman in the 1890s," *Nineteenth-Century Fiction* 33 (1979): 445.

177. Philip Gibbs's *The New Man: A Portrait Study of the Latest Type* (London: Sir Isaac Pitman and Sons, 1913) opens by setting the emergence of the New Man against the history of the New Woman from the 1880s onwards. For Gibbs, the New Man "has been profoundly affected by the changing ideals and characteristics of his women." While I concur with Gibbs that men responded to women, this chapter has argued against his assertion that "the New Man . . . has been created largely by the New Woman" (3–5). On the New Man, see George Robb and Nancy Erber, eds, *Disorder in the Court: Trials and Sexual Conflict at the Turn of the Century* (London: Macmillan, 1999), 1.

178. *Oxford Magazine*, June 4, 1884, 281. On Browning's views of male friendship and love and their relationship to "sympathy" for inferiors, see Oscar Browning, "Sympathy in Common Life," *Humanitarian* (February 1897), 88–92; "The Love of Plato," *Humanitarian* (April 1897), 253–256. On the sexual controversies surrounding Browning and his friendships with "young working lads," see H. Montgomery Hyde, *The Love That Dared Not Speak Its Name: A Candid History of Homosexuality in Britain* (Boston: Little, Brown and Company, 1970), 116–120.

179. J. A. Symonds as quoted in *Toynbee Record* (April 1890), 78.

180. Symonds's revelation that "some at least of the deepest moral problems might be solved by fraternity" occurred to him in 1877. He had picked up a "brawny young soldier" with "frank eyes" on the street and later met him in a private room where he "enjoyed the close vicinity of that splendid naked piece of manhood." But rather than having sex, they sat and talked. Presumably Symonds paid him for his time. Symonds was not able to fully understand the extent to which the unequal economic conditions of their encounter posed its own set of moral problems. See Phyllis Grosskurth, ed., *The Memoirs of John Addington Symonds* (New York: Random House, 1984), 253–254. Cross-class sex was an ongoing fascination for Symonds. I analyzed his response to Greenwood's workhouse scandals in chapter 1.

181. Forster was presumably referring to Cambridge House in South London. On Lytton Strachey's cross-class sexual fantasies, see Julie Anne Taddeo, *Lytton Strachey and the Search for Modern Sexual Identity: The Last Eminent Victorian* (New York: Harrington Park Press, 2002), ch. 2.

182. See E. M. Forster, *Maurice* (New York: Norton, 1971). Forster was well acquainted with the philanthropic projects and many of the men discussed in this chapter. He believed that Ashbee "had a gift for practical organization and for sympathetic contact with the working class." See Forster, *Goldsworthy Lowes Dickinson*, 35. On Forster's "foreclosing" the radical potential of his own proj-

ect, see Sara Suleri's analysis of Forster's *A Passage to India* in *The Rhetoric of English India* (Chicago: University of Chicago Press, 1992), ch. 6, esp. p. 137.

183. See T. A. Ross, "A Case of Homosexual Inversion," *Journal of Neurology and Psychopathology* 7 (April 1927), reprinted in Lucy Bland and Laura Doane, eds., *Sexology Uncensored: The Documents of Sexual Science* (Chicago: University of Chicago Press, 1998), 66–67. Ross wholly pathologized homosexuality, and the case study concludes with Ross successfully restoring his patient to normal heterosexuality.

184. In this respect, I follow Christopher Lane, who warns that "queer theory increasingly *assists*–rather than avoiding—this eclipse of historical difference by substituting terms such as 'deviance' and 'perversion' for the dissimilarities, aporias, and discontinuities [between past and present] they only partially represent." Lane continues that "historical differences immediately get lost and sexual meaning buckles under a demand for interpretive certainty." Christopher Lane, *The Burdens of Intimacy: Psychoanalysis and Victorian Masculinity* (Chicago: University of Chicago Press, 1999), 227.

185. As a citadel for the purification of the slums, Toynbee Hall was a space *not* subject to the surveillance of purity crusaders and the police. Gustav-Wrathall argues that the YMCAs served as important meeting places for homosexual men in late Victorian and early-twentieth-century America. But unlike London settlement houses, YMCAs were subject to policing. See John Donald Gustav-Wrathall, *Take the Young Stranger by the Hand: Same-Sex Relations and the YMCA* (Chicago: University of Chicago Press, 1998).

186. There is a vast and sophisticated theoretical literature about the emergence of homosexuality as well as the differences between terms such as "sexual identity" and "sexual subjectivity," "homosexuality" and "homoerotic desire," "masculine types" and "masculine personae." The work of Michel Foucault has been the starting point for much of this discussion. On Foucault and the need to refine his arguments, see David Halperin, "Forgetting Foucault: Acts, Identities, and the History of Sexuality," *Representations* 63 (1998): 93–120.

187. Ashbee recorded his reflections on Winnington Ingram in two extended entries, which I have combined. See C. R. Ashbee, March 1901 and July 23, 1901, journal, vol. 1, Ashbee Papers.

188. An example of his political caution but openness was his eventual conversion to women's suffrage in 1914. See *Extracts from Speeches by the Bishop of London and the Bishop of Oxford in Behalf of the Woman Suffrage Bill in the House of Lords, London, England, May 7, 1914* (Richmond, VA: Equal Suffrage League, 1914).

189. See minutes of the Guild of Handicraft, vol. 1, mss. English 86.DD.15, entries for October 16, 1890; July 10, 1891; October 23, 1891; and October 27, 1891, Victoria and Albert Museum Library.

190. See ibid., July 23, 1891, and May 12, 1892.

191. See Charles Booth, *Life and Labour of the People of London*, First Series, vol. 1, "Poverty" (New York: AMS Press, 1902, 1970), 100. For a naïvely appreciative account of the clubs at Oxford House, see Francis Eardley, "A Workmen's Club in the East End," *Good Words* 36 (1895), 227–231. One of

Eardley's hosts from Oxford House must have told him about the failed attempt to allow University Club men to manage their own club because he noted that "working men are excellent managers if they have a controlling hand over them. . . . left alone on committees, petty squabbles will arise on very trivial pretexts."

192. Winnington Ingram outlined his ideas about working men's clubs in "Working Men's Clubs," in J. M. Knapp, ed., *The Universities and the Social Problem* (London: Rivington, Percival and Co., 1895). He had noted the challenges of steering between "the Scylla of despotism and the Charybdis of anarchy" in managing the clubs (43).

193. In 1890, Oxford House experimented with and then abandoned self-rule by club members. See General Meeting, University Club, January 21, 1890, as reported in *The Trumpet* (February 1890). I have located only one set of the club's journal, *The Trumpet*, at the Bodleian Library, Oxford. On the history of working-men's clubs, see Laurence Marlow, "The Working Men's Club Movement, 1862–1912: A Study of the Evolution of a Working Class Institution," Ph.D. diss., University of Warwick, 1980. See also, T. G. Ashplant, "London Working Men's Clubs, 1875–1914," in Eileen and Stephen Yeo, eds., *Popular Culture and Class Conflict, 1590–1914* (Sussex: Harvester Press, 1981); Richard Price, "The Working Men's Club Movement and Victorian Social Reform Ideology," *Victorian Studies* 15 (December 1971): 117–147; and John Taylor, *From Self-Help to Glamour: The Working Men's Club,* History Workshop Pamphlet No. 7 (Oxford: History Workshop, 1972).

194. For this debate, see the Minutes of the Oxford House Club and the Minutes of the Council of Oxford House, July–September 1897. Oxford House University Settlement Papers.

195. Ibid.

196. A. F. Winnington Ingram, *New Testament Difficulties*, 1st ser. (London: Society for Promoting Christian Knowledge, 1901), 70.

197. See Arthur F. Winnington Ingram, "One Bread," in *Banners of the Christian Faith* (London: Well Gardner, Darton and Co., 1899), esp. 166–169.

198. The phrase comes from Gerard Fiennes's description of the need for male settlers to balance "perfect equality" with deference in their dealings with working-class men. See Gerard Fiennes, "The Federation of Working Men's Social Clubs: What It Is, And What It May Be," in Knapp, *The Universities and the Social Problem*, 218–219.

199. Gertrude Himmelfarb stresses Toynbee Hall's role as a beacon of civic communitarian values and its shaping of a "citizenship that made tolerable all those other social distinctions which were natural and inevitable." While I concur with Himmelfarb that in many respects Toynbee was "an experiment in democracy—which was no mean feat at that time and place," she minimizes the constraints and limitations of this vision and ignores entirely the gender and sexual politics of the settlement movement. In part, this is because Himmelfarb's analysis is based entirely on the idealistic rhetoric of the movement and not on its social history. See Gertrude Himmelfarb, *Poverty and Compassion: The Moral Imagination of the Late Victorians* (New York: Alfred A. Knopf, 1991), 235–243. Standish Meacham, by contrast, stresses the hierarchical nature of Toynbee

Hall and its failure to live up to its own communitarian ideals. But Meacham obscures the negotiated character of relations between rich and poor and the evolution of the settlement over time, as well as the settlement's daring experimentation with new conceptions of masculinity. See Standish Meacham, *Toynbee Hall and Social Reform 1880–1914: The Search for Community* (New Haven, CT: Yale University Press, 1987).

200. Tape-recorded interview, Mandy Ashworth interviewing Sir Guy and Molly Clutton-Brock, 1984. Tape and transcript, Oxford House University Settlement Papers.

201. The quote comes from Morris's 1885 "Manifesto for the Socialist League," reprinted as appendix 1 in E. P. Thompson, *William Morris* (London: Lawrence and Wishart, 1955).

202. There is a strong body of scholarship on imperial manliness that considers a similar configuration of issues in organizations such as the Boy Scouts and among bachelor imperial military warriors. See contributions by John Springhall, Jeffrey Richards, J. A. Mangan, John MacKenzie, and Allen Warren in an early and still important contribution to the study of masculinity, J. A. Mangan and James Walvin, eds., *Manliness and Morality: Middle-Class Masculinities in Britain and America, 1800–1940* (New York: St. Martin's Press, 1987). Many settlers praised the heroic sacrifices of bachelor imperial war heroes, especially General Gordon. See Winnington Ingram's homage to Gordon in "Self-Sacrifice unto Death," in Arthur F. Winnington Ingram, *The Attractiveness of Goodness* (London: Wells Gardner, Darton and Co., 1913), 64–80; Toynbee settler Robert Morant likewise worshiped Gordon and read his "Noble Diary" for inspiration. See Bernard M. Allen, *Sir Robert Morant: A Great Public Servant* (London: Macmillan, 1934), 63. On the tensions between the "primitive" and "civilization" in sexology's construction of desire, see Merl Storr, "Transformations: Subjects, Categories, and Cures in Krafft-Ebing's Sexology," in Lucy Bland and Laura Doan, eds., *Sexology in Culture: Labelling Bodies and Desires* (Chicago: University of Chicago Press, 1998), 14.

203. Edward Cummings "University Settlements," *Quarterly Journal of Economics* (April 1892), 257.

204. On Knight-Bruce and Carey's contributions to the church in South Africa, see Peter Hinchliff, *The Anglican Church in South Africa* (London: Darton, Longman & Todd, 1963), chs. 6–8; James R. Cochrane, *Servants of Power: The Role of English-Speaking Churches in South Africa, 1903–1930* (Johannesburg: Ravan Press, 1987), esp. ch. 5. See also Edward Norman, *Christianity in the Southern Hemisphere: The Churches in Latin America and South Africa* (Oxford: Clarendon Press, 1981), ch. 4.

205. See Walter Carey, *Liberty, Equality, and Fraternity* (London: Allen, 1918), 91.

206. Walter Carey, *Good-Bye to My Generation* (London: A. R. Mowbray, 1951), 37, 50, 52, 57. I should add that Carey *did* defend the rights of people of color in South Africa against many of the worst abuses of the emerging system of apartheid.

207. Tape recorded interview, Mandy Ashworth interviewing Fred Gore, April 3, 1984, Oxford House University Settlement Papers.

CONCLUSION

1. From the outset, the media framed debates around *Faith in the City* as a struggle over Victorian values. See "Higher Capital, Current Spending Key to Rescue, Church of England Report 'Faith in the City,'" *Guardian* (December 3, 1985). The term Urban Priority Area (UPA) was a self-conscious attempt to break away from the word "slum" with its links to the Victorian past and the world of slumming.

2. Controversy surrounded the use of the word "Marxist" to describe the report's findings. See Colin Brown, "Minister Attacks Church on Inner City Aid," *Guardian* (December 2, 1985). Runcie denied that the report was Marxist and claimed that "its enthusiasm for small business and local enterprise could be described as Thatcherite." Runcie as quoted in Walter Schwarz and James Naughtie, "Church Confident Attack on Report Has Flopped," *Guardian* (December 4, 1985). Ian Aitkin described the Faith in the City affair as a "deliberate carefully planned self-inflicted wound" to the Conservative party. See Ian Aitken, "Agenda: Points of Order, Church of England Report on Inner Cities," *Guardian* (December 6, 1985). Aitken traced the short history of the use of the word "Marxist." See John Torode, "Working Brief: The Gospel with a Sense of Salvation, The Church of England's Inner Cities Report," *Guardian* (December 17, 1985). Most articles in the *Times* were highly critical of the report, criticizing it for murky theology and moonshine optimism. Its initial leader article on the report claimed that the latter did not even represent the views of the church itself. See "A Flawed Faith, Focus on Report from Archbishop of Canterbury's Commission on Inner Cities," *Times* (December 3, 1985); see also Ronald Butt, "No Faith in This Cure for Poverty," *Times* (December 5, 1985); see also David Watt, "Church Report—The Real Flaw, Faith in the City Controversy," *Times* (December 20, 1985).

3. *Faith in the City, A Call for Action by Church and Nation* (London: Church House Publishing, 1985), 25.

4. See George Carey, Archbishop of Canterbury, "Christianity and Citizenship," Roscoe Century 21 Lectures, Liverpool John Moores University, February 23, 2000. As he campaigned to unseat the Conservative government in the autumn of 1996, Tony Blair declared that "the essential challenge posed by *Faith in the City* remains unanswered: do we have the confidence and the ideas as a nation to achieve prosperity with fairness in the next century?" See Tony Blair, "Battle for Britain," *Guardian* (January 29, 1996). The leader of the Conservative opposition, William Hague, criticized *Faith in the City* in his Wilberforce Lecture in November 1998. See William Hague, "Podium—We Are a Nation of Churches," *Independent* (November 20, 1998). *Faith in the City* spawned many local studies and publications as well such as H. Russell, ed., *Faith in Our City* (1987) on Liverpool and *Faith in the City of Birmingham* (1988). For an assessment of its impact, see Anthony Dyson, "Faith in the City, Ten Years On," *The Way: Identity and Change* (January 1994), 210–220.

5. *Faith in the City*, xiv, 9.

6. See Hugo Young, "Commentary: No Government Answer to Faith in the City," *Guardian* (December 5, 1985).

7. *Faith in the City*, 5, 31.

8. George Lansbury, *My Life* (London: Constable and Co., 1928), 129–131.

9. See G. S. Jones, *Outcast London: A Study in the Relationship between Classes in Victorian Society* (Oxford: Clarendon Press, 1971; New York: Pantheon Books, 1984); Standish Meacham, *Toynbee Hall and Social Reform 1880–1914: The Search for Community* (New Haven: Yale University Press, 1987); Asa Briggs and Ann Macartney, *Toynbee Hall: The First One Hundred Years* (London: Routledge & K. Paul, 1984).

10. George Dangerfield, *The Strange Death of Liberal England, 1910–1914* (New York: H. Smith and R. Haas, 1935), 56.

11. See Arthur Mejia, "Lord Hugh Cecil: Religion and Liberty" for the first and as yet only academic analysis of Cecil's ideology, in J. A.Thompson and Arthur Mejia, eds., *Edwardian Conservatism: Five Studies in Adaptation* (London: Croom Helm, 1988). For Conservative views on social service, brotherhood, and democracy reminiscent of Hugh Cecil's, see Stanley Baldwin, *Our Inheritance: Speeches and Addresses* (Garden City, NY: Doubleday, Doran and Co., 1928), 239–254. As Baldwin explained, "we are not all equal, and never shall be; the true postulate of democracy is not equality but the faith that every man and woman is worthwhile" (252). For Baldwin on the "handclasp of brotherhood," see report of a speech he gave in Merthyr Tydfil, July 18, 1938, in *Times* (July 19, 1938), 9.

12. Speeches reprinted in "Oxford House in Bethnal Green, Meeting in New College Hall," *Oxford House Chronicle* (June 1907), 3.

13. See Clement Attlee, "A Speech at a Luncheon of the National Association of Boys' Clubs," in *Purpose and Policy, Selected Speeches by the Rt. Hon. C. R. Attlee* (London: Hutchinson, [1947]), 87–90.

14. See Clement Attlee, "A Speech to the House of Commons on the Second Reading of the National Insurance Bill," in *Purpose and Policy*, 98.

15. See Attlee's contribution to *Why I Am a Democrat, A Symposium*, ed. Richard Acland (London: Lawrence and Wishart, 1939); on cultural values and class, see Clement Attlee, *The Social Worker* (London: G. Bell and Sons, 1920), esp. 129–130.

16. William Beveridge to Annette Beveridge, January 25, 1903, and May 11, 1903, IIa, Beveridge Papers.

INDEX

All clergymen are listed as "Rev." regardless of the clerical office held.

gelizing in, 90, 138; charities in, 92–93; Charrington's evangelizing in, 91–92; dirtiness of, 211; and philanthropy, 128; pleasures of, 127; Scott Holland on, 253; and Schreiner, 199; women journalists in, 163; working men's clubs in, 277

Echo, 141

Economic Journal, 164

Education (Feeding of Necessitous School Children) Act (1906), 132, 225

Edwards, David: undercover inspecting by, 11–12

Elberfeld system, 59

Elephant Man. *See* Merrick, Joseph

Ellis, Edith Lees: on Hinton, 16; and same-sex love, 17

Ellis, Havelock: and Hinton, 16, 299n54; on lesbianism, 209; and sexology, 87; on sexual inversion, 73; and Symonds, 72–74

Ellis, Ralph, 102

Elmy, Elizabeth Wolstenholme, 225

emigration: to Canada, 85

empire, 125; in Caribbean, 123; obligations of, 124; tropes of, in slum writings, 237, 254

Engels, Frederick: on literary realism, 341n103

English Illustrated Magazine, 164–165

English Woman's Journal, 151

Englishwoman's Review, 151

ethnography: and slum dwellers, 15, 37

Eton: and Oscar Browning, 274

evangelical charity: concepts of truth in, 93–103, 110, 117; conflicts within, 91–94; doctrine of atonement in, 232; and dream narratives, 110; in London: 90, 94, 111, 129; and Meade, 216; and ritualism, 256; principles of, 58, 99–100; scope of, 321n16; and sex, 104–105; sin and salvation in, 100, 138

evangelical party: decline of, in 1870s, 94

Eyre, Edward John, Governor, 62

Fabian society, 16, 208

Factory act: laundresses on, 165

Fairfax-Cholmeley, Hugh, 265

Faith in the City (1985), 282–284

fallen women. *See* prostitution

Family Welfare Association, 283. *See also* Charity Organisation Society

Farnall, H. B.: inspection by, 66; and Lambeth workhouse, 45, 56, 311nn103 and 109

Farrel, Mick, 109–110

Fegan, James W. C., 101–102, 115

Fellowship of the New Life, 208; and Hinton, 16

femininity: Banks's performance of, 147, 150, 160, 166; bourgeois, 100; debates about, in 1890s, 142; and womanliness, 141. *See also* gender, womanliness

feminism: rise of, as political movement, 222

fenianism, 26, 231

Field Lane Refuge, 77

Fitzgerald, Edward, 106–108, 133

flogging: in Barnardo's Home, 121–122

Flowers, William, 277

Flynt, Josiah, 73

Following Fully (Shipton, 1872), 95

Ford, Emily, 208

Forster Education Act (1870), 152

Forster, Edward Morgan, 219–220, 275; on slum philanthropy, 372n182

Foucault, Michel: on discourse and human agency, 293n7; on history of homosexuality, 373n186

Fox Talbot, William Henry, 117

Francis of Assisi, Saint, 252

fraternalism, 236

fraternity: language of, 229; and male reformers, 21; among Oxford men, 228; "unnatural," 264. *See also* brotherhood; cross-class brotherhood

freak show, 126–127

Fremantle, Rev. William Henry: and charity reform, 59

Freud, Sigmund: on benevolence and sexuality, 298n44

France: press in, on "A Night," 26–27

friendly visiting, 101, 225; by women, 191

friendship: cross-class, 2, 4, 7, 200, 225–226; between men, 263; romantic, 203–204, 217–221, 269, 368n138; and social reform, 240; Trumbull on, 263; between women, 191, 193, 202

Friendship, the Master Passion (Trumbull, 1892), 263

friendship-love: definition of, 265; and homosexuality, 269. *See also* friendship, romantic